FOUNDATIONS OF
QUALITATIVE
RESEARCH

INTERPRETIVE AND CRITICAL APPROACHES

JERRY W. WILLIS
LOUISIANA STATE UNIVERSITY

WITH

MUKTHA JOST
NORTH CAROLINA AGRICULTURAL
AND TECHNICAL UNIVERSITY

REMA NILAKANTA
IOWA STATE UNIVERSITY

SAGE Publications
Thousand Oaks ▪ London ▪ New Delhi

For information:

 Sage Publications, Inc.
2455 Teller Road
Thousand Oaks, California 91320
E-mail: order@sagepub.com

Sage Publications Ltd.
1 Oliver's Yard
55 City Road
London EC1Y 1SP
United Kingdom

Sage Publications India Pvt. Ltd.
B-42, Panchsheel Enclave
Post Box 4109
New Delhi 110 017 India

Printed in the United States of America

Library of Congress Cataloging-in-Publication Data

Willis, Jerry, 1942-
Foundations of qualitative research : interpretive and critical approaches / Jerry W. Willis.
     p. cm.
Includes bibliographical references and index.
ISBN-13: 978-1-4129-2740-6 (cloth)
ISBN-13: 978-1-4129-2741-3 (pbk.)
   1. Social sciences—Research. I. Title.

H62.W537 2007
001.4'2—dc22

                                     2006027192

This book is printed on acid-free paper.

07 08 09 10 11 10 9 8 7 6 5 4 3 2 1

Acquisitions Editor:	Lisa Cuevas Shaw
Editorial Assistant:	Karen Greene
Production Editor:	Catherine M. Chilton
Copy Editor:	Carol Anne Peschke
Typesetter:	C&M Digitals (P) Ltd.
Proofreader:	William H. Stoddard
Indexer:	Diggs Indexing Services
Cover Designer:	Edgar Abarca
Marketing Manager:	Stephanie Adams

Brief Contents

Detailed Contents

List of Definitions

Chapter 7

List of Articles of Interest

Chapter 9

Preface

There are many genres of books about qualitative research. Two broad genre families are *method* books and *conceptual* books. Method books emphasize how to do the various types of qualitative research, from participant observation to interviewing to participatory action research and emancipatory research. Method books typically emphasize the process of doing one or more forms of qualitative research. They come in many varieties, from those that try to cover all the major methods to specialty books that cover one method, such as interviewing. Even books on interview research may be specialized so that you learn the ins and outs of doing one major form of the method, such as open interviews, semistructured interviews, focus groups, or life story interviews.

Method books, especially those that focus on a single research method, generally offer many valuable tips, tricks of the trade, and professional practice knowledge—information that Aristotle might have called phronesis, or practical wisdom. I advise novice qualitative researchers to carefully study one or more method books before starting a research project that requires them to use a new research method. For example, the *Handbook of Interview Research,* edited by Jaber Gubrium and James Holstein (2002), contains chapter after chapter on how to do many types of interview research such as focus groups and life story interviews. It also has chapters on how to do interview research with different groups (children, adolescents, men, women, older adults, elites, and the ill) and for different types of research (e.g., forensic investigation, medical, education, therapy). Another aspect of this handbook points to another type of qualitative research book, one that focuses on the foundations and conceptual underpinnings of different paradigms of qualitative research.

Like most large, encyclopedic books of its type, the *Handbook of Interview Research* also has chapters that deal with conceptual and theoretical issues that influence how we think about qualitative research. For example, there are chapters or sections on *postmodern* interviewing, interviewing in *grounded theory* research, *poetic* representation, *feminist* approaches, and *interpretive and constructionist* research and interviewing. Method books tend to emphasize the *how to* of research, but they cannot completely avoid dealing with the conceptual and theoretical foundations of qualitative research because those foundations guide the researcher at every stage of the process, from deciding what to study to selecting the method of research to analyzing the data and drawing conclusions. For example, whether you would consider using participatory action research methods or emancipatory research methods depends to a great extent on the *paradigm* of research you have adopted. A paradigm is a broad conceptual framework that addresses foundational questions such as "What is the nature of knowledge?" "What sources of knowledge warrant our attention?" "How confident can we be that we know something?" and "What should the relationship between research and practice be?"

Like the method books discussed earlier, this book also includes content on methods *and* content on conceptual and theoretical issues. The difference is that this book focuses on the conceptual foundations rather than the methods of qualitative research. Knowledge of methods and conceptual knowledge are both important, even crucial to good research, however that is defined. With the help of two talented graduate students who have now begun their own academic careers, Muktha Jost and Rema Nilakanta, I wrote this book with an emphasis on the conceptual foundations of qualitative research because I thought there were many good books that emphasized the methods of qualitative research but not many that provided a broad overview of the major contemporary intellectual foundations that guide our thinking about qualitative research. The book is organized around three major paradigms or frameworks: positivism and postpositivism, critical theory, and interpretivism. Other books may use different names, but most of the literature on alternative paradigms for qualitative research deals with these three paradigm families or subgroups within them. An understanding of those paradigms, and their relatives, is essential if you are to become a thoughtful and informed qualitative researcher. You also need to understand them if you plan to be a *consumer* of qualitative research because, to an extent we are reluctant to admit, the paradigm adopted often determines the findings and the conclusions of the research. Different paradigms lead us to ask different questions, use different methods to study those questions, analyze our data in different ways, and draw different types of conclusions from our data. They are so powerful, and so often taken for granted or even used without awareness, that I wrote this book to help both researchers and consumers of research explore and understand them. I have done that from a viewpoint that is antipositivist, antifoundational, and prointerpretivist (with sympathy for the critical paradigm as well). However, my goal in the book is not to convert you to my particular mix of qualitative research dogma. It is to help you explore the issues, options, and implications of the different paradigms and frameworks that compete for your attention and allegiance. You may disagree strongly with some of the positions I take in this book. If, after studying this book, you can better articulate why you disagree and what you think is a better position, I will feel a basic goal has been accomplished.

The author of any book must make many choices about what to include, what to leave out, and what to treat generally or in depth. Those decisions often are difficult, and they must be made over and over during the writing process, particularly when a book makes it to a second edition. I welcome your comments and suggestions on this book, particularly when it comes to ways of improving it. As an instructor, can you think of topics that should have been included that were not? Topics that should be expanded, reduced, or cut? As a student, do you have suggestions about how to improve the book? Any suggestions you have are more than welcome. You can send them to me at my academic e-mail address (jerryw@lsu.edu) or my permanent e-mail address (jwillis@aol.com).

—Jerry W. Willis
Louisiana State University

Acknowledgments

My understanding and awareness of the issues and ideas discussed in this book emerged gradually from discussions and interactions with colleagues at three universities: the University of Houston, Iowa State University, and Louisiana State University. I used a rough draft of the entire book in a course at Iowa State University and selected chapters in several courses at Louisiana State University. I benefited greatly from the suggestions students generously took the time to make. My students helped improve understanding, flow, and clarity. I also benefited from the suggestions of two sets of reviewers. One group looked at the initial proposal and the sample chapters. Another group read the rough draft of the entire manuscript. The depth and thoughtfulness of the reviewers' comments indicated that they took their task seriously. The reviewers will see that I did not agree with all their suggestions and that I sometimes responded to their comments in ways different from their suggestions. However, I cannot enumerate all the improvements made to the book that are directly attributable to the quality of the reviewers' comments. To these anonymous reviewers I can only say, "Thank you."

Finally, I want to thank Lisa Cuevas Shaw, the acquisitions editor for research methods and evaluation at Sage Publications. This will be my 60th book (plus or minus five or six; I am not a very quantitative researcher), and the support, encouragement, and structure Lisa and her staff provided were outstanding. It was her idea to include summaries of Articles of Interest in the text and then provide a link to all the articles mentioned on a Web site for the book. This feature makes the book a core of basic content that is linked to a large web of additional, relevant material that expands on the basic coverage in this textbook. She also offered many other very useful ideas and helped me work through all the reviewer comments, decide what was most relevant and important, and make plans for revising the manuscript. Thank you, Lisa! Finally, Carol Anne Peschke was the copyeditor for this book. It is humbling to receive a chapter with more than a hundred major and minor revisions. My initial response to all those red marks was, "There couldn't possibly be that many things that need to be changed in 45 pages!" But there were. Her excellent work made this book more readable and more understandable. Thank you, Carol!

CHAPTER 1

World Views, Paradigms, and the Practice of Social Science Research

Case 1. Quantitative Research

Dr. James Jackson was concerned about whether a particular approach to teaching undergraduate courses is effective. The approach is called the personalized system of instruction (PSI), developed by Fred Keller, a Columbia University psychologist and personal friend of B. F. Skinner. PSI (Martin, 1997) has been used for several decades in the sciences, but Dr. Jackson was not able to find convincing research about the suitability of PSI for humanities courses.

Personalized System of Instruction (PSI)

The PSI method of teaching was popular in the 1970s and is still used in many science classes. The content to be learned is divided into units or modules. Students get assignments with each module. When they think they have mastered a module, they come to class and take a test on that module. If they make 85% or more on the test, they get credit for the module and begin studying the next module. When they pass all the modules they are finished with the course and receive an A. In a course with 13 modules, anyone who completes all 13 might receive an A, students who finish 11 would receive Bs, and so on. The approach was called "personalized" because students could go at their own pace and decide when they wanted to be tested. Critics argued that PSI wasn't very personalized because all students had to learn the same content, which was selected by the instructor, and everyone was evaluated with the same objective tests.

Professor Jackson believed PSI would be a good format for humanities courses, and to test his hypothesis he and his colleagues conducted a research study. The course, "History of Western Cultural Traditions," was popular and had several sections. Dr. Jackson designed a PSI version of the course, and half the sections were taught using the PSI format whereas the others were taught using a standard lecture and discussion format. The sections were randomly assigned to treatment conditions (traditional or PSI).

The PSI sections were all taught by Dr. Jackson, and the traditional sections were taught by three experienced professors who had regularly taught the course using that format. At the end of the course all sections completed a 150-item objective test on the core content of the course. That content was agreed upon by all the instructors. Dr. Jackson analyzed the end-of-course test results. He used a statistical procedure called analysis of variance (ANOVA). The results were as follows:

- Students in the PSI sections scored significantly higher on the test than students in the traditional sections.
- Within each of the two groups of sections (traditional and PSI) some sections scored significantly higher than others. In the case of the traditional sections this may have resulted from the use of different instructors. However, there were also differences between the four PSI sections, which were all taught by Dr. Jackson.

Dr. Jackson concluded that the results of this study support the hypothesis that PSI is a viable format for humanities courses. He concluded his paper on the research by recommending that more humanities courses be taught using PSI.

Case 2. **Qualitative Research**

Dr. Joan Jackson was concerned about the quality of the humanities courses in her department. In talking with other faculty she found that they too were worried about their programs. All of them thought that although the courses were well organized and the teachers knowledgeable, the students simply were not getting as much as they should from the courses.

To explore this issue Joan organized a study group, with support from the department chair, who also became a group member. They met twice a month and eventually concluded that they might need to make major changes in the way the courses were taught. They also decided to get input from current students and graduates before making any changes. With that in mind they invited three groups of students to their sessions to talk about the courses: current students, students who had just graduated, and students in the graduate program who had completed their undergraduate work in the department. These meetings were not very fruitful. The group realized that even the students who had graduated from the program and were no longer affiliated with the department were reluctant to talk freely with professors about needed changes in the courses. One member of the group suggested a different approach: Do individual interviews with students using a semistructured format that involved providing some guiding questions but allowed students to express their opinions on many topics related to the courses. The interviewer, who was a graduate student known for her comfort working with both students and faculty, conducted the interviews. She assured each participant that the report based on the interviews would not "name names," nor would it single out individual professors or students.

The results of the interviews were very helpful, and the faculty began to develop ideas about some of the problems in the courses. However, another faculty member suggested that students should not be the sole source of input to the group. He suggested that input be sought from several faculty members at similar universities who were known for their success as undergraduate teachers. Another suggested that they select humanities faculty by looking for winners of "excellence in teaching" awards. Over a 2-month period seven award-winning faculty from humanities departments around the country were interviewed, mostly by phone. They were asked about innovative methods of teaching. They also reviewed the course syllabi for several of the humanities courses that were of particular concern. The result was another very useful report that summarized the suggestions and opinions of the star faculty members from other universities.

The two reports and a review of the literature on teaching in the humanities were all valuable. After a number of extensive discussions the group decided to experiment with one course: "History of Western Cultural Traditions." The group agreed that three innovative teaching strategies were promising: problem-based learning (Savin-Baden, 2000), case-based learning (Christudason, 2003), and an approach called Assisting Small Group Learning Through Electronic Resources (ASTER), developed in Britain at Oxford University (Condron, 2000; Jelfs & Coburn, 2002).

Instead of selecting one idea and using it in several sections, the group decided that enthusiastic faculty teaching a section of the course would implement one of the three innovations. At the end of the first experimental semester, the faculty talked to the group about their impressions, and they presented the findings of the more formal evaluations of the innovation. The evaluations consisted of reflective notes written by the instructor over the course of the semester, interviews with students at critical points during the semester, and observations and evaluations by other faculty who visited the class. Generally, the results of this first semester were that all three innovations showed promise, but they needed refinement and adaptation to work well in the course. Over two more semesters the ASTER approach and the case-based learning approach gradually evolved into mature innovations that were used in most of the other sections of the course. Problem-based learning was dropped because faculty decided it did not fit the content and goals of the course. Instead, several instructors tried new methods of facilitating class discussions that involved several interesting questioning techniques (Beaudin, 1999; George, 2004; VanVoorhis, 1999). The professors reported that these worked well and were also valued by the students and the observers who sat in on some of the classes.

Reflection

This term has many meanings, but the *reflective notes* that were an important part of the research in this example are a product of thinking about issues, problems, and successes that occurred as the instructor taught the course. The idea of thinking seriously about what you are doing and then using your reflections to plan future action is not new. The idea can be traced back to Plato. However, the best-known modern advocate of *reflective practice* was Donald Schon (1987), who suggested that practitioners such as psychologists, social workers, teachers, and architects engage in two forms of reflection. *Reflection in action* happens when someone encounters a unique problem or decision that cannot be solved by the application of routine or standard solutions or rules. Instead the professional must reflect on the fly and decide what to do. The other type of reflection, *reflection on action,* happens when practitioners think through their previous work. For example, a psychotherapist might mentally run through a recent therapy session, analyze it, evaluate the impact of different steps taken in the session, and come to a conclusion about what to do differently in the next session with that patient. That is reflection on action, and it is the type illustrated by the reflective notes the instructors took.

After 2 years of experimentation the group decided the three successful methods might be worth trying in other humanities courses as well. They held workshop sessions for other faculty and helped them try out the teaching and learning methods in their courses. At the same time, the group decided to become a permanent aspect of the department. Each semester they tried out some interesting innovations and then reported to the humanities faculty on the results.

Joan Jackson published several papers on this work. One dealt with the process of selecting innovations and trying them out. Three other papers were also published, one on each of the successful methods. All were qualitative, which means they described the context of the work—the course, type of students, background of the instructors, and so forth—and the papers provided detailed information on the innovation and the story of how it evolved from the first implementation to the current incarnation. Evaluations by the professors, students, and observers were included, as were suggestions about issues to think about. Each paper concluded that the experiences of Dr. Jackson and her colleagues might be helpful to humanities faculty at other universities.

Article of Interest

Throughout this book there are boxes like this that alert you to an article of interest. Each article is briefly introduced in the box, but the full article is available on the publisher's Web site for the book. To read the entire article, please go to http://www.sagepub.com/willis_aoi.

Melanie Jasper. (2005). Using reflective writing within research.
Journal of Research in Nursing, 10(3), 247–260.

Jasper distinguishes between notes about research progress and "reflective writing" as part of the research process. She points out that many more quantitatively oriented researchers tend to prefer research notes that are very objective. Reflective writing during a research project is much more subjective and may be considered detrimental to research by some. In the main portion of her article, Jasper argues that reflective writing can contribute to the trustworthiness of a study and facilitate "creativity, critical thinking and strategies for analysis and innovative discovery" (p. 248). She then describes the nature of reflective writing and how to use it in the research process. She even introduces the idea of reflective writing as additional data to be analyzed.

The two fictional cases that begin this book represent two distinct *paradigms,* or world views about what research is and how it is to be conducted. The first case is in the *quantitative* tradition and the second is in the *qualitative* tradition. The terms *qualitative* and *quantitative* are widely used today to describe two ways of thinking about research in the social sciences, but the terms are not always clearly understood.

What This Book Is and Is Not About

This book is not an attempt to prepare you fully to use any research method. If you decide to do research using a particular method such as *focus groups,* you will need to immerse yourself in the growing body of literature on the use of focus groups. Our goal is more modest when it comes to methodology. It is to make you aware of several established and several emerging methods, how they work, and what sorts of issues are involved in their use. Furthermore, the goal is to deal with a particular group of emerging methods that are particularly appropriate for researchers who want to base their work on an *interpretivist* world view or a critical world view. The terms *interpretivist* and *critical theorist* will be explained and explored in detail in the coming chapters.

Interpretivism

This approach to social science research rejects the positivist idea that the same research methods can be used to study human behavior as are successfully used in fields such as chemistry and physics. Interpretivists argue that when you study the behavior of a metal, the primary causes of changes in the metal are in the environment (e.g., heat, stress). Humans behave the way they do in part because of their environment. However, that influence is not direct as it is with a piece of metal. Humans are also influenced by their subjective perception of their environment—their subjective realities. We do not worry about the subjective impressions of a steel bar, but if we are to fully understand the behavior of an 18-year-old delinquent we must understand her view of the world around her. We must also understand the subjective perceptions of her by others in her social and cultural context. Thus, for interpretivists, what the world means to the person or group being studied is critically important to good research in the social sciences. Interpretivists favor qualitative methods such as case studies, interviews, and observation because those methods are better ways of getting at how humans interpret the world around them. Some of the philosophical foundations of interpretivism can be found in Immanuel Kant's *Critique of Pure Reason* (1781/2003), in which he argued that humans interpret their sensations; they do not directly experience the "out there" world as it is. In the 18th century Wilhelm Dilthey added to the foundations of interpretivism by arguing that *verstehen* (understanding) was the goal of social science research and that the proper topic of social science research was the lived experiences of humans. He was reacting against contemporary ideas that the social sciences should emulate the positivist methods of the natural sciences because humans could be treated as complex machines. For him, natural reality was not the same as social reality, and that meant that different methods of research were needed to study social reality.

In our view, however, any exploration of qualitative research methods cannot be meaningfully accomplished without attention to the underlying assumptions, or "givens," that guide the use of a particular research method. The terms *quantitative* and *qualitative* are popularly used to describe two different world views or paradigms for research. Using those terms implies that the big difference between the two paradigms is in the type of data collected: Quantitative researchers use numbers as data, whereas qualitative researchers do not. In fact, that is not true. Number-based research methods often are used by qualitative researchers, and a growing number of quantitative researchers use qualitative data.

The major difference between these approaches is not the type of data collected. It is in the foundational assumptions, the givens that are assumed to be true. A focus of this book is those foundational assumptions, and they will be explored in some detail. The paradigms of research therefore are the primary focus, especially the interpretivist and critical theory paradigms. Only after the major paradigms are explored will the focus shift somewhat to research methods.

Article of Interest

Jaan Valsiner. (2000). Data as representations: Contextualizing quantitative and qualitative research strategies. *Social Science Information, 39,* 99–113.

This chapter has presented the traditional view that qualitative data tend to be associated with critical and interpretive paradigms of research, whereas studies that rely on quantitative data tend to be couched in a positivist or postpositivist paradigm. Furthermore, the important difference between paradigms is not the type of data preferred but the underlying beliefs and assumptions of each paradigm. In this article Valsiner takes a closer look at qualitative and quantitative data and the quantitative and qualitative paradigms in the social sciences. In contrast to many scholars who see these two paradigm families as mutually exclusive and in opposition, Valsiner concludes that *quantitative* is actually a derivative of *qualitative*. You may find his reasoning fascinating.

To read the entire article, please go to http://www.sagepub.com/willis_aoi.

Just What Is a Paradigm?

Chalmers (1982) defines a paradigm as "made up of the general theoretical assumptions and laws, and techniques for their application that the members of a particular scientific community adopt" (p. 90). Chalmers (1982, p. 91) points out that a paradigm has five components:

- Explicitly stated laws and theoretical assumptions.
- Standard ways of applying the fundamental laws to a variety of situations.
- Instrumentation and instrumental techniques that bring the laws of the paradigm to bear on the real world.
- General metaphysical principles that guide work within the paradigm.
- General methodological prescriptions about how to conduct work within the paradigm.

A paradigm is thus a comprehensive belief system, world view, or framework that guides research and practice in a field. Today, in the social sciences, there are several competing paradigms. Some discussions are organized around the idea that there are two paradigms, quantitative and qualitative, but that is an oversimplification that emphasizes data rather than foundational beliefs and assumptions. The exact number of world views (paradigms) and the names associated with a particular paradigm vary from author to author, but one generally accepted list includes three paradigms (Cupchik, 2001; Gephart, 1999; Greene, Benjamin, & Goodyear, 2001; Guba, 1990; Smith, 1989):

- Postpositivism
- Critical theory
- Interpretivism

A paradigm is not just a philosophy of science, such as postpositivism. It is also the related social science theory, such as behaviorism, and the associated research framework. Finally, it is the application of that entire framework to practice. Each level influences and is influenced by all the other levels. At the basic or fundamental level there is a philosophy of science that makes a number of assumptions about fundamental issues such as the nature of truth (ontology) and what it means to know (epistemology). Although many researchers and practitioners ignore this foundational layer of assumptions, it is an essential aspect of a paradigm. Many of the basic tenets of behavioral psychology (and information processing theory and cognitive science), for example, would make very little sense without the assumptions of post-positivism. That is because positivism or postpositivism is the philosophy of science that is the foundation for these paradigms. Their methods and practices are based on the assumption that positivism, or at least postpositivism, is the true and correct way to look at the world. And the use of the scientific method as a framework for conducting research would not make sense unless proponents adopt a realist ontology: "Reality exists 'out there' and is driven by immutable natural laws and mechanisms. Knowledge of these entities, laws, and mechanisms is conventionally summarized in the form of time- and context-free generalizations" (Guba, 1990, p. 20). Similarly, there are research frameworks such as cooperative inquiry (Heron, 1996; Tan, 2002) that attempt to see problems from multiple perspectives. Such methods would not make much sense without a relativist ontology—"Realities exist in the form of multiple mental constructions, socially and experientially based, local and specific, dependent for their form and content on the persons who hold them" (Guba, 1990, p. 27)—and an assumption that the goal of research is understanding in context instead of the discovery of universal, lawlike truths.

Ontology and Epistemology

These two terms often put students off philosophy for life. Ontology and epistemology are the two major aspects of a branch of philosophy called metaphysics. Metaphysics is concerned with two fundamental questions. First, what are the characteristics of existence? Or, put another way, what are the characteristics of things that exist? Or what are the universal characteristics of things that exist? These are ontological questions. The second aspect of metaphysics is the question, "How can we know the things that exist?" This is an epistemological question. Unfortunately, these definitions are too abstract and ephemeral to be of much use when the concepts are new to you.

Ontology is concerned with the nature of reality (or being or existence), and various ontological positions reflect different prescriptions of what can be real and what cannot. For example, someone who takes a materialist ontological position (e.g., all that is real is the physical or material world) would reject the idea that ghosts or spirits can influence the physical world. Why? Because ghosts cannot exist if all that is real is physical. Materialism is one of the major ontological positions, and it is the foundation for much of the research conducted in the natural sciences. However, a competing view of reality is idealism, which proposes that reality is mental and spiritual rather than material (Craig, 1998). Another ontological position is metaphysical subjectivism. Proponents of that position assert that perception, what we perceive through our senses, creates reality and that there is

(Continued)

(Continued)

no other reality than what is in our heads. That is, there is no reality other than what humans create in their own minds. You can see how different ontological positions can lead to very different positions on many issues. Today, for example, there are debates in the field of medical informatics that come down to whether medical terms and diagnoses reflect a materialistic reality that is external to the mind and that exists independent of the mind versus a more subjective view that they are constructions of the minds of medical specialists (Hajdukiewicz, Vicente, Doyle, Milgram, & Burns, 2001). Most of Western natural science is based on modern versions of Descartes's dualism, the idea that both material and mental entities exist.

Epistemology is concerned with what we can know about reality (however that is defined) and how we can know it. At the risk of oversimplification, ontology is about what can exist or what is real, and epistemology is about knowledge. In fact, the English term comes from the Greek word *episteme,* which means "knowledge." When you ask questions such as "What is knowledge?" "How do I acquire knowledge?" "How can I be sure of my knowledge (if I can at all)?" and "What are the limits of human knowledge?" you are asking epistemological questions.

Epistemology is a crucial foundation for research in both the natural and the social sciences. The traditional scientific method, for example, is based on an empirical epistemology: You can come to know about the world (which, ontologically, is a physical or material world) through properly done experiments. An alternative is feminist epistemology, which argues that much of the research in the social sciences has been conducted from a male perspective. To a feminist epistemology this is important because all knowledge is situated in the experiences and context of the researcher. Thus, the knowledge produced by a male-dominated sociology or anthropology will not be the same as the knowledge produced by female-oriented researchers. Thus, feminist epistemology is based on a more subjective ontology and also rejects the idea that research is a way of coming to know what is objectively "real." Instead, the knower is always influenced by her or his situation, and thus all knowledge is also situated (Harding, 1998).

Article of Interest

Penelope Vinden. (1999). Gathering up the fragments after positivism: Can Ratner make us whole again? *Culture & Psychology, 5*(2), 223–238.

This article is actually a review and commentary on a book written by Carl Ratner (1997). The book lays out a foundation for building an approach to studying culture within psychology that uses qualitative research methods. Vinden tends to prefer positivist approaches (which are called postpositivism in this book), whereas Ratner rejects them and proposes what Vinden calls postmodernism but is probably closer to what is called critical theory in this book. She acknowledges that positivism has lost ground as a significant foundation for psychological research, and she makes the point that "with the demise . . . of traditional science has come a rejection of its time-honored methodology, quantitative methods" (p. 224). She questions whether this is a good idea, and she analyzes Ratner's case for adopting another paradigm (postmodernism or interpretivism) and another type of data (qualitative). For example, Vinden takes issue with Ratner's assertion that psychological phenomena have a cultural context and foundation. As a discipline psychology, more than other social sciences, has tended to equate quantitative research with positivist and postpositivist philosophies of science. That is the compass point Vinden is coming from. And although I do not agree with every position Ratner takes, he does come from the general direction of interpretivist and critical theory philosophies of science and qualitative research.

Vinden works hard to associate Ratner with names and terms such as *Marx, Engels, Leontiev, Luria, Vygotsky, Marxist,* and *new left,* and she concludes that his "formulation of cultural psychology has a Marxist flavor" (p. 225). In fact, much of her objection to Ratner's approach boils down to the two psychologists operating from two different paradigms. He is concerned, as critical theorists are, with linking research to the idea of emancipation, of freeing people from beliefs that restrict and control them in the name of movements and groups that do not have their best interests at heart. He is also more comfortable with the idea that our understanding of culture and behavior is not definitive and objective. What we know is subjective and tentative. Vinden is a bit worried about that; she wants more clear-cut ideas, theories, and answers. Otherwise, "there is no room to advance, nothing to study" (p. 227).

In the last half of her review Vinden addresses Ratner's critique of positivism as a poor foundation for psychological research. As you read Vinden's comments, consider whether you are most comfortable with her view or Ratner's. And, after you have read the article, ask yourself how many times you saw the basic or fundamental beliefs of Vinden or Ratner being expressed in the positions they take on various issues. Also notice how much overlap there is between the psychological theories they espouse and social-political theories. This overlap is nicely illustrated in Vinden's last comment: "Capitalism and positivism may not have provided an answer to these questions [how to determine what is good for people], or may have given answers with which many of us are not happy. It is not clear, however, that socialism and humanitarianism will guarantee more satisfactory answers" (p. 237).

To read the entire article, please go to http://www.sagepub.com/willis_aoi.

Family Resemblances Within Paradigm Groups

Qualitative research sometimes is described as ethnographic, interpretive, critical, or postmodern research (Creswell, 1997). Quantitative research, on the other hand, is often called empirical, positivist, postpositivist, or

objectivist (Henrickson & McKelvey, 2002). There are important differences between positivism and postpositivism or between postmodernism
and interpretivism, for example. However, these differences are less
important than the similarities. Positivism and postpositivism are members
of a group of related ways of thinking about and doing research. The relationship between empirical, positivist, postpositivist, and objectivist
frameworks for conducting research probably is best characterized as a set
of *family resemblances* (Wittgenstein, 1973). Just as members of a particular family may have unique appearances but still resemble each other, all
members of the empirical, positivist, postpositivist, and objectivist family
have enough resemblances to make it obvious that they are members of
the same family. That family dominates quantitative social science research,
and it is sometimes called positivism, although the most influential
version today is a variant called postpositivism. Two other families, critical
theory and interpretivism, are the most important ones in the qualitative
tradition.

Positivism

Seventeenth-century French philosopher Auguste Comte established positivism in
Western philosophy. He believed societies passed through three stages of explanation. In the first and least enlightened stage, *theological* explanations dominate.
In the second and more enlightened stage, *metaphysical* or philosophical explanations emerge. For example, a person might say that a particular drug puts
people to sleep because it has "dormative powers." Certain characteristics are
attributed to items and treated as explanations in the metaphysical stage. And in
the third and highest stage, *positivism,* scientific explanations are the rule. Comte
advocated the emerging sciences, such as astronomy, biology, physics, and
chemistry, but he was also a founder of sociology and was concerned that this
field of human study should be based on a solid scientific foundation. He sometimes called sociology "social physics" and argued that the methods that were so
successful in the natural sciences should also be applied to the human sciences.
He advocated the use of the scientific method to validate theories of human
behavior:

> Scientifically speaking, all isolated, empirical observation is idle, and even
> radically uncertain; . . . science can use only those observations which are
> connected, at least hypothetically, with some law; that it is such a connec-
> tion which makes the chief difference between scientific and popular
> observation, embracing the same facts, but contemplating them from

different points of view: and that observations empirically conducted can at most supply provisional materials, which must usually undergo an ulterior revision. . . . The observer would not know what he ought to look at in the facts before his eyes, but for the guidance of a preparatory theory. . . . This is undisputed with regard to astronomical, physical, and chemical research, and in every branch of biological study. . . . Carrying on the analogy, it is evident that in the corresponding divisions . . . of social science, there is more need than anywhere else of theories which shall scientifically connect the facts that are happening with those that have happened. (Comte, 1854)

Thinking About the Foundations and Practice of Research

Some books on research concentrate on the tools for doing certain types of research. For example, there are thousands of books on the use and interpretation of statistical analyses (e.g., Lockhart, 1997; Ott, Longnecker, & Ott, 2000; Roussas, 2002; Sprinthall, 1996). The more general statistical books are supported and extended by thousands of books on specialized statistical methods of data analysis such as regression analysis (Montgomery, Peck, & Geoffrey, 2001; Von Eye, Schuster, & Schiller, 1998), multivariate statistical analysis (Johnson & Wichern, 2002), and structural equation modeling (Mueller, 1996; Schumacker & Lomax, 2004). These are but a few of the several hundred specialized statistical methods that are used in the social sciences today.

Statistics are used in social science research for two main reasons:

• To help us come to conclusions about what the data from our research say. The ubiquitous *t* test, for example, is used to compare the average (mean) scores of two groups. One of the groups has generally served as some sort of control group, and the other has been administered some form of treatment. If the treatment group's mean score is higher that the mean of the control group, and the *t* test is significant, then the researcher can suggest that the treatment used may have been effective.

• A second reason for using statistics is to deal with common, and often unavoidable, problems that crop up in research. For example, suppose you are going to study the impact of two alternative approaches to providing support services to new immigrant families. Unfortunately, it is not possible to randomly assign students to control and experimental groups. That is a problem because random assignment to experimental and control groups usually is an important requirement of the scientific method. A statistical procedure called analysis of covariance (ANCOVA) has been developed to even out the effects of initial differences between control and experimental groups and thus give you a more accurate picture of the impact of your treatment (Huitema, 1980; Rutherford, 2000). Statistical procedures are used to compensate for violations in the basic requirements for scientific research (such as random assignment of subjects to groups). Similarly, analysis of variance procedures have been developed to improve statistical power (the ability to see real differences even when there is much random variation in the data; Lindman, 1992; Milliken & Johnson, 2001). Finally, nonparametric statistics have been developed to deal with data that do not meet some of the minimum standards of traditional *parametric* statistical analysis (Siegel & Castellan, 1988).

Statistics is a nearly universal aspect of traditional quantitative research. A second aspect of research, qualitative or quantitative, that must be considered is research design, or the way the study is organized. The term *methodology* generally is used to describe several aspects of a study: the design, the procedures for data collection, methods for data analysis, selection of subjects, and details of the specific treatments, if any. Many books are available on methodology or design from a traditional perspective (Campbell & Stanley, 1963; McBurney & White, 2003; Montgomery, 2004).

Statistics and methodology or design guides are at one end of a continuum of publications about how to conduct traditional or quantitative research. At the other end of the continuum are books that deal with the broad theoretical and philosophical frameworks that guide practice. Chalmers (1982, 1990, 1995, 1999), for example, compares the characteristics of several philosophies of science: positivism, postpositivism, sociological theories of science, and Feyerabend's (1993) *anything goes* philosophy of science.

The interconnectedness of the various levels of a paradigm is discussed throughout this book. Chapter 2 looks at the history of the three paradigms (postpositivism, interpretivism, and critical theory), with an emphasis on what the founders were reacting to when the paradigm emerged as a research framework. Chapter 3 introduces postpositivism, the dominant paradigm today. The chapter also discusses one of the alternative paradigms: critical theory. Chapter 4 covers the interpretive paradigm. The final four chapters of this book focus on methodology. Chapter 5 covers alternative frameworks for interpretivist and critical research, chapter 6 presents general principles or guidelines for doing research, and chapter 7 gets down to specific methods and covers in some detail broad methods of interpretive and critical qualitative research. Finally, chapter 8 deals with data collection and analysis, and chapter 9 looks at the future of social science research.

This book focuses on the qualitative research tradition from *interpretive* and *critical* approaches. However, the dominant quantitative frameworks for research will be addressed frequently for three reasons:

- Quantitative research remains the dominant paradigm in many areas of the social sciences. Some researchers and policymakers even consider quantitative research the only *real* research. The recent emphasis on traditional quantitative research in the second Bush administration's Department of Education is one example of an effort to make quantitative research methods based on the scientific method the only way to answer many important questions. The second Bush administration created the Institute of Education Sciences, and that agency's guide to deciding which educational innovations are supported by rigorous research illustrates this point (IES, 2003). Innovations with *strong* evidence should be supported by several well-designed research studies involving random assignment of students to control and experimental groups. Those with *possible* evidence of effectiveness should be supported by randomly assigned control–experimental group studies that are good but have some flaws or by comparison studies that involve closely matched groups. If an innovation does not have either strong or possible evidence (e.g., evidence based on research in the positivist or postpositivist tradition), then "one may conclude that the intervention is not supported by meaningful evidence" (p. 7). (Note: Although quantitative social science research normally is practiced within a postpositivist paradigm, which is discussed in the next two chapters, there is an emerging approach to quantitative research based on a alternative paradigm, critical theory.)

- Much of what has happened in the field of qualitative research has been in response to shortcomings, perceived or real, of quantitative research.

- There is a tradition in qualitative research that adopts the framework and belief systems of quantitative research. In that tradition qualitative research (or the collection of qualitative data) is really an extension of the quantitative paradigm. As you will see in this book, critical and interpretive qualitative research involves much more than that.

There is a significant tension between postpositivism, critical theory, and interpretivism.

What Warrants Our Attention?

At the American Educational Research Association (AERA) meeting in New Orleans a few years ago, Elliot Eisner quoted another Stanford professor, D. C. Phillips, as saying, "Worry about warrant will not wane." Phillips and Eisner were referring to the current state of affairs in education and the social sciences with regard to what is and is not research. Scholars have perspectives, beliefs, ideas, and theories they would like to share with others in their field. However, all of us are besieged with papers, books, and presentations on the topics that interest us. We all develop ways of deciding what we will ignore and what we will pay attention to. That is what D. C. Phillips (2000; Phillips & Barbules, 2000) was talking about: warrant. All of us decide what types of material warrant our attention and what types do not.

My graduate experience, like that of most psychologists who were trained in American doctoral programs between 1930 and 1985, provided a precise, clear-cut answer to the question of warrant. Only properly conducted quantitative research that was based on the scientific method warranted our attention. Case studies, papers based on experience in a particular area of professional practice, and a hundred other types of studies that used qualitative data or were based on methods other than the scientific method were simply outside the pale. They were not research and did not warrant my attention. I must admit that I left graduate school in 1970 with great confidence about research. I could comfortably decide what warranted my attention both as a consumer of research and as a producer of research.

Now, more than 30 years later, I consider the confidence I had when I graduated as arrogance that kept me from attending to and learning from a whole range of scholarship that is outside the boundaries of traditional quantitative research. I am not alone in this predicament, however. Several generations of social scientists are reevaluating their long-established notions about what warrants their attention and what does not.

The Traditional Canon

Consider some of the chapter titles of a typical quantitative research and statistics book used in the 1980s (Welkowitz, Ewen, & Cohen, 1982):

Frequency Distributions and Graphs

Measures of Central Tendency

Measures of Variability

The Normal Curve Model

Testing Hypotheses About the
Differences Between the Means of
Two Populations

Linear Correlation and Prediction

Other Correlation Techniques

Introduction to Power Analysis

One-Way Analysis of Variance

Although more sophisticated methods for quantitative analysis are available today, thousands of research courses still teach these topics. They are topics I was taught in graduate school, topics I am comfortable with and understand. I have used the knowledge from my graduate school quantitative courses to conduct many research studies over the past 30 years. But there is something I did not learn in graduate school, something I should have learned along with the quantitative paradigm and its associated methods and techniques.

Alternative Paradigms

What I did not know when I finished graduate school was that the things I was taught about research—from how to decide what warrants my attention to how to interpret an analysis of variance summary table—were all based on one paradigm. That paradigm was *postpositivism,* and it takes very specific, very strong positions on everything from the acceptable reasons for doing research to the proper methods for collecting and analyzing data.

Postpositivism, which is also known as postempiricism, is no longer the only game in town when it comes to social science research. It never was. That fact gradually dawned on me over the past three decades. Awareness emerged as I became more and more dissatisfied with what I could and could not do with traditional scientific method research. It seemed to me that traditional research based on the scientific method forced us to study some of the least important issues because we could quantify the variables and control the experimental context. While we were publishing plenty of methodologically sound studies, we seemed to be publishing too few papers on the topics that were really important. So I began to explore other options and discovered the emerging field of qualitative research. The following is a list of topics covered in the fourth edition of Bogdan and Biklen's (2002) book on qualitative research:

Phenomenology	Modified Analytic Induction
Symbolic Interaction	The Constant Comparative Method
Ethnomethodology	Participant/Observer Research
Cultural Studies	Developing Coding Categories
Case Studies	Action Research
Observational Case Studies	Applied Qualitative Research
Life Histories	

There is almost no overlap between the content of this qualitative research textbook and the quantitative book mentioned earlier. That is true even though the qualitative book takes a conservative approach. Bogdan and Biklen selected research methods primarily from social sciences, such as sociology and anthropology, and from education. Eisner (1997) makes the point that until recently "discussions of qualitative research methods almost always were reduced to doing ethnography" (p. 1) because ethnography was the established method for a social science, cultural anthropology. However, the interpretive paradigm is increasingly drawing on disciplines that are further afield. The humanities, for example, are often looked to for appropriate methods. An issue of the journal *Qualitative Inquiry* (1[4], 1996) includes an article on "Dance as a Mode of Research Representation" by Donald Blumenfeld-Jones. The same issue contains an article by Robert Donmoyer and June Yennie-Donmoyer titled "Data as Drama: Reflections on the Use of Reader's Theater as a Mode of Qualitative Data Display." As social science researchers get in touch with the methods of the humanities and social sciences besides their own specialty, we are all likely to find ourselves considering a wide range of methods for collecting new forms of data and new ways of representing our interpretations of that data. This point was made by education researcher Elliot Eisner (1997) when he said, "The assumption that the languages of social science—propositional language and number—are the exclusive agents of meaning is becoming increasingly problematic, and as a result, we are exploring the potential of other forms of representation for illuminating the educational worlds we wish to understand" (p. 4).

Propositional Logic

When Eisner mentioned "propositional language" in his discussion of research, he was talking about this type of logic:

If A is true (proposition or declarative or "atomic" statement)

and B is true (proposition or declarative or "atomic" statement)

then C must (logical statement or compound sentence) be true

The first two lines are each propositions about the world, also called declarative sentences or atomic statements. The third line is a logical statement or compound sentence that must be true if A and B propositions are true. Whereas sentences A and B are empirically verifiable statements, C is proved logically rather than empirically. Here is a concrete example that is often used to illustrate the importance of the first two propositions being true:

All swans are white.

This bird is black.

Therefore, this bird is not a swan.

If the first two statements are true, then it is logically impossible for the bird to be a swan. It turns out, by the way, that every European swan thus far observed is white, but when explorers arrived in Australia, they found black swans. That means statement A is false (not all swans are white), and thus the logical conclusion in the third statement may be false as well. The bird could be a black swan from Australia. There is much more to propositional logic than presented here, but this is the basic idea.

New Techniques or New Paradigms?

The emergence of a qualitative research paradigm as a viable alternative to quantitative, postpositivist methods is not simply an expansion of options at the technique level. We have not simply added to control group and experimental group research a few additional methods such as case studies. Qualitative research can be, and usually is, based on a different paradigm or *world view*. It has different fundamental assumptions, different reasons for doing research, different beliefs about what types of data are the most worthwhile to collect, and decidedly different approaches to analyzing the data collected. Such differences are at the heart of the current debate about what type of research warrants our attention and energy.

In the AERA symposium mentioned earlier the focus was the question, "Could a novel ever be a dissertation in a college of education?" Elliot Eisner, among others, spoke eloquently in favor of that possibility because the purpose of research is to inform and convince people, and a novel might do that better than many other forms of research. Jere Brophy facetiously said that perhaps it could be used for an Ed.D. but not for a Ph.D. Then he and Howard Gardner argued forcefully that there are standards for what research is and that a novel does not fall within those standards. Eisner, Brophy, and Gardner disagreed in part because they were operating from different paradigms. Eisner is one of the best-known advocates of the interpretive paradigm in educational research, whereas Brophy is an established proponent of a more traditional view of research based on the postpositivist paradigm.

Alternative paradigms have become a major focus of debate in research circles over the last 20 years, and there is already a healthy body of literature on the topic. Two of the best books on the philosophies of science that are the foundation for research today were written by Alan Chalmers (1990, 1995). He roughly divides the alternatives into five general philosophies of science: empiricist, postempiricist, critical theory, sociological (e.g., Kuhn, 1970, 1996; Kuhn, Conant, & Haugeland, 2000; Lakatos & Musgrave, 1970), and anarchistic (e.g., Feyerabend, 1975, 1993). More specialized books written specifically for readers in the social sciences have generally covered the same ground but with more attention to the implications for research and practice in the areas of human and cultural endeavor. In a 1989 book, Smith roughly divided the options into two categories: empiricism and interpretivism. After a bit more thought, in a book titled *After the Demise of Empiricism: The Problem of Judging Social and Educational Inquiry,* Smith (1993) discussed four alternatives: empiricism, postempiricism, critical theory, and interpretivism. In *The Paradigm Dialog* (Guba, 1990), the alternatives were conventional positivism (or empiricism, which is generally agreed to be outmoded), postpositivism (or postempiricism), critical theory, and constructivism. Those same four paradigms were used by Guba and Lincoln (1994) in the *Handbook of Qualitative Research* (Denzin & Lincoln, 1994, 2000), a book that extensively covers the large and growing family of qualitative research models and paradigms.

The paradigm debates are more than intellectual exercises that waste time and energy. Let me cite just three examples that I ran across recently. In one case graduate students were told by a professor that their work, which was excellent scholarship within the interpretive paradigm, was not "real research." Such a comment from an authority figure is likely to discourage students from pursuing qualitative approaches to research even if they seem most appropriate to the student. In another case, a student developed a research proposal that focused on the collection of rich qualitative data. Her advisor refused to accept the proposal and required her to redesign the study to focus on quantitative data. She made the changes but still thought her research question was more amenable to qualitative approaches. In the third case, a department chair at a midlevel research university disagreed with the qualitative method being supported by one of his faculty. He did not have the power to forbid the particular research method, but he did suggest to the faculty member that a special departmental faculty meeting be called so that members of the faculty could vote on whether the method was acceptable to the department. If the majority of faculty voted against the method, students would be officially forbidden to use the method in their dissertations. For all these examples, differences in the underlying paradigm were at the bottom of the disagreement.

I am not troubled about one scholar expressing an opinion about what is considered research and what is not. Expressing different viewpoints and engaging in a discussion of the differences is a time-honored way of expanding our understanding of important, critical issues. The art of stimulating discourse, and the ability to listen to the perspectives of others who disagree with you, is probably more central to the highest purposes of scholarship than any traditional form of research.

What bothers me about these three examples is that they all involved assumptions and givens that people took for granted without acknowledging that others operating within different paradigms would not accept them. In each of the three examples, the positions taken are appropriate and meaningful in one paradigm of research, but they do not make sense if you accept an alternative paradigm. As described in the next chapter, there are three active paradigms that guide research in the social sciences today, and

- They differ on the question of the nature of reality.
- They offer different reasons or purposes for doing research.
- They point us to quite different types of data and methods as being valuable and worthwhile.
- They have different ways of deriving meaning from the data gathered.
- They vary with regard to the relationship between research and practice.

These three paradigms—postpositivism, interpretivism, and critical theory—are the dominant guiding frameworks in the research literature in the social sciences. However, there is no legitimate way of asserting with absolute confidence that one paradigm is better than another. Because of that inability to make a final choice with supreme confidence, scholars and research consumers should be willing to acknowledge that the viewpoints and procedures based on other paradigms are accepted and used by "reasonable" scholars even if they do not agree with them. This last point is one with which proponents of all the paradigms have difficulty (although we all tend to think that people who do not use "our" paradigm have more difficulty than we do).

However, there is a difference between limiting the work of others because it does not fit our criteria for acceptable research and working out in our own minds what we believe and arguing forcefully for that. I am an interpretivist, and I believe that paradigm affords the best framework within which to interpret and conduct research in my field. I also believe that the interpretive and critical perspectives overlap and that critical theory is an important and productive research tradition of the social sciences. (That said, I must also acknowledge that research in the quantitative postpositivist tradition has supplied a rich vein of knowledge as well. However, this book focuses on qualitative research in the interpretive and critical traditions.)

Implicit in this book is a view of the relationship between our preferred paradigm and other paradigms. This book focuses on certain ways of researching an issue without asserting that other alternatives are valueless. Again, there is a difference between deciding what you believe and being so confident you are "right" that you try to impose your views on others. As a journal editor, for example, I do not feel I have the right to judge an article submitted to my journal as "right" or "wrong" on the basis of whether it adheres to the paradigm I currently use. The question is not whether it fits my paradigm. The proper question is, "Would scholars within the paradigm used in this article consider it a contribution to the literature? Do they support it being published?" None of us, regardless of the paradigm we adhere to, can be so confident we are right that we can justify limiting the practice of others. There are serious flaws in the logic of all three of the major paradigms (see Chalmers, 1990, 1995; Smith, 1993). There is no absolute winner in any effort to find the paradigm that has no flaws or weaknesses, although some authors continue to argue that there is. For example, D. C. Phillips and Nicholas Barbules (2000) continue to assert, "We need disciplined, competent inquiry to establish which of our beliefs are warranted and which are chimerical. And the philosophy that will serve us best in our endeavors is postpositivism" (p. 92).

Like Phillips and Barbules, I will make an effort to convince you that the paradigm choices I have made are good ones you should also consider. However, I do not think the choices are so straightforward that everyone who thinks about them will make the same choices I have. Thus, my goal for readers is not to convert you to my choices. It is to help you make better-informed and thoughtful choices as both a producer and a consumer of social science research.

Summary

In the social sciences there are a number of general frameworks for doing research. The terms *qualitative* and *quantitative* often are used to describe two of these frameworks. However, these terms imply that the main difference between the different frameworks is the type of data collected: numbers or something else such as interviews or observations. Actually, the differences are much broader and deeper than type of data. They involve assumptions and beliefs on several different levels, from philosophical positions about the nature of the world and how humans can better understand the world they live in to assumptions about the proper relationships between social science research and professional practice. Terms such as *world view* and *paradigm* better capture the nature of the differences between different approaches to social science research, and this book focuses on three of the most popular paradigms or world views today: positivism or postpositivism, interpretivism, and critical theory.

Questions for Reflection

1. Consider your own history of contact with research in the social sciences and education. Have you been exposed to several different paradigms or primarily to one? As you start reading this book, what is your paradigm—what are your beliefs about critical issues such as the nature of the world and sources of knowledge about the world? For example, do you accept a materialistic view of the world, that the only thing that exists is the physical world? Or do you believe there is something else, a mental or spiritual element? What is the basis for your beliefs? And what are the ways humans can understand the world better? Is scientific research the only way? What other ways, if any, of knowing the world do you accept or reject? Intuition? Subjective experience? Religious visions? Holy books? Poetry? Ancient wisdom? Prophesy? Folk wisdom?

2. The knowledge and skills needed to be a good consumer of qualitative research are a subset of those needed to do qualitative research. Are there particular types of qualitative research you would like to learn to do? Are there particular types you would like to become a good consumer of? Why?

3. How does your answer to question 1 stack up to Chalmers's criteria for a paradigm? Are there areas of your paradigm that are undeveloped or underdeveloped? If so, why are they undeveloped or underdeveloped?

References

Beaudin, B. (1999). Keeping online asynchronous discussions on topic. *Journal of the Adult Learning Network, 3*(2), 41–55.

Bogdan, R., & Biklen, S. (2002). *Qualitative research for education: An introduction to theories and methods* (4th ed.). Boston: Allyn & Bacon.

Campbell, D., & Stanley, J. (1963). *Experimental and quasi-experimental designs for research.* Chicago: Rand McNally.

Chalmers, A. (1982). *What is this thing called science?* Queensland, Australia: University of Queensland.

Chalmers, A. (1990). *Science and its fabrication.* Minneapolis: University of Minnesota Press.

Chalmers, A. (1995). *What is this thing called science? An assessment of the nature and status of science and its methods* (2nd ed.). Indianapolis: Hackett.

Chalmers, A. (1999). *What is this thing called science?* (3rd ed.). Indianapolis: Hackett.

Christudason, A. (2003). A case for case-based learning. *Ideas on Teaching, 24.* Retrieved November 13, 2005, from http://www.cdtl.nus.edu.sg/Ideas/iot24.htm

Comte, A. (1854). *The positive philosophy* (H. Martineau, Trans.). New York: D. Appleton. Retrieved November 13, 2005, from http://www2.pfeiffer.edu/~lridener/DSS/Comte/comte.html

Condron, F. (2000, Spring). A survey of small-group teaching in the humanities: The ASTER Project. *Computers & Texts, 18/19,* 14–17. Retrieved November 13, 2005, from http://info.ox.ac.uk/ctitext/publish/comtxt/ct18-19/14condron.pdf

Craig, E. (1998). Metaphysics. In E. Craig (Ed.), *Routledge encyclopedia of philosophy.* London: Routledge. Retrieved November 13, 2005, from http://www.rep.routledge.com/article/N095

Creswell, J. (1997). *Qualitative inquiry and research design: Choosing among five traditions.* Thousand Oaks, CA: Sage.

Cupchik, G. (2001, February). Constructivist realism: An ontology that encompasses positivist and constructivist approaches to the social sciences. *Forum for Qualitative Social Research, 2*(1). Retrieved November 13, 2005, from http://www.qualitative-research.net/fqs-trexte/1-01/1-01cupchik-e.htm

Denzin, N., & Lincoln, Y. (Eds.). (1994). *Handbook of qualitative research.* Thousand Oaks, CA: Sage.

Denzin, N., & Lincoln, Y. (Eds.). (2000). *Handbook of qualitative research* (2nd ed.). Thousand Oaks, CA: Sage.

Eisner, E. (1997). *The enlightened eye: Qualitative inquiry and the enhancement of educational practice.* Columbus, OH: Merrill.

Feyerabend, P. K. (1975). *Against method.* London: Verso.

Feyerabend, P. K. (1993). *Against method* (3rd ed.). London: Verso.

George, N. (2004, March). Teaching at post-16. *British Journal of Educational Technology, 35*(2), 248.

Gephart, R. (1999, Summer). Paradigms and research methods. *Research Methods Forum, 4.* Retrieved November 13, 2005, from http://www.aom.pace.edu/rmd/1999_RMD_Forum_Paradigms_and_Research_Methods.htm

Greene, J., Benjamin, L., & Goodyear, L. (2001). The merits of mixing methods for evaluation. *Evaluation, 7*(1), 25–44.

Guba, E. (Ed.). (1990). *The paradigm dialog.* Newbury Park, CA: Sage.

Guba, E., & Lincoln, Y. (1994). Competing paradigms in qualitative research. In N. Denzin & Y. Lincoln (Eds.), *Handbook of qualitative research* (pp. 105–117). Thousand Oaks, CA: Sage.

Hajdukiewicz, J. R., Vicente, K. J., Doyle, D. J., Milgram, P., & Burns, C. M. (2001). Modeling a medical environment: An ontology for integrated medical informatics design. *International Journal of Medical Informatics, 62*(1), 79–99.

Harding, S. (1998). *Is science multicultural?: Postcolonialisms, feminisms, and epistemologies*. Bloomington: Indiana University Press.

Henrickson, L., & McKelvey, B. (2002, May). Foundations of a "new" social science: Institutional legitimacy from philosophy, complexity science, postmodernism, and agent-based modeling. In *Proceedings of the National Academy of Science* (Suppl. 3), 7288–7295. Retrieved November 13, 2005, from http://www.pubmedcentral.nih.gov/articlerender/fcgi?artid=128599

Heron, J. (1996). *Co-operative inquiry: Research into the human condition*. Thousand Oaks, CA: Sage.

Huitema, B. (1980). *The analysis of covariance and alternatives*. New York: Wiley.

IES (Institute of Education Sciences). (2003). *Identifying and implementing educational practices supported by rigorous evidence: A user friendly guide*. Washington, DC: Author. Retrieved November 13, 2005, from http://www.ed.gov/rschstat/research/pubs/rigorousevid/rigorousevid.pdf

Jelfs, A., & Colburn, C. (2002). Do students' approaches to learning affect their perceptions of using computing and information technology? *Journal of Educational Media, 27*(1–2), 41–53.

Johnson, R., & Wichern, D. (2002). *Applied multivariate statistical analysis* (5th ed.). New York: Prentice Hall.

Kant, I. (2003). *Critique of pure reason*. Mineola, NY: Dover Philosophical Classics. (Originally published 1781)

Kuhn, T. S. (1970). *The structure of scientific revolutions*. Chicago: University of Chicago Press.

Kuhn, T. S. (1996). *The structure of scientific revolutions* (3rd ed.). Chicago: University of Chicago Press.

Kuhn, T. S., Conant, J., & Haugeland, J. (2000). *The road since structure*. Chicago: University of Chicago Press.

Lakatos, I., & Musgrave, A. (Eds.). (1970). *Criticism and the growth of knowledge*. New York: Cambridge University Press.

Lindman, H. (1992). *Analysis of variance in experimental design*. New York: Springer Verlag.

Lockhart, R. (1997). *Introduction to statistics and data analysis for the behavioral sciences*. San Francisco: W.H. Freeman.

Martin, N. (1997). *Introduction to the personalized system of instruction*. Retrieved November 13, 2005, from http://www.cs.rochester.edu/u/www/courses/108/Fall-98/psi-intro/psi-intro.html

McBurney, D., & White, T. (2003). *Research methods*. Belmont, CA: Wadsworth.

Milliken, G., & Johnson, D. (2001). *Analysis of messy data: Volume III analysis of covariance*. Boca Raton, FL: CRC Press.

Montgomery, D. (2004). *Design and analysis of experiments* (6th ed.). New York: Wiley.

Montgomery, D., Peck, E., & Geoffrey, G. (2001). *Introduction to linear regression analysis* (3rd ed.). New York: Wiley.

Mueller, R. (Ed.). (1996). *Basic principles of structural equation modelling: An introduction to LISREL and EQS*. New York: Springer Verlag.

Ott, L., Longnecker, M., & Ott, R. (2000). *An introduction to statistical methods and data analysis*. New York: Duxbury.

Phillips, D. C. (2000). *The expanded social scientists bestiary*. Lanham, MD: Rowman & Littlefield.

Phillips, D. C., & Barbules, N. (2000). *Postpositivism and educational research*. Lanham, MD: Rowman & Littlefield.

Ratner, C. (1997). *Cultural psychology and qualitative methodology: Theoretical and empirical considerations*. New York: Springer.

Roussas, G. (2002). *An introduction to probability and statistical inference*. San Diego: Academic Press.

Rutherford, A. (2000). *Introducing ANOVA and ANCOVA*. Thousand Oaks, CA: Sage.

Savin-Baden, M. (2000). *Problem-based learning in higher education*. Philadelphia: Open University Press.

Schon, D. (1987). *Educating the reflective practitioner*. San Francisco: Jossey-Bass.

Schumacker, R., & Lomax, R. (2004). *A beginners guide to structural equation modeling*. Mahwah, NJ: Erlbaum.

Siegel, S., & Castellan, J. (1988). *Nonparametric statistics for the behavioral sciences*. New York: McGraw-Hill.

Smith, J. (1989). *The nature of social and educational inquiry: Empiricism versus interpretation*. Norwood, NJ: Ablex.

Smith, J. (1993). *After the demise of empiricism: The problem of judging social and educational inquiry*. New York: Ablex.

Sprinthall, R. (1996). *Basic statistical analysis* (5th ed.). Boston: Allyn & Bacon.

Tan, S. (2002, March). Is public space suited to co-operative inquiry? *Innovation: The European Journal of Social Science Research, 15*(1), 23–31.

VanVoorhis, J. L. (1999). The evaluation of teaching and effective questioning in college teaching: An interview with Wilbert J. McKeachie. *Journal of Excellence in College Teaching, 10*(1), 77–90.

Von Eye, A., Schuster, C., & Schiller, F. (Eds.). (1998). *Regression analysis for social sciences*. San Diego: Academic Press.

Welkowitz, J., Ewen, R., & Cohen, J. (1982). *Introductory statistics for the behavioral sciences* (2nd ed.). San Francisco: Academic Press.

Wittgenstein, L. (1973). *Philosophical investigations* (3rd ed., G. E. Anscombe, Trans.). New York: Prentice Hall.

CHAPTER 2

History and Context of Paradigm Development

In his book *The Lysenko Effect: The Politics of Science,* Nils-Roll Hansen (2004) tells the story of Trofim Denisovich Lysenko, an uneducated horticulturist who achieved fame by claiming that Darwinian evolution was wrong and that the older theory of evolution proposed by French scientist Jean-Baptiste Lamarck was correct. Essentially, Lamarck proposed that physical changes in an organism could be passed on to the next generation. For example, if short-necked giraffes stretch their necks to eat leaves high in a tree, their offspring could inherit longer necks. The leaders of the Soviet Union found the Lamarckian view appealing. A model of improvement based on the idea that changes in the environment could cause changes in animals and plants that would be passed on to the next generation was very attractive. It meant that "the working class were not slaves of the past but creators of the future" (Sheehan, 1993, p. 218).

In the 1920s the Soviet government supported research on both Darwinian and Lamarckian evolution. However, there were strong disagreements among Soviet scientists, especially about the "inheritance of acquired characteristics," the central theme of Lamarckian theory. While scientific evidence around the world was accumulating in favor of Darwinian evolution, in the Soviet Union proponents of the Lamarckian view began to cite the writings of Engels and Marx to support the theory. Essentially, their argument was that Marx and Engels's idea of *scientific determinism* was incompatible with Darwinian evolution because Darwin's theory relied on chance. The debate within Soviet science was fierce, but in the late 1920s it took an ominous turn.

Scientific Determinism

Classical Marxist ideology can be boiled down to a few main points. One is that there is an inherent conflict between those who own and control the means of production and the workers (the owners vs. the proletariat). Another main point is that traditional governments developed to protect and extend the control and power of the ruling class over the proletariat. Another pillar of Marxism is *scientific determinism* (also called hard determinism), the view that anything in the future is, in principle, predictable. That is, using the correct scientific procedures you can accurately predict what is going to happen. This has a number of implications. If everything is scientifically predictable, that means there is no room for things such as divine intervention, which means any claims to the contrary on the part of a religion are nonsense. And by eliminating the spiritual and divine aspects of existence, scientific determinism supports the materialist position (e.g., nothing exists except physical matter) of Marxism. Scientific determinism also allowed Marx and Engels to claim they had discovered laws of social development that assured us society was inexorably moving toward the collapse of capitalism and the development of socialist (communist) forms of social and economic organization. It was a matter not of whether but of when. By grounding in scientific determinism their belief in the inevitable triumph of their theories, they were able to reject not only religious beliefs but also many forms of liberal politics that could be defined as wrong because they violated Marx and Engels's scientifically derived laws of social development.

Trofim Lysenko, a Ukrainian agronomist, became famous for his work in Azerbaijan on ways to treat seeds so that they behaved differently and also passed on their new characteristics to the next generation of seeds. Lysenko made extravagant claims for the process he called "vernalization" and was promoted to more and more powerful positions despite the concerns of many scientists that his experiments were sloppy, his data faked, and his conclusions inaccurate. By 1935 he was a popular and respected figure in Soviet agriculture, and he proposed a broad theory of heredity that rejected the existence of genes and held that the basis of heredity did not lie in some special self-reproducing substance. On the contrary, "the cell itself . . . developed into an organism, and there was no part of it not subject to evolutionary development. Heredity was based on the interaction between the organism and its environment" (Sheehan, 1993, p. 223). Furthermore, he asserted that Darwinian and Mendelian genetics was "reactionary, bourgeois, idealist and formalist. It was held to be contrary to the Marxist philosophy of dialectical materialism" (Sheehan, 1993, p. 224). A Darwinist approach made evolutionary change in genetics a slow process that occurred almost by accident over many generations of a species, whereas Lysenko's approach allowed genetic changes to occur over a single generation. Lysenko captured Stalin's interest, and the result was a series of purges that sent many opponents of Lysenko's views to gulags or to undocumented deaths after the secret police arrested them in the middle of the night. In the 1930s Lysenkoites converted a scientific debate into a political one and accused scientists with Darwinian and Mendelian leanings of being racists, fascists, saboteurs, terrorists, Trotskyites, "powers of darkness," and "handmaidens of Goebbels" (Sheehan, 1993, p. 225). Helena Sheehan's book *Marxism and the Philosophy of Science* (1993) tells what happened to Nikolai Vavilov, perhaps the most respected and outspoken critic of Lysenko:

> In 1940, Vavilov was himself arrested, and Lysenko replaced him as director of the Institute of Genetics of the Academy of Sciences. In 1941, Vavilov stood trial and was found guilty of sabotage in agriculture, belonging to a rightist conspiracy, spying for England [because he published papers in British scholarly journals], and a string of other charges. Although he denied all accusations and the "evidence" consisted of false testimony, he was sentenced to death. After spending several months in a death cell, Vavilov's sentence was commuted, but he died in prison in 1943 of malnutrition. (p. 225)

Dialectical Materialism

Marx borrowed from German philosopher Hegel the idea that the world is not a static entity; instead, it is active and ever changing. In that process, development happens through contradictions in which some things are destroyed, and from which new things emerge. It is thus a *dia-electic* process. Marx used Hegel's concept of the dialectic, but he did not accept Hegel's proposition that the process was started by an Ideal Power (e.g., God), nor did he agree with Hegel's idealistic position that *ideas* are primary over physical things. Instead Marx adopted the materialism of another German philosopher, Ludwig Feuerbach, who believed the world was made up only of matter. Feuerbach rejected the notion that a supreme being created the world. Feuerbach was a materialist; he saw *matter* as primary rather than ideas. Marx's combination of the dialectics of Hegel and the materialism of Feuerbach produced *dialectical materialism,* which became the foundation not only for Marxist–Leninist political theory but for science in the Soviet Union.

Many others who resisted Lysenko's theories were arrested.

> Of these some were shot, while others simply died in prison. Others were witch-hunted, lost their jobs, and were forced into other areas of work. Institutes were closed down. Journals ceased to appear. Books were removed from library shelves. Texts were revised. Names became unmentionable. The 7th International Congress of Genetics, which was scheduled to be held in Moscow in August 1937 was cancelled. When the congress did take place in Edinburgh in 1939, no Soviet scientists were present, not even Vavilov who had been elected its president. (Sheehan, 1993, p. 226)

There are many lessons to be learned from the Lysenko affair. It is certainly an example of what can happen when scientists let political ideology intrude on science. It also illustrates what can happen when one paradigm is so entrenched that disagreeing with it is considered traitorous. In this case, the paradigm was Marxist–Leninist political and scientific philosophy, which was officially and brutally supported by the Soviet bureaucracy. Many Westerners are not aware that the Soviet government made it a point of faith that their system of government had been "scientifically proven" to be the best, and until 1991 almost every college student in the Soviet Union, regardless of major, took a required course on scientific communism.

In the Soviet system, the purpose of all science was to advance the cause of "scientific socialism," to use Engels's term. There was no question of whether science should be value free; it must be infused with the values of Marxist–Leninism. As J. D. Bernal (1937) put it,

> The relevance of Marxism in the development of science is both theoretical and practical. It removes science from its imagined position of complete detachment and shows it as part, a critically important part, of economic and social development. The complete revolution of the history of science as the result of Marxist analysis . . . is one of the first results of this new attitude. But for Marxism understanding is inseparable from action, and the appreciation of the social position of science leads at once in a socialist country, such as the U.S.S.R., to the organic connection of scientific research with the development of socialized industry and human culture. The organization of science in capitalist countries has gradually molded itself in the service of big business, but because the process is not understood or appreciated its service is poor and incredibly wasteful. In any case production for profit can never develop the full potentialities of science except for

destructive purposes. The Marxist understanding of science puts it in practice at the service of the community and at the same time makes science itself part of the cultural heritage of the whole people and not of an artificially selected minority.

That meant science was based on a materialistic, monistic view of the world; God and similar metaphysical concepts were rejected. Science was also incorporated into the broader world view of Marxism: dialectical materialism.

Much of the impact of dialectical materialism in the social sciences is expressed through a derivation called historical materialism. Marx referred to what we call historical materialism as "the material conception of history." In essence, he meant that the changes in human and social behavior across history are caused by material things and the efforts of different groups to obtain more material goods at the expense of other groups. Historical materialism is thus the conceptual foundation of Marxism.

Stalin's Great Terror in the 1930s was an extreme example of what totalitarianism can do to a society, and at the heart of totalitarianism is the idea that there is one world view or paradigm that must be accepted by everyone. Thousands of priests, intellectuals, military officers, party members, actors, musicians, students, and ordinary citizens (and their families) were arrested and murdered or sent into exile by the NKVD (precursor to the KGB). Sometimes there were "show trials," but often the people just disappeared. Stalin justified his approach by referring to aspects of dialectical materialism that predict that as the development of revolution progresses, contradictions increase, and therefore resistance increases. To accomplish great things calls for fighting the enemy. Furthermore, as dialectical materialism posits, if we are to understand why Stalin behaved the way he did we must understand the context in which he operated. Contextual understanding is also the focus of two of the three paradigms that guide social science research today. This chapter takes a contextual tour of all three of the major paradigms covered in this book. You will see that all were, perhaps more than anything else, a response to problems their creators saw in society and in science.

Article of Interest

Marlène Laruelle. (2004). The discipline of culturology: A new ready-made thought for Russia. *Diogenes, 51,* **21–36.**

With the collapse of the Soviet empire, Russia entered a period of uncertainty. Established and official foundational beliefs such as dialectical materialism were swept out of their privileged places. However, Russians had become accustomed to an official orthodoxy from the 80 years of Communist rule and the hundreds of years of Czarist rule. Marlène Laruelle's article documents the rise of a new discipline, *culturology,* in Russia that may be popular now in part because it can replace some of the discarded doctrines such as dialectical materialism and provide Russians with "ready-made thought." In universities where courses with names such as "Scientific Communism" and "History of the Communist Party of the USSR" were required of all students, they now are required to take a course in culturology. Laruelle's analysis of the roles culturology plays in Russian culture and of the origins and structure of the discipline makes interesting reading. Is culturology a continuation of Leninist–Marxist thinking? Is it an effort to provide yet another orthodoxy that defines what Russia is? Or is it a break with the past and a move toward Western social science?

To read the entire article, please go to http://www.sagepub.com/willis_aoi.

Three Paradigms

In many ways the major paradigms of social science research have separate histories. They were responses to different problems, and they adopted different ways of addressing those problems. They were influenced by the cultures in which they grew, and they made radically different assumptions about issues such as the nature of truth. The next two chapters deal with the question of foundational assumptions and how they influence conceptions of research. Before that, however, this chapter addresses another point: the problems that founders of the three different paradigms saw as barriers to human progress. To understand these paradigms, some understanding of the cultural and social context in which they emerged is essential. Each of the major paradigms makes much more sense if you understand what the founders were responding to in the culture around them.

Positivism: A Response to Metaphysical and Magical Explanations

A fundamental assumption of positivism is that the use of the scientific method is the primary or only way of discovering truths about the world. Positivism, or empiricism, assumes we can discover universals about human behavior if we do a good job of scientifically and objectively studying them in well-controlled contexts. This perspective emerged during the Renaissance (about 1450–1600) and the Enlightenment (1600–1800) as part of a general move toward the use of experiments and observations to discover truths about the world. During that period, William Harvey discovered that blood circulates through the body, and Copernicus proposed that the planets, including Earth, revolve around the sun. Few question the accomplishments of science during the Renaissance and Enlightenment, but it is important to recognize that the use of more objective and "scientific" approaches to all sorts of topics, both physical and social, was a marked departure from the methods of the era preceding the Renaissance, namely the Middle Ages.

The Middle Ages (330–1450)

The Middle Ages lasted from about 330 to 1450 in Europe, and intellectual life in the latter part of this period was dominated by two characteristics: a reverence for the knowledge of Greek and Roman scholars such as Aristotle and an emphasis on the value of the Christian religion as a source of truth about the world around us. Scholastics, or *schoolmen,* often tried to uncritically apply the thinking of Greek and Roman philosophers, and they often used religious texts and beliefs as a source of knowledge about everything from the place of Earth in the universe to the way humans think. Scholasticism even combined these two characteristics by asserting that the Greek and Roman philosophers were expressing an eternal, God-given truth and therefore could not be fallible. Furthermore, given the assumption that the writings of Aristotle were inspired by God, it followed that they could not be in conflict with the Gospels because they too were God-given. Scholastic scholars were more likely to write books to communicate the thinking of Aristotle than conduct original experiments or carry out systematic observations. Thus, although much of the specifics of Greek and Roman science was incorrect, the Scholastics did little to discover those errors and advance what we know about the world. However, attributing what we believe, our truths, to a god is a traditional road to all sorts of problems and disasters. The Crusades in the Middle Ages (1096–1270) are an example of conflicts based on different religious beliefs. People on both sides justified their barbarity by saying it was for God and thus sanctioned by God. The problems Galileo had with the Catholic Church when he proposed that the earth revolved around the sun illustrate this problem in science. Galileo based his conclusion on observations he had made, whereas his opponents based their conclusions on religious beliefs and church policy. And because his opponents were positive their beliefs and policies were God-given, they had difficulty giving them up without also having to question their entire religious belief system. Science in the modern sense was severely restricted by the power of religion and the reverence for ancient sources of knowledge.

The Renaissance (1450–1600): The Beginning of Empiricism

The end of the Middle Ages and the beginning of the Renaissance was marked by a change in the roles of three sources of knowledge. Greek and Roman scholarship and the Christian religion became less important in efforts to discover how the world really is. The Renaissance was also a period in which another source—experimentation and observation—became critically important. Roger Bacon advocated this shift as early as 1268:

> Having laid down the main points of the wisdom of the Latins as regards language, mathematics and optics, I wish now to review the principles of wisdom from the point of view of experimental science, because without experiment it is impossible to know anything thoroughly.

Bacon was also clearly aware that other forms of knowing were still competing with the scientific method:

> Authors write many things and the people cling to them through arguments which they make without experiment, that are utterly false. . . .
> Experience is of two kinds. One is through the external senses: such are the experiments that are made upon the heaven through instruments in regard to facts there, and the facts on earth that we prove in various ways to be certain in our own sight. . . .
> And because this experimental science is a study entirely unknown by the common people, I cannot convince them of its utility, unless its virtue and characteristics are shown. . . . If we would attain to experiments precise, complete and made certain in accordance with the proper method, it is necessary to undertake an examination of the science itself, which is called experimental on our authority.

These quotes from Bacon incorporate nearly all the foundations of a positivist (and postpositivist) paradigm of research:

- Experimentation is the method for learning about the world.
- Much error is perpetuated by authors, philosophers, theologians, magicians, and others who confidently express truths that are false and that have not been subjected to experimental evaluation.
- Good research must be quantitative; it must use numbers because no science can be known without mathematics. Armchair reasoning or thinking about an issue is inferior to quantitative experimentation as a way of acquiring knowledge.

Bacon's discussion incorporates the essential elements of the scientific method as it is practiced today. However, it is important to consider Bacon's advocacy of the scientific method in context. That context includes the sources of knowledge that were considered credible in the 13th century. In his book he mentions some of them, including magicians. It is not an overstatement to say that the growing reliance on scientific method during this era was a response to a culture that accepted the pronouncements of magicians, the beliefs of the Scholastics and the church hierarchy, and ancient texts as supremely credible sources of universal knowledge about many aspects of the world. The early empiricists, such as Galileo, found the methods of the Scholastics unsatisfactory as a means of learning more about the world. Galileo sought knowledge in a different way: scientific. However, it was not an easy transition. McCleary (1998) tells the story this way:

> As a young mathematics professor at the University of Pisa, Galileo Galilei (1564–1642) designed a simple experiment to test Aristotle's assertion that heavier objects fall faster than lighter objects; he dropped light and heavy objects from the Leaning Tower and measured the time they took to reach the ground. This research was controversial in two respects. First, crude empiricists like Galileo were a minority among physicists of that period.
>
> Second, the experimental results challenged Aristotle's Physics. Because his colleagues were largely Aristotelians, Galileo was fired. Moving to the University of Padua, Galileo concentrated on astronomy. . . . Now in those days, there were two competing models of the solar system. The prevailing Aristotelian–Ptolemaic geocentric model held that the earth was a fixed center-point around which the planets orbited in perfect concentric circles. The newer Copernican heliocentric model held that earth and the other planets followed elliptical orbits around the sun. Since Galileo's work cast doubt on the prevailing model, it came under attack by Aristotelian scholars. In 1614, this work was denounced as heresy by a local priest. Galileo responded with an open letter that challenged the relevance of Biblical passages to scientific fact; Galileo argued that the Church should have no opinion on questions that could be answered empirically. In 1616, all Copernican books were censored and Galileo was ordered to recant his heliocentric beliefs. Galileo remained silent until 1632 when he published an essay on the implications of ocean tide data for the two competing solar system models. Although Church censors had licensed this essay, Galileo was tried for heresy by the Inquisition and was sentenced to life imprisonment; his essay was burned, and a denunciation was read publicly

in every university. Under house arrest and blind, Galileo died in 1642. More than 200 years later, in 1979, Pope John Paul II reopened the inquiry into the charges against Galileo. Thirteen years later, in 1992, a papal commission acknowledged the Church's error in condemning Galileo.[1]

The Age of Enlightenment (1600–1800): Empiricism as a Major Source of Knowledge

During the Renaissance, empiricism flowered. The Renaissance was followed by the Age of Enlightenment (1600–1800). During this era systematic observation and a rudimentary scientific method became a major source of knowledge, and competing sources continued to decline in influence.

Empiricism and Rationalism

The broadest meaning of the term *empiricism* is that what we know about the world comes from experience. The idea is often traced back to Aristotle, who advocated the careful observation and study of nature in order to understand it. Aristotle's emphasis on careful study of the world was in contrast to Plato's idealistic approach. For Plato, the things in the world were no more than flawed and inaccurate copies of ideal forms. For example, any horse that Aristotle might study would have some flaws or imperfections that the perfect or ideal horse would not. For Plato the way to understand the ideal form of a horse was to think about it, not study many horses in the physical world. Plato's approach is called rationalism because the path to understanding is rational thinking rather than intensive observation. Aristotle thus supported a materialist ontology and an empirical epistemology. In contrast, Plato advocated an idealist ontology and a rational epistemology. These two approaches lead to very different conclusions about many basic issues. For example, Aristotle's materialism and empiricism lead to the conclusion that we derive all our ideas from experience. Plato's idealism and rationalism support the proposition that there are innate ideas, ideas humans already have in their minds when they are born. Later, people such as English philosopher John Locke (1632–1704) followed the path laid down by Aristotle and asserted that humans are born a blank slate (*tabula rasa* in Latin) and that experience determines what a person thinks and believes.

Since the Enlightenment the term *empiricism* gradually has come to mean the use of the scientific method to learn about the world. The term *scientific method* was rather loosely defined in the beginning, but it has gradually acquired a very detailed set of concepts, procedures, and techniques that must be followed before a study will be accepted as scientific.

Although empiricism has dominated Western thinking since the Enlightenment, rationalism has remained a potent force. For example, German philosopher Immanuel Kant (1724–1804) made innate ideas a foundation of his philosophical system. In the 20th century the long-running debate over whether nature (e.g., inherited characteristics) or nurture (the experiences of a person) determines what humans become reflected questions Aristotle and Plato raised 2,500 years ago. In the late 20th century, linguist and political activist Noam Chomsky became famous arguing that languages have both a surface structure, which can vary widely from one language to another, and a deep structure, which is common across all human languages. He argued that the deep structure of language was universal because it was innate.

Finally, Harvard psychologist Steven Pinker, in a book titled *The Blank Slate: The Modern Denial of Human Nature* (2002), forcefully argued that humans are born with a large set of inborn predispositions that influence everything from learning of language to gender bias and political beliefs. Pinker uses Darwinian evolutionary theory to explain how humans come to possess innate tendencies or characteristics, and he uses those characteristics to explain many things in contemporary society, from rape and violence to music and art.

Pinker deals with one aspect of the difference between traditional empiricism and traditional rationalism: whether humans come into the world with innate ideas. The alternative is Locke's blank slate view. Pinker comes down solidly on the nature side of the nature–nurture debate. As one reviewer put it,

> A juggernaut of data has finally put the nature/nurture controversy to rest, at least from a scientific standpoint, and the final score is pretty much nature one, nurture zero. Fifty to seventy percent of the variation between individuals—in intelligence, in personality, in political leanings, or just about any other mental character you care to name—derives from the genes; zero to ten percent derives from the home environment; and the mysterious remainder is due to chance or to non-parental environment. (Buehler, 2002)

Pinker thus comes down on the rationalist side of the nature–nurture debate. However, Pinker is neither a thoroughgoing empiricist nor a rationalist. He draws on both rationally developed evidence and conclusions from empirical research to support his thesis. This combination of rational and empirical perspectives is typical among scholars today, who generally acknowledge that good research involves both rational decision making and interpretation and empirical data gathering. In fact, the modern conception of scientific method combines experimentation (e.g., experience or empiricism) with rational thought (e.g., the selection of topics, methods, data to be collected, the process of interpretation).

Eighteenth-century philosophers called their century the Age of Enlightenment. From our perspective, however, there is good reason to include the 17th century in this period. During that earlier century, the debate between rationalists (e.g., Descartes, Spinoza) and empiricists (e.g., Bacon, Locke) came into sharp focus, early scientists (e.g., Galileo, Newton) wrote new rules of inquiry, and faith in the power of human reason (humanism) prevailed. The Enlightenment is generally thought to have ended with the French Revolution or the end of the 18th century. Before the Enlightenment, the dominant way of knowing was an appeal to authority, particularly the church, the state, the Bible, or a classical philosopher (ironically, Aristotle). After the Enlightenment, the dominant way of knowing was empirical observation, particularly science; Kant suggested *"Sapere Aude!"* or "Dare to know!" as a motto for the Enlightenment (McCleary, 1998).

In the early part of the Enlightenment Francis Bacon made eloquent statements about knowledge coming from perception and observation, and Thomas Hobbes talked about the mind as a machine. Later, John Locke and George Berkeley refined the concept of research as a quantitative, scientific process. Although some form of empiricism can be traced back to Aristotle (at least), it is most closely associated with English philosophers John Locke and Francis Bacon. By 1800, the fantastic successes of science in fields such as biology, chemistry, and physics had elevated empirical science to a position well above that of its competitors as a source of truth.

That prestige also influenced the social sciences, which emerged as separate disciplines in the late 19th century. Although not all the founders were empiricists, that persuasion eventually carried the day. Since the founding of the first psychology laboratory by Wilhelm Wundt at Leipzig University in 1875, empiricism has been one of the dominant forces, first in the German conception of psychology and then in the American tradition of psychology. (Ironically, Wundt's first lecture was called "The Influence of Philosophy on the Experiential Sciences.") Other fields of social science, such as sociology and anthropology, were also influenced by the scientific revolution but not as thoroughly as psychology.

Since its inception psychology has focused on experimentation. One reason for psychology's emphasis (and that of other social sciences) on the scientific method was the tremendous success of the natural and physical sciences, both in areas of basic knowledge and in the application of that knowledge to important problems.

Another reason for the adoption of a scientific approach was psychology's desire to be accepted as a "real" science like the physical sciences. The scientific method is the dominant source of knowledge in the physical sciences, and for much of the 20th century psychology has attempted to emulate those fields, particularly physics.

Psychology in the 20th century, especially American psychology, was heavily influenced by logical positivism and other empiricist philosophies of science. Logical positivism can be described as the modern direct descendant of Locke and Bacon's empiricism (McCleary, 1998). The logical positivists were the most extreme of the positivists. They defined both subject matter and methods in terms of a very strict empiricism. Their efforts to develop a paradigm in the empiricist tradition was based on naive positivism. Naive positivists assumed that by conducting proper experiments you make conclusive deductions about how the world really is (this is sometimes called the correspondence theory of truth). The naive positivist position assumes that if you follow the rules set down for good research, your data will reveal the truth about the world. This is called a correspondence theory of truth because research is supposed to tell you which theories correspond to what is in the external world.

> The key aim of the logical positivists who flourished in Vienna in the 1920s and 1930s, and whose considerable influence persists into the 21st century, was to defend science and to distinguish it from metaphysical and religious discourse, which most of them dismissed as non-scientific nonsense. They endeavored to construct a general definition or characterization of science, including the methods appropriate for its construction and the criteria to be appealed to in its appraisal. (Chalmers, 1990, p. 4)

In the 1930s and 1940s Sir Karl Popper and others published devastating criticisms of logical positivism, or naive positivism as it is sometimes called. For example, Popper pointed out that logical positivism assumed that through well-constructed experiments, you could arrive at the truth about something. Popper showed that you could not because there is always the possibility that the data gathered do not represent reality. Data that disprove a hypothesis are more definitive than data that support a hypothesis. In Popper's view, then, you can definitively disprove a hypothesis but you can never prove it beyond any doubt. An example often used to illustrate this point is an empiricist turkey living in North America who heard that humans ate turkeys. The empiricist turkey gathered data on this question for many days, weeks, and months, beginning in January. After gathering data for 10 months the turkey considered the data definitive; it was clear that humans did not eat turkeys. Then, on the fourth Thursday in November (or the second Monday in October if the turkey was living in Canada) one data point proved he was wrong: Humans do eat turkeys.

Faced with a number of effective critiques, many social scientists moved to a modified version of positivism, now called postpositivism.

Postpositivism accepts the idea that you can never do enough research to be absolutely sure your theory is correct because there are all sorts of reasons why a particular study or group of studies might yield false results (e.g., experimenter bias, poor instruments, improper subject selection, misinterpretation of the data). Postpositivism in the Popper tradition takes a falsificationist approach. That is, confirming studies do not "prove" anything; they simply add to the evidence that supports a theory. On the other hand, a well-done study that does not turn out the way your theory predicts suggests strongly that your theory is incorrect. This form of positivism, generally called postpositivism, will be explored in more detail in the next chapter.

By the end of the 18th century the natural sciences such as chemistry, physics, and astronomy were well established. Although most of the leaders in these fields professed strong religious beliefs, they rejected the dominance of religious authority and Greek wisdom in the natural sciences. Instead, they elevated the scientific method to the position of supreme arbiter of what was and was not true.

Logical Positivism

Sometimes called the Vienna Circle because the scientists and philosophers who made up the group often met at cafes in Vienna, the logical positivists emerged at a time (the 1920s) when many people still regarded religion, myth, and metaphysics as reliable sources of scientific knowledge. (Metaphysics is anything outside the realm of the physical world, such as ideals, thoughts, mind, consciousness, and spirit.) The group was also known as *logical empiricists, logical neopositivists,* and *neopositivists*. Moriz Schlick was founder, and Rudolf Carnap, Otto Neurath, and Carl Gustav Hempel were leaders. When the Nazis came to power in Austria in the 1930s, several logical positivists, including Carnap, came to America and had a profound influence on American philosophy during the prewar and postwar period. (Schlick was murdered in 1936 by a Nazi student on the campus of the University of Vienna.)

A major concern of the Vienna Circle was to precisely define and prescribe how knowledge should be acquired. They began with the assertion that there were only two sources of knowledge: logical reasoning (i.e., analytic a priori) and experience (i.e., synthetic a posteriori). Logical knowledge is basically knowledge that is true within a specified framework. Mathematics is an example because $2 + 2 = 4$ according to the prespecified logic of mathematics (at least base-10 mathematics). However, the logical positivists were particularly interested in knowledge that comes from experience.

They developed a very precise version of the scientific method that specified how experience could be used to develop valid knowledge in any discipline, from anthropology to zoology. They proposed that this method was universal, that all disciplines must use their method of research if they were to develop valid knowledge. After he came to America, Neurath was even the editor of an ambitious publication called the *International Encyclopedia of Unified Science*.

By limiting sources of knowledge to logic and experience, the logical positivists excluded synthetic a priori knowledge. That is, no knowledge was accepted as given regardless of the source (but especially if the source was religion or traditional philosophy). Instead they proposed the famous *verifiability principle*. A statement of fact was meaningless unless it could be validated—established as true or false—through experience (at least in principle). If you could not specify a way to test whether a statement was true or false, then the statement had no meaning and no place in science. (This principle has been used to reject two popular theories, Marxism and Freud's psychoanalysis, because both theories are flexible enough to explain almost any outcome of an experiment to test the truth of the theory.) Thus, much of philosophy, which relies on the relationship between the meanings of different words, was relegated to metaphysics and rejected as meaningless because there was no way to test it empirically. Even topics such as ethics fall outside the realm of science according to the logical positivists because the rules of ethics are not subject to verification. In essence, logical positivists took the position that the *only* knowledge that was valid was scientific knowledge.

The logical positivists developed a framework for creating scientific theories and then developing hypotheses from those theories. They used the form "If Theory X is true, then Result Y should occur when this experiment is conducted in this manner." They accepted that some content of a theory might be untestable, but they insisted on a tight link between the "theoretical" parts of a theory and the "observable" parts that could be tested. For example, if an aspect of a theory could not be empirically verified, Carnap proposed that there must be empirical laws that are logically deduced from it that could be tested. If the empirical law turns out to be true, then that aspect of the theory is supported. This approach makes science a deductive process: You begin with a broad theory, deduce specific, testable hypotheses from the theory, and then empirically test the truth of that hypothesis. For example, if an implication of a theory is that crowded conditions in a city cause certain types of crime, a study that supports that hypothesis would also support the underlying theory.

The logical positivists also emphasized the need to use language carefully so that terms and concepts were tied precisely to observable aspects of the physical world. They thought religion and other forms of metaphysical belief were barriers to knowledge, and their famous maxim for a sentence to have cognitive meaning required that it could be demonstrated to be either true or false by either being logically (e.g., analytically) consistent or inconsistent or being subject to empirical verification.

(Continued)

(Continued)

> To summarize, the logical positivists were materialists and realists in that they believed only the physical or "real" world existed, they were empiricists in that they judged the truth of statements by comparing them to what actually happened in the real world, and they were positivists in that they believed the scientific method was the sole source of valid knowledge.

Positivism and postpositivism are foundations for most of the research in the natural sciences. They also became foundations for the social sciences in the 19th and 20th centuries. Smith (1989) traces the importing of positivism into the social sciences to French philosopher Auguste Comte. As noted earlier, the 17th and 18th centuries were ones in which some sources of absolute truth—religion and ancient texts—became less influential. Comte's approach offered another absolutist perspective:

> Comte was a figure to reckon with in the second half of the nineteenth century. He appealed to many reflective people who had given up traditional Christianity but needed a psychological replacement; Comte offered a scheme in which humankind advanced from a religious sensibility to a scientific one. The latter provided a means for ameliorating our social estate. In some interpretations a corporate scientific and bureaucratic community was the basis for Comte's famous "religion of humanity." This secular church would generate the political leadership for a utopian, if conservative, cultural order. (Kuklick, 1995, p. 1227)

Comte's positivism was an effort to replace the confidence that had been placed in religion, and other ancient sources, with science (Steele, 2002). By using the scientific method, we could come to know how the world really is. This approach is called naive realism (naive because it ignores a whole host of problems that make it difficult to say that the results of an experiment are perfect reflections of an out-there reality). Smith (1989) points out that Comte's positivism was in part an extension of the Enlightenment with its rejection of religion and metaphysics as sources of scientific knowledge. However, Comte was also responding to a development he considered quite negative:

> Along with the traditionalists . . . he believed that the Enlightenment had brought about an excessive individualism that was leading to a

general disintegration of European society. To prevent this disintegration required a return to order and stability, but this could not mean a return to what he called a "retrograde" theological system that was advocated by many conservatives. (Smith, 1989, p. 41)

The answer to the need for more stability was positivism, the idea that science and the scientific method can be used as the final arbiter of what is correct and incorrect in society. Even before Comte, John Locke and John Stuart Mill built most of the foundations for what we call empiricism and the scientific method today. The relationship of basic beliefs to research practice is obvious in the work of these early empiricists. For example, Locke accepted the duality of mind and body (following Descartes), which meant you could separate the feelings and opinions of the mind from the real or physical world. Without that belief, you could not justify the scientific method because it requires that research be conducted objectively, without the influence of personal values, feelings, and beliefs.

By the late 19th century, an approach to the study of social life modeled on the natural sciences was being firmly established. The desire to master social life expressed itself in a concern for the discovery of social laws; in the development of methods that stressed the observation of experiences, experiments, and comparisons; in the separation of facts from values; and in the separation of the cognizing subject from the object of cognition (Smith, 1989, p. 45).

The social sciences emerged in the late 19th century. Comte coined the term *sociology*, Wundt established psychology at Leipzig University, and Durkheim established a base for sociology (and the other social sciences) that was largely in the image of the natural sciences. That the social sciences tried to emulate the natural sciences is illustrated by Smith's (1989, p. 48) summary of Durkheim's vision of the foundation of social sciences:

• Social science should be "a neutral, objective, and value free process."

• Dualism of mind and body is possible. You can separate cognitions about an object from the object itself.

• The goal of social science research "was to use the knowledge obtained from observation to discover reality and find the causes of social phenomena. This required a scientific language, different from a lay language."

Today, social scientists who adopt a positivist position would still agree with the three characteristics of Durkheim's position. The possible exception would be the idea that social science should be neutral and objective. Most positivists today agree that the process of research should be objective, but some argue that the way a topic of research is selected or a theory developed may involve subjective decisions.

To summarize, positivism and a belief in the scientific method as the best or only source of valid knowledge in the sciences began as a response to other sources of knowledge, especially religion and ancient sources, that were considered inferior. Dissatisfied with the lack of progress during the Middle Ages, scholars such as Galileo began to base their conclusions about reality on observations and experiments. By the time the social sciences emerged as separate disciplines in the 19th century, the natural sciences had adopted positivism. They had also been spectacularly successful, and many of the founders of the social sciences wanted to adopt the same approach when studying human behavior. The next section explores another paradigm, critical theory.

Critical Theory: A Response to Inequities in Society

Some of the origins of a Marxist–Leninist philosophy of science were discussed at the beginning of this chapter. This section focuses on the modern expression of that tradition: critical theory (Rush, 2004). *Critical theory* is a broad term that can apply to a number of movements in the social sciences. Guba (1990) prefers the term *ideologically oriented inquiry* because a major focus of the critical approach is the analysis of data through the lens of an ideology. Guba points out that several terms are associated with this approach, including *neo-Marxism, materialism, the Frankfurt School,* and *Freireism.* All these approaches have links back to classical Marxism, and that common ancestor is the source of many of the shared perspectives between these different frameworks.

The beliefs of critical theory are discussed in more detail in the next chapter, but they are tied intimately to the emergence of Marxism in the 19th century. Critical theory was built on the foundation of Marxism by scholars who thought that classical Marxist theory was not sufficient to deal with the complex social and economic structure of modern societies.

What Did Marxism Respond To?

Marxism matured in the 19th century, when industrialization was sweeping Europe. Industrialization profoundly changed the relative status of workers, who, instead of toiling on a farm as the serfs of a landowner, now moved into towns and began to work in factories. Ken Follett's 1995 novel *A Place*

Called Freedom is fictional, but it documents the awful living and working conditions of Scottish workers in the coal mines of absentee owners in the 18th century. For example, a person who was working in a mine when he reached the age of majority was owned by that mine until death and could not legally work anywhere else without the owner's permission. The condition of the oppressed factory workers during this period was as bad as or worse than that of the serfs under feudalism. In fact, Marxism is based on the assumption that the Haves are always going to oppress the Have-Nots and even introduce policies and procedures designed to keep the Have-Nots from ever becoming equals. Engels's book *The Origin of Family, Private Ownership, and Exploitation of Man by Man* laid the social and philosophical foundations for classical Marxism, and Marx's *Das Kapital* provided the economic theory. At its heart Marxism is a theory of how those who are oppressed can free themselves from oppression.

> Before capitalism, in Western Europe, and in China and Japan before the arrival of the Europeans, the system which existed was feudalism. Instead of today's capitalists who own firms and employ workers for a wage, under feudalism the ruling class was the aristocratic nobility—the lords—based on large estates in the countryside. The oppressed class, instead of workers earning a wage, were the peasants (serfs) doing agricultural work on the lord's estate. They had their own plots of land, but they had to work for the lord for part of the week or give part of their own produce to the lord. (*The Militant,* 1998)

Class conflict is at the base of Marxist theory. As Marx and Engels put it in *The Communist Manifesto,*

> The history of all hitherto existing society is the history of class struggles. Freeman and slave, patrician and plebeian, lord and serf, guild-master and journeyman, in a word, oppressor and oppressed stood in constant opposition to each other, carried on an uninterrupted, now hidden, now open fight, a fight that each time ended, either in a revolutionary reconstitution of society at large or in the mutual ruin of the contending classes. (Cited in *The Militant,* 1998)

Thus, from a Marxist perspective there is a conflict between classes in society, and if we allow the conflict to run its course the result will be the ruin of all classes. What is needed is a radical reformation of society. Classical Marxism (or historical materialism) saw revolution as the most likely means of reformation because those in power are rarely willing to give it up except by force.

Because of their ideology Marxists may look at the same data and come to radically different conclusions than postpositivists. Consider a Marxist perspective on the American Civil War that was published on a Web site for *The Militant,* an Australian Marxist journal.

> Take for example the American Civil War of 1861–65. What do most people know about this war? Northern Americans, the Union, fought against the Southern Confederates; Bluecoats fought Greycoats. Why?
>
> Most people would say, well, it was about slavery. The Union president, Abraham Lincoln, was against slavery, while the southerners were in favour of it. That's the myth; the northerners fighting slavery out of the goodness of their hearts. But Marxists would say there was a lot more to it than that. In fact the northern industrialists behind the Union were in bitter conflict with the big southern farmers who owned the slaves; most of these industrialists were racists and not very sympathetic to black slaves. The basic causes of the war were in this economic conflict between the two different sections of the US ruling class. (*The Militant,* 1998)

The Marxist explanation of the reasons for the American Civil War illustrate the primary characteristic of this family of paradigms: interpretation of data based on ideology, in this case Marxist ideology, which emphasizes class conflict and control over society's means of production.

Classical Marxism emerged in the 1800s, when raw capitalism was an especially oppressive influence on society. Ideas we accept today as virtually guaranteed rights were commonly denied to workers in the 19th century:

> In the first half of the 19th Century the working classes in the newly industrializing countries of England and Germany suffered under many forms of exploitation. The old feudal restrictions which had fixed peasants in place on the land and limited their income had also guaranteed them a place in the world. They may not have prospered, but they were often able to fend off starvation and homelessness simply because they had been born onto estates from which they could not be removed against their wills.
>
> The dissolution of this old order meant that workers could be hired and fired at will and had to sell their labor for whatever the going rate was—and that rate was determined by their competition with each other to work cheaply enough to gain them an advantage

in the job market. Traditional rules and protections went by the board in the new factories, which often ran for twenty-four hours a day (two twelve-hour shifts), seven days a week under the most inhumane conditions. Women and children were absorbed into the work force as well, often preferred because they cost much less than men. Living standards and educational levels actually declined in many areas. (Brian, 1998)

Classical Marxism was a response to the conditions of workers in early capitalist societies. It put their sad and exploited state into a broad theoretical framework and proposed specific ways of correcting the situation. Just as the rise of empiricism, positivism, and the scientific method was a reaction against other sources of knowledge, the rise of classical Marxism was a reaction against another set of truths. In this case it was widely accepted truths that oppressed the bulk of humanity to benefit the few.

Marxism was and is a political theory, a theory of social science, and a philosophy of science. Classical Marxism is now more interesting to social scientists as a historical influence than as a modern influence, however. On the other hand, approaches that are based in part on classical Marxism are influential today, and their influence is growing in many areas of the social sciences.

The Frankfurt School: The Beginnings of Critical Theory

The Frankfurt School, or the Institute for Social Research, was founded in 1923 at the University of Frankfurt (Wiggershaus & Robertson, 1995). The members were unusually gifted scholars who helped to define the future of Marxist thought. The term *neo-Marxism* is sometimes applied to the ideas and concepts that emerged from the Frankfurt School. Until the members of the school fled Nazi Germany in the 1930s, the group included well-known scholars such as Erich Fromm, Theodor Adorno, Max Horkheimer, and Herbert Marcuse. The Frankfurt School accepted much of the theory expressed by Karl Marx, including historical materialism, but also changed it in radical ways. For example, as nations developed in the 1800s and early 1900s, the issue of means of production as a central or core issue became less important. The Frankfurt School expanded the focus beyond the capitalist–working class struggle to include many other aspects of society. They were quite concerned about mass media in society, for example, because they were the vehicle through which a national mind developed. Whoever controlled the media could control what a nation thought and therefore what it did. The Frankfurt School saw modern mass media as another tool by which the ruling class could keep groups who were disenfranchised from developing their own emancipatory consciousness. Instead, oppressed groups were encouraged to develop beliefs that justified the status quo and kept the ruling class in power. This aspect of the Frankfurt School has become a significant part of several modern disciplines, such as cultural studies, race and gender research, and visual literacy.

The work of the Frankfurt School led to a paradigm that is generally called *critical theory*. This paradigm is not housed primarily in one particular social science, as behaviorism is in psychology. Instead, it is multidisciplinary. There are critical theory movements in anthropology, art criticism, economics, education, history, literary criticism, psychology, political science, sociology, and theology.

If critical theory were defined briefly, a central point would be the "emancipatory imperative directed towards the abolition of social injustice and . . . [the focus] principally on a critique of ideology, showing how repressive interests underlie the ostensibly neutral formulations of science, politics, economics, and culture in general" (Underwood, 1998).

This emphasis on both making domination and subjugation obvious and helping oppressed groups to free themselves led critical theorists to use established research methods in quite different ways and also to develop new methods. This aspect of critical theory will be discussed in the next chapter along with foundational beliefs. What is important here is the reason critical theory developed in the first place. It is a modern expression of classical Marxism that emerged in an era when those who owned the means of production often oppressed the workers. Contemporary expressions of this paradigm remain focused on oppression, but the paradigm has broadened to include oppression and marginalization based on many factors, including gender, race, nationality, ethnicity, sexual orientation, social class, and work.

Interpretivism: A Response to the Excesses of "Scientific" Social Science

The interpretivist paradigm is enjoying a resurgence (Heshusius & Ballard, 1996), but it has always been at least a minor force in the social sciences. The paradigm combines two essential threads of thought that can be traced back at least to Greek and Roman philosophy. One is the idea that the experience of the senses (empiricism) is not always the best way to know something. *Rationalism,* as you will see, has been proposed as an alternative to empiricism for thousands of years.

The second thread is *relativism*. Relativism is the idea that the reality we perceive is always conditioned by our experiences and our culture. We can never be sure that what we think is real is a true reflection of the out-there reality. Humans are social animals, and so they construct their views of reality in groups. Each individual has constructed his or her own version of reality, but individuals are influenced by their culture and context. Another term commonly used to describe the second idea is *antifoundationalism,* which is the argument that there is no secure foundation that humans can use to decide what is true and what is not.

Rationalism, the idea that you can come to know reality by thinking about it, was an important element of Plato's philosophy. One reason that Plato, in contrast to Aristotle, emphasized thinking and reflection in preference to observation and hands-on study was his view of the objects in the physical world. As noted earlier, for Plato the objects in the physical world were imperfect and flawed reflections of the ideal form of that object. Therefore, you could not study the physical objects in your world and empirically arrive at a full understanding of an object because all the physical representations of the object were flawed. Instead, you had to think your way to an understanding of the ideal form of that object. That ideal form does not exist in the physical world. George Hein (1998) made the point that Plato's perspective, and alternatives to it, are at the core of many of today's debates in the social sciences:

> Our beliefs about the nature of knowledge, our epistemology, profoundly influence our approach to education. It makes a difference whether we believe that knowledge exists independently of the learner, as an absolute, or whether we subscribe to the view that knowledge consists only of ideas constructed in the mind. Plato believed in the existence of ideal forms, independent of the learner. Thus, for him, learning consisted of arriving at knowledge through an intellectual process. Conversely, Berkeley believed that knowledge existed only in the mind of the knower. Thus, he answered in the negative the hypothetical question about the sound of a tree falling in the forest when no one is there to hear it. We can represent this epistemological dichotomy as a continuum [from knowledge as something that exists independently of the learner (realism) on one end to knowledge that is constructed in the mind of the learner on the other.]

> Plato's perspective is an important one in the history of science. As Losee (1993) put it, "Plato sometimes has been condemned for supposedly promulgating a philosophical orientation detrimental to the progress of science. The orientation in question is a turning away from the study of the world as revealed in sense experience, in favour of the contemplation of abstract ideals." (Hein, 1998, p. 17–18)

Most interpretivists follow Plato's perspective that reality cannot be experienced directly through the senses. However, they typically do not agree with the idea that ideal forms exist in some mental form. On the other hand, Plato's ideal forms are similar to Piaget's mother structures, Jung's archetypes, ethology's concept of imprinting, and the general concept of innate tendencies that are a foundation for sociobiology. All share the idea that there is some preexisting mental or nonphysical structure that has not been learned through experience. This idea is also reflected in Chomsky's view that there is an innate deep structure to language, as mentioned earlier. Von Glaserfeld (1998) pointed out the link between modern and Platonic forms:

> Plato's theory . . . the notion that the gods instilled all "real" knowledge into the first human beings and that it is transmitted with their souls from generation to generation, seemed too fanciful to most modern philosophers. Yet, Chomsky succeeded in launching an analogous theory, replacing the gods with the principle of genetic determination. According to the new version, abstract knowledge is supposed to lie dormant in the human genome, waiting to be triggered by experiential stimuli.

Regardless of whether they accept ideal forms in the Platonic sense, most interpretivists do adopt the rationalist approach: Reality is not available to us solely through direct experience. For rationalists, thinking and reflecting are important aspects of the process of knowing. This approach became known as armchair psychology in the early 20th century, when empiricism and the scientific method dominated American psychology. The derogatory term *armchair psychology* was used to indicate that people who took this approach were not conducting real research because they were not conducting scientific experiments.

Plato's rationalism is idealistic because it posits the existence of truth (ideal forms). Admittedly, Plato's truth is a mental or metaphysical one rather than the truth of physical reality proposed by the empiricists. But it is a form of reality that exists outside the minds of individuals. Instead of an idealistic rationalism, most interpretivists are relativists instead of idealists:

> Interpretivists also tend to be relativists. Relativist accounts argue that what science "takes" to be a universally enframing account of knowledge of the world is always, in fact, located within an institutional and socio-culturally determined community. Moreover, what that community takes to be a universal epistemology is always a particularised epistemology which can claim no greater worth (as

knowledge) than any other competing claims to truth. The immediate implication of this critique for the design and execution of
empirical methodology is that, whilst structured and designed to be
"neutral" or "value-free," methodology is only ever neutral insofar as
it conforms to the world-view of the community which develops it.
Therefore, according to a relativist thesis, knowledges produced
by scientific method are not "transferable" or "translatable"
knowledges—they can exhibit consistency with the epistemological
foundations of a particular "science"—but cannot be taken to be
universally true. They acknowledge that there can be an external
world (a reality) that is separate from, and not dependent on, the
human mind. However, they do not believe humans can ever come
in direct contact with that reality. Our experiences, our tools such as
language, and our culture are filters that shape and help define the
reality that we construct. (Every, 1998)

The relative rationalism of interpretivists represents a line of thinking
that goes back at least to Plato. But it has often been overshadowed, especially in the 18th, 19th, and 20th centuries, by other perspectives, especially
realism. This is in part because of the advances made by the natural sciences
through the use of the scientific method. Many social theorists wanted to
transfer over to the social sciences the research paradigm of the natural
sciences. And, of course, the underlying philosophy of science was also
adopted because the research methods made little sense without the supporting philosophy.

The Response to Objectivism: Interpretivism

The idea that the social sciences are like the natural sciences did not go
unchallenged. In fact, there was a strong reaction against this view, and it
originated in Germany (Gregor, 2002). It began with the philosophy of
Immanuel Kant, who argued that you could not be objective about subject
matter because we come prewired, so to speak, with "categories of understanding" that then influence our perceptions. It is therefore not possible,
according to Kant, to conduct objective research from which your views and
subjective opinions are completely separate.

Wilhelm Dilthey, a German historian and philosopher who helped establish the social sciences (which he called the cultural or human sciences),
rejected the objectivism of the natural sciences in relation to the social
sciences. While discussing the discipline of history in his 1883 book
Einleitung in die Geisteswissenschaften (*Introduction to the Human*

Sciences), he addressed the irrelevance of the empirical approach in the social sciences. Dilthey proposed a subjective base for social science:

> In my own work I was troubled by questions which face every thoughtful historian, student of law, or political theorist. Thus there arose in me both a need and a plan for the foundation of the human sciences. What is the system of principles which provides a basis for the judgments of the historian, the conclusions of the political economist, and the concepts of the jurist, and which at the same time assures their certainty? . . .
>
> The answers given to these questions by Comte and the positivists and by J. S. Mill and the empiricists seemed to me to truncate and mutilate historical reality in order to assimilate it to the concepts and methods of the natural sciences.
>
> Only inner experience, in facts of consciousness, have I found a firm anchor for my thinking, and I trust that my reader will be convinced by my proof of this. All science is experiential; but all experience must be related back to and derives its validity from the conditions and context of consciousness in which it arises, i.e., the totality of our nature. . . .
>
> Previous epistemology—Kant's as well as that of the empiricists—has explained experience and cognition in terms of facts that are merely representational. No real blood flows in the veins of the knowing subject constructed by Locke, Hume, and Kant, but rather the diluted extract of reason as a mere activity of thought. A historical as well as psychological approach to whole human beings led me to explain even knowledge and its concepts (such as the external world, time, substance, and cause) in terms of the manifold powers of a being that wills, feels, and thinks; and I do this despite the fact that knowledge seems to be woven of concepts derived from the mere contents of perception, representation, and thought. (Dilthey, 1883)

These quotes from the Preface of *Introduction to the Human Sciences* summarize the essence of Dilthey's philosophy of social science:

- He rejects the sterile objectivism some attempted to import from the natural sciences.

- He argues that understanding can occur only in context. History is understood in part by a "sympathetic immersion in the details."

- He emphasizes that true understanding is a holistic rather than atomistic process.

- He emphasizes that empirical facts do not exist separate from our mental or conscious activities. The objectivism required by empiricism is simply not possible. Following the rationalist tradition, he proposes that we must think in order to know reality.

The Rise of Verstehen *and Hermeneutics in the Social Sciences*

To Dilthey's four foundations of social science, we can add one more:

- Dilthey rejected the empiricist purpose for science: the discovery of generalizations and laws. Instead, as Smith (1989, p. 121) notes, he felt we should "undertake an interpretive understanding of the individual or the type."

Although Dilthey's break with empiricists on the purpose of research happened more than a hundred years ago, the issue has not been settled, and it is at the heart of many discussions and debates today. Most social science research in the 20th century was in the empirical tradition, an effort to find lawlike generalizations that derive from theories that are tested through the scientific method. Dilthey's alternative, the idea that the purpose of social science research is to understand (*verstehen* in German) what is studied, is a fundamental tenet of interpretivism and, to a lesser extent, critical social science research today. *Understanding* here means understanding of context, both historical and contemporary. A number of movements in the late 19th century and 20th centuries followed this tradition:

- *Existentialism* emphasized the need to make "leaps of faith" into the unknown because you have no way of knowing the world in any direct or empirical sense.

- *Phenomenology* focused on the subjectivity and relativity of reality, continually pointing out the need to understand how humans view themselves and the world around them. Following Kant, phenomenologists distinguished phenomena (the perceptions or appearances from the point of view of a human) from noumena (what things really are).

- *Gestalt psychology* made the critical point that breaking things down into parts destroys some of the meaning, which is contained in the whole. The whole is greater than the sum of its parts.

- *Constructivism* asserts that reality is socially constructed and can be understood only in context.

Interpretivism, which encompasses a number of more specific and focused movements, was thus a response against positivism and empiricism. Interpretivism is essentially a reaction against the idea that you can use the same research methods and paradigms in the social sciences as are used in the natural sciences. Interpretivists have proposed alternatives to those methods and paradigms.

This chapter has covered the historical context of the three major paradigms or world views that influence social science today. It would make sense to move now to the next chapter because it deals with the specifics of the paradigms, their fundamental beliefs and values. However, doing so would omit two significant movements that are quite influential today in the social sciences: postmodernism (Best & Kellner, 2001) and feminism (Campbell & Wasco, 2000). The last section of this chapter briefly outlines these two movements and their influence on research.

The Special Cases of Postmodernism and Feminism

This chapter singles out two movements, postmodernism and feminism, for special attention because they are both active influences today on the social sciences. Also, they cut across the two alternative paradigms presented in this book: critical theory and interpretivism.

Postmodernism

Except in art, modernism is generally defined as a belief in the goodness of science and the findings of science. All progress is assumed to be good for humanity, and there is a tendency to uncritically support scientific and technical advances, from the development of urban centers to the creation of powerful antibiotics. Modernism also raises to a privileged position the use of the scientific method as a way of knowing. Modernism had a major influence on the social sciences. Gergen (1983, 1986, 1991) highlights some of the primary characteristics of a modernist psychology:

- *A basic subject matter.* "At the core of modernism lies the belief in a knowable world" (1991, p. 19).

- *Universal properties.* "In addition to presuming a knowable subject, modernist psychology has also fallen heir to a belief in universal properties.

That is, it is presumed that there are principles, possibly laws, that may be discovered about the properties of the subject matter" (p. 19).

- *Empirical method.* "Following the rational justification of logical empiricist philosophy, modernist psychology has also been committed to a belief in truth through method. In particular, the pervasive belief is that by using empirical methods, and most particularly the controlled experiment, one could derive obdurate truths about the nature of the subject matter and the causal networks in which it is embedded. Further, it is believed, the results of such methodology are impersonal [e.g., objective]" (p. 20).

- *Research as progressive.* "Derivative of the preceding assumptions is the final modernist belief, a belief in the progressive nature of research. As empirical methods are applied to the subject matter of psychology, we learn increasingly about its fundamental character" (p. 20).

Postmodernism, on the other hand, refers to

[an] age which has lost the Enlightenment belief in emancipation and progress through more knowledge and scientific research. Postmodern society consists less of totalities to be ruled by preconceived models than by decentralization to heterogeneous local contexts characterized by flexibility and change. . . . It is an age in which the multiple perspectives of new media tend to dissolve any sharp line between reality and fantasy, undermining belief in an objective reality. (Kvale, 1992, p. 2)

Postmodernism thus questions the benefits of progress and challenges the idea that the scientific method is the sole source of knowledge. Postmodernism has influenced both critical theory and interpretivism. Postmodernism has been *critical* because it highlights the negative results of progress on oppressed peoples. It points out the impact of different forms of progress, such as industrialization in the 19th century and urbanization in the 20th, on the poor, women, and different racial and ethnic groups. It is *interpretive* because it proposes that "to separate disembodied ways of knowing from embodied ones, assigning an epistemologically privileged status to the former" (Heshusius & Ballard, 1996, p. 1) is incorrect. For postmodernists true knowledge comes from knowing in context, and we acquire this type of knowing in many ways, including the use of "nonscientific" research methods.

In his influential book *Psychology and Postmodernism,* Steinar Kvale (1992) concludes that a postmodern psychology would differ in seven ways from a modernist psychology:

- *Knowledge.* "There is a move from knowledge as abstract, universal and objective to socially useful, local knowledge. More practical forms of knowing are advocated elevating the practical embodied knowledge of everyday life over theoretical knowledge" (p. 12).

- *Practice.* "The professional practice of psychologists is today coming to be regarded as an important generator of psychological knowledge" (p. 12).

- *Research.* "The legitimacy of modern psychology has rested heavily on the application of alleged natural science methods. . . . [Today] there is a changed conception of research—from a method-centeredness to a discursive practice. The research process is not a mapping of some objective social reality; research involves a co-constitution of the objects investigated, with a negotiation and interaction with the very objects studied. . . . A multi-method approach is advocated by several authors, with an emphasis on qualitative, interactive and involved research. Narrative, hermeneutical and deconstructive approaches are advocated. . . . With the research process embedded in a concrete and local situation, research becomes a negotiated practice" (p. 13).

- *Deconstruction.* Deconstruction "represents an effort to construct by destruction. Old, obsolete concepts are demolished to erect new ones. Deconstruction focuses on the self-contradictions in a text, on the tensions between what the text means to say and what it is none the less constrained to mean" (p. 13).

- *The vanishing subject.* An object of study (the subject) requires a researcher who looks for eternal truths in the responses of the subjects. Postmodern psychology is more likely to invite the "subjects" into the research endeavor, where they participate in meaning making in ways that would be considered blasphemous by positivist, modernist psychologists.

- *Humanism and naturalism.* "A postmodern approach to the relation of the human being to the world goes beyond a familiar opposition of psychology as a natural or a humanistic science. Postmodern thought is far from the mechanical picture of the natural sciences provided by positivist philosophers. It is closer to the current emphasis on the interpretative, interactive and relative nature of knowledge in the natural sciences" (p. 14).

- *From inside to outside.* "In current understanding of human beings there is a move from the inwardness of an individual psyche to being-in-the world with other human beings. The focus of interest is moved from the inside of a psychic container to the outside of the human world" (p. 15).[2]

You should find much that is familiar in Kvale's seven characteristics of postmodern psychology. Most are assumptions of the interpretivist paradigm, the critical paradigm, or both. Note, however, that Kvale argues that when the social sciences emulate the natural sciences by adopting a modernist positivist or postpositivist philosophy of science, they are actually adopting an old view, whereas the current emphasis in the natural sciences is on an approach more in tune with the postmodern approach he proposes for psychology. This topic is not discussed further here, but it is an interesting argument.

Although there is an extensive literature on social science research from a postmodern perspective (Hollinger, 1994; Macmillan, 2001; Rosenau, 1991), this book does not present a separate postmodernist research paradigm or describe postmodern methods. That is because postmodern perspectives are represented in both critical and interpretivist frameworks, which are covered in detail in this book. A similar perspective applies to feminism.

Feminist Theory and Research

Feminist theory is a broad, diverse movement in academia that covers almost every level of scholarship, from foundations such as philosophies of science (Duran, 1997) to activist research and practice in an effort to achieve equality for women (Hesse-Biber & Yaiser, 2003; Landrine, 1995; Leatherby, 2003; Potter, 2004). In some quarters of feminism the research focus is on the topics to be studied. Gender equity, programs of empowerment, and similar topics are championed.

In other quarters feminists have adopted an approach to research and practice that reflects an ideological or philosophical slant. For example, feminist pedagogy (Cohee et al., 1998; Luke & Gore, 1992; Maher & Schwiender, 2001; Mayberry & Rose, 1999) proposes approaches to teaching and learning that are in line with feminist theory. These "principled" approaches to feminism are difficult to define and explain, in part because some are based on critical theory whereas others are in the interpretive tradition. Some are associated with a postmodern stance.

In the influential book on feminist theory she edited, Sandra Harding (1987) posed the question, "Is there a distinctive method of inquiry?" She then answered the question by identifying ways a feminist researcher can transform methodology:

- *Additive approaches.* These approaches include women in studies where they have traditionally been excluded. Harding rejects this approach because she believes traditional research methods often misrepresent women.

- *Women's contributions.* The purpose of this type of feminist research is "to examine women's contributions to activities in the public world which were already the focus of social science analysis" (p. 4). Through this type of research "we now can see that women, too, have been the originators of distinctively human culture, deviants, voters, revolutionaries, social reformers, high achievers, wage workers, and so forth" (p. 4). Harding criticizes this approach as well: "This focus still leaves some powerfully androcentric standards firmly in place, thereby insuring only partial and distorted analyses of gender and women's social activities. It falsely suggests that only those activities that men have found it important to study are the ones which constitute and shape social life" (p. 4).

- *Victimologies.* This approach is based on the "study of women as victims of male dominance" (p. 5). Harding does not totally reject this approach, but she points out that it tends to "create the false impression that women have only been victims, that they have never successfully fought back, that women cannot be effective social agents on behalf of themselves or others" (p. 5).

After criticizing these three ways of doing feminist research, Harding defines three broad characteristics that typify much of the feminist research she feels is the best and most useful examples of this genre:

- *Women's experiences guide the development of research.* Harding points out that postpositivist philosophies of science do not specify how a topic of study is to be selected. The topic can arise from many sources. Harding finds this unacceptable, in part because in American social science it has led to research agendas that are set by men. She argues that feminists should challenge the idea that selecting topics for research is a value-free process. "Defining what is in need of scientific explanation only from the perspective of bourgeois, white men's experiences leads to partial and even perverse understandings of social life. One distinctive feature of feminist research is that it generates its problematics from the perspective of women's experience" (p. 7).

- *Research for women.* Harding asserts that much of the research to date has been for men. Even studies of women often were based on "desires to pacify, control, exploit, and manipulate women. Traditional social research has been for men" (p. 8). Feminist research can be for women as well.

- *The subjective objective.* Harding supports quantitative research methods, but she argues that the traditional method of doing the research—asserting that the researcher must maintain an objective, neutral stance—hides the biases and influential experiences that guide research regardless of whether we acknowledge them or not. She proposes a much more open acknowledgment of the subjectivity of our research: "The class, race, culture, and gender assumptions, beliefs, and behaviors of the researcher her/himself must be placed within the frame of the picture that she/he attempts to paint. . . . Thus the researcher appears to us not as an invisible, anonymous voice or authority, but as a real, historical individual with concrete, specific desires and interests. . . . Introducing this 'subjective' element into the analysis in fact increases the objectivity of the research and decreases the 'objectivism' which hides this kind of evidence from the public" (p. 9).

Harding's approach to feminist methodology is generally in line with the critical theory paradigm discussed in this chapter and the next. Much of what defines feminist research is an ideological perspective rather than the use of a particular method of research. In fact, some scholars see feminism as a branch of critical theory. However, much of Harding's perspective is also compatible with the viewpoint of interpretivism. The same is true of the work of Fonow and Cook (1991). Although they maintain and support many of the critical themes in Harding's book, the four typical themes of feminist research from their perspective are quite different from those of Harding:

• *Thoughtful, reflexive (reflective) research.* "By reflectivity we mean the tendency of feminists to reflect upon, examine critically, and explore analytically the nature of the research process" (p. 2). Reflexive research involves more than the approach the researcher takes to thinking about the study. It may also include consciousness raising, which involves helping the participants in research and the readers of research to become aware of hidden restrictions and controls. Ideally, becoming aware of false consciousness leads to ways to eliminate oppression.

• *Collaborative scholarship* means that feminist scholars tend to work in groups rather than alone.

• *Action orientation.* Feminist research often is empancipatory. It is aimed at helping members of an oppressed group take control of their lives. Action may be direct (the study itself leads to change) or indirect (policy or historical studies point to strategies for reform and revolution).

• *Attention to the affective components of the research act.* "Another major feature of feminist epistemology is its refusal to ignore the emotional dimensions of the conduct of inquiry. Feminist researchers often attend specifically to the role of affect in the production of knowledge" (p. 9).

• *Use of the situation at hand.* Feminists consider it "legitimate to study the taken-for-granted, mundane features of everyday life. For women, these routine aspects of everyday life help to sustain gender inequality. Analysis of 'common courtesies,' linguistic practices, commercial advertisements, and even tombstone inscriptions have revealed the cultural norms and assumptions governing gender relations. This concern with the ordinary extends itself to the selection of research settings such as beauty parlors, children's playgrounds, weight watchers meetings, and shopping malls, and research topics such as volunteerism, meal preparation, and husband maintenance. . . . Feminists seem particularly adept at recognizing the opportunities available in unforeseen settings to study otherwise-hidden processes" (p. 12).

This also extends to the study of the research process itself. A third aspect of reflexive research involves looking for hidden aspects of the research process.

> Feminists pay particular attention to . . . ignored phases of inquiry for a variety of reasons. First, women have been unfairly excluded from full participation in scholarship because of events that occur during such states as obtaining funding or presenting their results to others. (p. 5)

Fonow and Cook's general characteristics of feminist research have major critical theory elements, but they also have a great deal in common with the topic of chapter 4, interpretivism. There are many good books on feminist methodology (Hesse-Biber & Yaiser, 2003; Leatherby, 2003; Reinharz, 1992), but this introductory text integrates this work into two broader frameworks: critical theory and interpretivism.

Summary

The three popular paradigms in social science research were all developed in response to a perceived problem in society. Positivism was a response to the use of metaphysical and religious sources of knowledge about everything from astronomy and chemistry to human behavior. Critical theory emerged as an expansion of traditional or classical Marxism. It extended the original theory to social and cultural factors other than control of the means of production and the relationship between owners (capitalists) and workers. Critical theory was a response to the complexities of modern nation-states that often lead to domination and exploitation of one group by another.

By the 19th century the idea of science as a means of progress was well established. Being scientific was good, and being unscientific was bad. Being scientific generally meant that you used the experimental method, you gathered quantitative data, and you looked for universals or laws that were expressed in theories that could be tested. (Actually, the theory is not tested directly; hypotheses derived from the theory are tested.)

The social sciences, which developed in the 19th century, have generally been held in less esteem than the natural sciences, and there has been a continuing effort to make the social sciences more like the natural sciences by adopting the same philosophy of science (e.g., positivism or postpositivism) and the same approach to acquiring knowledge (e.g., the scientific method). One extreme version of positivism that developed in the early 20th century is logical positivism. It was very influential in the social sciences, especially psychology. Logical positivism is generally discredited today. There is general agreement that the assumptions of this form of empiricism are not tenable. It has been replaced by a less confident (some would say less arrogant) philosophy of science: postpositivism.

Today postpositivism is the most commonly adopted philosophy of science in many of the social sciences, and quantitative research based on the scientific method often is considered the highest-quality work a scholar can do. In the last 50 years, however, two important alternatives have emerged: critical theory and interpretivism. Critical theory is, at its base, ideological. Interpretivism is an approach based on the idea that humans cannot come to know how the world really is, regardless of the research method used. Interpretivism proposes that we abandon the search for generalizable truths and laws about human behavior and concentrate instead on local understanding.

The next two chapters explore in much more detail the three paradigms that guide social science research today: postpositivism, critical theory, and interpretivism.

Questions for Reflection

1. When they were developed, the three paradigms discussed in this chapter were thoughtful responses to the contemporary social and historical contexts. Would this help explain why different people support different paradigms today? Do we see the world differently and have different

world views? Do we respond to different perceived problems and issues? Take the area of interest to you and describe the views proponents of the three paradigms would hold toward that topic.

2. The chapter discusses the Greek and Roman period, the Middle Ages, the Renaissance, and later periods that have supported the idea of progress through science (modernism). Do the characteristics of these periods have their counterparts in contemporary society? In world politics? In education? Do those shared characteristics today result in similar responses that share beliefs with earlier periods in history?

3. Some might say the role of the Scholastics or schoolmen is quite similar to the role of practitioners who read the research of the scientists and then follow the implications of that research. Good practice follows the directions of the experts—the scholars. What are some alternatives to this researcher–practitioner relationship? Is the schoolmen model a good one? Are there drawbacks and weaknesses? Are they dealt with by your alternatives?

4. Create a short story that describes the lives of two characters in the 17th century. One has come to see the scientific method as a grand source of truth and knowledge. The other character maintains that the old ways of knowing are still valid. Describe their lives and the way they deal with assaults on their viewpoints.

5. Is it true that each of the three philosophies of science was responding to conditions in society? Locate and summarize some original sources related to the philosophies of science that shed some light on why they were developed and the authors' opinions about problems in society at that time.

6. Consider the interpretivist philosophy of science. What do you see as the most significant departure from postpositivism? Why? What aspects of interpretivism do you find most difficult to accept? Why?

7. Consider a topic of research in an area of interest to you. What would be the purpose of research on the topic if it were conducted from a postpositivist perspective? Critical? Interpretive?

Notes

1. From *Methodological Principles of Social Science*. Copyright © 2006, Richard McCleary.

2. From S. Kvale (Ed.), *Psychology and the Postmodern*, copyright © 1992. Reprinted with permission by Sage Publications, Inc.

References

Bacon, R. (1268). Cited in O. Thatcher (Ed.), *Medieval sourcebook: On experimental science.* Milwaukee: The Library of Original Source. Available from University Research Extension Co. (1901), *Vol. V: The early medieval world* (pp. 369–376). Retrieved December 3, 2005, from http://www.fordham.edu/halsall/source/bacon2.html

Bernal, J. D. (1937). Dialectical materialism and modern science. *Science and Society, 2*(1). Retrieved November 13, 2005, from http://www.marxists.org/archive/bernal/works/1930s/dsams.htm

Best, S., & Kellner, D. (2001). *The postmodern adventure: Science, technology, and cultural studies at the third millennium.* New York: Guilford.

Brian, P. (1998). *Introduction to 19th-century socialism.* Retrieved December 3, 2005, from http://www.wsu.edu/~brians/hum_303/socialism.html

Buehler, R. E. (2002). *Because we're all relatives, it's not all relative.* Retrieved December 3, 2005, from http://www.amazon.com/exec/obidos/tg/detail/-/0670031518/104-6362272-3901545?v=glance

Campbell, R., & Wasco, S. (2000). Feminist approaches to social science: Epistemological and methodological tenets. *American Journal of Community Psychology, 28*(6), 773–791.

Chalmers, A. (1990). *Science and its fabrication.* Minneapolis: University of Minnesota Press.

Cohee, G., Daumer, E., Kemp, T., Krebs, P., Lafky, S., & Runzo, S. (1998). *The feminist teacher anthology: Pedagogies and classroom strategies.* New York: Teachers College Press.

Dilthey, W. (1883). *Introduction to the human sciences.* Retrieved December 3, 2005, from http://werple.net.au/~gaffcam/phil/dilthey.htm

Duran, J. (1997). *Philosophies of science/feminist theories.* Boulder, CO: Westview.

Every, P. (1998). *Incommensurability, relativism, methodology.* Retrieved December 3, 2005, from http://www.csad.coventry.ac.uk/IDN/neopraxis/psci.htm

Fonow, M., & Cook, J. (Eds.). (1991). *Methodology: Feminist scholarship as lived research.* Bloomington: Indiana University Press.

Gergen, K. (1983). *Local knowledge: Further essays in interpretive anthropology.* New York: Basic Books.

Gergen, K. (1986). The social constructionist movement in modern psychology. *American Psychologist, 40,* 266–275.

Gergen, K. (1991). *The saturated self: Dilemmas of identify in contemporary life.* New York: Basic Books.

Gregor, S. (2002). A theory of theories in information systems. In S. Gregor & D. Hart (Eds.), *Information systems foundations: Building the theoretical base* (pp. 1–20). Canberra: Australian National University.

Guba, E. (Ed.). (1990). *The paradigm dialog.* Newbury Park, CA: Sage.

Hansen, N. (2004). *The Lysenko effect: The politics of science.* Amherst, NY: Humanity Books.

Harding, S. (Ed.). (1987). *Feminism & methodology.* Bloomington: Indiana University Press.

Hein, G. (1998). *The constructivist museum.* Retrieved December 3, 2005, from http://www.gem.org.uk/hein.html

Heshusius, L., & Ballard, K. (Eds.). (1996). *From positivism to interpretivism and beyond.* New York: Teachers College Press.

Hesse-Biber, S., & Yaiser, M. (Eds.). (2003). *Feminist perspectives on social research.* Oxford: Oxford University Press.

Hollinger, R. (1994). *Postmodernism and the social sciences.* Thousand Oaks, CA: Sage.

Kuklick, B. (1995, December). Comte rendu/A review. *Journal of American History,* 1226-1227. Retrieved December 3, 2005, from http://hgx-hypersoft.com/clotilde/biblio/harprvw.htm

Kvale, S. (1992). Introduction. In S. Kvale (Ed.), *Psychology and postmodernism* (pp. 1–16). Newbury Park, CA: Sage.

Landrine, H. (1995). *Bringing cultural diversity to feminist psychology: Theory, research, & practice.* Washington, DC: American Psychological Association.

Leatherby, G. (2003). *Feminist research in theory and practice.* Philadelphia: Open University Press.

Losee, J. (1993). *A historical introduction to the philosophy of science* (3rd ed.). New York: Oxford University Press.

Luke, C., & Gore, J. (Eds.). (1992). *Feminisms and critical pedagogy.* New York: Rutledge.

Macmillan, A. (2001). *Deconstructing social and cultural meaning: A model for education research using postmodern constructs.* Altona, Victoria, Australia: Common Ground Publishing.

Maher, F., & Schwiender, N. (2001). *Feminist pedagogy: An update.* New York: Feminist Press.

Mayberry, M., & Rose, E. (1999). *Meeting the challenge: Innovative feminist pedagogies in action.* New York: Routledge.

McCleary, R. (1998). *Philosophy of science.* Retrieved December 3, 2005, from http://mrrc.bio.uci.edu/se10/philosophy.html

The Militant. (1998). *The Marxist view of history (historical materialism).* Retrieved December 3, 2005, from http://www.werple.net.au/~militant/ed/hismat.htm

Pinker, S. (2002). *The blank slate: The modern denial of human nature.* New York: Penguin Putnam.

Potter, E. (2004). *Feminist philosophy of science: An introduction.* New York: Routledge.

Reinharz, S. (1992). *Feminist methods in social research.* Oxford: Oxford University Press.

Rosenau, P. (1991). *Post-modernism and the social sciences.* Princeton, NJ: Princeton University Press.

Rush, F. (Ed.). (2004). *The Cambridge companion to critical theory.* Cambridge, UK: Cambridge University Press.

Sheehan, H. (1993). *Marxism and the philosophy of science.* Latham, MA: Humanities Press.

Smith, J. (1989). *The nature of social and educational inquiry: Empiricism versus interpretation.* Norwood, NJ: Ablex.

Steele, T. (2002). The role of scientific positivism in European popular education movements: The case of France. *International Journal of Lifelong Education, 21*(5), 399–413.

Underwood, M. (1998). *Critical theory.* Retrieved December 3, 2005, from http://www.ndirect.co.uk/~cultsock/MUHome/critical.html

von Glaserfeld, E. (1998). Scheme theory as a key to the learning paradox. Invited paper presented at the 15th Advanced Course, Archives Jean Piaget, Geneva, September 20–24, 1998. Retrieved December 3, 2005, from http://www.umass.edu/srri/vonGlasersfeld/onlinePapers/pdf/vonGlasersfeld_258.pdf

Wiggershaus, R., & Robertson, M. (1995). *The Frankfurt School.* Cambridge: MIT Press.

CHAPTER 3

Foundational Issues

Postpositivist and Critical Perspectives

Traditional textbooks on research in the social sciences tend to fall into two broad but related categories: statistics and research methods. A great many texts are available that detail the statistical procedures that can be used to analyze quantitative data. *Basic Statistical Concepts* (Bartz, 1998) is a good example of this type of book. It introduces the general concepts of quantitative analysis and common concepts such as nominal, ordinal, interval, and ratio data. Then it covers a wide range of statistical concepts and techniques such as

- Frequency distributions and the standard curve
- Measures of central tendency such as mean, median, and mode
- Normative scores such as percentages, age and grade scores, and standard scores
- Measures of variability: range, standard deviation, variance
- Relationship tests such as correlation and regression
- Difference tests such as *t* tests and analysis of variance

Bartz's book also covers some *nonparametric* statistical procedures such as the Mann–Whitney *U,* and it devotes some attention to the design of research studies. However, it is primarily a book on standard or parametric statistics. Although it and books like it are regularly used to introduce students to social science research methods, it concentrates on one type of data: quantitative. However, the statistical procedures described in Bartz's book do not work well with interview data, with journals and life histories, with observations in the field, and with case studies. It focuses on certain types of quantitative data.

Parametric and Nonparametric Statistics

The statistical analysis of data is an integral part of research in every social science. The thousands of statistical procedures used by social scientists fall into two broad families: parametric and nonparametric. Parametric statistics are based on the assumption that the data being analyzed have a particular pattern, or distribution. Specifically, parametric statistics assume that most of the data points will be clustered in the middle. For example, suppose you gather data on extroversion, and the scores you obtain range from 10 to 90. If the pattern of scores is parametric, you would expect many of the scores to be in the middle of that range, say around 50, and that the number of scores would decrease as you move further away from that middle. Your data might have 120 scores around 60 but only 35 around 75 and just a few close to 90. Also, there might be around 120 scores near 40, far fewer around 25, and a very small number near the extreme lower end of the range of scores. This pattern is often called the normal distribution, often represented graphically as a bell-shaped curve.

If your data meet the criteria for parametric distributions, you can use parametric statistics to test hypotheses. For example, suppose you are studying the impact of a social skills training program on the "sociability" of people who complete the program. If you have an experimental and a control group, one of the things you will want to know is whether the sociability scores of the people in the experimental group who completed the training program are higher than the scores for similar people who did not participate in the training. If your data are parametric you can use a parametric statistic such as the t test to compare the average scores in the two groups. But what if your data aren't distributed parametrically? What if, instead, most of the scores on the measure of sociability are near the bottom of a range of scores? Perhaps more than half of the scores are from 31 to 45, with 31 being the lowest score in your data and the highest being 145. This distribution of scores is not parametric. The distribution violates one of the assumptions of parametric distributions.

When you have a nonparametric distribution, there are two commonly used solutions. The first is to simply ignore the nonparametric nature of the data and use parametric statistics such as the t test anyway. Many researchers do, and quite a few studies show that parametric statistics are reasonably accurate even when there are violations of the assumptions. However, when the distribution of data grossly violates the assumptions on which parametric statistics are based, there is another option: nonparametric statistics. These statistics do not make assumptions about how the data are distributed. Therefore, they can be used with data that have an odd or nonparametric pattern. A nonparametric equivalent of the *t* test, for example, is the Mann–Whitney *U* test.

You may be wondering why you would even try to use parametric statistics if there are nonparametric statistics that do the same job but don't have so many pesky assumptions behind them that are often violated by data gathered on humans. The answer is *power*. If the data are parametric in their distribution pattern, the *t* test will be able to detect differences between the two groups better than the Mann–Whitney *U*. If your treatment group has a mean of 45 and the control group had a mean of 39, a Mann–Whitney *U* test might not tell you that difference was significant, but a *t* test would. Therefore, researchers generally use parametric statistics whenever possible because they are usually more powerful. They use nonparametric statistics when the distribution of data drastically violates the assumptions that underlie parametric statistics. At a more personal level, I like nonparametric statistics because they tend to have more exotic names such as the Wald-Wolfowitz runs test, the Kolmogorov-Smirnov two-sample test, the jackknife resampling method, and the bootstrap estimation method. They sound so much more exotic than parametric statistics such as the analysis of variance and the correlation coefficient.

Another common type of text used in research classes today is the method book. Paul Cherulnik's (2001) *Methods of Behavioral Research* is typical of this type. Instead of concentrating on statistical tests and procedures, a method book emphasizes design. The book attends to basic topics such as criteria for good research (e.g., internal validity, reliability, and generalizability or external validity). However, the bulk of the text introduces a range of research designs. In his book Cherulnik even organizes them according to their quality, based on a set of standards. He divides studies into three general families: preexperimental designs, true experimental designs, and quasiexperimental designs. In his value system a case study is a preexperimental design that rates very, very low on his set of criteria.

A bit further up the methodological food chain are quasiexperimental designs. They are often used in the social sciences for applied research because it is often impossible to meet all the criteria for a true experimental design. For example, in educational studies it is rarely possible to randomly assign subjects to treatment and control groups. In a true control group–experimental group study the subjects would be randomly assigned to either the control condition or the experimental condition. Those subjects would also represent the general population to which you want to generalize the results. When subjects cannot be randomly assigned to treatment conditions, the researcher often uses a quasiexperimental design instead. For example, you might use intact groups such as students in eight existing classrooms. The use of intact groups violates the random assignment rule of traditional experimental research, and the study is thus quasiexperimental instead of experimental. Some research methodologists treat quasiexperimental research with disdain. However, the choice of using an experimental or quasiexperimental research design often involves balancing two important values: validity and meaningfulness. Suppose you are studying the courtship behavior of humans and you are concerned with whether adolescent males court females who are from their neighborhood differently from females from other neighborhoods. You could do a completely randomized experimental study using another species, such as *Drosophila* flies. Actually, this type of study has been done, and female flies respond differently to males from their immediate geographic area (homotypic or within strain) compared to males who are "not from around here" (heterotypic or between strain). In fact, the research in this area shows many differences in the courtship and mating patterns with "local" and "foreign" potential partners. For example, Long, Montgomerie, and Chippindale (2006) found that females who had already had sex with one partner "were significantly less likely to remate . . . if the second males they had the opportunity to mate with were from their local population than if those second males were from a foreign population" (p. 6). In trying to explain why this happened, the authors concluded, "It seems most likely that foreign males, or their courtship signals, were in some way more attractive to females than were local males, rather than that males expended more energy in courtship when they encountered unfamiliar females" (p. 9). Foreign males also had another advantage in that they

> were 80% more successful than local males, on average, at maintaining sperm in the female's reproductive tract following remating. . . . This finding suggests better sperm binding in the female reproductive tract by foreign males conferring resistance to either (i) the challenge of second male sperm and accessory proteins or (ii) lower sperm dumping . . . by females during remating. (p. 10)

This study involved several thousand flies that came from genetically controlled populations that had been "kept under identical environmental conditions for greater than 600 generations" (Long et al., 2006, p. 1). The experimental process was also tightly controlled: "Adult flies of both sexes were collected as virgins under light CO_2 anaesthesia as they eclosed from pupae on day 9. . . . Adults were allowed to mate and freely interact in the females' natal vials for the next five days" (p. 3). The study was thus highly controlled in ways that would not be thinkable in a human population.

The purpose of this research was to contribute generally to the study of animal mating behaviors, but what if we try to apply the findings to humans? The study is very well controlled and is clearly an experimental rather than a quasiexperimental study. We can probably believe the results of this study, which means it has high *validity*. Is it also *meaningful* in the sense that we can apply the findings to human courtship and mating behavior? Clearly, meaningfulness of that sort is in question. Does research on flies kept in artificially controlled environments have a lot to say about human behavior "in the wild"? This is the big question, and different scholarly traditions answer it in diverse ways. My opinion is that although well-controlled cross-species research may add to the discussion, both qualitative and quantitative research on humans in natural environments may be more meaningful even if it is quasiexperimental or of some other type that is held in low esteem on the traditional hierarchy of research methods. In their somewhat critical commentary on contemporary research about sex differences and social behavior, Rabinowitz and Valian (2000) pointed out that many different research methods have been used, including experimental and quasiexperimental methods, qualitative studies of behavior in natural environments, and qualitative analyses of archival data. Rabinowitz and Valian use the example of research on jealousy to emphasize the importance of individual cognitive and social characteristics that may be overlooked in cross-species and purely experimental research. The available research indicates that "women are more likely than men to report distress at emotional infidelity; men are more likely than women to be upset about sexual infidelity" (Rabinowitz & Valian, 2000, p. 197). This suggests that the characteristics of jealousy may be sex-linked and genetically based. However, more detailed studies (that explore many issues best studied using qualitative research methods) found that an individual's perception of the meaningfulness of an action is very important. "For men more than women, a partner's sexual infidelity implies emotional commitment whereas for women more than men, a partner's emotional infidelity means that sex is in the air. Most people choose as most distressing the type of infidelity that more implies the existence of the other" (pp. 197–198). In this finer-grained research, biological sex did not appear to be the core determinant of what was upsetting. Instead, it was the individual's beliefs about how these two types of behavior (emotional infidelity and sexual infidelity) interact.

The issue of validity is a major one, but there are actually many criteria for a good research study in the postpositivist tradition, and very few studies in the social sciences meet all of them. Therefore, most of the quantitative studies you read will be quasiexperimental rather than true experimental studies.

The value system, the examples used, and the designs proposed in Cherulnik's book (and hundreds like it) are all based on a postpositivist paradigm that includes the assumption that the traditional scientific method is the only reasonable way to think about research. This is succinctly expressed in Cherulnik's (2001) introduction to research designs: "Every research study is a comparison between what happens under one set of conditions and what happens under another or a number of others" (p. 144). This position dominated social science research for much of the 20th century, and it is explored in this chapter.

Social Science Research: The View From the Postpositivist Paradigm

The paradigms that will be discussed in this chapter and the next take distinctive positions on five issues:

- The nature of reality
- The purpose of research
- The methods of research and types of data that are acceptable
- The types of meaning achieved and the way meaning is derived from the data gathered
- The relationships between research and practice

These five issues are similar to the three Guba (1990) used to distinguish research paradigms: *ontological, epistemological,* and *methodological.* Table 3.1 summarizes the positions taken by the postpositivist paradigm and the older paradigm that it replaced, positivism.

Table 3.1   Differences Between Positivism and Postpositivism on the Five Major Issues

	Empiricism or Positivism	*Postempiricism or Postpositivism*
Nature of reality	External to human mind	External to human mind
Purpose of research	Find universals	Find universals
Acceptable methods and data	• Scientific method • Objective data	• Scientific method • Objective data
Meaning of data	• Mirror to reality • Use to develop theory	• Falsification • Use to test theory
Relationship of research to practice	• Separate activities • Research guides practice	• Separate activities • Research guides practice

In the admittedly oversimplified comparison of positivism and postpositivism in Table 3.1, there are only two differences between these two paradigms. First, as regards the meaning of data, positivism takes the position that you can discover the way things really are by conducting scientific research. That is, if you do enough research and it verifies your theory, you can be confident your theory reflects the true nature of the world. This is sometimes called a *correspondence theory* of truth. Postpositivists, on the other hand, argue that you can never be sure that the next research study will not be the one that shows your theory is wrong (Popper, 1937). Thus, there is never enough research to permit you to eliminate all doubt about your theory. On the other hand, if one study produces data that contradict your theory, that is enough to falsify the theory. You then look for a better theory, or modify your current theory, in response to the falsification. This extreme version of falsification is not widely used today. Most researchers who work in the positivist or postpositivist tradition have adopted a modified falsification approach in which failures may result from a number of things—instrumentation, misinterpretation of the data, misapplication of the theory, poor sampling, and so on—and therefore do not always mean your core theory is wrong.

The other difference between these two paradigms is the relationship of theory to data. Positivism proposes that theory be derived from research observations. This "raw empiricism" assumes that you can collect objective data that are theory free and then use them to develop a theory. The data are "unpolluted" by theory. Postpositivists reject this assumption and accept that any collection of data is based on theory. Data and the interpretation of data are thus theory dependent. Postpositivists can develop a theory in any way they want; theory need not be based on data. However, they test their theories by doing scientific research.

Postpositivism has largely replaced positivism today in the social sciences, and the remainder of this section focuses on postpositivism. As you can see from Table 3.1, the purpose of postpositive research is the discovery of universals or laws. As Guba (1990) puts it, "The business of science is to discover the 'true' nature of reality and how it 'truly' works" (p. 19). The way those universal laws are to be discovered is by use of the scientific method. Again quoting Guba (1990),

> Once committed to a realist ontology [e.g., the basic nature of the world is material], the positivist is constrained to practice an objectivist epistemology [e.g., we can come to know something only by experience in the real world, such as empirical research]. If there is a real world operating according to natural laws, then the inquirer

must behave in ways that put questions directly to nature and allow nature to answer back directly. (p. 19)

The Foundations of Postpositivist Research

Most paradigm debate literature makes the assumption that the research being done is basic research on fundamental issues such as the nature of human learning or the truth about how children's cognitive development takes place. However, much of the research in the social sciences is applied rather than basic. Even though positivism and postpositivism were developed primarily to guide basic research, the majority of studies in the social sciences—basic and applied—are based on one of the variants of postpositivism. Although there is a difference between testing a broad general theory about how humans learn and comparing the success of two ways of teaching reading, research on these two questions, if it is based on a postpositivist paradigm, shares some critical elements. The most important probably is the tendency to look for truth. The goal of postpositivist research, basic or applied, is to find the truth about something. Postpositivists do not believe you can convincingly find truth with one study, but each study is part of a broader effort to get closer and closer to the truth through a series of research studies. That is one characteristic of postpositivist research that distinguishes it from other types. There are many others, and our discussion of them has been organized around the five basic or foundational issues discussed earlier.

Nature of Reality

All research grounded in this paradigm is based on the assumption that there is an accessible, external, physical reality. Accessibility does not necessarily come easily, however. In this paradigm many of the rules for research were developed to give researchers more confidence in their assertions about an external reality. For example, many areas of postpositivist research have developed very specialized jargon to allow researchers to use words to precisely and accurately describe the "real world." That is one reason the language of the postpositivist researcher often differs from both ordinary or "street" language, and the language of practice.

Another reason postpositivists invest so much energy in trying to develop unambiguous language is the assumption that all problems can and should be clear cut. Reflecting the line of thought expressed by Newell and Simon (1972) on both the nature of real-world problems and how problems are formulated, postpositivist researchers assume that all meaningful problems can be framed in clear-cut, unambiguous ways. That is why post-positivists require students to write very precise hypotheses for dissertation research. There are no fuzzy, ambiguous problems, only fuzzy ambiguous formulations of problems. And, likewise, the paradigm assumes there are clear-cut solutions to clear-cut problems. However, the problem must be properly framed before we can fruitfully search for a solution, and the search must be conducted in an objective, scientific manner. For example, it would not be appropriate for a postpositivist to begin a research study without knowing exactly what is to be studied and how the research will be conducted. You need precisely stated hypotheses and well-defined methods.

Article of Interest

Bruce A. Ryan. (1999, August). Does postmodernism mean the end of science in the behavioral sciences, and does it matter anyway? *Theory & Psychology, 9,* 483–502.

Bruce Ryan is a psychologist at the University of Guelph in Canada. His article is about different definitions of reality and their impact on the discipline of psychology and on the social sciences in general. Ryan distinguishes between what he calls a modernist view of reality—that it is independently knowable and external to the knower—and a postmodernist conception that posits reality as something constructed by humans. Ryan traces the history of these two conceptions of reality from Plato and Aristotle to contemporary philosophers of science. He also devotes much of the last half of his article to the implications of adopting a postmodern definition of reality in the social sciences. Opinions vary, from the end of social science research as we know it, to the flowering of social science research in a new era of usefulness and impact. What is your view of the impact of adopting a postmodern view of reality in your field?

To read the entire article, please go to http://www.sagepub.com/willis_aoi.

Purpose of Research

With postpositivism, the search for universals is not limited to basic research. That search extends to applied research as well. As noted earlier, both the basic researcher studying cognitive functioning and the applied researcher studying methods of teaching reading may be looking for universals. The postpositivist paradigm searches for those universals:

beliefs, concepts, and ideas that can be applied to many different situations. Consider this question: Will teacher education students be more likely to use technology in their own classrooms when they graduate if their computer experiences in teacher education focus on developing strong basic operational skills or their computer experiences emphasize ways technology can be integrated into the classroom? Postpositivist research on this question would look for a general and universal answer. The purpose of research is to find universals that allow you to generalize across contexts.

Article of Interest

Frances E. Racher & Steven Robinson. (2003, August). Are phenomenology and postpositivism strange bedfellows? *Western Journal of Nursing Research, 25,* 464–481.

Frances Racher is a nurse practitioner, and this article is a reflective analysis of her struggle with the paradigms she used to guide her research and practice. She is particularly concerned with postpositivism and interpretivism, especially phenomenology practiced within an interpretive framework. Whereas much of the literature takes the position that postpositivism and interpretivism are incompatible because they take radically different positions on topics such as the nature of reality and the purpose of research, Racher and Robinson argue that they are, in fact, quite compatible. How do they come to that conclusion? Do their positions on fundamental issues reflect the views of postpositivists? Interpretivists? Or do they manage to merge the two perspectives?

To read the entire article, please go to http://www.sagepub.com/willis_aoi.

Acceptable Methods and Data

Good research must meet the established, objective standards for both the design and the analysis of data. In the early 20th century a group of scientists in Vienna established the Vienna Circle, a solidly positivist group that argued there is one acceptable way of discovering the truth: the scientific method. Rudolph Carnap, one of the founders of the Vienna Circle, argued forcefully that all science, including social science, must use the same scientific method. His 1934 book *The Unity of Science* is a clear statement of this position. If standards for what constitutes good research are universal, they are the same for basic and applied research in all fields, from physics to anthropology to history.

In this paradigm the technical standards of good research are of paramount importance. If the technical standards are not met, the research does not warrant our attention. For the postpositivist the goal is objectivity and precise control of the research situation. The opposite, subjectivity, must be avoided at all costs.

Article of Interest

Stephen C. Yanchar & Jack R. Hill. (2003, January). What is psychology about? Toward an explicit ontology. *Journal of Humanistic Psychology, 43,* 11–32.

Both positivist and postpositivist philosophies of social science emphasize the need to pay particular attention to the rigor of the research design. Yanchar and Hill point out that this has often resulted in *methodolatry:* the worship of research design over other important issues in the research process. They believe that the privileging of research method (e.g., a favored epistemology) has harmed psychology because the emphasis has let psychology drift along without a real subject matter of its own (e.g., it does not have specific answers for ontological questions). For example, some psychologists study observable behavior, others study cognition, and still others study the unconscious. As Yanchar and Hill put it, "We have no idea of what psychology is about" (p. 16). Furthermore, the level at which these topics of study are explained ranges from the chemical and biological levels to the social or group levels. The authors think this crisis in psychology should be redressed through an ontology of psychology that points to the topics that interest psychology as a discipline. Their solution begins with a rejection of much of the positivist framework. They then argue for the adoption of an alternative ontological position. What do you think of the position they adopt and the arguments they use to support it?

To read the entire article, please go to http://www.sagepub.com/willis_aoi.

Meaning of Data

Postpositivist research is based on a theory-first model. Before conducting a standard study, the researcher would develop specific hypotheses to be tested. In fact, the entire study would be planned in detail because the logic of this type of research calls for everything to be clearly and precisely stated before the data are collected. Ad hoc conclusions are viewed with suspicion. Through statistical analysis, data are interpreted relative to the implications of a theory. The theory comes first, then you conduct the research to test your theory.

Relationship of Research to Practice

Inherent in this paradigm is the assumption that research is a special activity that is quite different from practice. Professional practice is an inherently subjective activity. Thus, a teacher, psychologist, or urban planner will not be able to conduct good research as a part of professional practice. Research must be conducted under very stringent, well-controlled conditions by an objective researcher. Few practitioners work in settings where the requirements for good research can be satisfied (e.g., random assignment to groups, to name just one), and they are not objective about their students, patients, or clients. You must step out of the professional practitioner role in order to take on the role of researcher. In the researcher role you look for universals that, when found, can be communicated to others, who use them to guide practice. In the postpositivist paradigm, there is an inherent hierarchical relationship between research and practice. Research generates the rules of practice that practitioners are to follow.

Article of Interest

Matthew O. Howard, Curtis J. McMillen, & David E. Pollio. (2003, March). Teaching evidence-based practice: Toward a new paradigm for social work education. *Research on Social Work Practice, 13,* 234–259.

The postpositivist model of empirical research guiding practice is aptly expressed in the contemporary concept of evidence-based practice. Over the past decade this concept has gained in popularity so that there are organizations to promote evidenced-based health care, evidence-based education, and evidence-based just about everything else. This article, written by three professors of social work at Washington University in St. Louis, lays out a rationale for evidence-based social work practice and describes how students in the master's degree program in social work at Washington University are prepared to base their professional decisions on the best available empirical evidence. Compare the beliefs of these authors with those of Yanchar and Hill in the previous Article of Interest. How would the recommendations and suggestions be different in each article if the foundational beliefs of the authors were swapped?

To read the entire article, please go to http://www.sagepub.com/willis_aoi.

Examples of Postpositivist Research

A good example of an applied postpositivist research study is the work of Waxman and Huang (1996). They asked whether "1) classroom interaction, 2) selection of activities, 3) instructional activities, 4) organizational setting of the classroom, and 5) student on-task and off-task behaviors in the classroom significantly differ according to the degree of use of technology in mathematics classrooms" (p. 157). Such studies are conducted in many fields, from studies of different forms of psychotherapy to the impact of different medical treatments on a particular disease. Such questions have many practical implications, but they are also inherently theoretical questions. In this case the question is, "Does using computers in the classroom change important classroom patterns?" Waxman and Huang studied more than 2,000 randomly selected middle school students in a large school district. Trained observers visited the classrooms four times in one year. They used a well-validated and reliable classroom observation instrument to gather data on a wide range of student and teacher behaviors in the classroom. Waxman and Huang used part of the observation data to categorize classrooms into three levels of technology use: moderate, slight, and infrequent. Then they used multiple analysis of variance (MANOVA) and analysis of variance (ANOVA) procedures to analyze the rest of the classroom observation data. The results were interesting:

> Instruction in classroom settings where technology was not often used tended to be whole-class approaches where students generally listened or watched the teacher. Instruction in classroom settings where technology was moderately used had much less whole-class instruction and much more independent work. (p. 157)

In their discussion Waxman and Huang also comment that the overall level of use of technology in the classrooms they studied was not high even though the school district had provided technology resources for the classrooms:

> The mere presence of computers or any other type of instructional technology in the classroom does not mean that it will be effectively used. The results from the present study clearly indicated that the wide availability of technology in these mathematics classrooms did not ensure that teachers would use them in their classrooms. Technology needs to be combined with properly trained teachers before it can be really beneficial for students. (p. 165)

The authors also point out that although preservice teacher education usually covers topics such as instructional strategies and classroom management, such topics are generally addressed in contexts that do not involve technology use. However, if the use of technology does change the dynamics of the classroom, then preservice teachers need exposure to and experience in technology-enriched classrooms if they are to teach successfully in that environment.

The Waxman and Huang study meets many of the criteria for a good scientific study, but, like most applied studies conducted in a real-world environment, it does not meet all of them. For example, the researchers used intact groups that were conveniently available rather than randomly assigning each of the 2,000 students who participated to an experimental group. Another education study (Brush, 1997) did randomly create control and experimental groups specifically for the research study. Brush was concerned with the way integrated learning systems (ILSs) are commonly used in schools. (ILSs typically diagnose students' academic deficits and then focus on teaching students what they do not know through drills, tutorials, and practice.) Typically, students work alone at their ILS computers. Brush cited literature indicating that this isolated approach to ILS work can lead to increased anxiety, hostility, and boredom. His study "examined achievement and behavior differences between students completing ILS activities in a traditional, individualized format, and students completing the same activities in cooperative learning groups" (p. 51). He randomly assigned 65 fifth graders to one of two groups, cooperative or individual, and after several weeks of work in the math section of the Jostens ILS, he administered an achievement posttest and an attitude scale. The attitude questionnaire had questions such as "Do you like math?" and "Do the computer math lessons help you with your math classwork?" Students in the cooperative group scored significantly higher on the achievement test and had significantly better attitudes toward both math and the computer math lessons.

These two studies point out some of the problems of dividing up research by paradigms. Postpositivist research often is associated with teaching strategies based on behavioral and information processing theories. However, Waxman and Huang's study used objective methods to demonstrate that classrooms with higher levels of technology use tend to be more "constructivist." Thus "technology can be the catalyst that helps teachers shift from traditional lecture and drill approaches to more student-centered, authentic approaches that emphasize teaching for understanding" (Waxman & Huang, 1996, p. 166). This study thus uses objectivist methods to demonstrate that technology may well support a move toward more subjective teaching and learning environments. Brush's study, on the other hand, attempts to compare a very structured, objective approach to teaching and learning (e.g., ILSs) with a constructivist strategy, cooperative learning. However, in Brush's study the definition of cooperative learning is that pairs of students worked at the computer on the ILS assignments. They helped each other with the ILS lessons. This is a bit like saying you are using cooperative learning strategies if you allow students to work in pairs while they complete the math drill sheets you duplicate and hand out for seatwork. Constructivist educators would argue that cooperative learning involves more than children working together; it involves them working on quite different types of activities than are typical of the tasks found in integrated learning systems. The Brush study illustrates one significant problem of crossing paradigms: The meaning of critical terms and phrases may be subject to debate.

Social Science Research: The View From the Critical Theory Paradigm

In their chapter on critical theory Nichols and Allen-Brown (1997) comment that "the language of critical theory is at times difficult to understand" (p. 227). Similarly, Smith (1993) begins his explanation of critical theory with the comment that "of the three major philosophical tendencies now competing for the attention of social and educational researchers, critical theory is probably the most difficult to understand and, as a result, the most difficult to coherently summarize" (p. 91). This section attempts to capture some of the essence of this paradigm, although most critical theorists will find this effort less than satisfactory.

Proponents of critical theory are a loose collection of scholars and practitioners who tend to focus on the impact of power relationships in human cultures. Critical theory emerged from Marxism in the first half of the 20th century and differs from classical Marxism in its willingness to explore a wide range of power relationships, including those involving gender, race, and ethnicity, whereas classical Marxism tended to focus on capitalist–worker relationships and control of the means of production. Leading proponents of critical theory as a philosophy include Jürgen Habermas. He is a contemporary advocate of a tradition that goes back to a movement called the Frankfurt School, which included both social scientists and philosophers associated with the Institute for Social Research that began in Frankfurt, Germany, in 1929. Examples of scholarship in this tradition include Apple (2003), Giroux (2001a, 2001b) Sloan (2001), and Nightingale and Cromby (1999). Members of this group are generally known today as *critical theorists*. The terminology and the framework of critical theory research are unfamiliar to many people. Consider this explanation by a critical theorist:

> Critical research assumes the necessity of critique of the current ideology, seeking to expose dominating or oppressive relationships in society. It illuminates power relationships between individuals and groups of

individuals, enabling the researcher and participants to critique commonly-held values and assumptions. It requires the researcher and participants to be willing to become aware of how a false understanding contributes to oppression and resistance.

Critical theory is also concerned with human action and interaction. When action takes place, the historical context changes and we must critique our assumptions again. Critical theory is a continuous process. Its goal is Utopia and its reality is that although Utopia may not be possible, our struggle to achieve it will at least create something better than our current existence. (Kilgore, 1998)

In simpler terms, critical theory research tends to emphasize relationships that involve inequities and power, and a desirable aspect of critical research involves helping those without power to acquire it.

Kilgore (1998) explains research in the critical theory tradition this way:

Critical research begins with identifying a specific organization of people whose needs are not satisfied within the current system, and who are willing and able to put research findings into practice. Researchers then enter the participants' world to gain an interpretive understanding of their intersubjective meanings; the culture that has been created by all groups of actors in their world. Researchers then figure out how the current social condition came to exist with historical and empirical analyses.

Understanding the current social condition and the events and actions leading up to the present, the researcher then tries to illustrate the "dialectical tension between historically created conditions of action and the actors' understanding of these conditions" (Comstock, 1982, p. 383). This model reveals social contradictions under which human beings work for a society that no longer works for them. The researcher tries to educate participants and enable them to see the situation in a different light and themselves as capable of transforming a culture that they participated in creating. Finally, the researcher participates in a program of action that will change the current social condition.

Many of the research methods you will study later in this book are used by critical theorists. In fact, some are almost unique to them.

Although the rhetoric of critical theorists is quite different from that of both postpositivists and interpretivists, they are also defined, to a great extent, by the positions they take on the five foundational issues discussed earlier.

Nature of Reality

Table 3.2 suggests that critical theory shares only one common foundation with postpositivism: a belief in an external, knowable reality. There is actually even less agreement than is implied by the table. Yes, both are materialists and thus agree that there is an external reality, but the form that reality takes is quite different in the two paradigms. Critical theory's external reality has little in common with the external reality of postpositivism, and this is only the beginning of the differences between these two paradigms. For example, postpositivist researchers might study the impact of a new method of teaching certain business skills to students. Critical theorists might analyze the impact of the skills themselves and conclude that education is being used as a tool of business to subjugate workers and prepare them to fit into boring jobs created by industry. Although critical theorists might not argue with the findings of the postpositivist who is studying better ways to teach certain skills, they would probably question whether those skills are really important and whether teaching them is a good or bad idea. They might also assert that such research supports a system that is itself in need of reform or revolution. Thus, the reality of the postpositivist is quite different from the reality of the critical theorist.

Table 3.2   Differences Between Postpositivism and Critical Theory on the Five Major Issues

	Postpositivism	*Critical Theory*
Nature of reality	Material and external to the human mind	Material and external to the human mind
Purpose of research	Find universals	Uncover local instances of universal power relationships and empower the oppressed
Acceptable methods and data	• Scientific method • Objective data	Subjective inquiry based on ideology and values; both quantitative and qualitative data are acceptable
Meaning of data	• Falsification • Use to test theory	Interpreted through ideology; used to enlighten and emancipate
Relationship of research to practice	• Separate activities • Research guides practice	• Integrated activities • Research guides practice

┌───┐

Article of Interest

Steve Fleetwood. (2005, March). Ontology in organization and management studies: A critical realist perspective. *Organization, 12,* **197–222.**

The State Museum of Russian Art in Kiev, Ukraine, houses an interesting painting. The name of the picture is *Easter Procession in a Village,* and it shows the poor peasants of the village marching down the street in an Easter procession while the drunken village priest stands unsteadily on the steps of a house (you can view the picture at http://www.abcgallery.com/P/perov/perov23.html). At his feet is another religious official, who is so drunk he has fallen down. The two are moving from one house to another, blessing the inhabitants and receiving the customary and expected gifts of food and drink. The painter, Vasily Perov, was part of the critical realist movement in art. This group used art to point out the poverty and oppression of the poor by those in power. Perov painted his village procession scene in 1861. He was one of the leaders in the critical realist movement that attempted to influence the power structure of tsarist Russia to reform the system and improve the lot of the peasants.

Although the term *critical realism* has a number of different meanings today, there are still elements of the meaning that led Vasily Perov to try to use his artistic talent to help emancipate and empower the peasants of Russia. In this article Steve Fleetwood, from Lancaster University in the United Kingdom, takes a critical realist view of the world and applies it to business research.

Fleetwood does not find positivist realist positions on the nature of the world very appealing. However, he is also not very happy with the fuzzy, subjective nature of an interpretivist's or postmodernist's world. He rejects a subjective foundation for research and proposes instead a realist foundation. However, his is a critical realism rather than a postpositivist realism. As you read the article, note that he rejects aspects of both subjective and positivist versions of what we can know. For example, he argues that the world is knowable as something separate from the mind of the knower. However, he does not believe there is any possibility of humans having unmediated access to the external world (external to the human mind). All our access is mediated by our prior experiences and beliefs. Thus, Fleetwood neither totally rejects nor totally accepts either positivism or interpretivism (postmodernism). However, his strongest criticisms are aimed at postmodern or interpretive subjectivism. Do you find his version of critical realism an appealing alternative to positivist realism and interpretive subjectivism? Why?

To read the entire article, please go to http://www.sagepub.com/willis_aoi.

└───┘

Purpose of Research

Critical theory is less focused on methodology than it is on the reason for doing research. In fact, as noted in chapter 2, Guba (1990) thinks the phrase *ideologically oriented inquiry* is a much better name for this approach than *critical theory* because it emphasizes the focus on ideology as a guide to research. Critical theorists do accept that there is an external reality, but as noted in Table 3.2 they do not pretend to be objective about how they go about discovering that external reality. They *know* that power relationships are critical factors in society, and they know the research they conduct will find specific examples of the negative influence of those relationships. Much of the research within this paradigm is aimed at uncovering these hidden relationships and making us aware both that they exist and that they disenfranchise some groups while giving excessive power and resources to others.

Although critical theorists tend to conduct research that makes us aware of issues such as gender bias in corporate hiring, many critical theorists argue that it is not enough simply to point out problems. The research must also empower the oppressed and help them overturn or overcome the oppression. As Smith (1993) puts it, "The regulative ideal of critical social and educational inquiry is to integrate theory and practice in a way that not only makes transparent to people the contradictions and distortions of their social and educational lives, but also inspires them to empower and emancipate themselves. Critical theorists and critical inquirers have embraced the Marxian injunction that the idea is not merely to interpret or understand the world, it is to change it" (p. 92). Research and practice are thus integrated activities in the critical paradigm. Paulo Freire (1995; Freire & Barr, 1995) probably is the best-known theorist in education who advocated this more active form of critical theory.

Critical theory's idealized version of what research should be is based on the concept that the research process is interwoven with practice in such a way that it helps those who are oppressed to free themselves from the oppression. However, thus far the critical theorists have demonstrated much more skill at criticizing than at empowering and freeing. Most research projects within this tradition are cogent critiques of the current state of affairs. A minority of the critical studies detail successful efforts to bring about change.

Article of Interest

Gaile S. Cannella & Yvonna S. Lincoln. (2004, April). Epilogue: Claiming a critical public social science—Reconceptualizing and redeploying research. *Qualitative Inquiry, 10,* 298–309.

Cannella and Lincoln have written an aggressive defense of the critical research agenda in the social sciences that puts the issue squarely in the political and ideological arenas. They make their critical theory foundation clear by declaring, "First, research as construct was/is conceived and practiced as a political act that generates power for particular groups" (p. 302). Critical research is to support a left-wing view of both the way things are and the way things should and can be (e.g., "engaging in a struggle for liberatory social transformation," p. 304). The authors define the type of research that needs to be done and argue that social scientists must make a concerted effort to get the message of critical social science research to the public and to counter the right-wing research agenda, supported mostly by the positivist and postpositivist paradigm. Would the field of social science that interests you be better if it adapted a critical realist paradigm? A postpositivist paradigm? Why?

To read the entire article, please go to http://www.sagepub.com/willis_aoi.

Acceptable Methods and Data

Because the heart of critical theory is ideological rather than methodological, the research from this paradigm is not limited to a narrow range of methods. Critical theorists sometimes criticize the "objective" methods of postpositivism because the approach tends to treat people and social phenomena as things or objects. Critical theorists also argue that the whole process of research—from the selection of research topics to the creation of research instruments and the interpretation of the data gathered—is not a value-free activity. Each step of the research process is based on the values and beliefs of the researcher. Therefore, there can be no "objective" research. However, there are examples of both quantitative and qualitative research in this tradition.

Meaning of Data

The difference between critical theory research and other paradigms, especially interpretivism, is not so much in the methods used as in the way the data are interpreted and understood. Both critical theory and interpretivism often use qualitative research methods but in different ways. Carspecken's (1995) book on qualitative research methods is a clear-cut explanation of how several qualitative methods are used within the critical paradigm. Carspecken does not introduce readers to ethnography; he presents the case for *critical* ethnography. The difference between critical use of a method and an interpretive or postpositivist use is important but difficult to explain. If they used a qualitative method, postpositivists would conduct research to get at "the way things are," but critical theorists do not view the data as having significant meaning in themselves. The interpretation of data from a critical perspective entails thoughtful analysis and reflection.

The purpose of that analysis and reflection is "to critique or make transparent the false consciousness and ideological distortion" (Smith, 1993, p. 106). Critical theorists believe current social and political systems distort reality and create in individuals a false consciousness that keeps them from seeing the real structure of society. It is only through critical self-reflection that we can free ourselves of these distortions and move toward a truly emancipated society. Research in the critical tradition is thus part of the process of fostering and nurturing self-reflection, which is a necessary step in the course of moving society toward the empowerment of all citizens. For more information on critical methodology, see Gitlin (1994), Morrow and Brown (1994), and Lather (1991).

Relationship of Research to Practice

There are several aspects of the critical theorist's view of research and practice. Unlike postpositivists, critical theorists tend to emphasize scholarship that occurs in context. If they study gender bias, for example, they are likely to do it in a setting such as a classroom, a factory, a university, or an organization. Postpositivists are more likely to study it in artificial, more controlled environments. For example, postpositivists might study gender bias in a psychology lab at a university (rather than studying the patterns of gender bias in the promotion and hiring practices of the psychology department).

Critical theory's emphasis on meaningful research in context is supported by the emphasis on going beyond knowing something. To be useful the research also has to be emancipatory. Emancipatory research helps free individuals and groups from oppression and control. Thus, critical theorists tend to see research and practice as interwoven rather than separate activities.

However, research conducted by a critical theorist generates knowledge that is superior to the knowledge of people the researcher studies. One purpose of research is to free those studied from their mistaken beliefs so they can achieve goals generally set by the researcher. Therefore, although critical research and critical practice commingle, there is an inherent assumption that the knowledge developed by the research is superior to that of subjects in the research. A goal is thus to get the subjects to believe as the researcher does.

Examples of Critical Research

Michael Apple (1991, 1995, 2003; Bromley & Apple, 1998; Carlson & Apple, 1999) is one of the best-known critical theorists in education. He also writes regularly about issues related to technology in education. In 1990 he made a presentation to the annual meeting of the Society for Technology and Teacher Education. His paper was subsequently published (Apple, 1991) and is a good example of the type of conceptual work many critical theorists do. Apple did not describe in his article a single "study," nor did he summarize the results of a series of individual studies. Instead, he stepped back and took a broad view of the field. He argued that too many of the discussions about technology in education focus on the "how to" questions rather than the "why" questions. He then explored a number of political and economic issues and discussed in detail whether teaching as a profession will be enhanced and empowered by the advent of technology. His conclusion was that if current trends continue the profession may well be disempowered and deskilled as teaching is redefined as a management job that focuses on keeping the computers running while the machines deliver specific, skill-based instruction to students who are being prepared for boring, demeaning jobs in a capitalist society that views people as resources to be used as the employer sees fit.

Apple's broad-stroke research draws from the methods of the historian and essayist as well as of the critical educational researcher. This is a common approach among critical theorists because they are often concerned with larger and more complex issues. C. A. Bowers (1988) uses a similar approach in his article "Teaching a Nineteenth-Century Mode of Thinking Through a Twentieth-Century Machine." In the article he argues that the way personal computers are being used in education reinforces certain types of social interaction and legitimizes certain types of knowledge at the expense of others. Bowers argues that in a computer-intensive learning environment the role of the teacher as an interpreter, clarifier, and amplifier of cultural knowledge becomes critical because of the bias built into the computer as an educational tool.

Critical theorists also use more traditional qualitative and quantitative research methods. For example, Monke (1999) used a detailed case study of the diffusion of technology into the public schools of Des Moines, Iowa, to highlight the significant and serious hidden costs to teachers and administrators of such efforts. A modified case study method was also used by Ann De Vaney (1993) to analyze the gender issues inherent in a popular piece of educational software, *The Oregon Trail.*

Critical theorists have also used several types of quantitative methods. For example, Chappell (1996) used a procedure called content analysis to study gender representation and the amount of violence and competition in the most popular math educational software. Her results indicated that 4.2% of the activities in preschool math software were violent, and 46% of the activities in high school programs were violent. Similarly, none of the activities in the preschool software involved competition against peers, whereas 31% of the activities at the high school level were competitive. Chappell points out that some research suggests that the attitude of girls toward computers is positive in preschool but becomes more negative over the years. She suggests that the amount of violence and competition in software may be one factor in that trend. Her study also found that whereas 39% of the characters in preschool math software were female, only 13% were in high school programs.

Another critical theorist, Jonathan Rees (2003), analyzed the use of standardized testing in American schools, with a focus on American history. He analyzed the American history section of the National Assessment of Educational Progress. Rees offers a thoughtful and careful critique of the test itself and many of the ways the results are used. However, his approach is informed and guided by a critical theory of education. Consider these comments from his article:

- The test's "structural flaws and problems with question design make any standardized history test a bad measure of student understanding. Worse still, because the framework of this exam limits test subject areas to a narrow consensus, it defeats the purpose of learning historical knowledge to promote informed democracy and encourages the misuse of history for partisan political purposes."

- The questions "tend to stress the importance of institutions over individuals, conservative actors over reformers and agreement over dissent. In other words, they tend to reflect conservative political values."

- "By defining . . . American history . . . in the most uplifting terms, conservatives, including President Bush, can then use history to promote their political agenda. Under the cover of promoting citizenship, they want to limit American history to information that reinforces their point of view."

- "Rather than recognize the inherent flaws . . . conservative politicians and educational reformers exploit standardized test scores to promote the idea that a crisis exists in history and civics education. They insist that the house is on fire so that they can sell their version of fire prevention. Teaching conservative values is how they want to stop historical and civic ignorance from reoccurring, and by using standardized tests they can claim their methods are scientifically measured and objective. . . . The crisis over the failure of American students to learn the component knowledge of an unattainable consensus is nothing but a political smokescreen."

- The National Assessment of Educational Progress "reflects the conservative consensus championed by the test's political backers. And because these views are cloaked under the auspices of a supposedly objective test, parents, students and other segments of the American public don't realize how their understanding of history is being manipulated."

In an analysis of the "correct" answers to questions, Rees used the question, "What is the purpose of labor unions?" as an example. The answer counted as correct ("to protect jobs and interests of workers") reflects the "consensus desire for upward mobility" but "wobblies, communists and socialists [who supported labor unions for other reasons] are therefore not worth noticing."

Rees's research is a very good example of how ideology guides research in the critical paradigm. Of course, Rees and other critical theorists would argue that ideology also guides research in other paradigms, but that fact is often hidden (something he accuses conservative educators of doing).

One final comment on critical theory research: Critics, including other critical theorists, often chastise this paradigm because it often seems "to be aimed at building individual careers by criticizing the work of others, and it emphasizes the ways in which people are oppressed and despairing" (Nichols & Allen-Brown, 1997, p. 229). The critical theory literature can indeed be a downer, with too much doom and gloom and far too few examples of positive work done from a critical perspective. However, that is changing. More and more critical theorists are taking initiative and developing approaches to problems in our field that reflect the values and perspectives of critical theory.

Article of Interest

Susan Birden. (2004, August). Theorizing a coalition-engendered education: The case of the Boston Women's Health Book Collective's body education. *Adult Education Quarterly, 54*(4), 257–272.

Despite our implication that critical theorists don't do much more than criticize, this article by a professor at Buffalo State College illustrates just the opposite: a critical approach that is emancipatory and change focused. The main emphasis is on the use of an approach called coalition-engendered education, which the author illustrates by discussing the origins and operation of the Boston Women's Health Book Collective. The author, Susan Birden, contrasts this approach with a more established approach to emancipatory research based on literacy that was developed by Paulo Freire. After reading the article, do you see the approach advocated by Birden as an extension of Freire's work or a different approach to emancipation? Why? Do you agree with Birden's criticism of mainstream adult education as being too much like schooling? Why? Finally, would you consider work to establish and grow a coalition-engendered education group to be community activism, research, or both? Why?

To read the entire article, please go to http://www.sagepub.com/willis_aoi.

Summary

These two research traditions, postpositivism and critical theory, are quite different. Postpositivist research is separate from practice. It is conducted in an *objective* way using objective methods. Critical theory research often is subjective, conducted with emotion and ideological bias in the "real world." (Note, however, that critical theorists would argue that postpositivist research is not objective but rather is controlled and directed by the values and beliefs of the researchers and their supporters.) These two forms of research have different purposes, different methods, and different ways of looking at the data of the research project. Critical theorists often criticize postpositivists for studying unimportant things simply because they can be quantified and for studying things that prop up and maintain systems that should be torn down. Postpositivists often criticize critical theorists for confusing ideological practice with "real" research and for coming to the research table with preconceived biases about what will be learned.

In the next chapter you will learn about another framework: interpretivism. It has some things in common with the postpositivist paradigm but shares more with the critical theory paradigm. Interpretivism is also roundly criticized by proponents of both the competing paradigms.

Questions for Reflection

1. A scholar's view of the nature of reality has a major impact on the research she or he does. Select a topic of research that interests you and link views on the nature of reality to aspects of the research endeavor: purpose, acceptable methods, data analysis, and the research–practice link.

2. Consider the five areas of difference discussed in this chapter. Develop your own position on each of them. Does your personal perspective fit one of the established philosophies of science? Do you differ on any of the foundational issues with the paradigm you are closest to? Why?

3. Consider the relationship between research and practice. What is the typical pattern in your field of practice or interest? Is the typical pattern a good one? Or would a different pattern be more useful? Why?

4. Create three imaginary studies of a particular topic that typify research in each of the three paradigms. Include information on the purpose of the study, the design and data analysis, and the relationship of the researcher to practitioners.

References

Apple, M. (1991). The new technology: Is it part of the solution or part of the problem in education? *Computers in the Schools, 8*(1/2/3), 59–81.

Apple, M. (1995). *Education and power.* New York: Routledge.

Apple, M. (2003). *The state and the politics of knowledge.* London: Falmer.

Bartz, A. (1998). *Basic statistical concepts* (4th ed.). New York: Macmillan.

Bowers, C. A. (1988, Winter). Teaching a nineteenth-century mode of thinking through a twentieth-century machine. *Educational Theory, 38*(1), 41–46.

Bromley, H., & Apple, M. (Eds.). (1998). *Education, technology, power: Educational computing as a social practice.* Albany: State University of New York Press.

Brush, T. (1997). The effects on student achievement and attitudes when using integrated learning systems with cooperative pairs. *Educational Technology Research and Development, 45*(1), 51–64.

Carlson, D., & Apple, M. (1999). *Power-knowledge pedagogy: The meaning of democratic education in unsettling times.* Denver: Westview.

Carnap, R. (1934). *The unity of science.* London: Kegan Paul.

Carspecken, P. (1995). *Critical ethnography in educational research : A theoretical and practical guide.* New York: Routledge.

Chappell, K. (1996). Mathematics computer software characteristics with possible gender-specific impact: A content analysis. *Journal of Educational Computing Research, 15*(1), 25–35.

Cherulnik, P. (2001). *Methods of behavioral research.* Thousand Oaks, CA: Sage

Comstock, D. (1982). A method for critical research. In E. Bredo & W. Feinberg (Eds.), *Knowledge and values in social and educational research* (pp. 370–390). Philadelphia: Temple University Press.

De Vaney, A. (1993). Reading educational computer programs. In R. Muffoletto & N. Knupfer (Eds.), *Computers in education: Social, political, and historical perspectives.* Cresskills, NJ: Hampton.

Freire, P. (1995). *Pedagogy of the oppressed* (M. Ramos, Trans.). New York: Continuum Publishing Group.

Freire, P., & Barr, R. (1995). *Pedagogy of hope: Reliving pedagogy of the oppressed.* New York: Continuum Publishing Group.

Giroux, H. (2001a). *Stealing innocence: Corporate culture's war on children.* New York: Palgrave Macmillan.

Giroux, H. (2001b). *Theory and resistance in education: Towards a pedagogy for the opposition.* New York: Bergin & Garvey.

Gitlin, A. (1994). *Power and method: Political activism and educational research.* New York: Routledge.

Guba, E. (1990). The alternative paradigm dialog. In E. Guba (Ed.), *The paradigm dialog* (pp. 17–27). Newbury Park, CA: Sage.

Kilgore, D. (1998). *The critical paradigm: A transforming approach.* Retrieved December 3, 2005, from http://www.stedwards.edu/newc/kilgore/critical.htm

Lather, P. (1991). *Getting smart: Feminist research and pedagogy with in the post-modern.* New York: Routledge.

Long, T., Montgomerie, R., & Chippindale, A. (2006). Quantifying the gender load: Can population crosses reveal interlocus sexual conflict? *Philosophical Transactions of the Royal Society B, 1098,* 1–12.

Monke, L. (1999). *Tools of transformation: The ideological role of computer technology in education.* Ph.D. dissertation, Iowa State University, College of Education.

Morrow, R., & Brown, D. (1994). *Critical theory and methodology.* Thousand Oaks, CA: Sage.

Newell, A., & Simon, H. A. (1972). *Human problem solving.* Englewood Cliffs, NJ: Prentice Hall.

Nichols, R., & Allen-Brown, V. (1997). Critical theory and educational technology. In D. Jonassen (Ed.), *Handbook of research for educational communications and technology* (pp. 226–252). New York: Macmillan.

Nightingale, D., & Cromby, J. (1999). *Social constructionist psychology: A critical analysis of theory and practice.* Philadelphia: Open University Press.

Popper, K. (1937, reissued 2001). *The logic of scientific discovery.* New York: Routledge.

Rabinowitz, V., & Valian, V. (2000, April). Sex, sex differences, and social behavior. Evolutionary perspectives on human reproductive behavior. *Annals of the New York Academy of Science, 907.* Retrieved December 3, 2005, from http://maxweber.hunter.cuny.edu/psych/faculty/valian/rabinowitz&valian.pdf

Rees, J. (2003). A crisis over consensus: Standardized testing in American history and student learning. *Radical Pedagogy, 5*(2). Retrieved December 3, 2005, from http://radicalpedagogy.icaap.org/content/issue5_2/03_rees.html

Sloan, T. (Ed.). (2001). *Critical psychology: Voices for change.* New York: Palgrave Macmillan.

Smith, J. (1993). *After the demise of empiricism: The problem of judging social and educational inquiry.* New York: Ablex.

Waxman, H., & Huang, S. (1996). Classroom instruction differences by level of technology use in middle school mathematics. *Journal of Educational Computing Research, 14*(2), 157–169.

CHAPTER 4

History and Foundations of Interpretivist Research

T he third paradigm, interpretivism, is sometimes viewed as a part of, or at least closely related to, critical theory. However, major differences between these two paradigms are pointed out in this chapter, beginning with an exploration of the five basic questions that framed the discussion of postpositivism and critical theory. They are summarized in Table 4.1.

Nature of Reality

Interpretivists do not necessarily deny that there is an external reality. Most are quite comfortable accepting the existence of an external, physical

Table 4.1   Differences Between Postpositivism and Interpretivism on the Five Major Issues

	Postpositivism	*Interpretivism*
Nature of reality	External to human mind	Socially constructed
Purpose of research	Find universals	Reflect understanding
Acceptable methods and data	Scientific method	Subjective and objective research methods are acceptable
Meaning of data	• Falsification • Use to test theory	• Understanding is contextual • Universals are deemphasized
Relationship of research to practice	• Separate activities • Research guides practice	• Integrated activities • Both guide and become the other

reality. What they have difficulty with is the assertion that it is an independently knowable reality. Interpretivists do not accept the premise of postpositivism that the scientific method is a way of objectively learning about that external world. On the contrary, interpretivists assert that all research is influenced and shaped by the preexisting theories and world views of the researchers. The terms, procedures, and data of research have meaning because a group of scholars has agreed on that meaning. Research is thus a socially constructed activity, and the "reality" it tells us about therefore is also socially constructed.

This is a fundamental issue in social science and research. Gall, Borg, and Gall (1996) make it the defining characteristic of positivist and postpositivist research:

> Some researchers assume that features of the social environment . . . have an objective reality, which means that these features exist independently of the individuals who created them or who observe them. . . . Researchers who subscribe to a positivist epistemology make this assumption of an objective social reality. Sally Hutchinson (1988), for example, states, "Positivists view the world as being 'out there,' and available for study in a more or less static form. The task of positivist scientific inquiry, then, is to make bias-free observations of the natural and social world 'out there'." We define positivism as the epistemological doctrine that physical and social reality is independent of those who observe it, and that observations of this reality, if unbiased, constitute scientific reality. (pp. 17–18)

Gall et al. (1996) go on to discus an alternative view of reality:

> An opposing epistemological position to positivism is based on the assumption that social reality is constructed by the individuals who participate in it. . . . This view of social reality is consistent with the constructivist movement in cognitive psychology, which posits that individuals gradually build their own understanding of the world through experience and maturation. . . . Educational researchers who subscribe to this constructivist position believe that scientific inquiry must focus on the study of multiple social realities, that is, the different realities created by different individuals as they interact in a social environment. They also believe that these realities cannot be studied by the analytic methods of positivist research. (p. 19)

The authors name the idea of socially constructed meaning *postpositivism* because it was "a reaction to the positivist approach to social science inquiry" (p. 19). This meaning is sometimes used in the literature, but as was noted earlier, the term *postpositivism* is generally used to describe a philosophy of science that is an adaptation of positivism or raw empiricism based on the work of Karl Popper rather than a distinctly different philosophy. Gall et al. are referring to the approach called interpretivism in this book and in many others (Berger & Luckman, 1967; Creswell, 2002; Heshusius & Ballard, 1996; Maxwell, 2004; Smith, 1989, 1993). The interpretive paradigm is not the dominant model of research today, but it is gaining influence. There are even articles on the use of interpretive research in areas many of us would think of as solidly quantitative and postpositivist, such as accounting (Chua, 1986), health care (Horton, 1998; Koch, 1995; Young, 2003), computer engineering (Fischer, Nakakoji, Ostwald, Stahl, & Sumner, 1993), computer software design (Thanasankit & Corbitt, 1999), management information systems (Kosaka, 2002), requirements engineering (Atkinson, 2000), the history of chemistry (McEvoy, 2000), and management (Dyer & Wilkins, 1991).

Gall et al. are also slightly off on their description of how meaning is constructed according to interpretivists. They place much emphasis on the work of the individual in constructing a personal and unique reality. This position leads to the "problem of other minds" (Morick, 1967) because anyone who accepts the idea that every individual constructs his or her own unique and mental version of reality runs immediately into the problem of how two such individuals can communicate and know what the other means. The very idea of research, if it includes communication of information to others, becomes impossible if everyone has his or her own unique version of reality. Fortunately, most interpretivists do not accept this version of how knowledge is constructed. They argue instead that making meaning is a group or social process. Humans in groups, and using the tools and traditions of the group (including language), construct meaning and thus are able to share their understanding with other members of the group. What this means is that the research you conduct and disseminate is likely to be understood better by those who are also members of your group. Members of other groups who do not share the same socially constructed version of what research is and how it is to be conducted will find your research more difficult to understand and harder to accept as real research.

Whether you call it interpretive research or qualitative research, a core belief of this paradigm is that the reality we know is socially constructed. Researchers therefore have access only to a socially constructed reality. None of us, including those who conduct research using the scientific method, has direct access to external reality. This position often is counterposed to positivism, but it also differs from critical theory. Critical theorists believe they can uncover and make obvious local examples of broad truths such as oppression, bias, and the abuse of power. For an interpretivist, however, what the critical theorist finds is not truth in any absolute sense. It is a view from a group that shares certain beliefs and expectations. This is perhaps the most upsetting aspect of interpretivist theory. Postpositivists need an external reality and research methods that bring them closer to knowing what that reality is. Critical theorists need an external reality and methods to empower people to overthrow oppression. Neither is comfortable with the socially constructed reality of interpretivism.

Article of Interest

Nini Praetorius. (2003, August). Inconsistencies in the assumptions of constructivism and naturalism. *Theory Psychology, 13,* 511–539.

Praetorius, who teaches at the University of Copenhagen, compares the basic assumptions of constructivist (interpretivist) and naturalist (positivism or postpositivism) philosophies of social science. She is particularly concerned with how the two approaches handle the mind–body question and the mind–reality question. Both these questions are couched in the dualist philosophy of René Descartes. For Descartes, mind and body exist as separate entities, and the mind can comprehend an externally existing reality. Praetorius points out that different answers to the basic questions about mind and body are the foundation for different research traditions in psychology. What is your response to Praetorius's explanations of why both naturalism and constructivism are based on indefensible fundamental assumptions? Are her arguments sound? And is the solution she offers better than constructivism? Better than naturalism? Why?

To read the entire article, please go to http://www.sagepub.com/willis_aoi.

Purpose of Research

Perhaps the most obvious implication of an interpretivist view of reality has to do with the purpose of research. Whereas postpositivism looks for universals and critical theory looks for local instances of universals, interpretivism looks for understanding of a particular context. Interpretivists believe an understanding of the context in which any form of research is conducted is critical to the interpretation of the data gathered. Consider the study by Waxman and Huang mentioned in chapter 3. Whereas some postpositivists might use the data from that study to make a general statement about the relationship between computers and teaching strategies, interpretivists might argue that an understanding of the context of the study could call that general conclusion into question. In their article Waxman and Huang mention that the school district where the data were collected had provided training for teachers. The district training tended to emphasize the use of constructivist approaches to teaching and learning. Would the results have been the same if the data had been collected from a district where the teachers were provided extensive training on the use of integrated learning systems or some other nonconstructivist teaching method? In his review of the literature Zhu (2003) attributes the differences found in the Waxman and Huang study simply to greater use of technology. However, ironically, Zhu's own research led him to conclude that

> Regardless of variations across schools, however, most schools tend to use computers in traditional ways. This indicates if school and district policy-makers believe transformational use of computers will help reform and restructure public schools, they may consider building up or strengthening characteristics that enhance transformational ways of computer usage, such as organizing professional workshops on technology use and model classroom sessions to demonstrate how computers are used for classroom instruction [which is precisely what the district was doing in the Waxman and Huang study]. Squandering money on installing computers may not serve the purpose. (pp. iii–iv)

This question of interpreting data in context highlights the concern interpretivists have about the *situatedness* of knowledge. Thus, the goal of interpretive research is an understanding of a particular situation or context much more than the discovery of universal laws or rules.

It is difficult to overemphasize the importance of the difference between postpositivist views of the purpose of research and that of interpretivists. Research as a search for generalizations, laws, and rules is supported by behavioral and information processing theories of learning and by positivist and postpositivist philosophies of science. On the other hand, several philosophical traditions support the idea that research in the social sciences leads to the construction of contextual knowledge, or local knowledge, rather than laws. The general framework of an interpretive philosophy of science has already been discussed. Here we will deal with three other movements that support understanding as the purpose for doing research: *verstehen,* hermeneutics, and phenomenology.

Verstehen

As a reason for doing research, the German word for "understanding," *verstehen*, expresses the idea that understanding the particulars of a situation is an honorable purpose. This goal is quite different from that of positivist research: to explain (erklären) and find lawlike rules or generalizations that can be used well beyond the situation studied.

At the end of the 19th century Dilthey (see Harrington, 2000) distinguished between two types of knowledge: understanding (*verstehen*) and explanation (erklärung). He proposed that there are two types of sciences: naturwissenschaft, or natural sciences, and geisteswissenschaft, or the cultural (human, moral, or social) sciences. Finding lawlike generalizations is fine for the natural sciences but it is not a suitable goal for the cultural (social) sciences. Dilthey saw the goal of research in the natural sciences as explanation, whereas in the social sciences the purpose was understanding. Associated with Dilthey's idea of *verstehen* was his belief that the legitimate topic of study was lived experience. Thomas Schwandt (1994) uses these two ideas, understanding and lived experience, to explain the essence of interpretive qualitative research:

> Proponents . . . share the goal of understanding the complex world of lived experience from the point of view of those who live it. This goal is variously spoken of as an abiding concern for the life world, for the emic point of view, for understanding meaning, for grasping the actor's definition of a situation, for *Verstehen*. (p. 118)

Emic and Etic

Emic and *etic* refer to two contrasting ways of approaching the study of cultures. The emic approach looks at things through the eyes of members of the culture being studied. What is valid or true is what members of the culture agree on. The etic approach uses structures or criteria developed outside the culture as a framework for studying the culture. From an etic perspective, what is true may be judged through comparison of the cultural practices to an external standard or structure. With etic research the scientists doing the study are the judges of what is true because they are the ones who select the external standards or structures that will be used. Lett (2005) points out that the ways *emic* and *etic* are defined have both ontological and epistemological implications. She suggests epistemological definitions for emic knowledge and etic knowledge that are widely but not universally accepted.

The terms "emic" and "etic" should be seen as adjectives modifying the implicit noun "knowledge." Accordingly, the distinction between emics and etics has everything to do with the nature of the knowledge that is claimed and nothing to do with the source of that knowledge (i.e., the manner by which it was obtained). Emic constructs are accounts, descriptions, and analyses expressed in terms of the conceptual schemes and categories that are regarded as meaningful and appropriate by the members of the culture under study. . . . The validation of emic knowledge thus becomes a matter of consensus—namely, the consensus of native informants, who must agree that the construct matches the shared perceptions that are characteristic of their culture.

Etic constructs are accounts, descriptions, and analyses expressed in terms of the conceptual schemes and categories that are regarded as meaningful and appropriate by the community of scientific observers. An etic construct is correctly termed "etic" if and only if it is in accord with the epistemological principles deemed appropriate by science (i.e., etic constructs must be precise, logical, comprehensive, replicable, falsifiable, and observer independent).

Schwandt (1994) links current interpretivist research foundations to several movements: "the German intellectual tradition of hermeneutics and the *verstehen* tradition in sociology, the phenomenology of Alfred Schutz, and critiques of scientism and positivism in the social sciences [including] the writings of ordinary language philosophers critical of logical empiricism" (p. 119).

Article of Interest

Austin Harrington. (2000). In defense of *verstehen* and *erklären*. Theory & Psychology, 10(4), 435–451.

Harrington, a sociologist at the University of Leeds, deals with a much-debated issue in this article. It is whether the role of a social science such as psychology is understanding (*verstehen*) or explanation (*erklärung*). He traces the history of this debate and its relationship to the idea that the natural sciences (*naturwissenschaften*) and the social sciences (*geisteswissenschaften*) are fundamentally different and thus entail quite different research methods. A strength of this article is Harrington's ability to situate the origin of the major ideas in the historical setting where they were developed. He shows that our understanding of

Dilthey's use of the terms *verstehen* and *erklären* will be different if we understand the state of psychology when he was writing.

As you read about the different positions on whether there is a difference between the natural and social sciences, develop your own opinion. Are you close to the idea that there are universal research methods and purposes and that they are best illustrated in the practices of the natural sciences? Or do you believe Dilthey's distinction between them is appropriate and correct? Or would you accept the argument that there is a difference between the natural and cultural sciences but that psychology should be a natural science? Or, finally, do you agree with Rorty and others that all the sciences are subjective and that the natural sciences would fare better if they acknowledged the subjectivity inherent in their work?

To read the entire article, please go to http://www.sagepub.com/willis_aoi.

Ordinary Language Philosophers

In the 20th century philosophers such as Bertrand Russell at Cambridge University and Alfred Tarski in Poland tried to develop specialized languages that allowed thinkers to convey precisely what they meant to say. Behind these efforts was the belief that ordinary or everyday language was not precise enough for scholarly work. Ordinary language left too much open to interpretation on the part of the reader or listener. This looseness worked for normal communication, but it was not acceptable in areas such as scientific research and philosophy. What was needed was a precise and accurate language that was *transparent*. That is, the message to be communicated passed from one person to another, via language, without the language adding to or subtracting from the intended meaning. This approach is called *ideal language philosophy*.

Although efforts to build specialized languages that are both transparent and precise continue, what many people call the "linguistic" turn in philosophy occurred in the first half of the 20th century. This turn was initiated by Ludwig Wittgenstein, an Austrian philosopher who spent much of his academic life at Cambridge University in England. First, however, Wittgenstein was on the other side of the argument. In 1922 Wittgenstein published a revolutionary book that was, at Bertrand Russell's suggestion, titled *Tractatus Logico-Philosophicus*. In that book, Wittgenstein offered a philosophical foundation for what is now called a picture theory of meaning. Something said is correct if it is a picture of (e.g., accurately portrays) facts in the physical world. Wittgenstein and his book were a major influence on many groups, including the logical positivists, who were studying ways of communicating that were transparent and precise.

After a decade of reflection, in which Wittgenstein did many things including teach in a rural elementary school and donate to his siblings his share of a huge fortune (his grandfather established the steel industry in the Austro-Hungarian empire), Wittgenstein rethought his position on language and developed a very different theory of language and meaning. He argued that it is not possible to develop a transparent and precise language because the meaning of words depends on the context of use. Language thus has meaning through his famous concept of *family resemblances*. Just as the members of a particular family may resemble each other in a number of ways (but not have all the exact same characteristics such as a short nose or long, thin fingers), so words and phrases may have somewhat different but related meanings when used in different contexts. What was crucial in his idea of family resemblances is that this way of defining meaning does not depend on a set of core or required characteristics (just as a Smith without a stubby nose may still look like other Smiths because of her long thin fingers or the shape of her ears). Wittgenstein challenged anyone to come up with a set of core characteristics of the word *game* that is shared by everything we agree is a game.

One implication of the family resemblances concept is that the meaning of a word cannot be understood by looking it up in a dictionary. Meaning came from use, not definitions. The picture theory of meaning was not only wrong, it led us in the wrong direction. Meaning emerges from use in the real world, and what we do when we use words and phrases is play the "language game," which has an evolving set of rules that govern how the elements of language are used.

This idea of family resemblances and language games opened up many new vistas for both philosophers and scientists. For example, if meaning comes from use in a particular group of language users (e.g., cultural anthropologists or clinical psychologists), that means other groups of language users may play a different language game with the same words and thus have a different understanding of what the words mean. Much of interpretivist theory is based on this idea of a relativist definition of meaning, and many research projects in the social sciences have been conducted to understand the way meaning develops in different language communities.

For philosophy, the theories of the "later Wittgenstein" pushed the disipline toward the study of meaning in context and away from efforts to find a perfect language. Thus ideal language philosophy was rejected and "ordinary language" philosophy became an important focus. For example, Wittgenstein argued that many of the foundational arguments in philosophy were really simply confused uses of language that would disappear if his theories were adopted. Through the use of ordinary language many philosophical puzzles would "dissolve" instead of being solved because their roots were in the way language was used, not in philosophy. For example, a foundational question such as "What is truth?" has been the focus of thousands of years of philosophical thought, but for Wittgenstein it is a matter of language. How is the phrase used in ordinary language? Philosophers such as J. L. Austin, Gilbert Ryle, John Wisdom, and, more recently, Richard Rorty were heavily influenced by Wittgenstein.

Hermeneutics

Originally the term *hermeneutics* referred to the study of sacred texts such as the Talmud or Bible. You can see how study of a document that was originally written over a period of time in a number of different languages several thousand years ago might present some problems when it comes to understanding exactly what is meant by a particular passage. Efforts to get at the meaning might include the study of the meaning of terms and phrases from the document in other writings from the same era, the social and political context in which the passage was written, and the way the concepts discussed are used in other parts of the document. This is a simplistic explanation of the original idea of hermeneutics, but it will serve our purposes here. Gradually, hermeneutics has expanded beyond that original meaning to include understanding human action in context. Although there are many variations of hermeneutics, Smith (1989) concludes that they all share two common characteristics:

• An emphasis on the importance of *language* in understanding. Language makes possible what we can say, and it limits what we can say.

• An emphasis on the context, particularly the historical context, as a frame for understanding. You cannot understand human behavior and ideas in isolation; they must be understood in context.

Smith (1989) points out that there are at least three current versions of hermeneutics, "which can be labeled *validation (or objective), critical,* and *philosophical*" (p. 13). The first, validation, is based on postpositivism and assumes that hermeneutics can be a scientific way of finding the truth. The second, critical, is based on critical theory. Critical hermeneutics aims to make transparent and obvious the historical conditions that have led to oppression. "Critical hermeneuticists . . . are deeply suspicious of the validation perspective, because it fails properly to account for the possibility of historically formed ideological distortion and false consciousness" (p. 106). "The whole point of critical-hermeneutical self-reflection is to foster practical engagement or emancipation in the light of historical truth" (p. 107).

The third type of hermeneutics, philosophical, is based on interpretivist epistemology and aims at developing understanding. It rejects any form of foundationalism—that is, a sure way of finding truth. Interpretivists see validation hermeneutics as an effort to find truth through a research method. They see critical hermeneutics as foundational as well because the interpreter (researcher) is still given a privileged position to explain to the subjects of the research why their false consciousness is wrong and the researcher's view is more correct. Interpretivists do not accept either approach as a foundation for qualitative research. Instead, they push for understanding of the topic of study in context.

Foundationalism

Many different philosophical systems begin with the assumption that there are infallible, absolutely true facts that can serve as the starting point for our understanding of the world. For example, Aristotle believed that the primary or basic truths of science were self-evidently true. These he called *first principles* (Irwin, 1990). It was not necessary to prove that first principles were true; that was taken as a given. And, of course, Aristotle could not prove that the concept of first principles was true. This too he took as a given. Research (e.g., careful observation) allowed you to move from those self-evident truths to build other knowledge.

Aristotle's first principles can be understood by thinking about them, which means this is a form of rationalism. However, empiricists can also be foundationalists. If you take the position that the only way to obtain valid knowledge about the external world is through experience, that is a foundational assumption that cannot be proved. Thus empiricists are also foundationalists.

Many philosophers of science have taken an *antifoundationalist* position. This group is very diverse, but they hold in common the idea that there is no dependable foundation on which you can build a philosophy of science. In the 20th century, Sir Karl Popper wrote extensively about foundationalist views and argued forcefully that you cannot ever prove anything beyond a shadow of a doubt. The best you can do is falsify or cast doubt on a theory. His emphasis on doing empirical research to falsify a theory meant that science progressed by finding the flaws in theories and coming up with better theories that were not so easily falsified. Richard Rorty is a contemporary antifoundationalist philosopher who argues that humans do not have access to a God's-eye view of the world that is inherently infallible.

The results of taking either a foundationalist or antifoundationalist position are significant:

> If foundationalism is the thesis that we can construct knowledge with absolute certainty starting from nothing, then the denial of this can give us various possible theses: (1) knowledge cannot be constructed, (2) there is no absolute certainty, and (3) knowledge cannot be started from nothing. The first thesis gives us the idea of "deconstruction" to describe and symbolize the failure of foundationalistic projects. The second thesis, that we cannot have absolute certainty, is now accepted

(Continued)

(Continued)

> by all but everyone outside a few Aristotelians. But the third thesis is the best clue to an alternative theory: If knowledge cannot be started from nothing, what does it start with? With previous knowledge, of course. But what is to count as previous knowledge? Why, just whatever it was that we thought we knew before whatever happened that changed our minds. And if there is no certainty to knowledge, and no permanent, fixed system can be constructed, then the new knowledge will be what we think we know until something else happens to change our minds again.
>
> This process ends up being described by the "hermeneutic cycle." "Hermeneutics," from Greek hermêneuô, "to interpret or translate" (from the messenger of the gods, Hermes), is the theory and practice of interpretation, originally the interpretation of texts, especially religious texts. The "hermeneutic cycle" is the process by which we return to a text, or to the world, and derive a new interpretation—perhaps a new interpretation every time, or a new one for every interpreter. It is clear that this happens all the time. We can understand a book, a movie, etc. a little differently each time we read or see it. (Ross, n.d.)

The term *hermeneutic circle* is sometimes used to refer to the process of developing meaning or understanding. It always involves going back and forth between the topic of study, the context, and our own understanding. When the topic is human behavior we have a double hermeneutic because we are humans and we are trying to understand ourselves.

Qualitative research methods are used by hermeneuticists from all three persuasions, but they are particularly useful to critical and philosophical (interpretive) researchers. In a passage that is less than clear, Schwandt (1994) explains philosophical hermeneutics:

> In contrast [to approaches based on positivist paradigms], the philosophical hermeneutics of Heidegger, Gadamer, and Taylor is concerned with ontology (being). The hermeneutical condition is a fact of human existence, and philosophical hermeneutics is concerned with a phenomenological (i.e., existential) explication of *Dasein* (condition of existence or being-in-the world). (p. 121)

Terms such as *Dasein* and *being-in-the world* drive postpositivists up a wall, but that tends to support the assertion of the philosophical hermeneuticists, that we can understand only by understanding the context of the other person and our own context, both historical and contemporary. For this group there is no solid ground where an objective or "true" perception of what is real is available.

Article of Interest

Anshuman Prasad. (2002, January). The contest over meaning: Hermeneutics as an interpretive methodology for understanding texts. *Organizational Research Methods, 5*(1), 12–33.

This article by Anshuman Prasad, who teaches management courses at the University of New Haven, is a good overview of the current status of and issues related to hermeneutic research methods within the interpretive tradition. He provides a brief history of the method, explains the concepts and introduces current issues, and explores the actual methods of hermeneutic research. Although written for organizational researchers in business, his article is also appropriate for any social science researcher. As you read this article make sure you understand the words and phrases that have special meaning in hermeneutic research. These include *text, fusion of horizons, language as a metainstitution, interpretation, the hermeneutic horizon, critical or depth hermeneutics, critical self-reflexivity,* and the *non–author-intentional view of meaning.* Do any of the various forms of hermeneutics discussed in the article appeal to you more than others? Why? If you find hermeneutics appealing, is the appeal that of a research method or of a paradigm with certain epistemological and ontological beliefs?

To read the entire article, please go to http://www.sagepub.com/willis_aoi.

Phenomenology (and Existentialism)

Another supporting theory for interpretive qualitative research is phenomenology and a related movement, existentialism. Phenomenology is the study of people's perception of the world (as opposed to trying to learn what "really is" in the world). The focus is thus on understanding from the perspective of the person or persons being studied. The modern emphasis on this concept resulted in large part from the work of a German philosopher, Edmund Husserl. Through a student of his, Martin Heidegger, he also influenced the existential movement that was popularized by French philosopher Jean-Paul Sartre (who was a student of Heidegger). Alan Woods (1998), a British Marxist philosopher, summarizes phenomenology and existentialism in his critical dismissal of these approaches:

> Existentialism has its roots in the irrationalist trend of 19th century philosophy, typified by Nietzsche and Kierkegaard. It has assumed

the most varied forms and political colouring. There was a religious trend (Marcel, Jaspers, Berdyayev and Buber) and an atheistic trend (Heidegger, Sartre, Camus). But its most common feature is extreme subjectivism, reflected in its preferred vocabulary: its watchwords—"being-in-the-world," "dread," "care," "being towards death," and the like.

It was already anticipated by Edmund Husserl, a German mathematician turned philosopher, whose "phenomenology" was a form of subjective idealism, based on the "individual, personal world, as directly experienced, with the ego at the centre."

Woods dismisses both these movements as part of the "irreversible decline in 20th century philosophy," primarily because his critical stance still holds onto the belief that you can know an external reality, whereas existentialism and phenomenology accept that there are no universals that humans can know without doubt. Interpretivism owes an intellectual debt to both these movements. They form part of the basis for justifying social science research that attempts to understand the local context rather than find universals or laws of human behavior.

Understanding often calls for different forms of research and different ways of reporting the results of research. In fact, some research methods that attempt to get at the perceptions of the person being studied often are called phenomenological research methods. In general, interpretivists tend to use more qualitative methods such as case studies and ethnography, and the reports they write tend to be much more detailed. Rich reports are necessary because the context is needed for understanding. The interpretivist approach to understanding the data generated in a research study sometimes is called the hermeneutic approach. It is difficult to explain. D. C. Phillips (1992), a strong opponent of the interpretivist paradigm, comments that the growing literature on hermeneutics "is more a repository of enthusiasm than of enlightenment," and "the literature is full of claims, . . . and there is a dearth of examples. . . . Like the Scarlet Pimpernel, hermeneutical issues are claimed to be everywhere" (p. 1). Phillips's view of research based on "understanding" is itself understandable because his postpositivist approach does not find understanding of the local context very fulfilling. He is looking for something a bit more universal. Hermeneutic understanding has much in common with the reflective practitioner model of Donald Schon (1984, 1987, 1990; see also Atweh, Kemmis, & Weeks, 1998), and researchers familiar with and comfortable with that approach to professional practice probably will find the interpretivist approach to research a compatible framework.

┌─ **Article of Interest** ─────────────────────────────────────┐

Kate Caelli. (2000, May). The changing face of phenomenological research: Traditional and American phenomenology in nursing. *Qualitative Health Research, 10,* **366–377.**

Caelli, who teaches at the University of Alberta, responds to criticisms of nursing research using a phenomenological framework. Some critics argue that it is not really phenomenological because it does not adhere to the European standards of phenomenological ideology. Her response is to point out that North American nursing research in the phenomenological tradition often is based on American, not European, phenomenological thought. She traces the development of both American and European strands of phenomenology and links current research practice in North America and Australia to the influence of phenomenological philosophy, particularly American. Which tradition do you find most appealing? Why? Do the implications of American and European phenomenology that Caelli talks about in nursing also have implications for research in your area of interest? How?

To read the entire article, please go to http://www.sagepub.com/willis_aoi.

└───┘

Acceptable Methods and Data

Interpretivists are antifoundationalists; they believe "there is no particular right or correct path to knowledge, no special method that automatically leads to intellectual progress" (Smith, 1993, p. 120). That position is particularly troubling to postpositivists who believe no progress can be made unless certain standards of research are upheld. Interpretivists don't have a problem with standards that guide research; it is just that they do not believe those standards are in any way universal. They are, instead, the products of a particular group or culture. This is in marked contrast to the view of many postpositivists. B. F. Skinner (1953) succinctly stated the alternative when he said that achieving the goal of psychology, to "predict and control the behavior of the individual organism . . . must be done within the grounds of a natural science. We cannot assume that behavior has any peculiar properties which require unique methods" (pp. 35–36). For Skinner and many postpositivists today, the scientific method, as practiced in the natural sciences, is the only path to truth. Interpretivists don't always abandon standards such as the rules of the scientific method; they simply accept that whatever standards are used are subjective, and therefore potentially fallible, rather than objective and universal. Interpretivists accept almost all the types of quantitative methods that positivists use, but they differ in how they interpret the results of quantitative research. Quantitative research is one of many potential sources of understanding. And in many cases, quantitative research is not the preferred mode of research. Interpretivists also use a broad range of qualitative methods.

Saying that interpretivists use both quantitative and qualitative research methods does not tell the entire story, however. They also accept reflective discussions of professional practice. In fact, the thoughtful reflections of experienced practitioners are a prized source of knowledge and understanding for interpretivists. So are the stories of people with relevant experiences. This is in contrast to postpositivists, who generally consider practitioner reflections and personal stories to be unacceptable as research because they are neither scientific nor objective. Sigmund Freud's use of case studies to develop and validate psychoanalytic theory is one reason that most academic psychologists in America refused to take his work seriously for decades. In a similar vein, Jean Piaget's use of research methods that were well outside the bounds of the traditional scientific method is a reason that American psychologists lagged behind European academics in giving him serious consideration. For example, in 1985 and 1987 the American Psychological Association (APA) filed amicus briefs with the U.S. Supreme Court in a case involving the issue of whether teenagers should be able to make their own decisions about whether to have an abortion. The APA argued that teens should have that right because their thinking was as sophisticated as that of adults. The briefs were based in part on Piaget's theory of cognitive development, especially the assertion that the final stage of cognitive development, formal operations, begins at about 12 years. That stage ends in late adolescence, and the APA therefore argued that teens should not be denied their rights on the grounds that teens did not think at the same level of sophistication as adults, citing Piaget's work as evidence. However, in 1989 Gardner, Scherer, and Tester wrote an article in the *American Psychologist* titled "Asserting Scientific Authority: Cognitive Development and Adolescent Legal Rights." They pointed out that the APA later became concerned that the use of Piaget's work, and that of others, lacked scientific rigor. What was needed before such assertions could be made were well-controlled experimental studies that compared the thinking of adolescents with that of adults.

That American positivist and postpositivist psychology still regards the research methods of both Freud and Piaget as suspect is not surprising. Jacques Vonèche (2003) points out that Piaget, perhaps because of his own adjustment problems in adolescence, had a strong interest in psychoanalysis and that some of his research methods are similar to those of Freud.

Piaget's research methods, and Freud's, were well outside the bounds of traditional positivist psychology, and Piaget managed to make things even worse (from the perspective of the positivist) by studying his own children.

Interpretivists have no problem with this because they do not consider any form of research to be truly objective. And because context is so important in the interpretation of data, they tend to prefer data sources that are close to the point of application. For those two reasons—the abandonment of the quest for objectivity and emphasis on the importance of context—professional practice knowledge is elevated to a position that is often considered superior to knowledge based on out-of-context empirical research (e.g., studies of the learning patterns of college sophomores [or pigeons] that are conducted in small austere rooms on university campuses).

Article of Interest

Margarete Sandelowski & Julie Barroso. (2003, July, 2003). Writing the proposal for a qualitative research methodology project. *Qualitative Health Research, 13,* 781–820.

Sandelowski and Barroso are professors of nursing at the University of North Carolina at Chapel Hill. The focus of their article is on how to write a proposal for a qualitative research project. However, it emphasizes the issues that must be addressed because qualitative research does not typically use planned research methods that cannot be changed once the study has begun. Instead, the methods emerge across the research project. Throughout this article you will see suggestions for addressing the emergent nature of qualitative research methods. How would a person who believes in any research, including qualitative studies, respond to the suggestions in this article? How would they respond to a proposal that describes an emergent model if they were serving on an institutional review board that must approve studies before research begins? Would you agree if you were on the review board? Why? Why not?

To read the entire article, please go to http://www.sagepub.com/willis_aoi.

Meaning of Data

As noted earlier, the purpose of interpretivist research is not the discovery of universal laws but rather the understanding of a particular situation. Even this goal is subjective. Interpretivists eschew the idea that objective research on human behavior is possible.

Most of Anglo-American psychology in the 20th century has sought to emulate the outlook and methods of the natural sciences in order to achieve a similar kind of success. To this end, they have adopted an outlook, worldview, and metatheories which is perhaps best termed as *naturalistic*, . . . with the view that human life is fundamentally a part of nature and nothing other than nature, to be studied and explained by disciplined, objective sciences that rely mainly on controlled experimentation and seek, so far as possible, strictly objective, "value free," "value neutral," or "culture free" accounts of human phenomena. . . . (Christopher, Richardson, & Christopher, 2001, pp. 3–4)

Knowledge can never be objective because of our inescapable historicity. We are always situated in a particular "horizon" of understanding that is based on a combination of cultural and personal presuppositions (prejudices). . . . (p. 12)

Instead of trying to ground truth and representation through method as objectivism does or dismiss the whole notion of truth as much of postmodern thought does, hermeneutics substitutes a dialogical form of truth. Hermeneutics sees the pursuit of truth as essential to human existence, but suggests we can never have certainty we have found truth. For instance, while statistically significant correlational findings are often assumed to indicate universal, ahistorical truths about the human condition, Bernstein observes that they could simply reflect "regularities or systematic interrelationships in the personal or social existence of particular historical communities." . . . We can never be certain about our theories, our research findings, our epistemic principles, our values, or our ontological commitments. In consequence, hermeneutics substitutes . . . our "best accounts" for the quest for timeless, universal laws of human behavior. We can only offer our best accounts, our best interpretation, our best arguments, and our best reasons for the ongoing historically situated dialogue in which we are necessarily immersed. (p. 20)

You can see elements of both postpositivism and critical theory in the perspective on what research data mean. Like the postpositivists who adhere to Popper's falsificationist theory, interpretivists do not believe you can ever be sure that what you think to be true is true. And, like the critical theorists, interpretivists emphasize that context, *historicity,* is an essential aspect of understanding your data.

However, that does not mean that there is no way to apply or use the results of interpretivist research in settings other than the one in which the data were gathered. Postpositivists generally expect their research to be applied through a process that Schon (1987) calls "technical rationality." According to the technical rational approach, research leads to general rules that are then applied by practitioners to particular situations. Technical rationality is implicit in a postpositivist research paradigm. Interpretivists reject this way of thinking because they do not believe the situation in which the research findings are to be applied is a simple, easily understood context in which preexisting formulas can be routinely applied. They argue that research results must be applied at a higher, conceptual level. Research adds to our understanding of different contexts and situations, but our application of that understanding is not a technical process; it is reflective. That is, we must thoughtfully make decisions in our own practice, and those thoughtful decisions must be based on all our understanding.

The interpretivist's understanding is not quite the same as that of a postpositivist. It is not a single understanding of the "right" way of viewing a particular situation. Instead, it is an understanding of multiple perspectives on the topic. Smith (1993) makes this point by saying that postpositivist research searches for theories that provide us with abstract principles or rules that can then be applied in practice, whereas interpretivist research "expresses a practical tradition of inquiry based on the listing of exemplars" (p. 140). Postpositivists are generally uncomfortable with the idea of leaving lists of exemplars as the final product of research; they would like to transform them into theories that represent universals.

> Interpretivists, of course, will have none of this at any level. They agree with Feyerabend (1981) when he says that, for certain traditions . . . "a list is not a mistaken first step on the way to a more appropriate definition: it is the only adequate form of knowledge." . . . One learns to use a list, and thereby becomes part of a practical tradition, by playing around with or applying the list in interaction with others. (Smith, 1993, p. 141)

However, lists are not simply different forms of postpositivist universals. "Items on a list are not rules that foreclose or predetermine the kind of judgments people make, they are values that influence those judgments" (Smith, 1993, p. 141). An example of the use of exemplars, or list of examples, is Kuhn's (1962) use of the word *paradigm*. In his book *The Structure of Scientific Revolutions,* paradigm is a central concept. In the book he defines the word in many different ways—so many, in fact, that you cannot find one, authoritative dictionary-style definition that is informative and comforting. As Masterman (1970) notes in her article "The Nature of a Paradigm," "Kuhn, . . . with that quasi-poetic style of his, makes paradigm-elucidation genuinely difficult for the superficial reader. On my counting, he uses 'paradigm' in no less than twenty-one different senses, . . . possibly more, not less" (p. 61). However, Kuhn is not really trying to define the word *paradigm* in the traditional way, by offering a precise definition. Instead, the meaning of *paradigm* emerges from Kuhn's use of examples that illustrate what he means by the term. That is perhaps appropriate because the English word *paradigm* comes from the Greek word *paradeigma*, which roughly means "example."

To some, this use of fuzzy, ill-defined lists and exemplars as suitable outcomes of research is unacceptable, even dangerous. For example, after pointing out that Kuhn defines *paradigm* in many different ways, whereas Foucault uses the term frequently but never defines it, Göktürk (2005) devotes his article to defining the term *paradigm*. Many social scientists fear that the loss of an objective foundation for research and practice results in a wimpy relativism that treats every opinion and theory equally because there is no way to make objective decisions about what is right. This is one of the most common misconceptions of interpretivism: that because you cannot be sure of a right answer, all answers must be treated as equal. We can still advocate a position, argue forcefully for what we believe, and urge others to accept our views. What we cannot do is assert that we have found the truth in any absolute sense and that there is no need to explore and understand alternative views and perspectives. To do so would be to yield to a dangerous tendency that philosopher Richard Rorty (1991) calls ethnocentrism. Rorty's brand of interpretivism goes beyond the simple assertion that everything is subjective. Because we cannot escape our own backgrounds and experiences, he believes we must practice, conduct research, and develop theories within that framework; it is our only option. We cannot work in a vacuum, and we cannot shed our background. We need not remain totally within our own group, however. If we are empiricists who scientifically study the impact of different forms of psychotherapy, we need not remain completely ignorant of other forms of scholarship, such as case studies of people in therapy. As Rorty (1991) put it,

> I urge that whatever good the ideas of "objectivity" and "transcendence" have done for our culture can be attained equally well by the idea of a community which strives after both intersubjective agreement and novelty—a democratic, progressive, pluralist

community of the sort which Dewey dreamt. If one reinterprets objectivity as intersubjectivity, or as solidarity . . . then one will drop the question of how to get in touch with "mind-independent and language-independent reality." One will replace it with questions like "What are the limits of our community? Are our encounters sufficiently free and open? Has what we have recently gained in solidarity cost us our ability to listen to outsiders who are suffering? To outsiders who have new ideas?" These are political questions rather than metaphysical or epistemological questions. Dewey seems to me to have given us the right lead when he viewed pragmatism not as grounding, but as clearing the ground, for democratic politics. (p. 13)

Rorty's (1979, 1982, 1991) democratic pragmatism thus accepts the subjective nature of both research and professional practice, but he argues that we can reduce the danger of ethnocentrism by encouraging free and open discussion within our own group and by making a special effort to seek out and understand the truths of other groups.

One consequence of antirepresentationalism is the recognition that no description of how things are from a God's-eye point of view, no skyhook provided by some contemporary or yet-to-be-developed science, is going to free us from the contingency of having been acculturated as we were. Our acculturation is what makes certain options live, or momentous, or forced, while leaving others dead, or trivial, or optional. We can only hope to transcend our acculturation if our culture contains (or, thanks to disruptions from outside or internal revolt, comes to contain) splits which supply toeholds for new initiatives. Without such splits—without tensions which make people listen to unfamiliar ideas in the hope of finding means of overcoming those tensions—there is no such hope. The systematic elimination of such tensions, or the awareness of them, is what is so frightening about *Brave New World* and *1984*. So our best chance for transcending our acculturation is to be brought up in a culture which prides itself on not being monolithic—on its tolerance for a plurality of subcultures and its willingness to listen to neighboring cultures. This is the connection which Dewey saw between antirepresentationalism and democracy.

We should not look for skyhooks, but only for toeholds (Rorty, 1991, pp. 13–14).

Antirepresentationalism

American philosopher Richard Rorty uses the concepts of representationalism and antirepresentationalism to express some of his views on epistemology (Boros, 1998). Representationalism is, essentially, the idea that human knowledge is a way of representing the external world. This is a subject–object relationship. That is, the human is the subject, and the object is some aspect of the external world. Representationalism is a fundamental assumption of many forms of the scientific method, and it is also implicitly assumed by many natural and social scientists.

Rorty's antirepresentationalism is based on the view that you cannot separate the subject from the object:

> Antirepresentationalism does not try to see the world as it is, it does not investigate knowledge or accurate representation of reality, since in every statement about the world there is an inseparable "mixture" and "cohabitation" of the subject and the object. That means if we think that we know something about the world, we can never exactly [make the distinction between] what part of it comes from us and what part comes from the "outside world." (Boros, 1998)

Rorty's view of human knowledge is thus subjective: We can never be absolutely sure that what we think is true about the world is actually true. In this his antirepresentationalism is similar to Sir Karl Popper's (and postpositivism's) adoption of falsification as a criterion for judging theories instead of confirmation. Both have given up the idea that you can ever prove that human knowledge accurately portrays external reality. However, Rorty's ideas have become a stone in the foundation of interpretivism, whereas Popper's are an important foundation for an empiricism that still searches for the truth about the external world.

Efforts to retrieve representationalism from the criticisms of Rorty and others often involve accepting that there is no firm foundation on which our knowledge about the external world can be based but arguing that it is still good to pursue our studies as if there were. For example, philosopher Hillary Putnam proposed a "quasi-realism" (the term used by Boros, 1998) or "internal realism" (the original term used by Putnam, 1981) that is, in a way, halfway between representationalism and antirepresentationalism. Rorty has argued against all efforts to salvage representationalism.

Whereas interpretivists agree strongly with Rorty's position, critical theorists have problems with this approach. Part of the problem has to do with what type of knowledge can be generated or created by research. As Kilgore (1998) puts it,

Critical theorists reject an exclusive emphasis on either predictive knowledge generated in the positivist paradigm or constructed meaning generated in the interpretive paradigm. Instead, these are viewed as dialectically interrelated—thesis and antithesis—providing a foundation for a third type of knowledge (Bredo & Feinberg, 1982) that seeks to resolve their conflict. Allowing a place for both positivist and interpretive knowledge, critical theorists seek to show that they are driven by human interest. They believe that knowledge can never be value-free and that in claiming that it has no interest, it has already become distorted.

Habermas describes three kinds of interest that produce knowledge: technical, practical, and emancipatory. A technical interest in prediction and control arises from a society's interaction with nature to produce an existence (Welton, 1993). In modern societies, technical knowledge arises in the positivist paradigm. . . . Interpretive research studies how humans make meaning out of their interactions, producing practical knowledge. Finally, an emancipatory interest derives from a desire to be freed from domination. Emancipatory knowledge is a consciousness of the contradictions between our beliefs and our aspirations to be free from domination.

Critical theorists believe that the predictions generated in the positivist paradigm or the descriptions constructed in the interpretive paradigm are not adequate by themselves. Emancipatory knowledge, generated in the critical paradigm, focuses on the correct use of the technical and practical modes of learning and on the adequacy of the knowledge.

The concepts of technical, practical, and emancipatory knowledge are very useful, but in our view both interpretive and critical research have the potential to produce emancipatory knowledge. (However, critical theorists may want to assert that when interpretivists do research that is emancipatory they become critical theorists.) The difference is more in how much of an imperative there is to discover emancipatory knowledge. For critical theorists it is essential. For interpretivists it is important if the context calls for it, but it is not a requirement of good research.

Relationship of Research to Practice

As has been noted already, in the interpretive paradigm the divide between interpretive research and practice is not great. As Christopher et al. (2001) put it,

In the hermeneutic view, social theory is a form of practice. Psychology has always struggled to reconcile its insistence of pursuing a neutral form of inquiry with its mission of advocating human welfare. However, philosophical hermeneutics and other postmodern critiques have pointed out how the ideal of the "disinterested observer" is misguided, self-deceived and ultimately impoverishes the social sciences. (p. 21)

The debate over how research and practice relate is ongoing and it is not likely to be settled easily because the different views are based on differences in paradigmatic or fundamental beliefs. The April 1996 issue of *Educational Researcher* contains several articles on the role of research in guiding practice. Gage (1996) makes an eloquent plea for the use of social science research to guide practice from a technical rational perspective. Much of the defense offered by Gage is based on the assumption that social science research can lead us to long-lasting generalizations. Gage concludes that there are universals that "hold up over considerable variation across the individuals or other units studied, across different ways of describing and measuring those individuals or other units, across varied settings, and across decades" (p. 14). Thus Gage proposes that, through good empirical research, we can come to know how things are and thus base our practice on that knowledge. He refers to those who disagree with that view of social science research, and there are many today, as

counsels of despair [who] assert that, whereas the behavioral sciences once promised to reveal universal relationships between phenomena in the social world—generalizations that would hold true everywhere and forever—we should now realize that they have failed, and must inevitably continue to fail, to produce such generalizations. (p. 5)

Gage's worries are implicitly based on the assumption that if you cannot discover universals, there is no other meaningful purpose for social science research. This view of the purpose of research is solidly centered in the postpositivist, objectivist, and empiricist schools of thought. Schon (1987) makes the same point when he talks about reflective practice.

Technical rationality rests on an *objectivist* view of the relation of the knowing practitioner to the reality he knows. On this view, facts are what they are, and the truth of beliefs is strictly testable by reference to them. All meaningful disagreements are resolvable, at least in principle, by reference to the facts. And professional knowledge rests on a foundation of facts.

In the constructionist [e.g., interpretivist] view, our perceptions, appreciations, and beliefs are rooted in worlds of our own making that we come to accept as reality. Communities of practitioners are continually involved in what Nelson Goodman . . . calls "worldmaking. . . . When practitioners respond to the indeterminate zones of practice by holding a reflective conversation with the materials of their situations, they remake a part of their practice world and thereby reveal the usually tacit processes of worldmaking that underlie all of their practice." (p. 36)

The contrast between technical rational (postpositivist) and interpretive (reflective) views of research and professional practice has been around a long time. In the April 1996 special issue of *Educational Researcher,* two scholars from the University of Utrecht in the Netherlands, Kessels and Korthagen (1996), also address this issue from a historical perspective. They point out that for more than one hundred years theoretical, abstract knowledge has been considered superior to "concrete skills or the tacit knowledge of good performance" (p. 18). However, Kessels and Korthagen note that the ancient Greek concepts of *episteme* and *phronesis* are relevant to the issue of how research and theory interact with practice. Plato's knowledge, *episteme,* is general, abstract, and procedural. It is universal. The propositions or assertions of epistemic knowledge

are of a general nature; they apply to many different situations and problems, not only to this particular one. Consequently, they are formulated in abstract terms. Of course, these propositions are claimed to be true; preferably their truth is even provable. . . . Because they are true, they are also fixed, timeless, and objective. . . . It is this knowledge that is considered of major importance, the specific situation and context being only an instance for the application of the knowledge. (p. 18)

This is the type of knowledge that Merrill (1997; Merrill & ID2 Research Team, 1996) counts on for his form of research, and it is what Gage is talking about when he speaks of knowledge that allows us to make generalizations.

Tacit Knowledge Versus Explicit Knowledge

Talented professionals and artisans often develop ways of doing things that allow them to excel in their field. If they can explain and teach that knowledge, it is *explicit*. Often, however, they can use the knowledge but they cannot explain it or teach it to someone else. That is *tacit* knowledge.

The idea of tacit versus explicit knowledge was developed by Michael Polanyi (1967). As the social sciences and fields such as artificial intelligence began to take an interest in the differences between how experts solve problems and how novices solve the same problems, these two types of knowledge became useful concepts for explaining some of those differences. Faced with a problem, a novice may try to apply the principles and rules he has been taught explicitly. An expert may not even consciously think of the principles and rules for this type of problem; she may develop a strategy or select a problem solution on the basis of her tacit knowledge. And when asked to explain why she did what she did, she may not be able to communicate all the knowledge she used. Some psychologists, including R. J. Sternberg (Sternberg & Horvath, 1999), believe tacit knowledge is knowledge that has not been but could be converted to explicit knowledge. However, Polanyi's original concept was that tacit knowledge cannot be made explicit and cannot be converted into propositional logic statements (e.g., "When the patient has these symptoms, do treatment B").

In Polanyi's original sense, the idea of tacit knowledge has a number of implications. An important one is that you cannot completely break down a skill such as the practice of medicine into a set of rules that can then be taught to students. If exemplary practice is, in part, determined by tacit knowledge that is not translatable into explicit rules, then the teaching of rules gets at only part of what makes a great physician, a great artist, or a great scientist. Another implication is that if tacit knowledge is acquired through experience (rather than through learning rules), then the preparation of professionals and artisans should include a great deal of mentored, practical experiences (e.g., the physician's internship and residency or the architect's studio classes). Several groups in cognitive psychology have proposed learning methods such as anchored instruction, cognitive apprenticeships, contextual learning, problem-based learning, and informal learning that are justified in part because some of what is to be learned is tacit knowledge. (Note: In the field of business the term *tacit knowledge* has a different meaning. It often refers to the store of expertise and knowledge in the minds of employees of an organization.)

Aristotle's knowledge, *phronesis*, is situated in a context and is dependent on that context. It is practical wisdom rather than abstract, universal wisdom. This type of knowledge is knowledge of a different kind, not abstract and theoretical, but its very opposite: knowledge of concrete particulars. . . . In practical prudence, certitude arises from knowledge of particulars. All practical knowledge is context-related, allowing the contingent features of the case at hand to be, ultimately, authoritative over principle. (Kessels & Korthagen, 1996, p. 19)

For Aristotle, it is not possible to capture good practice in a system of rules. Kessels and Korthagen quote Aristotle: "Let this be agreed from the start, that every statement (*logos*) concerning matters of practice ought to be said in outline and not with precision" (p. 19). Kessels and Korthagen believe that knowledge about professional practice and research is best thought of as *phronesis* rather than *episteme*. Trying to precisely apply universal rules is doomed to failure. As Donmoyer (1996) puts it,

Aristotle's "practical" problems are as much about framing questions as finding answers and as much about values as facts. Problems, from a phronesis frame of reference, are also, by definition, about idiosyncrasy and uniqueness, about particular students or particular clients rather than about seeing particular students or clients merely as exemplars of a general category or ideal type. (p. 4)

With Platonic knowledge we can provide detailed steps about how to do a research study because we have what Gage calls universal or generalizable knowledge about methods. With Aristotelian knowledge we cannot do that because the context is so important to meaning. Most of the qualitative research methods discussed in this book are based on the assumption that knowledge of how to do research in the social sciences is more Aristotelian than Platonic. From an interpretive perspective the nature of the knowledge derived from research is also more Aristotelian than Platonic.

The result of a qualitative study is thus understanding in context rather than rules or laws. That *phronesis,* or understanding, can be communicated to others, who use it as part of their context for making decisions. It is not truth, however, and does not lead to laws of human behavior. The essential difference between understanding and truth is that truth can be exported to other settings and applied directly as a rule. Understanding informs a decision maker (teacher, physician, social worker, politician, economist, or researcher). Understanding of work completed in another context cannot be applied directly to a different setting. Some ideas or procedures from a study may even be tried out in practice, but they are used because the practitioner or researcher has thoughtfully considered the possibilities and thinks they are promising. I recently moved to a new home and, after buying some brown-and-serve bread, carefully read the directions for preparing the bread. The directions said to preheat the oven to 425 degrees. I dutifully followed the rules (directions), dialed 425 degrees, and created a black, carbonized mess. I tried several times to use the directions on the package as laws and failed to produce edible bread. Later, after my wife used the oven several times, the mystery was solved. She concluded that the oven was about 50 degrees hotter than the dial said. She adapted the directions, and the bread was delicious. Sometimes even laws have to be treated as general and adaptable guidelines.

Implications of an Interpretivist Approach

In many ways interpretivism is more difficult to understand than the other two paradigms because it is so open. For example, it does not specify a certain type of research method. But it does take a very strong position on the way research should be understood.

Interpretivism views all research as subjective, but proponents are not extreme relativists who see every viewpoint as just as good as any other. They are comfortable arguing for their particular viewpoint despite the subjectivity of their foundations. They simply argue that conclusions from any program of research could be wrong and that we should all be aware of and open to findings from other perspectives and traditions.

Complex and fuzzy as interpretivism is, the paradigm has a number of significant implications for researchers. Those implications are discussed in this section, but they are formulated as family resemblances rather than absolute truths about every version and variation of interpretivist social science. Varieties of interpretivism tend to reflect these implications.

Fields such as computer science and physics are naturwissenschaften; *studies of human behavior and learning are* geisteswissenschaften. Although much of the American thrust in both the philosophy of science and the development of the social sciences has placed the social sciences in a position of emulating natural science, there are traditions in German philosophy that distinguish between the natural sciences (*naturwissenschaften*) and the cultural sciences (*geisteswissenschaften*). Research in natural and cultural or social sciences may have different purposes, different methods, and different frames of reference. Thus, the objective scientific method that has allowed such progress in the natural sciences is not necessarily a universal method that should be used uncritically in the social (cultural) sciences. If the two types of science are different, then they may need different methods.

The search for universal truths ends, and efforts to find local truth and understanding accelerate. Nancy Davis, a sociologist at DePauw University, posed this question for one of her courses on social theory: "What if, as postmodernists posit, there is no grand narrative or driving force that organizes human history, only local narratives and local truths?" Faced with the need to give up the search for "grand narratives" and laws of social behavior that are universal, some social scientists refuse to accept an interpretivist ontology and epistemology. One such critic is William Matthews (n.d.) at the University of Massachusetts. His blunt rejection of interpretivism (which he calls postmodernism and radical social constructivism) nicely summarizes the attitude of many postpositivists:

> Radical social constructivism and its equivalencies of cultural constructivism, deconstructivism, feminist discourse, post-structuralism, post-modernism and the like have become, in my opinion, a serious blight on the American intellectual landscape. The argument, which I will refer to in general terms as post-modernism, is, as I will show, logically fallacious and with only reasonably close inspection falls under its own nihilistic weight. In essence, the post-modernist position is that truth is only relative and has no general application given that said truth is a mere construction created by a given social context. . . . Since truth is only relative and subject to various prejudices, the statement that all truths are relative and have no generalizability is itself simultaneously relative and absolute and as such offers us no reason to accept it. Relativism makes no distinction (because for such folks there is none) between objective (i.e., verifiable) knowledge and superstition (astrology, creationism, flat-earthers, to name but a few, come to mind) and is deeply flawed as an epistemology. It is, by definition, a direct attack on science, scientific method, and critical rationality. This view would offer us no way to distinguish between superstition and verifiable knowledge and as such is both nonsensical and intellectually dangerous.
>
> Post-modern thought has continued to gain prominence within certain circles of academia (e.g., certain aspects of feminist discourse, literary criticism, some advocates of multiculturalism, etc.) and increasing influence within some subsets of the psychological community. For example, with reference to the latter, Prilleltensky (1997) in his discussion of the assumptions of various models of therapy appeared to feel forced to elevate post-modernism to the status of a model of therapy in the absence of any empirically based evidence to support it.

Critical Rationality

This term takes on different meanings in different parts of the literature. For Marxists and neo-Marxists, it sometimes refers to the use of rational thought to expose and understand the Marxist–Leninist laws of social and economic development. For critical theorists, critical rationality may involve the analysis of oppression and acting to remove oppression and inequality so that dominated individuals and groups are free. Among positivists and postpositivists, in contrast, it means the use of rational thought to develop laws of behavior and to correctly evaluate the evidence for and against different theories and their implications. Although the term is most often used in a neo-Marxist or critical theory way, the preceding quote from Matthews uses the positivist or postpositivist meaning.

Interpretivism, at least the brand discussed here, is not quite as Matthews describes. He appears to have confused it with the anarchic or "anything goes" philosophy of science developed by Paul Feyerabend (1993). Perhaps the most important issue is Matthews's statement that local truth "has no general application." In this he is incorrect. If you are studying the relative importance of work and family among urban professionals in Germany, the findings, according to interpretivists, are not automatically applicable to urban professionals in, say, the United Kingdom or Canada. They may not even be applicable to German urban professionals 5 years later. However, the findings do become part of the contextual or local knowledge about this issue, and a scholar studying the same topic in the United Kingdom, Hong Kong, or Sierra Leone should be aware of the German study. Some of the findings of the German study may influence the questions asked and the interpretation of data in a new study. Researchers may even find similarities between the situation in Germany and other settings. Thus interpretivist research can be used outside the context in which it was conducted. The difference is in who makes the decision about what the use. Postpositivist researchers look for lawlike generalizations that can be applied in other settings. If the findings are laws, you will treat them differently than you would findings that are local truths. With local truths the user decides what seems applicable and what does not in a new context. With a law it is the job of the practitioner or user to correctly apply the law.

Another of Matthews's conclusions, which is commonly made by postpositivists, is that an interpretivist philosophy gives us "no way to distinguish between superstition and verifiable knowledge." This statement does apply to Feyerabend's anarchic philosophy. He suggests that if you look at the way scientists actually do scientific research, it is difficult to differentiate it from magic or witchcraft. That is not the case with interpretivism. Within this framework you can develop a strong belief in the correctness of your research method and your research findings. What you cannot do is argue that your research method is the only method that may be useful or that your findings are undoubtedly a reflection of external reality.

Messy, in-context research becomes much more valuable, and well-controlled research conducted out of context is devalued. Much of the model for an instructional approach called programmed instruction, which was popular in the 1960s, was generalized from studies of pigeons. Even then, the pigeons were not even living the normal life of a pigeon. Instead, they were kept in small metal cages, isolated from one another, and starved to keep their motivation high. A shift to an interpretivist framework would encourage more work in the authentic environments of humans (other than college sophomores taking psychology courses, who are already studied more than pigeons). The shorter the step to generalization the better. The higher technical quality and the better control that are typical of out-of-context research would not outweigh the leap needed to generalize from the artificial environment to the lived experiences of people. In an interpretivist milieu, interest in traditional quantitative research methods would wane because they are not suited to in-context research, and a range of qualitative methods would become much more popular.

Sources of truth would expand well beyond the traditional research study. Research in the social sciences, using an interpretive approach, could involve data such as diaries, journals, debriefings, interviews, case studies, textual analysis, reflections, and much more. Control–experimental group studies would be only one of the many acceptable methods. The *Handbook of Qualitative Research* (Denzin & Lincoln, 1994, 2000) introduces many different methods and data-gathering strategies. Interpretivists do not reject traditional research, however. Instead, traditional postpositivist research is simply one of many sources of knowledge, and it does not hold a privileged position over other ways of understanding.

Awareness and understanding of alternative traditions would become a virtue. In an age of information overload it is very easy to narrow our search for new knowledge down to the sources we have come to agree with. An interpretivist perspective calls for more attention to work in traditions different from the one we find most comfortable.

Article of Interest

Charles Teddlie. (2005). Methodological issues related to causal studies of leadership. *Educational Management Administration & Leadership, 33*(2), 211–227.

Teddlie, a professor at Louisiana State University, is a well-known advocate of mixed-method research. That is, not only does he believe that we should be aware of research methods other than those we use, he also argues that we should both use the research from other paradigms and actually *do* research using methods from a variety of paradigms. His focus is educational research, but almost all the content of the article also applies to most social science research. Teddlie uses the term *constructivism* for what we call interpretivism in this book, and he tends to equate qualitative research with the interpretive paradigm. Teddlie divides research into three types: qualitative, quantitative, and mixed. He criticizes the "paradigm purists" who work only within one paradigm and proposes, instead, that we all become mixed-method researchers. Although Teddlie focuses on research methods, he does link a philosophy to mixed methods. That philosophy is a uniquely American creation: pragmatism. Does Teddlie's pragmatic mixed method paradigm offer us a comfortable way of using the research methods of both qualitative and quantitative research? If it does, we have argued that both interpretive and critical paradigms do as well. That is because it is the foundational beliefs, not the research methods, that distinguish the different paradigms. Quite a few postpositivists use qualitative data, but they do not analyze it in the same way interpretivists or critical theorists do. Does Teddlie's approach allow you to use the foundational beliefs of both postpositivism and critical or interpretive philosophies of social science? This is a more difficult question. He proposes a pragmatic definition of causality, for example, to bridge the gap between postpositivist causality and the *verstehen* of interpretivism. Does he actually accomplish his goal? Does using qualitative research to draw causal conclusions violate the fundamental assumptions of the interpretive paradigm? Finally, does Teddlie's approach simply ignore critical theory, or does he lump it in with constructivism and instructivism?

To read the entire article, please go to http://www.sagepub.com/willis_aoi.

Some goals of research would become nonsense. Wittgenstein's expansion of logical choices from a binary choice of *true* or *false* to three choices, *true, false,* or *nonsense,* allows us to ignore and move beyond some questions because they are nonsense. Consider this question: "Is computer-based learning more effective than traditional learning?" That question, which has been "answered" in the literature hundreds of times, is nonsense, and we need not spend any more time on it. The reason it is nonsense is because there is no such thing as "computer-based learning." There are many forms of computer-based learning, and the different forms do not have enough in common to justify treating them all as representatives of some hypothetical construct called "computer-based learning." The choices we must make in education are much more complex than that, and worthy questions should reflect that complexity. We do not ask, "Is prescription medicine more effective than folk cures?" There are too many types of prescription medicines and folk cures for such a question to make sense. It is a question that does not lend itself to a yes-or-no answer. It is a nonsense question.

Hypothetical Construct

A hypothetical construct is something you cannot touch or feel. Instead, it is assumed to exist because of logical or empirical evidence. For example, you cannot see a self-concept or a person's intelligence, but some social scientists base their research on the assumption that they exist because they believe rational or empirical evidence points to their existence. A number of theories reject the use of hypothetical constructs. For example, behaviorism asserts that the only legitimate topic of study is observable behavior. Behaviorists reject any effort to inject mentalistic and unobservable concepts into social science. However, some scholars have argued that a hypothetical construct may be used in research without becoming mentalistic if you define it in a different way. For example, intelligence quotient might be defined as "what an IQ test measures," and the value of both measuring IQ and using it in practice (e.g., for admission to college or special education programs) could be justified by showing that IQ scores are related to things such as academic success. This operational way of defining a hypothetical construct was used in the mid-20th century but has gradually faded. In essence, the question of whether hypothetical constructs such as intelligence can be considered real, regardless of how they are defined, is a replay of the shift from structuralism to poststructuralism that was discussed in an earlier chapter. As an inherent characteristic of individuals (as structuralism might describe it), intelligence is often challenged today as something that is influenced by many things other than innate factors. These other influences include the cultural and educational history of the individual. Thus, intelligence, as measured by IQ tests, is not an innate characteristic of individuals.

In the social sciences and associated professional fields such as social work and education, research becomes less an effort to support theory and more of a collaborative effort to create successful instruction and successful treatment.

The theory-driven debates of American social science over the past 90 years have generated thousands of studies designed to support one theory over another. This is certainly true even of a very "applied" field such as psychotherapy. Therapy journals contain many studies of a particular therapeutic approach that is found to work. However, the conclusions drawn from many of these studies often are less about that specific instance of therapy than about the class of psychotherapy. For example, we say that cognitive psychotherapy (or family therapy, or psychoanalytic therapy, or client-centered therapy, or humanistic therapy, or any of 30 or 40 other forms of psychotherapy) probably is good and should be used more often because a research study supports a version of that psychotherapy. We may well be wrong in making this type of generalization because the specific instance of therapy studied may be very different from many other therapies that carry the same general name. The generalizations made often are based on the assumption that the shared characteristics of all the therapies called cognitive behavioral, or psychoanalytic, are at the core of what those therapies are all about. Differences are minor and not as important. Interpretivists are skeptical of this sort of reasoning, especially when it involves comparisons of systems of human behavior. To illustrate this point, consider the study reported by Keller et al. (2000) in the *New England Journal of Medicine*. The research compared three treatment groups of clinically depressed patients. The first group received only drug treatment. Each person in the second group received at least 16 sessions of cognitive–behavioral analysis psychotherapy, and the third group received both the drug treatment and the psychotherapy. The researchers found that about half the patients in the psychotherapy and drug treatment groups improved, but in the combination group about 85% of the patients improved. This difference was statistically significant.

How do we interpret the results of this study? It is difficult to say. One of the treatments (the antidepressant nefazodone, also known by the brand name Serzone) is more of a physical treatment, whereas the cognitive behavioral therapy involves significant interaction between humans. It is probably easier to standardize the drug treatment so that the same drug in the same dosage is used across many studies. That may make us more comfortable accepting the idea that Serzone is a promising treatment for clinical depression, especially when used in conjunction with cognitive–behavioral therapy. However, accepting the generalization is not so easy when it comes to psychotherapy. Different practitioners of cognitive–behavioral therapy approach the therapeutic process somewhat differently, and it is well known that different therapists are not equally effective. Because so many things are likely to affect whether a particular therapy is effective, including unique characteristics of the local implementation, it would be much more difficult to draw strong conclusions about psychotherapy than about drug treatment.

That may be giving too much credit to drug research, however. Nemeroff et al. (2005) conducted a study similar to the one discussed earlier, using the same antidepressant drug. They found similar general results, but when they looked at subgroups of patients they concluded that patients with a history of early childhood trauma such as the death of a parent or physical abuse benefited more from psychotherapy alone than drug therapy alone, and combined treatment was only slightly more effective than psychotherapy. Thus, characteristics of the patient being treated may be a factor in whether a method is effective; there may be no universal law to discover. Finally, this message was posted on a mental health Web site (http://www.mentalhealth.com):

Important News: Discontinuation of Sales of Nefazodone (Serzone)

On 10/02/2003 Bristol-Myers Squibb announced: "It has come to the attention of Health Canada that nefazodone (Serzone) has been associated with adverse hepatic events including liver failure requiring transplantation in Canada. Following discussions with Health Canada, Bristol-Myers Squibb Canada has decided to discontinue sales of nefazodone, effective November 27, 2003."

The drug was also withdrawn from the Dutch and Swedish markets but not the American market. Therefore, in 2004 the consumer advocacy group Public Citizen sued the federal government to halt the sale of Serzone in America. Public Citizen documented 55 cases of liver failure and 20 deaths caused by the drug. The organization claimed that the Food and Drug Administration had had information on liver damage caused by Serzone for 17 months but had allowed the drug to stay on the market.

Given that we cannot accept much knowledge, if any, as a universal law or dependable generalization, it may be prudent to encourage a much closer relationship between research and practice. The two studies cited earlier on the treatment of clinical depression did that. They were conducted with real patients, and the treatments provided were similar to those provided in clinics around the world. They also compared and combined therapies across different conceptual frameworks (drug therapy and cognitive–behavioral therapy) and found in one study that a combination therapy was more effective. Many of the problems of humans that the social sciences attempt to address may be best approached from combinations of approaches that cut across theoretical frameworks. Seeking good treatment instead of proofs of theory may well lead to more such cross-paradigm combination treatments.

Can we take the approaches used in the two studies of clinical depression further? Yes. An interpretive (and a critical) approach suggests we should take the results of such studies as local knowledge, not general knowledge. Thus, when similar treatments are used in another local setting, the therapeutic efforts should be carefully followed and studied. The researcher–practitioner may well find that the patients he or she treats do not seem to be responding as the patients in previous studies did.

In the applied social sciences, making research and practice more like each other might also help us avoid the distasteful and destructive tendency to adopt an us (researchers) versus them (teachers or therapists or social workers or economists) approach that is expressed in this quote from a researcher in the 1960s who was concerned about studies of programmed instruction that showed it did not work:

> Further refinement of research methodology in school settings is needed. Important as programming [programmed instruction] techniques are in inquiry, they have not assured satisfactory control in all respects. Teachers, for instance, may influence the results of experiments even when they are not directly present. Pupils' performances may be lower in programmed instruction because of an influential teacher who conveys to them her antagonism toward research, programming, or both. By way of example, one teacher is reported to have affected results with a sardonically expressed comment (spoken as she brandished a screwdriver), "Children—the age of automation has arrived. Go to your teaching machines!" (McNeil, 1963, pp. 79–80)

This quote involves a contradiction that is difficult for the postpositivists to escape. The author clearly feels that finding the truth about programmed instruction must be accomplished by conducting research. Yet the heart of the quote is a conclusion that teacher sabotage is the source of negative results. That conclusion is not based on extensive research using the scientific method. It is based on hearsay, rumors, and innuendo (and perhaps the biases of the researcher). Interpretivists argue that all research is embedded in values and beliefs. It is better, they say, to acknowledge those values and beliefs and to use a range of research techniques than to deny they are there and to limit yourself to a few ways of knowing. Furthermore, in this example, they might argue that it is more important to create better learning environments than to do research that supports one particular method over another.

Instead of requiring that all research begin with hypotheses and predictions, approaches that leave open the opportunity to discover things as the research progresses would be accepted. The main reason for requiring detailed research hypotheses is to avoid the dreaded subjectivism that could creep in if predictions are not made before data are gathered. This problem is eliminated in the interpretivist approach because all research is subjective. You cannot avoid it and should not pretend that you have.

Article of Interest

Judith Wuest. (2000, January). Negotiating with helping systems: An example of grounded theory evolving through emergent fit. *Qualitative Health Research, 10,* 51–70.

Judith Wuest's article is about emergent models of theory building. That is, she describes a type of research that may begin with a tentative theory she hopes will explain the data she collects, but she is more than willing to discard, modify, or replace that theory as her research progresses. Wuest, who is a feminist researcher at the University of New Brunswick, uses the concept of emergent fit to describe a process in which new data help the researcher accept or change an existing theory. The approach is iterative, which means the researcher cycles through the same process over and over. New data are compared with the predictions of the theory, then the theory is changed as needed, and more new data are compared with the predictions of the revised theory. This article, which uses a grounded theory method, produces explanatory theories of why things happen the way they do. Wuest uses women's roles in caring as her research topic, and she develops a theory to explain how caring happens. Does her explanation of the type of theory she is developing fit with an interpretivist paradigm? Are the theories she develops acknowledged as subjective, or are they presented as general truths? Local truths? How can you tell?

To read the entire article, please go to http://www.sagepub.com/willis_aoi.

What Sorts of Research Are Worthwhile?

In a very interesting analysis of our notions of learning, Iran-Nejad, McKeachie, and Berliner (1990) propose that we think of learning theories as having one of two basic thrusts. One type assumes that the best way to learn anything is based on the "assumption of simplification by isolation" (p. 509). This approach, which is generally associated with behavioral and information processing theories, is heavily criticized by these authors. They trace it back to the work of Bartlett (1932) and characterize it as an approach in which one simplifies the learning environment by isolating one variable for study while holding everything else constant:

> The roots of the assumption of simplification by isolation are as firm in practice [as in theory building]. Schools break down complex skills like reading into their components (sounds, letters, words, etc.). The assumption is, to rephrase Bartlett (1932), that component skills are easier to learn when they are separated from other skills with which they are ordinarily integrated. Similarly, it is often assumed that basic concepts, facts, and definitions must be mastered in isolation before authentic real-world aspects of complex subject matters can be learned. (Iran-Nejad et al., 1990, p. 510)

Iran-Nejad et al. (1990) argue that simplification by integration is a more promising approach to designing learning environments. Such environments are based on the assumption that "the more meaningful, the more deeply or elaboratively processed, the more situated in context, and the more rooted in cultural, background, metacognitive, and personal knowledge an event is, the more readily it is understood, learned and remembered" (p. 511). In many ways research is a form of learning, and if we take the advice of Iran-Nejad et al. and base our research on the simplification by integration principle, then interpretive research has much to recommend it.

Examples of Interpretive Research

It is impossible to select a few "typical" interpretivist research studies from the social sciences because there is so much diversity that you cannot really select two or three studies and even illustrate all of the resemblances among the large family called interpretive social science research. Instead, this section describes studies that illustrate the breadth and diversity of interpretivist research.

The first study was conducted by Holbrook, Bourke, Lovat, and Dally (2004) at the University of Newcastle in Australia. At that university students who complete a "research doctorate" do a dissertation study as the main element of their Ph.D. work. This is different from the "taught doctorates" that are more common in American universities. Newcastle's Ph.D. program is more like the research doctorates at Cambridge and Oxford in England.

Thus, in a research doctorate the dissertation (thesis) "is the primary and, in many cases, the only evidence of the candidate's learning and skills development" (p. 126). There may be no oral examination of the student. Instead, the written thesis is submitted to examiners who evaluate the work. Some of these may be at the student's university, but others may be external evaluators. Holbrook and his group analyzed the examiner reports on 101 doctoral theses from several Australian universities. Previous research had shown that in such reports the criteria used by most examiners were that the study be original and make a scholarly contribution to the field. However, these broad criteria were interpreted in different ways by different examiners. Prior research in America, the United Kingdom, and Australia also suggested that examiners came to the task with positive expectations that students would pass and that poor writing quality and presentation problems would be the focus of most criticisms.

To develop a better understanding of the process the authors carried out a qualitative study that involved several stages:

- *Coding.* Using some of the reports from examiners, they developed a set of codes for different types of comments. Once a stable set of codes had been created, all 303 evaluation reports (three for each thesis, with 53% written by Australians and 47% written by international scholars) were coded using NUD*IST 5, one of the more popular computer programs for analyzing qualitative data.

- *Search for common elements.* When all the reports were coded the researchers used the computer software to look for common elements in the reports. They found what might be expected: Evaluators commented on things such as the scope and significance of the study, breadth and quality of the literature review, methods, data analysis and reporting, and quality of writing ("substantial issues of communicative competence" was how the authors put it). However, *common elements* does not mean every review contained comments on a particular issue. For example, only 53% included any comment on the review of the literature. On the other hand, 73% of the examiners commented on communicative competence, and it was often to point out significant issues. Here is one example. "In contrast to Mr. X's impressive analytical work, its documentation, as well as the presentation of his results are marred by some editorial flaws. The structure of the thesis could have been tighter with less repetition and better integration of cause and effect. His literary style is patchy, ranging from rather eloquent prose to unedited laboratory jottings. There are some grammatical problems and too many cases of wrongly placed or missing punctuation marks" (p. 134).

- *Evaluative elements.* Another aspect of the study was an analysis of the evaluative elements of the reviews. The analysis of the coded data brought out four categories of evaluation. *Summative* comments "tend to be stand-alone and succinctly sum up the examiner's feelings about the whole thesis or a particular sub-section of it" (p. 135). They could be positive (9% of the total comments of any sort), negative (1%), or neutral (3%). Two other types of comment, *formative* and *instructional*, were efforts to tell "the candidate, and/or possibly the supervisor, to do something to improve the thesis or its products" (p. 135). Such a comment was coded as formative if it combined "information for the reader (commentary), detail about how to proceed (direction and/or action) and involvement or engagement with the topic" (p. 135). About 39% of all comments were either formative or instructional. A particular type of formative comment, prescriptive, was 7.5% of the total. Prescriptive comments provided explicit directions, such as "The opening argument needs to be re-argued. It needs operational definitions, critical comments on the two concepts of culture and management style. At least in this section if not throughout, updated references are required" (p. 137). The final type of evaluative comment, other judgment (14%), was more general ("Again I congratulate the candidate on this excellent effort") and more an expression of feelings ("an honest, and at times courageous, attempt at a complex and difficult topic"; p. 139).

- The data analysis also included *examiner and process categories* and *organization elements,* but there was little of interest in these areas.

- *Dialogic elements categories.* The final area of analysis had to do with the dialog involved in evaluating another person's research. As the authors noted, the other coding categories "do not do justice to the richness of the text they capture. . . . In a situation such as a final examination, one might expect the examiner to evince distance. It is a mark of the extraordinary nature of Ph.D. assessment that so little distance is evident in the examiner reports. . . . The conversational tone in 69 per cent of the reports . . . and the use of the first person . . . in 82 per cent of them was our earliest indication that many examiner reports contain something akin to parallel discourse. Given that accounts are highly context specific, the construction of academic identify is more in evidence . . . in examiner reports than we would have anticipated in that medium. . . . Where conversation occurs in a report, it may exhibit overt or subtle changes as the examiner moves from one role to another (arbiter, colleague, supervisor) and one audience to another. Candidates are assisted and often chided, supervisors may be admonished, administrators addressed and colleagues hailed. The form of address can move from the formal to the informal, from aloof distance to familiarity" (p. 141).

The study by Holbrook and his colleagues in Australia illustrates a traditional *code and retrieve* type of qualitative study. Data were coded and then retrieved (organized) to reveal broader categories of meaning. In an earlier era this work might have been done using notecards or even pieces of paper cut with scissors from a sheet and then coded by writing the appropriate codes on each one. Holbrook avoided that grueling work and, instead, used a computer program to do the clerical work. In the next study, the research process is much less standardized and structured. It is, instead, a synthesis of thinking that emerged from professional practice.

Terri Eynon (2002) is a psychotherapist in the Freudian tradition, and she works at the Nottingham Psychotherapy Unit in England. Her particular interest is in the use of a theory called cognitive linguistics in psychotherapy. Cognitive linguistics takes a different view of metaphor and metonymy (e.g., substituting the name of a feature or characteristic of something for the name of what you are talking about, as in "counting heads" to mean counting the number of people or saying "Wall Street" is bullish when you mean the American financial markets). Eynon points out,

> Until relatively recently it was assumed that it must be possible to provide an accurate, objective (i.e., literal) description of reality for the purpose of scientific advancement. For the modernist, metaphors characterize rhetoric, not scientific discourse. They were vague, inessential frills, appropriate for the purpose of politicians and poets, but not for those of scientists.

That status put some theories of human behavior, such as psychoanalytic theory, outside the boundaries of scientific discourse because there is so much emphasis on "metaphor, symbolization and transference." However, over the past 30 or so years linguists such as George Lakoff have come to believe that linguistic tools such as metaphor are not simply rhetorical flourishes; they are instead reflections of how humans perceive and construe the world. They are, in fact, the means by which we understand abstract ideas. As Eynon puts it, "If we do not acknowledge metaphor, it may destroy our understanding of the nature of abstract concepts." Eynon links the idea of metaphors and related linguistic tools to Freudian concepts such as transference and shows how the cognitive scientist's concepts of metaphor may have similar meanings to some Freudian concepts.

The main part of Eynon's article is about the use of cognitive linguistic theory in psychotherapy. She gives a number of case vignettes from her practice, including this one:

An anxious patient had a fear of losing control of her bladder. Behavioural analysis suggested that her problem might be related to fear of losing control, per se, but therapy was made difficult by her rather irritable personality. Although it was evident that her difficulties became worse when she had to relate to people she disliked, she was reluctant to accept an emotional basis for her urinary problem.

Her fear of wetting herself extended to a reluctance even to discuss words related to urine. As behavioral exposure therapy progressed, the therapist was able to suggest that the patient's fear of losing control of her bladder might be related to her fear of losing control of her temper. She might be rather *pissed off* (loss of control of self is loss of control of bodily functions). This interpretation not only injected some humor into the sessions and enhanced the therapeutic alliance but also gave the patient a metaphor that made sense of her symptoms and how they might relate to her moods.

Eynon also suggested that patient poetry and criminal behavior can sometimes be better understood through an understanding of metaphors that are expressed in the poetry or the behavior. Another of her cases illustrates how metaphor may facilitate dream interpretation:

A patient who had been admitted with a severe depressive illness made considerable improvements on antidepressants. In the multidisciplinary ward round, her consultant suggested that she might be ready for trial leave. The next day, the patient reported a dream to one of the nursing staff. A ship had sunk to the bottom of the ocean. It was being raised, but was still only halfway up to the surface.

The terms "depression" and "low mood" are directly related to the conceptual metaphors Good is Up, the state of depression is a location, the sea the place the patient now finds herself in her life, which is a journey. An "interpretation" by tracing the metaphorical route from source to probable target using idiomatic language derived from the same sources puts the images into words.

The patient's mood is clearly further *up* than it was, but she is not *out of the water* yet. She is not ready to *sail* through her life and is afraid that if the staff *let her go* too soon that she will *sink* into depression again.

The work of Eynon illustrates one way of integrating interpretive research into professional practice in a flexible way. Also, she used her preferred theoretical orientation, psychoanalysis, as a broad framework for interpreting and understanding what she was studying. Her theoretical orientation probably even influenced what she thought was important to study.

The final example of an interpretivist study falls between Holbrook's structured study of thesis evaluations and Eynon's looser and more conceptual development of psychotherapeutic theory. It is an interview study from the United Kingdom.

Peter Collins (1998) was concerned with the perceptions of adults experiencing chronic job insecurity. His research involved a series of open or unstructured interviews with people who worked for a local government in the United Kingdom that was undergoing a major restructuring. The changes dislocated many workers. Some were transferred to other agencies, some lost their jobs, and many were caught for months in the bureaucratic wasteland between the announcement that changes were coming and the arrival of those changes. Collins, who teaches qualitative research methods, pointed out that many students see interviews as smash-and-grab opportunities "in which they accost some innocent bystander and relieve them of whatever useful 'data' they may have." The purpose of interviews in this framework is for an expert to locate and mine factual information, which can then be reported to other experts. Collins argues that this concept of interviewing is encouraged by much of the literature on how to conduct interviews. He believes it is based on a number of assumptions, including a structuralist model of language that sees language "as external, determined and determining, rather than language as an emergent social activity."

> The interview serves to facilitate the process wherein messages are conveyed from one mind to another. The interviewer encodes a thought in words and the interviewee decodes them to discover the thought and then similarly transmits a thought in turn. . . . Language is reduced to little more than a medium or transparent system which conveys messages from one mind to another. The structuralist model is essentialist, ignoring the way in which people actually talk, and obscures the processes by which language is socially constituted. It perpetuates the myth that interviews are, above all else, opportunities for collecting objective facts. (Collins, 1998)

Collins (1998) sees interviewing as a process of creating and constructing data rather than simply collecting it. To him, the interviews

> are social interactions in which meaning is necessarily negotiated between a number of selves (and in which power may be *more*

or *less* shared). The interviewer need be neither "objective" nor "detached," but should rather be "engaged." Engagement implies a willingness on the part of the interviewer to understand the interviewee's response to a question or prompt in the wider context of the interview(s) as a whole.

For Collins, the interviews he conducts are not fact-finding missions; they are negotiations between people who are creating understanding through the conversation.

> My interviews comprise accounts of events together with attempts to interpret them on the part of interviewer and interviewee, but the process is haphazard and tentative. Rather than facts (which have an existence independent of the means of their discovery), such exchanges precipitate narrative: narrative that is emergent and indexical. Events and experiences are constituted, partly at least, in their telling (and re-telling). To describe a situation is to constitute it (as ethnomethodologists might put it).

Collins uses the term *indexical* to describe discourse in which terms and phrases used at one point are representations of or references back to other parts of the discussion. The narrative story he is building is *emergent* because it does not spring forth fully formed after Collins has gathered his data. Instead, it gradually emerges as he reads and rereads his data and thinks about it.

What does Collins publish when he finishes his research? It cannot be facts because they are not available in any absolute sense. What Collins publishes is *narrative,* or life stories. But if these stories are not truth, what are they? Collins quotes Chase (1996):

> The aim of narrative analysis is not to impose immutable or definitive interpretations on participants' stories or even to challenge the meanings participants attach to their stories. Rather, its goal is to turn our attention elsewhere, to taken-for-granted cultural processes embedded in the everyday practices of storytelling. (p. 55)

Chase's emphasis on seeing the givens or assumptions in a story, and pointing them out, is one way of adding value to the story told by an interviewee. However, Collins points out that this is not the only way the researcher influences the story that is told:

In encouraging the interviewee to tell me these stories and in asking them to develop a sub-plot here and a character there, I am encouraging them to construct and reconstruct themselves and contribute to this by exchanging stories of my own. . . . As I take less seriously the manuals' advice to maintain a lofty silence, I am increasingly moved to contribute my own stories, to hold them up for contrast or comparison to those of the interviewee.

Collins does not try to remain an objective outsider who maintains a degree of distance and objectivity. Instead, as the interviews progressed it "was increasingly difficult to remain passive, merely a listener. I was expected to participate, to contribute, to comment, to help in the development of stories which grow ever more intricate."

These three examples of interpretivist research illustrate a number of things. One is diversity: The methods used in interpretive research may be structured, very open, or semistructured. However, the studies were *emergent*. The meaning of the data was not apparent, for example, when one crucial statistic popped up on the computer screen. Instead, it emerged from the process of data collection and analysis. Another thing the studies illustrate is that interpretivism cuts across a number of disciplines and areas of application. Holbrook is an educational psychologist studying the Ph.D. process, Eynon is a Freudian psychotherapist studying ways to improve practice, and Collins is a sociologist seeking to better understand how people deal with a traumatic event in their lives.

Summary

This and the previous chapter make it clear that the three research paradigms point us to different reasons for doing research, different types of methods, and different ways of doing research. A critical theorist researching the way office automation affects the workplace is going to select different questions, use different methods, and come to different types of conclusions than a researcher who has adopted a postpositivist paradigm to study the same topic.

The differences between the paradigms are not cosmetic, and they are not surface issues. Their origins are deep in the core of the paradigms. Does that mean, then, that both producers and consumers of research should make a clear, informed choice and work within one paradigm? Some authors have certainly taken that position, and there is logic to support such a decision. In a way, it does not make sense to do some research within an interpretivist paradigm and then do other work within a postpositivist paradigm. These two paradigms are based on opposing answers to some fundamental questions about research. And this "be true to your school" approach, to borrow the title from a classic Beach Boys song, simplifies life because you need not learn the methods of other paradigms, and you need not keep up with research produced by other paradigms.

However, there are two other ways of thinking about this question, and they both lead us to different conclusions. The first involves the ability to separate core paradigm issues from methodological issues. You may use methods from a paradigm without adopting the core beliefs of that paradigm. Several of the studies cited in this section used a method from one paradigm but studied a topic that fit another. In the critical and interpretive paradigms, there is plenty of room to use many different research methods. You are not restricted to a particular list of officially approved methods. Thus, critical and interpretive researchers may both consume and conduct research using methods normally associated with the postpositivist paradigm. Postpositivists have more difficulty admitting they are ecumenical, but even a cursory reading of the postpositivist literature will demonstrate that proponents often rely on other types of data, including professional practice knowledge. Using a method from another paradigm may involve reinterpreting the meaning of the results, but borrowing methods from a different paradigm is already common.

Yet another way of thinking about this issue is to consider both what we believe to be right and our degree of confidence in the rightness of our beliefs. Both postpositivism and interpretivism assert that we cannot ever be totally sure that our external reality is the correct view. In postpositivism this is expressed through Popper's falsification theory (Chalmers, 1982, 1990; Sovacool, 2005): You can falsify a theory conclusively, but you can never demonstrate that it is true beyond any doubt. There is always the possibility that a new study will illuminate flaws and errors in a theory. Interpretivism argues that knowledge is socially constructed, and therefore truth is relative to the groups that produce and consume the research.

Whatever the reason, postpositivists and interpretivists make fundamental assumptions about the uncertainty of our knowledge. Critical theorists sometimes are much more confident that they are right (but would say the same of postpositivists and interpretivists). In such a situation Rorty's *democratic pragmatism* seems very appropriate as a framework for research: Do research within your own paradigm but remain open to methods and results from other paradigms. Make an effort to understand what others are saying and be willing to change your paradigm, or even give it up for another, if proponents of opposing views can convince you they have merit.

Questions for Reflection

1. What does interpretivism have in common with the critical paradigm? In your field which are more important: the commonalities or the differences? Why?

2. Take a study done in your area of interest that used a postpositivist paradigm. Then describe how a study on the same topic (or a related one) might be done from an interpretivist perspective.

3. Use the work you did for question 2 and link the differences in the interpretivist study to the five foundational issues. How would they influence what happened in the interpretivist study?

4. Are there drawbacks to interpretivists' acceptance of data from many different sources, including postpositivist research? On a journal whose editorial review board is half postpositivists and half interpretivists, what type of article would stand the best chance of being accepted (assuming all reviewers made decisions based on the paradigm they support): a postpositivist article or an interpretivist article? Why?

5. Two broad issues often are at the heart of discussions over the merit of a piece of research: relevance and technical quality. *Relevance* refers to how important and meaningful the study is. *Technical quality* involves meeting the criteria for good research in the paradigm you are using. Across the three paradigms, are there differences in the two criteria? Which is the most important in each paradigm? Why?

6. The difference between postpositivism's goal of identifying lawlike generalizations and interpretivism's goal of understanding in the local context is quite significant. Are there ways of thinking about this difference that can bridge the gap? What about postpositivism's criticism of interpretivism that if you aren't looking for generalizations or laws, why do the research in the first place? What about interpretivism's criticism that it doesn't matter whether you are looking for laws or not, you are not going to find them when studying human behavior?

7. Well-controlled, out-of-context research is a hallmark of postpositivism because you must do research "the right way." Messy, fuzzy, in-context research is the hallmark of interpretive research because meaning is made in a particular context. Therefore, meaning cannot be derived from out-of-context data. How do you feel about these two extreme positions? Develop a view of your own about this issue and defend it.

8. As a follow up to question 7, how is a list or set of exemplars that may emerge from interpretive qualitative research different from laws and generalizations that come from postpositivist research? Aren't these really the same thing?

9. The relationship of researchers to practitioners is something you will consider throughout this book. Use your background and experiences to describe the ideal relationship as you see it at this point.

10. What do you think about the distinction between *naturwissenschaften* and *geisteswissenschaften?* Is this a concept that makes sense? Defend your view.

11. What do you think warrants your attention as a consumer of research in your field? Is it research only from the paradigm you support? Why or why not? If you think looking at research from other paradigms is appropriate, defend your views.

References

Atkinson, C. (2000). Socio-technical and soft approaches to information requirements elicitation in the post-methodology era. *Requirements Engineering, 5*(2), 67–73.

Atweh, B., Kemmis, S., & Weeks, P. (1998). *Action research in practice: Partnerships for social justice in education.* New York: Routledge.

Bartlett, F. C. (1932). *Remembering.* Cambridge: Cambridge University Press.

Berger, P., & Luckman, T. (1967). *The social construction of reality: A treatise in the sociology of knowledge.* London: Penguin.

Boros, J. (1998). *Representationalism and antirepresentationalism: Kant, Davidson, and Rorty.* Paper presented at the 20th World Congress of Philosophy, Boston, Massachusetts, August 10–15. Retrieved January 27, 2006, from http://www.bu.edu/wcp/Papers/TKno/TKnoBoro.htm

Bredo, E., & Feinberg, W. (1982). The critical approach to social and educational research. In E. Bredo & W. Feinberg (Eds.), *Knowledge and values in social and educational research* (pp. 271–291). Philadelphia: Temple University Press.

Chalmers, A. (1982). *What is this thing called science?* (2nd ed.). St. Lucia, Queensland, Australia: University of Queensland Press.

Chalmers, A. (1990). *Science and its fabrication.* Minneapolis: University of Minnesota Press.

Chase, S. E. (1996). Personal vulnerability and interpretive authority in narrative research. In R. Josselson (Ed.), *Ethics and process in the narrative study of lives.* Thousand Oaks, CA: Sage.

Christopher, J., Richardson, F., & Christopher, S. (2001). *Philosophical hermeneutics: A metatheory to transcend dualism and individualism in Western psychology.* Retrieved January 27, 2006, from http://htpprints.yorku.ca/archive/00000163/01/HTP_Prints--Philosophical_Hermeneutics--A_Metatheory.pdf

Chua, W. F. (1986). Radical developments in accounting thought. *Accounting Review, 61,* 601–632.

Collins, P. (1998). Negotiating selves: Reflections on "unstructured" interviewing. *Sociological Research Online 3*(3). Retrieved January 27, 2006, from http://www.socresonline.org.uk/socresonline/3/3/2.html

Creswell, J. (2002). *Research design: Qualitative, quantitative, and mixed methods approaches* (2nd ed.). Thousand Oaks, CA: Sage.

Denzin, N., & Lincoln, Y. (Eds.). (1994). *Handbook of qualitative research.* Thousand Oaks: Sage.

Denzin, N., & Lincoln, Y. (Eds.). (2000). *Handbook of qualitative research* (2nd ed.). Thousand Oaks, CA: Sage.

Donmoyer, R. (1996). Educational research in an era of paradigm proliferation: What's a journal editor to do? *Educational Researcher, 25*(2), 4–10.

Dyer, W. G. Jr., and Wilkins, A. L. (1991). Better stories, not better constructs, to generate better theory: A rejoinder to Eisenhardt. *Academy of Management Review, 16*(3), 613–619.

Eynon, T. (2002). Cognitive linguistics. *Advances in Psychiatric Treatment, 8,* 399–407. Retrieved January 27, 2006, from http://apt.rcpsych.org/cgi/

Feyerabend, P. (1981). *Problems of empiricism* (Vol. 2). Cambridge: Cambridge University Press.

Feyerabend, P. (1993). *Against method* (3rd ed.). London: Verso.

Fischer, G., Nakakoji, K., Ostwald, J., Stahl, G., & Sumner, T. (1993). Embedding computer-based critics in the contexts of design. *Knowledge Engineering Review, 8*(4), 285–307.

Gage, N. (1996, April). Confronting counsels of despair for the behavioral sciences. *Educational Researcher, 25*(3), 5–15, 23.

Gall, M., Borg, W., & Gall, J. (1996). *Educational research: An introduction.* White Plains, NY: Longman.

Gardner, W., Scherer, D., & Tester, M. (1989, June). Asserting scientific authority. Cognitive development and adolescent legal rights. *American Psychologist, 44*(6), 895–902.

Göktürk, E. (2005). *What is "paradigm"?* Oslo: Norway: University of Oslo, Department of Informatics. Retrieved January 27, 2006, from http://folk.uio.no/erek/essays/paradigm.pdf

Harrington, A. (2000, August). In defense of *verstehen* and *erklären:* Wilhelm Dilthey's ideas concerning a descriptive and analytical psychology. *Theory Psychology, 10,* 435–451.

Heshusius, L., & Ballard, K. (Eds.). (1996). *From positivism to interpretivism and beyond.* New York: Teachers College Press.

Holbrook, A., Bourke, S., Lovat, T., & Dally, K. (2004). Qualities and characteristics in the written reports of doctoral thesis examiners. *Australian Journal of Educational and Developmental Psychology, 4,* 126–145.

Horton, R. (1998). The grammar of interpretive medicine. *Canadian Medical Association Journal, 158,* 245–249.

Hutchinson, S. A. (1988). Education and grounded theory. In R. Sherman & R. B. Webb (Eds.), *Qualitative research in education: Focus and methods.* New York: Falmer.

Iran-Nejad, A., McKeachie, W. J., & Berliner, D. C. (1990). The multisource nature of learning: An introduction. *Review of Educational Research, 60,* 509–515.

Irwin, T. (1990). *Aristotle's first principles.* Oxford: Oxford University Press.

Keller, M., McCullough, J., Klein, D., Arnow, B., Dunner, D., Gelenberg, A., Markowitz, J., Nemeroff, C., Russell, J., Thase, M., Madhukar, T., & Zajecka, J. (2000). A comparison of nefazodone, the cognitive behavioral–analysis system of psychotherapy, and their combination for the treatment of chronic depression. *New England Journal of Medicine, 342*(20), 1662–1670.

Kessels, J., & Korthagen, F. (1996). The relationship between theory and practice: Back to the classics. *Educational Researcher, 25*(3), 17–22.

Kilgore, D. (1998). *The critical paradigm: A transforming approach.* Retrieved January 27, 2006, from http://www.stedwards.edu/newc/kilgore/critical.htm

Koch, T. (1995). Interpretive approaches in nursing research: The influence of Husserl and Heidegger. *Journal of Advanced Nursing, 21*(5), 827.

Kosaka, T. (2002). The notion of diagrammatic expression in interpretive IS research. In *Proceedings of the 6th Asia-Pacific Conference on Information Systems.* Retrieved January 27, 2006, from http://www.ms.kuki.sut.ac.jp/KMSLab/kosaka/papers/icoa200411.pdf

Kuhn, T. (1962). *The structure of scientific revolutions.* Chicago: University of Chicago Press.

Lett, J. (2005). *Emic/etic distinctions.* Retrieved January 27, 2006, from http://faculty.ircc.cc.fl.us/faculty/jlett/Article%20on%20Emics%20and%20Etics.htm

Masterman, M. (1970). The nature of a paradigm. In I. Lakatos & A. Musgrave (Eds.), *Criticism and the growth of knowledge: Proceedings of the International Colloquium in the Philosophy of Science, London 1965* (pp. 59–90). Cambridge: Cambridge University Press.

Matthews, W. (n.d.). *Let's get real: The fallacy of post modernism.* Retrieved January 27, 2006, from http://www-unix.oit.umass.edu/~shamrock/recent_publications.htm

Maxwell, J. (2004). *Qualitative research design.* Thousand Oaks, CA: Sage.

McEvoy, J. (2000). In search of the chemical revolution: Interpretive strategies in the history of chemistry. *Foundations of Chemistry, 2*(1), 47–73.

McNeil, J. (1963). Programmed instruction and the elementary school curriculum. In R. Filep (Ed.), *Perspectives in programming* (pp. 70–83). New York: Macmillan.

Merrill, M. (1997, November/December). Instructional strategies that teach. *CBT Solutions,* 1–11. Retrieved December 4, 2005, from http://cito.byuh.edu/merrill/text/papers/Consistency.PDF

Merrill, M., & ID2 Research Team. (1996) Instructional transaction theory: Instructional design based on knowledge objects. *Educational Technology, 36*(3), 30–37.

Morick, H. (Ed.). (1967). *Wittgenstein and the problem of other minds.* New York: McGraw-Hill.

Nemeroff, C., Heim, C., Thase, M., Klein, D., Rush, A., Schatzberg, A., Ninan, P., McCullough, J., Weiss, P., Dunner, D., Rothbaum, B., Kornstein, S., Keitner, G., & Keller, M. (2005). Differential responses to psychotherapy versus pharmacotherapy in patients with chronic forms of major depression and childhood trauma. *Focus, 3,* 131–135.

Phillips, D. C. (1992). *The social scientist's bestiary: A guide to fabled threats to, and defenses of, naturalistic social science.* New York: Pergamon.

Polanyi, M. (1967). *The tacit dimension.* Garden City, NY: Anchor Books.

Prilleltensky, I. (1997). Values, assumptions, and practices: Assessing the moral implications of psychological discourse and action. *American Psychologist, 52,* 517–535.

Putnam, H. (1981). *Reason, truth, and history.* Cambridge, UK: Cambridge University Press.

Rorty, R. (1979). *Philosophy and the mirror of nature.* Princeton, NJ: Princeton University Press.

Rorty, R. (1982). *Consequences of pragmatism.* Minneapolis: University of Minnesota Press.

Rorty, R. (1991). *Objectivity, relativism, and truth: Philosophical papers* (Vol. 1). New York: Cambridge University Press.

Ross, K. (n.d.). Foundationalism and hermeneutics. In *Proceedings of the Frisian School, fourth series.* Retrieved January 27, 2006, from http://www.friesian.com/hermenut.htm

Schon, D. (1984). *The reflective practitioner: How professionals think in action.* New York: Basic Books.

Schon, D. (1987). *Educating the reflective practitioner: Toward a new design for teaching and learning in the professions.* San Francisco: Jossey-Bass.

Schon, D. (Ed.). (1990). *The reflective turn: Case studies in and on educational practice.* New York: Teachers College Press.

Schwandt, T. (1994). Constructivist, interpretivist approaches to human inquiry. In N. Denzin & Y. Lincoln (Eds.), *Handbook of qualitative research* (pp. 118–137). Thousand Oaks, CA: Sage.

Skinner, B. F. (1953). *Science and human behavior.* New York: Free Press.

Smith, J. (1989). *The nature of social and educational inquiry: Empiricism versus interpretation.* Norwood, NJ: Ablex.

Smith, J. (1993). *After the demise of empiricism: The problem of judging social and educational inquiry.* New York: Ablex.

Sovacool, B. (2005). Falsification and demarcation in astronomy and cosmology. *Bulletin of Science, Technology & Society, 25*(1), 53–62.

Sternberg, R. J., & Horvath, J. A. (Eds.). (1999). *Tacit knowledge in professional practice: Researcher and practitioner perspectives.* Mahwah, NJ: Erlbaum.

Thanasankit, T., & Corbitt, B. (1999). Towards understanding managing requirements engineering: A case study of a Thai software house. In *Proceedings of the 10th Australasian Conference on Information Systems.* Retrieved January 27, 2006, from http://www.vuw.ac.nz/acis99/Papers/PaperCorbitt102.pdf

Vonèche, J. (2003). The changing structure of Piaget's thinking: Invariance and transformations. *Creativity Research Journal, 15*(1), 3–9.

Welton, M. R. (1993). The contribution of critical theory to our understanding of adult learning. *New Directions for Adult and Continuing Education, 57,* 81–90.

Woods, A. (1998). History of philosophy. Retrieved January 27, 2006, from http://www.marxist.com/philosophy/index.asp

Young, S. (2003). Outsourcing and benchmarking in a rural public hospital: Does economic theory provide the complete answer? *Rural and Remote Health, 3*(1), Article 124. Retrieved January 27, 2006, from http://rrh.deakin.edu.au/

Zhu, J. (2003). *Application of computer technology in public school classrooms: Usage dimensions and influencing factors.* Dissertation submitted to Pennsylvania State University. Retrieved January 27, 2006, from http://etda.libraries.psu.edu/theses/approved/WorldWideFiles/ETD-327/thesisETD.pdf

CHAPTER 5

Frameworks for Qualitative Research

There are many ironies in qualitative research. One of the most interesting is that although selecting the right research method is far less important to qualitative researchers than it is to those with a quantitative bent, the field has produced an unbelievable number of research methods. For many qualitative researchers it is their general framework or paradigm that is most important to them. If they are devoted to a particular research method, it is often because that method is an expression of their paradigm.

If paradigms or frameworks are a central issue for qualitative researchers, why are there so many ways to do qualitative research? Do qualitative researchers place a primary emphasis on methodology? Perhaps some do, but another reason for the proliferation of research methods is that qualitative researchers have a number of conceptual frameworks from which to choose. These frameworks have much in common, but there are also many differences. Those differences often lead to the development and use of different research methods. The situation in qualitative research contrasts somewhat with the postpositivist paradigm, as you will see in the next section. There is more paradigm diversity in the qualitative genre than in the quantitative approach.

Postpositivist Research

Postpositivism has developed a detailed and highly technical approach to the process of conducting research. This approach matured and evolved over the 20th century. Postpositivist social science research at the beginning of the 21st century involves six basic steps:

1. *Find an idea you want to research.* Your idea for research can come from anywhere, even your experiences, or qualitative data you or someone else has collected.

2. *Develop or select a theory about the area you want to research.* It can be a metatheory that is grand and all encompassing, a midlevel theory that covers a single aspect of human behavior such as learning, or a minitheory such as learned helplessness (Peterson, Mailer, & Seligman, 1995) that predicts behavior only under certain conditions. (Note: Sometimes you pick a theory first and then look for an area to test it, so steps 1 and 2 may be reversed.)

3. *Develop specific, testable hypotheses* that derive from your theory. The hypotheses should be empirically testable, and they should be clear-cut derivations from the basic or core tenets of the theory you selected. This is often called the hypothetico-deductive model (Yore, Hand, & Florence, 2004).

4. *Design a scientific study* to objectively gather quantitative data under controlled conditions that allow you to draw conclusions about your hypotheses.

5. *Analyze the data* using standard statistical techniques and interpret the results using the guidelines of the scientific method. Using the postpositivist concept of *falsification,* a positive outcome must be reported as supporting the theory being tested. However, no study or series of studies can ever *prove* beyond any doubt that a theory is true. Falsification is potentially more plausible as a way of interpreting research results because the theory you are testing should be universal. Thus, any demonstration that it is inaccurate demonstrates it is false. On the other hand, a result that corresponds to the predictions of a hypothesis is simply *supportive* because a particular study is never an exhaustive test of the hypothesis. There could be other conditions under which the data would show the hypothesis to be false. However, not all postpositivists seem to accept falsification. D. C. Phillips, a leading proponent of the postpositivist paradigm in educational research, remarks (Phillips & Burbules, 2000) that "practical consequences often follow from the findings of educational research, and it behooves the researcher or evaluator to be certain that his or her account is not fiction and is not merely 'one reading' of many that are theoretically possible concerning the situation under investigation. It should be a good reading, a true reading" (p. 76). However, Phillips goes on to distinguish "a true reading" from a True reading of the data. "Those who believe (as we do) that

researchers should aim to discover the truth often are accused of thinking that there is *one* ('absolute') truth. But this is, of course, nonsense." Phillips argues that the point of view or the focus of a particular research study can be different from that of another even when they are studying the same topic. For example, someone on the fifth floor of a building might say that the third story is "below" them, and someone on the second story would say it is "above" them. Both have made a true statement about the situation. What Phillips seems to be missing is that many of the differences in statements about the outcomes of research are based on paradigmatic differences, not simple points of view. For example, in the 1950s and 1960s, studies of the psychological stability of homosexuals found that they were not as "well adjusted" as heterosexual people of similar backgrounds and age. Those who conducted their research assuming that homosexuality was a deviant and pathological personality trait treated the results as confirming their original viewpoint. Those who believed homosexuality was one of many "normal" sexual preferences saw the results as confirming the premise that society's rejection and persecution of homosexuals naturally led to difficulties adjusting in a hostile environment. The first and second editions of the American Psychiatric Association's *Diagnostic and Statistical Manual* (*DSM*) classified homosexuality as a disease. However, the third edition, which came out in 1976, classified homosexuality as a normal variation in sexual preference (the committee was influenced significantly by both the protests of gay rights groups and by respected gay psychiatrists). The current edition, *DSM–IV*, published in 2000, also considers homosexuality a normal variation, but practitioners who still consider it a disease use the more generic diagnosis "sexual disorder not otherwise specified." The change in *DSM–III* was not due to new research that refuted existing empirical studies; it was due to change in the underlying assumptions and beliefs of psychiatric researchers and practitioners. This is one of many such examples of a shift in psychological truths that have occurred over the past 100 years (another is the shift in the explanation of autism from "cold parents" to neurological factors). It is difficult to accept Phillips's assertion that "the problem for us researchers (assuming we are doing educational research and not gathering ideas for a novel) is, first, to comprehend. . . . There is a 'truth of the matter' . . . [and] it is our job to uncover it if we can" (p. 78). He then proposes that we move "not to the rigor mortis of relativism but to the rigor that is needed in a competent inquiry" (p. 78). Phillips goes on the make a strong case for the idea that finding truth, not understanding, is the goal of social science research. But he also calls on the authority of Sir Karl Popper, attributing to him the statement that "any fool can always find some evidence to support a favored theory" (p. 80), and Phillips then comments that "what serves as more genuine support is that no evidence can be found to *disprove* the account that is being given; it is up to the person giving the interpretation to convince the rest of us that such negative evidence has been sought vigorously" (p. 80). Thus, Phillips does seem to be accepting falsification. However, his writing is slippery on this point, as is his advocacy of truth as the goal of research. Near the end of his book he talks about *warrant* rather than proof and about beliefs that are *warranted* rather than truths that are proven. "The postpositivist approach to research is based on seeking appropriate and adequate warrants for conclusions, on hewing to standards of truth and falsity, that subject hypotheses (of whatever type) to test and thus potential disconfirmation, and on being open-minded about criticism" (pp. 86–87). "We need disciplined, competent inquiry to establish which of our beliefs are warranted and which are chimerical. And the philosophy that will serve us best in our endeavor is *postpositivism*" (p. 92). (Note: Although Phillips's approach is more common among quantitative researchers, there are qualitative researchers (Miles & Huberman, 1994a) who insist that they too are searching for truth, just as there are some quantitative researchers who use a critical or interpretive framework.)

6. *Report your work* in an objective manner. Typically the form of this report is a journal article, but larger studies may also be published as a monograph or book. Zigler and Muenchow's (1992) book on the impact of Head Start, the American preschool program for poor children, is an example of a book based on a large research study. That book was written for a lay as well as a professional audience. Many books based on research are written primarily for other scholars and academics. For example, the monograph (Crawford, 1990) on the Byzantine shops in the ancient city of Sardis is unlikely to make it to the *New York Times* hardcover bestseller list, but it is of immense interest to other specialists.

As has been noted many times, the positivist and postpositivist approach is based on a number of givens or foundational beliefs. One of the most important is that it is possible through the scientific method to study and learn about the real or external world. A supporting corollary is that there are basic rules and laws of human behavior in that world that we can discover. Qualitative research has an interesting history that shows it has, at times, taken on those same foundational beliefs.

Moments of Qualitative Research

It is not a method or research technique that determines whether something is qualitative research; it is how the study is conceived, what is to be accomplished, and how the data are understood. This question of what constitutes qualitative research is made more complex by the number of paradigms that can serve as foundations for qualitative research. Qualitative research emerged in the past century as a useful framework for social science research, but its history has not been the story of steady, sustained progress along one path. Denzin and Lincoln (1994, 2005) divide the history of 20th-century qualitative social science research, broadly defined, into eight moments.

The Traditional Period (Early 1900s–World War II)

During this period other cultures were studied from the perspective of the researcher's own culture. The classic ethnographic method involved going into another culture, making field notes of observations, and then writing conclusions. The works of Margaret Mead and Gregory Bateson reflect this period.

What the anthropologist was seeking was a positivist understanding of the way things really were, and there was thus a concern with providing "valid, reliable, and objective interpretations" (Denzin & Lincoln, 1994, p. 7). The four characteristics of this period of qualitative research were each the foundation for a reaction against this form of traditional postpositivist research.

- *A commitment to objectivism* was rejected later by interpretivists and postmodernists. Humans cannot get an objective, God's-eye view of the world. They are always influenced by their own experiences and culture.

- *Complicity in imperialism* was rejected by critical theorists who sought to uncover and make obvious the domination and subjugation of other cultures by the imperialist powers. Research during this period often supported imperialist notions.

- *The belief in monumentalism* ("ethnography would create a museum like picture of the culture studied" (Denzin & Lincoln, 1994, p. 7) was rejected by interpretivists because context is critical to understanding, so knowledge is local rather than universal. It was also rejected by the critical theorists because the conclusions presented were those of the dominant cultures that were imposed on those without power. "Today this image [of objectivism in fieldwork] has been shattered. The works of the classic ethnographers are seen by many as relics of the colonial past" (p. 7).

- Finally, a *belief in the timelessness or universal nature of findings* was rejected for the same reason monumentalism was. The truths of a particular study are not necessarily the only truths of the present, much less the future.

The Modernist Phase (1940s–1970s)

A core characteristic of the second moment of qualitative research was an attempt to put qualitative research on the same footing as quantitative—to make it a quantitative, objective, and statistical approach. "Thus did work in the modernist period clothe itself in the language and rhetoric of positivist and postpositivist discourse. This was the golden age of rigorous qualitative analysis" (Denzin & Lincoln, 1994, p. 8). The modernist phase attempted to improve on qualitative research as a method for accomplishing the goals of traditional period research. This approach remains a significant influence on qualitative research today. It is probably best represented in the work of Miles and Huberman (1994a, 1994b). They divide qualitative research methods and analysis procedures into two broad categories: "loose, inductively oriented designs, and 'tight,' more deductively approached ones" (1994a, p. 431).

> The former work well when the terrain is unfamiliar and/or excessively complex, a single case is involved, and the intent is exploratory and descriptive. Tighter designs are indicated when the researcher has good prior acquaintance with the setting, has a good bank of applicable, well-delineated concepts, and takes a more explanatory and/or confirmatory stance involving multiple, comparable cases. (p. 431)

Like traditional positivist and postpositivist researchers, Miles and Huberman tend to put the types of qualitative research methods covered in this book on the periphery of research; they see them as things you can do before you start to do "real" research. This is a convenient approach because postpositivism does not insist that the theories and predictions to be tested come from any particular source. Thus, concluding that less structured approaches to qualitative research can be good sources of ideas for more rigorous studies does not conflict with postpositivism because any source is acceptable.

Blurred Genres (1970s–1986)

Denzin and Lincoln's (1994) third moment marks the maturing of qualitative research.

Qualitative researchers had a full complement of paradigms, methods, and strategies to employ in their research. Theories ranged from symbolic interactionism to constructivism, naturalistic inquiry, positivism and postpositivism, phenomenology, ethnomethodology, critical (Marxist), semiotics, structuralism, feminism, and various ethnic paradigms. . . . Research strategies ranged from grounded theory to the case study, to methods of historical, biographical, ethnographic, action and clinical research. (p. 9)

Denzin and Lincoln credit sociologist Clifford Geertz with shaping this moment. Two of his books, *The Interpretation of Cultures,* published in 1973 at the beginning of this moment, and *Local Knowledge* (Geertz, 1983), published near the end, are still cited as valuable sources of perspective and method.

Essentially Geertz argues for an approach to social science research that rejects all four of the foundations of the traditional period (objectivism, imperialism, monumentalism, and timelessness). He proposes a social science based in "thick" descriptions and an approach that emphasizes seeking multiple perspectives, interpretive rather than positivist explanations and purposes, open-ended methods (Miles and Huberman's "loose" qualitative research methods), and the situatedness of knowing (the idea that we understand only in context).

With the arrival of this moment, "the golden age of the social sciences was over, and a new age of blurred, interpretive genres was upon us. The essay as an art form was replacing the scientific article" (Denzin & Lincoln, 1994, p. 9).

Crisis of Representation (Mid-1980s)

Social science leaders in this moment came to recognize that their methods, and the methods of a quantitative social science, were never going to represent a singular reality. Feminist and critical epistemologies grew in influence during this period, and the influence of traditional research methods that led us to some form of universal truth decreased.

Gathering data and writing up those data were generally separate activities until this moment. That approach was abandoned by some because data collection is determined in part by what we write and vice versa. Instead it became more acceptable to view

> writing as a method of inquiry that moves through successive stages of self-reflection. As a series of writings, the field-worker's texts flow

from the field experience, through intermediate works, to later work, and finally to the research text that is the public presentation of the ethnographic and narrative experience. Thus do fieldwork and writing blur into one another. There is, in the final analysis no difference between writing and fieldwork. (Denzin & Lincoln, 1994, p. 10)

A Triple Crisis (Today)

Denzin and Lincoln (2005) argue that the social sciences are in the middle of three crises today. They have to do with representation, legitimation, and praxis. The crisis of representation is about the inability of qualitative researchers to present in their written reports the lived experiences of those they study. Instead, "such experience . . . is created in the social text written by the researcher" (Denzin & Lincoln, 2005, p. 19). The second crisis, that of legitimation, is about warrant: What warrants our attention and why? In traditional positivist research warrant is about validity and reliability, but these concepts do not transfer over to many forms of qualitative research. The legitimation crisis thus addresses the question, "How are qualitative studies to be evaluated in the contemporary, poststructural moment" (p. 20)? Positivist research has the well-established and technically developed concepts of validity and reliability and a host of statistical and methodological procedures for establishing them. Qualitative research does not have one way of establishing warrant, it has many, and they are sometimes contradictory, debated, and dependent on different ideologies. The field of qualitative research has not yet arrived at a consensus on how to decide what warrants our attention and what does not.

The third crisis, that of praxis or practice, arises out of the first two and addresses the question, "Is it possible to effect change in the world if society is only and always a text?" (Denzin & Lincoln, 2005, p. 20). That is, if the results of our research are no more than a text that was created by the researcher and we have no established way of deciding which of many texts—views, perspectives, and understandings of human behavior and social life—warrant our attention, how can we actually bring about change in the world? Denzin and Lincoln propose that these three crises, of representation, legitimation, and praxis, are the background for four more moments in qualitative research. On further reflection and some distance from the period, Denzin and Lincoln may well decide that these four additional periods are less moments than aspects of a single, if complex, effort to deal with the maturing of qualitative research that must do more than react against positivist research. Before, the field was able to establish an identity by being against positivist methods and ideology while proposing alternatives. Now, however, it is becoming institutionalized rather than being on the outside of the power structure. And as institutionalization progresses, there is a growing need to reach some shared beliefs beyond simply being against positivism. That theme characterizes moments 6 through 8.

The Fifth or Postmodern Moment

In this moment qualitative researchers tried to deal with the crises of representation, legitimation, and praxis in a number of ways, from reporting their research in different ways to supporting the participation through the writing of members of groups that were traditionally silenced. The moment is characterized by further shifts from the idea of a research paper reflecting the reality of a particular context to the idea of the research paper as narrative and storytelling. And just as different people tell different stories, so do different qualitative methods. That is one of two major features of this moment. The other is an abandonment of the researcher as an aloof, privileged person who can decide what is true. There is movement toward an emphasis on cooperation and collaboration that

- Blurs the line between the researcher and the researched, with participation by all throughout the research process
- Operates in the real world instead of in artificially structured and simplified environments
- Includes both critiques of what is and efforts to change what is through "more action, participatory and activist-oriented research" (Denzin & Lincoln, 2005, p. 20)

In this context, any efforts to produce definitive statements of the way things are or to present a researcher's work as objective truth were abandoned. "The search for grand narratives was being replaced by more local, small-scale theories fitted to specific problems and specific situations" (Denzin & Lincoln, p. 20).

The Sixth or Postexperimental Inquiry Moment (1995–2000)

This period was characterized by high levels of excitement, new publishing options for qualitative scholars, and the encouragement of new ways of communicating qualitative research that does not make a strong distinction between social science and the humanities. For perhaps the first time there were publication outlets for social science scholarship expressed in poetry, drama, performative, visual, multimedia, and conversational modes.

The Seventh or Methodologically Contested Moment (2000–2004)

In this period a number of qualitative journals began publishing, but the period was one of conflict and anxiety as the field developed institutional components such as journals and thus needed ways of achieving consensus on topics such as how to decide which articles to publish.

The Eighth Moment: Methodological Backlash (2005–?)

When George W. Bush became president of the United States, he brought with him a group of social scientists and policymakers who imposed on the federal funding and support structure a decidedly positivist mode of thought. For social science and for projects aimed at dealing with the problems of education, poverty, and society in general, this meant that research tended to be narrowly defined as quantitative and experimental in the positivist, experimental tradition. To make an argument for a theory or intervention that was not accepted by the Bush team, the coin of the realm was high-quality experimental research. However, that was no guarantee of being heard because while the administration was demanding experimental research, it was also rejecting the results of just such research when it did not agree with the administration's ideology and when it would disturb groups that strongly supported the administration. The result was a period in which supposedly neutral scientific groups were stacked with administration supporters, reports from some scientific groups were actually rewritten by nonscientists in the Bush administration, and some government agencies produced "news reports" that were broadcast on cooperating television stations as if they were legitimate news done by real reporters instead of by public relations operatives producing propaganda. The administration even secretly paid fees (i.e., bribes) to supposedly independent journalists and media outlets to flog the administration's perspective. In all likelihood most administrations have been guilty of at least some selectivity in terms of the science they accept and promote, but the degree of duplicity by the Bush administration sets a new bar.

Denzin and Lincoln end their 1994 history of qualitative research with four conclusions (with a fifth added in their 2005 edition):

- "Each of the earlier historical moments is still operating in the present, either as legacy or as a set of practices that researchers still follow or argue against" (1994, p. 11).

- "An embarrassment of choices now characterizes the field of qualitative research. There have never been so many paradigms, strategies of inquiry, or methods of analysis to draw upon and utilize" (1994, p. 11).

- "We are in a moment of discovery and rediscovery, as new ways of looking, interpreting, arguing, and writing are debated and discussed" (1994, p. 11).

- "The qualitative research act can no longer be viewed from within a neutral, or objective, positivist perspective" (1994, p. 11). "Class, race, gender, and ethnicity shape inquiry, making research a multicultural process" (2005, p. 20).

- "We are not saying that the cutting edge is located in the present. We are saying that the present is a politically charged space. Complex pressures both within and outside of the qualitative community are working to erase the positive developments of the past 30 years" (2005, p. 20).

Denzin and Lincoln describe a dynamic, complex, confusing, and contradictory context for qualitative social science research today. We could wish for a context that is less confusing, more settled when it comes to foundational issues, and with fewer contradictions, but that is not the present. However, there are a number of general frameworks for approaching qualitative research. Actually, there are many, but only a few of the major ones are explored here.

Article of Interest

Martyn Hammersley. (1999). Not bricolage but boatbuilding:
Exploring two metaphors for thinking about ethnography.
Journal of Contemporary Ethnography, 28(5), 574–585.

Ethnography is a general term for research that involves observation in the field. The ethnographer may be observing the child-rearing patterns of a Pacific island tribe or the pickup lines used in a New York City bar, but in each setting the study will involve observing behavior in the natural context. This article focuses on the future of ethnographic research, but the ideas and conclusions can also apply to other forms of qualitative research. Hammersley begins with Denzin and Lincoln's fifth moment and their use of the concept of researcher as bricoleur or "jack-of-all-trades." He then questions whether the bricoleur metaphor is an appropriate one for a social science researcher. Hammersley prefers another metaphor, that of sailors rebuilding a ship while at sea, which he borrows from German sociologist Otto Neurath. He uses the contrast between bricolage and boatbuilding to raise an issue that concerns him. It is that whereas bricolage allows you to use and accept ideas and concepts that are contradictory or at cross purposes, boatbuilding does not allow you to design one part of the boat as a canoe and another part as a

Mississippi River steamboat. The boat will sink. Hammersley's vision of social science is one that is less influenced by the humanities ("we need to keep our distance from the others if we are to avoid collisions," p. 580), and that means doing research and writing in ways that clearly distinguish social science from literature or political journalism. He is also concerned with the loss of some positivist values such as "the obligation to produce value-relevant knowledge" (p. 581), and he believes that "denying that such knowledge is possible . . . represents a flouting of that obligation as generally understood" (p. 581). He longs for more certainty and more confidence in the results of social science research than the interpretivists allow. Using an interesting adaptation of a Wittgensteinian concept, he suggests that even though we cannot be sure of solid foundations, we should proceed as if we are and take them as givens. Thus, Hammersley argues that we should reject antirealism, subjectivism, and skepticism in favor of realism, even if we cannot be confident of our choice.

To read the entire article, please go to http://www.sagepub.com/willis_aoi.

Some General Frameworks for Qualitative Research

A framework is a set of broad concepts that guide research. Researchers working within interpretivist and critical paradigms have a number of frameworks from which to choose. From among the many available this chapter describes several that appeal to a number of researchers today. The first is analytic realism, which seeks to build a framework that is compatible with both critical and interpretivist paradigms.

Altheide and Johnson's Analytic Realism

Altheide and Johnson (1994) address the question of what criteria we should use to evaluate interpretive qualitative research. They point out that within the qualitative research community there are several approaches to deciding what warrants our attention, such as postpositivism, critical theory, and constructivism (interpretivism). They propose an alternative that is based on analytic realism with a general method called reflexive ethnography. "Analytic realism is an approach to qualitative data analysis and writing. It is founded on the view that the social world is an interpreted world. . . . Analytic realism rejects the dichotomy of realism/idealism, and other conceptual dualisms, as being incompatible with the nature of lived experience, and its interpretation" (p. 489).

They propose that reflexive qualitative research must attend to five different issues (the following list is an adaptation of Altheide and Johnson's list, which uses different terms for most of the issues):

• *Contextualization.* The relationship between what is observed and the larger context is critical.

• *Interaction.* The researcher, by being there, changes the setting and may well develop relationships with the participants. This is not bad, but it should all be spelled out and explained in the research report.

• *Perspective.* Some qualitative research is done from one perspective (e.g., union members who are striking while others are hired by the company to keep the plant open). At other times the research may include multiple perspectives (the new workers, the striking workers, the state's governor, and the company). Regardless of whether the research includes one or multiple perspectives, it is important to keep in mind that whatever is presented is a perspective and not truth in a postpositivist sense.

• *Reader roles.* If the purpose of a research report is not to pass on truth to readers, what is it for? If it is understanding rather than truth, the reader will play a major role in constructing meaning from the report. The roles you expect the readers to play should be kept in mind as you conduct your research, analyze your data, and communicate your results.

• *Style.* Until recently the typical research report was almost always a 10- to 30-page scholarly paper (or, occasionally, a monograph). Although papers are still important, the qualitative researcher may report findings in many diverse ways: a one-act play, a painting, a novel, a short story, a sculpture, a short video, or a multimedia document on the Web.

Altheide and Johnson's (1994) chapter goes on to discuss a number of issues related to what some would call validity in qualitative research. Their approach is somewhat similar to that of Denzin (1994) and Denzin and Lincoln (1994).

Article of Interest

Sharon Turnbull. (2002). Bricolage as an alternative approach to human resource development theory building. *Human Resource Development Review, 1*(1), 111–128.

In this article, Sharon Turnbull, a human resources scholar at Lancaster University, looks at the current debate in the field of human resources that pits positivists against constructivists (e.g., interpretivists) in her field of research. Her goal is to build theories concerning human resource development that reflect an understanding of the local context studied but will be helpful to others working in similar contexts. She believes the positivist–constructivist divide can be bridged using the concept of bricolage. In building her case Turnbull discusses alternative ways of increasing the believability or trustworthiness of qualitative inquiry, and she uses one of her case studies to demonstrate how bricolage can be used in an applied research context. The case study used Altheide and Johnson's framework of analytic realism. As you read this article, notice how the author determined what is real and should be reported. Are the results of a study based on analytic realism more like the "real" results of a postpositivist study or more like the results of a study that assumes all findings are subjective and contextual? Why?

To read the entire article, please go to http://www.sagepub.com/willis_aoi.

Denzin and Lincoln's Interpretive Perspective

Norman Denzin is a sociologist who writes extensively on qualitative research methods. He is also an editor of the journal *Qualitative Inquiry*. He advocates an alternative approach to deciding whether a qualitative study warrants our attention (Denzin, 1994). He begins with the assertion that postpositivism is being rejected and that the emphasis on objective research is untenable. "The age of putative value-free social science appears to be over. Accordingly, . . . any discussion of this process must become political, personal, and experiential" (p. 501).

For Denzin and other interpretivists, collection and interpretation of qualitative data on humans are inherently subjective. No matter how close we come to meeting detailed technical standards for research, the result is not an objective report of the truth of the matter.

Denzin (1994) describes some of the basics of interpretive research, especially data analysis. He views interpretation as

> an art; it is not formulaic or mechanical. It can be learned, like any form of storytelling only through doing. . . . Fieldworkers can neither make sense of nor understand what has been learned until they sit down and write the interpretive text, telling the story first to themselves, and then to their significant others, and then to the public. (p. 502)

When it comes to judging whether a study warrants our attention, Denzin (1994) suggests that the values we use to make that decision are ideological, political, moral, and personal. What is considered good research varies from paradigm to paradigm and perspective to perspective. "If the paradigm is positivist or postpositivist, the writer will present a text that stresses variables, hypotheses, and propositions derived from a particular theory that sees the world in terms of causes and effects" (p. 502). On the other hand, an interpretive or phenomenologically based text "would emphasize socially constructed realities, local generalizations, interpretive resources, stocks of knowledge, intersubjectivity, practical reasoning, and ordinary talk" (p. 502). Critical researchers focus on "the importance of terms such as action, structure, culture, and power, which are then fitted into a general model of society" (p. 502). And if the researcher works from a feminist perspective he or she "will attempt to tell a situated story stressing gender, reflexivity, emotion, and an action orientation" (p. 503).

According to Denzin (1994), qualitative research reports usually represent the multiple perspectives that are inherent in most human endeavors. They also provide detailed explications of the context in which the research was conducted. Finally, although Denzin offers some general guidelines for deciding whether research warrants our attention, he points to other nonresearch sources as the real frames that are used to judge qualitative research: "personal, interpersonal, economic, occupational, and rhetorical" (p. 503).

In a chapter coauthored with Yvonna Lincoln, a scholar at Texas A&M University (Lincoln & Denzin, 1994), they attempt to predict the future of qualitative research. In the current situation, the emphasis is on paradigms. However, they believe there is a core of common beliefs that will cut across the paradigms and provide a framework for thinking about qualitative research:

> There is an illusive center to this contradictory, tension-ridden enterprise that seems to be moving further and further away from grand narratives and single, overarching ontological, epistemological, and methodological paradigms. This center lies in the humanistic commitment of the qualitative researcher to study the world always from the perspective of the interacting individual. From this simple commitment flow the liberal and radical politics of qualitative research. Action, feminist, clinical, constructivist, ethnic, critical, and cultural studies researchers are all united on this point. They all share the belief that a politics of liberation must always begin with the perspectives, desires, and dreams of those individuals and groups who have been oppressed by the larger ideological, economic, and political forces of a society, or a historical moment. (p. 575)

This perspective seems to combine the goals of critical theory and some of the concepts of interpretivism. Lincoln and Denzin point out some of the issues that need to be addressed if this approach is adopted. For example, they support including participants in the process of research because it is their meaning, their constructed reality, that we are trying to understand.

Eisner's Connoisseurship Model of Inquiry

Eliot Eisner (1997), a professor at Stanford University, has a background in art and art education. He is the leading proponent of a qualitative research approach generally known as connoisseurship. It draws on methods from the arts and humanities and is an alternative to the postpositivist framework. Although Eisner is particularly concerned with qualitative research in education, his ideas apply to other types of qualitative research as well.

Eisner's approach is interpretive, but he makes room for critical approaches as well. In fact, his model has two major components: connoisseurship and criticism. Together, they constitute inquiry.

> I used inquiry rather than research and evaluation because I wish to include . . . efforts to reveal not only the qualities of classrooms and schools, but also the processes of teaching; teaching is a form of qualitative inquiry. In addition, inquiry is a broader concept than either research or evaluation. Research and evaluation are examples of inquiry, but not all inquiry is an example of research or evaluation. (Eisner, 1997, p. 6)

One characteristic of Eisner's approach is breadth. He advocates many different forms of qualitative inquiry, from writing fiction, to criticism in the style of the art or music critic, to quantitative research. He also advocates the use of many different forms of reporting, from plays, musical scores, paintings, and theatrical performances to traditional scholarly papers. In addition, he treats the communication of results not as an exercise in objective science but rather as a "magical and mysterious feat through which the content of our consciousness is given public form" (1997, p. 1). As you have probably already concluded, Eisner is a bit too fuzzy and metaphysical for postpositivists.

Eisner lists seven basic premises or givens that are the foundation for his model of qualitative research. They can also serve as the foundations for interpretive qualitative research in general:

- There are multiple perspectives, or ways of knowing about the world, and both artists and scientists can contribute to our knowledge of the world.

- Human knowledge is constructed, not discovered.

- The forms (e.g., scholarly paper, narrative, play, poem, painting) humans use to communicate their understanding influence what they can say.

- Effective use of any form requires intelligence.

- Selecting a particular form influences not only what we can say about the world but also what we as researchers see.

- Using multiple methods of research makes our studies "more complete and informative" (1997, p. 8).

- The forms that are accepted by the educational research community are determined in part by political as much as epistemological matters.

Eisner's two aspects of qualitative research, connoisseurship and criticism, are interrelated. A connoisseur is someone who can detect subtle differences in the topic. A wine connoisseur can sometimes tell the difference between wines from grapes in adjacent fields. For Eisner (1997), a connoisseur in research is someone who has the experience and skills to understand the subtle and not so subtle aspects of a situation, aspects that would be completely hidden to an observer who is not a connoisseur. "Connoisseurship is the means through which we come to know the complexities, nuances, and subtleties of aspects of the world in which we have a special interest" (p. 68). For Eisner connoisseurship is a private act. "One can be a connoisseur of fine wine without uttering a word about its quality" (p. 85). However, once the connoisseur communicates his or her views to others, it becomes criticism:

> The task of the critic is to perform a mysterious feat well: to transform the qualities of a painting, play, novel, poem, classroom or school, or act of teaching and learning into a public form that illuminates, interprets, and appraises the qualities that have been experienced. (p. 86)

Criticism in the arts and humanities forms the background for Eisner's ideas. Criticism may be negative, positive, or a mixture of both. And, like reviewers of a play, different critics may offer quite different criticisms. That is to be expected because different critics look at different aspects of a situation and bring different experiences and different frames of reference to the task. (Anyone who has served as the editor of a scholarly journal will recognize this pattern. It is not at all unusual for three reviewers of a paper submitted for publication to give the editor radically different recommendations—reject, accept as is, or substantially revise—for the same paper. This happens in all fields, from physics to cultural anthropology, and in both quantitative and qualitative research.)

The four aspects of criticism—description, interpretation, evaluation, and the explication of broad or general themes—are accomplished more through the methods of art and humanities criticism than through the scientific method.

Eisner (1997, pp. 32–40) lists six features of qualitative inquiry (QI) in his model:

- QI tends to be field focused.

- The researcher (self) is a major instrument of research.

- QI is interpretive.

- QI is presented in an expressive voice, with the researcher clearly present in the text. "The kind of detachment that some journals prize—the neutralization of voice, the aversion to metaphor and to adjectives, the absence of the first person singular—is seldom a feature of qualitative studies. We display our signatures" (p. 36).

- QI attends to particulars. Eisner's form of qualitative research does not, as a primary purpose, attempt to extract out of a study generalizations that can be used in other settings. When that is done, "the flavor of the particular situation, individual, event, or object is lost" (p. 38). This form of qualitative research tries, through providing details, to help the reader understand the topic of study in rich and revealing ways.

- Three criteria for appraising *transactive* accounts are coherence, consensus, and instrumental utility. Because Eisner emphasizes it so much, I have added a fourth criterion to his list: insightfulness.

The idea of transactive accounts requires some comment. Eisner does not see qualitative research as a top-down, subject–object relationship in which the researcher finds the truth about the subject. It is instead a transactive process that is

the locus of human experience. It is the product of the interaction of two postulated entities, the objective and the subjective. Since what we can know about the world is always the result of inquiry, it is mediated by mind. Since it is mediated by mind, the world cannot be known in its ontologically objective state. . . . Since what we know about the world is a product of the transaction of our subjective life and a postulated objective world, these worlds cannot be separated. (p. 52)

Eisner thus acknowledges that there is an external, objective world, but he denies that humans can ever know it in any absolute sense because our knowledge is the result of a transactive process that includes both objective and subjective elements. For Eisner, all research and all ways of knowing are transactive.

One reason Eisner emphasizes the concept of transactive accounts is to make room for many different sources of knowledge. He is concerned with the emphasis the scientific method places on one form of knowledge: propositional. In the social sciences propositional knowledge takes the general pattern of

If X is true → then Y must be true, too.

This abstract expression can be expressed in a basic and applied form:

If the results of the study are X → then theory Y must be true (or not true).

If the results of the study are X → then the professional practice Y must be true (or not true).

Although Eisner (1997) does not reject propositional knowledge, he does not find it such a useful form of knowledge for thinking about human behavior that it deserves a privileged position. This type of knowledge deals only with truth. For Eisner a broader concept is rightness, and there are many ways to seek rightness. "To dismiss the ways in which literature or poetry inform because they cannot be scientifically tested is to make a category mistake. We can live with many versions of rightness, truth being one" (p. 50).

Eisner's three criteria for evaluating qualitative research (and all research)—coherence, consensus, and instrumental utility—are essentially replacements for the postpositivists' concepts of validity and reliability. You could translate the term *validity* into *believability*. Can you believe the results reported? Reliability relates to stability. Are the results stable, or might the scores, results, or other data be quite different the next time the same study is done?

However, it is important to note that Eisner's three criteria are replacements only in the sense that they play similar roles in the interpretivist's framework. He does not propose these criteria as absolutes that must be achieved in all circumstances. Instead, they are considerations for the qualitative researcher.

Coherence

Does the study hang together as a whole? Are the conclusions and comments of the researcher supported by a number of sources? Eisner believes the research project, including the writeup, is an effort to persuade the reader. One aspect of that persuasiveness is whether the data and interpretations make sense as a whole.

> Qualitative inquiry . . . is ultimately a matter of persuasion, of seeing things in a new way that satisfies, or is useful for the purposes we embrace. The evidence employed in qualitative studies comes from multiple sources. We are persuaded by its "weight," by the coherence of the same, by the cogency of the interpretation. We try out our perspective and attempt to see if it seems "right". . . . In qualitative research there is no statistical test of significance to determine if results "count"; in the end, what counts is a matter of judgment. (1997, p. 39)

Consensus

A second criterion for appraisal is consensus, "the condition in which investigators or readers of a work concur that the findings and/or interpretations reported by the investigator are consistent with their own experience or with the evidence presented" (Eisner, 1997, p. 56). Consensus overlaps with coherence but extends the concept to consideration of both other researchers and the experiences of other scholars and readers. However, Eisner is quick to point out that consensus does not mean truth. Whole groups of researchers can reach consensus on an issue and then decide later that they were wrong. In the field of chemistry the famous polywater scandal (Franks, 1983) in the 1960s illustrates this point. After Soviet scientists reported the discovery of a "new form" of water that froze at a lower temperature than ordinary water and boiled at a temperature 100 degrees higher than ordinary water, researchers all over the world reported they had duplicated the original research. Many theories were developed to explain polywater, and many centers launched research programs to study it. However, some labs kept reporting failures to replicate the original research. Eventually, the whole line of research was discredited, and chemists today generally believe there is no such thing as polywater.

Instrumental Utility

For Eisner this is the most important test for a qualitative study. Is it useful? Usefulness can come in several forms. A study may "help us understand a situation that would otherwise be enigmatic or confusing" (1997, p. 58). It may also help us anticipate the way future situations will develop or assist us in understanding our past experiences better. Qualitative research may also serve as maps or "portrayals of terrain. They are designed to enable the traveler to anticipate (and to secure or avoid) particular encounters on the journey" (p. 59). However, Eisner believes qualitative scholarship less often provides a map and more often gives us guides.

> Guides, more than maps, are closely associated with the utilities of qualitative studies. Unlike maps, qualitative studies are general, they are not mathematically scaled to match the territory, and they are more interpretive and narrative. . . . Guides call our attention to aspects of the situation or place we might otherwise miss. (p. 59)

Insightfulness

Yes, the list at the beginning of this section said Eisner had three criteria. But he talks fervently about the idea of insight, and it is added to the list. Qualitative research data do not yield easily to automatic or technical analysis. The meaning of the data is not obvious. Eisner (1997) concludes that rationality is needed to get meaning from data.

> By rationality I mean the exercise of intelligence in the creation or perception of elements as they relate to the whole in which they participate. I do not restrict rationality to discursively mediated thought or limit it to the application of logic. Human rationality is displayed whenever relationships among elements are skillfully crafted or insightfully perceived. (p. 52)

Insightful research makes us aware of issues and ideas that we could not see for ourselves.

Coherence, consensus, instrumental utility, and insightfulness are not technical standards in the sense of the rules for conducting traditional experimental research. They are, instead, much more like Eisner's concept of guides.

Semiotics

Semiotics is the study of signs and their meaning for humans. Although the approach has much in common with phenomenology, hermeneutics, critical theory, and feminism, it also has a well-established history of its own (Deledalle, 2001). The framework has two fathers, one American and one European. Ferdinand de Saussure was the Swiss scholar who founded linguistics and semiotics. Saussure's form of semiotics is probably better known in the humanities than in the American social sciences. Saussure also contributed to some of the foundational ideas of another literary movement, deconstruction. At the core of his thinking is the idea that a sign or *signifier* (which is what carries meaning) and the *signified* (the meaning) are not related in any necessary or essential way. Therefore, all language and other forms of signs that carry meaning are arbitrary.

Deconstruction

French poststructuralist philosopher Jacques Derrida developed the idea of deconstruction from the work of Heidegger. Better known as a theory of literary criticism than as a concept in the social sciences, the core of deconstruction is the assertion that texts (which may be books or other documents as well as social and cultural processes such as women's fashion or rules about equal opportunity) can have more than one meaning or *voice*. Deconstruction is the process of uncovering these different voices and making them obvious. And some of the voices uncovered may be the opposite of what the author intended or contradictory to other voices expressed in the same text. Often the contradictions in a text can be traced to the history of the culture in which the text is situated. For example, in a text on the importance of equality in the workplace there may be vestiges of earlier cultural attitudes that reflect racial or gender biases.

The American father of semiotics was Charles Sanders Peirce. He distinguished between three types of signs:

- *Icons,* which derive their meaning from similarities between the sign and that which is signified

- *Indexes,* which have meaning based on cause and effect relationships
- *Symbols,* which have meaning based on agreement or convention

Peirce's system posits meaning that can come from more than the arbitrary associations of Saussure, but the two fathers have both been important influences in the arts. Semiotics has been used as a framework to study how we derive meaning from visual images and other types of signs. The scope of semiotics is broad, as a sampling of the general topics and presentations at the 1996 meeting of the Semiotic Society of America indicates:

William Pencak: Emily Dickinson: Post-Colonial Feminist, Post-Modern Semiotician

Mattie Scott: Sexual Harassment: A Semiotic Perspective

Josephine Carubia: Gender and Geometry in Virginia Woolf's *To the Lighthouse*

Almira Ousmanova: Gender Representation in Soviet Cinema: Fragmented Vision or Fragmented Image?

Nina Corazzo: The Garden Enclosed (*hortus conclusus*) and Its Vegetation as Sign

Linda McDonald: Cultivating the Garden: Growth and Change in Teachers' Practices

Vincent Colapietro: Peircean Reflections on Gendered Subjects

Tom F. N. Puckett: The Advent of Aristotle in the Soul of St. Thomas Aquinas: Rhetorica or Scientia?

John K. Sheriff: Literary Art/Artistic Women: Linking Subjectivity to Social Significance

John Deely: The Four Ages of Understanding Between Ancient Physics and Postmodern Semiotics

Mary C. Miles: From Elf to Pelf: Santa Claus in America

Scott Simpkins: "Role Stress" and Conflicted Masculinities in Byron's *The Corsair*

Karen M. Sheriff: Metonymical Re-membering and Signifyin(g) in Toni Morrison's *Beloved*

Lauro Zavala: A Semiotics of Film and Literary Fiction: Classic, Modern, and Postmodern

Charles Pearson: Peirce's Theorem: or the Characteristic Theorem of Semiotics

Another indication of the breadth of interests in this field is the statement of purpose of the journal *Semiotica:*

> SEMIOTICA, with a strictly scientific orientation, plans to publish studies in all fields in which the notion of signs is or can be recognized and discussed, such as logic, linguistics, information theory, analysis of social relationships, types of discourse (in epistemology, anthropology, psychoanalysis, etc.), poetics, esthetics in the arts.
>
> We invite contributions from all who are interested in developing semiotic concepts within the lines of the scientific approach we wish to encourage. (*Semiotica,* 1969)

Note that the editors of *Semiotica* indicated they were interested only in "scientific" papers, but their meaning of *scientific* is not the same as that of postpositivists. There is no particular method or form of data analysis that must be used in a semiotic study. This is indicated by the statement of purpose in the *American Journal of Semiotics:*

> The Discipline of SEMIOTICS studies signs and sign systems in order to describe, analyze, and interpret the full range of communication and culture experienced as discourse codes, events, messages, practices, and texts expressed and perceived as cultural, social, and natural subjects and objects. There are no subject matter or methodology restrictions in the journal, but all manuscripts are expected to meet a rigorous standard of scholarly research publication together with the particular application of a semiotic theory and method relevant to the author's chosen subject matter. Past issues of the journal may be consulted for examples of subject matters and methodologies ranging over the arts, humanities, and sciences. (*American Journal of Semiotics,* 1998)

Today the semiotics framework is used by scholars in many different fields including anthropology, linguistics, sociology, psychology, and education. The Web site of the Semiotic Society of America (http://www .uwf.edu/tprewitt/SSA.htm) is an excellent source of additional information on semiotics. The society sponsors the *American Journal of Semiotics* (http://www.pdcnet.org/tajs.html), holds an annual conference, and publishes a newsletter as well as the conference proceedings. There is also an

International Association for Semiotic Studies (http://www.arthist.lu.se/kultsem/assoc/IASShp1.html) that publishes the journal *Semiotica* and a series of books on semiotics. An excellent source of general information on semiotics and material specifically related to semiotic analysis of images is the Web site at the University of Newcastle (http://www.newcastle.edu.au/department/fad/fi/woodrow/semiotic.htm).

Article of Interest

Peter Teo. (2004). Ideological dissonances in Singapore's national campaign posters: A semiotic deconstruction. *Visual Communications, 3*(2), 189–212.

This study is an example of semiotic research. In this case, it is a semiotic analysis of three campaign posters used by the government of Singapore to promote different cultural practices. One poster encouraged productivity, another promoted the speaking of Mandarin, and the third advocated courtesy. In the article Peter Teo, who teaches at the national Institute of Education in Singapore, introduces and applies the approach of Kress and Van Leeuwen to analyze the three posters. It involves "reading images" along three dimensions of meaning making: the ideational metafunction, the interpersonal metafunction, and the textual metafunction.

Teo's method also included a deconstructionist approach, which looks for and makes apparent contradictions in the message of a text. For example, the productivity poster is aimed at all workers, but of the 10 workers represented, only two are female, and both of them are at the bottom of the illustration, "suggesting, perhaps, their lower status relative to that of the males" (p. 199). Although no study can be considered typical semiotic research, Teo's analysis of campaign posters illustrates one application of this framework to visual images.

To read the entire article, please go to http://www.sagepub.com/willis_aoi.

The Phenomenological Psychological Model (and Structuralism)

Across the history of psychology there have been movements that did not accept the positivist and postpositivist approaches to research (Giorgi, 1995). One such movement is phenomenology. It is based on the assumption that the subjects of psychological (and other social science) research have consciousness just as the researcher does, but that the subjects of natural science research (e.g., stars, rocks, plants, organs) do not. "This fundamental fact is missing in the natural sciences and it is not always appreciated that the concepts, methods and criteria of the natural sciences were introduced and developed in dialogue with phenomena that lacked consciousness" (Giorgi, 1995, p. 25). Phenomenology focuses on this point and is in many ways the study of consciousness.

Phenomenology uses a specialized vocabulary that helps emphasize its interests. To distinguish between real things (noumena) and our perceptions of them (phenomena), phenomenologists talk about the real thing that exists in the world versus our perception. The focus of phenomenology is the perceived thing. Another way they distinguish between external and internal things is through the concept of acts. Phenomenologists distinguish between

> acts of consciousness and the objects that are correlated by such acts. However, acts have to be understood in a two-dimensional way in order to be as faithful as possible to the dynamic characteristics of the life of consciousness. The word "act" refers . . . to the fact that by means of consciousness events and objects outside consciousness can be actualized for us. (Giorgi, 1995, p. 29)

Phenomenological psychology focuses on consciousness and perceptions. There is no effort to equate perceptions with external reality. Phenomenologists know that the perception of an external object is necessarily a partial, subjective, and incomplete one; it does not mirror reality. And because perception is different from the external object that is the subject of perception, "another term is needed, other than the thing itself and the series of acts of consciousness, to refer to the specific and precise awareness that one has of the 'real'" (Giorgi, 1995, p. 30) objects.

> Phenomenologists use the term "phenomenon" as a general term, to refer to the actual grasp that one has of the real things and events that exist in the world transcendent [the real world]. . . . When one begins to specify "phenomena," one begins to articulate objects such as precepts, memories, images, cognitions, etc. (Giorgi, 1995, p. 30)

The key focus of phenomenological research in its pure form is consciousness. Existentialists, who share a common intellectual heritage, may extend that to human existence, subjectively experienced.

What sorts of research do phenomenologists do? What are their methods? There is generally an emphasis on consciousness, subjective understanding, or psychological understanding.

> Basically, the phenomenological psychological method is one of the qualitative research strategies that have been emerging during the last 20 years or so. It is research based upon descriptions of experiences as they occur in everyday life by persons from all walks of life. These descriptions can be written by participants initially or the data could be obtained by means of an interview and then transcribed. The procedures could also be combined by first having the participant write a response to the research question and then have the researcher obtain more data by a follow-up interview based on the initial description provided by the participant. The descriptions are the raw data. These descriptions are then systematically and methodically analysed so that the implicit or explicit psychological meanings contained in them can be identified or made explicit and organized to reveal the underlying psychological structures. (Giorgi, 1995, pp. 39–40)

Interviews and questioning are the primary means of obtaining data. What is the purpose? It is not to find out about an external reality. It is to understand the meaning a conscious person has developed. Furthermore, it is to understand the structure of that consciousness. Giorgi (1995) believed this method is scientific because

> the claim can be made that these structures (the underlying psychological structures that are discovered by this type of research) are the result of processes that are systematic, critical, general and methodical and that they are open to intersubjective verification by the community of psychologists. (p. 40)

Intersubjective verification suggests these are universals. You can discover them in one subject and, if they are true, you can then find them in other subjects as well. Even other researchers will be able to find them. This is, of course, a positivist perspective applied to qualitative data. This perspective is not shared by most interpretivists. The search is more for individual and contextualized understanding rather than for universal cognitive structures.

The approach described by Giorgi is part of a larger approach, structuralism, that has a long history in psychology and other social sciences. The basic goal of structuralism is to identify and map out the topic being studied. Freud's concept of id, ego, and superego is an attempt to map out the unconscious part of the mind. Piaget's stages of cognitive development represent one of many efforts to describe the structure of human development across different periods of life. For more information on phenomenological research methods, see Cohen, Kahn, and Steeves (2000), Heidegger and Dahlstrom (2005), Karlsson (1993), and Kvale (1983). Christine Bruce and Ron Gerber (n.d.) at the University of Queensland in Australia have also produced an interesting annotated bibliography in book form that lists and cross-indexes hundreds of studies from this perspective. Their book is also available on the Internet (http://sky.fit.qut.edu.au/~bruce/anabib/intro.html).

Poststructuralism and Postmodernism

Structuralism and the form of phenomenology described by Giorgi have been criticized in recent years for looking at structures—whether they be in society or in the mind—as if they are simply there. Poststructuralists and postmodernists, among others, have argued that what structuralists find are not givens to be accepted as the standard or normal way things are but are instead products of a particular culture, context, and set of experiences. Thus, although these new ways of thinking exist within the broad framework of phenomenology, they tend to reject the structuralist idea that what is being discovered is in any way universal or common across individuals or groups. This shift in viewpoint is the source of much of the tumult in the social sciences today.

> The postmodern turn in ethnography, and in the social sciences more generally, has inspired commentators to identify and to explore a range of ways to report and represent the social or the cultural. In recent years there has emerged a dual process of destabilization: taken-for-granted categories and methods of data collection have become problematic; so have taken-for-granted methods of representing the outcomes of social research. . . .
>
> The once stable category of ethnography, a well-established approach to social research in anthropology and some schools of sociology (such as symbolic interactionism), has recently undergone a process of fragmentation. Centrifugal forces have given rise to a multiplicity of standpoints. One can now identify an almost carnivalesque variety of approaches, sometimes inspired by a departure from former analytic traditions. While the sources of that

polymorphous diversity should not be reduced to a simple list of "issues," one can recognize the interplay of poststructuralism, post-modernism, feminism and postcolonialism. Throughout those various standpoints runs a discursive turn, treating as central but problematic the relations of language, knowledge and power. Many of these perspectives indeed give rise to analyses that render ethnography itself, at least in any conventional mode, highly prob-lematic, if not all-but-impossible. (Coffey, Holbrook, & Atkinson, 1996)[1]

Denzin (1994) expressed a similar viewpoint when he discussed the challenges of feminism and poststructuralism to another framework, sym-bolic interactionism. Denzin believes that traditional

interactionists have persisted in believing in the presence of a con-crete real subject. . . . Language (and the verbal reports it permits) has been taken as the window into the inner life of the person. A behaviouristic theory of the sign, symbol and language, unrespon-sive to Charles Sanders Peirce's semiotic of the sign, has given inter-actionists a weak theory of the symbolic. (p. 50)

Symbolic interactionism will be discussed later, but the point to be made here is that the rise of interpretive and critical foundations for qualita-tive research brings into question some of the assumptions about what we can know from research. Can psychologists plot the structure of the human mind by studying a few humans and then generalizing to all? Can sociolo-gists study patterns of relationships between men and women and then pro-pose universal patterns? Can educational technologists study the success of failure of a few distance education programs, or multimedia simulations, and then propose universal conclusions? In general, the new theories shout "No." They argue that you can use the methods of approaches such as struc-turalism and phenomenology, but you cannot accept the idea that the meth-ods will lead you to bedrock truth. Feminists, for example, have argued for years that how women and men relate is not innate but socially and cultur-ally conditioned in many complex ways. And there will be multiple perspec-tives on that complexity. The age of universal truths is over. As Coffey et al. (1996) put it,

It is not necessary to endorse all the criticisms of postmodernists, feminists and postcolonialist critics in order to recognize the value of research and representations that allow for a plurality of analyses and interpretations. Likewise, it is not necessary to subscribe to the most extreme versions of textualism in ethnography to recognize that there is room for representations that are more open and more complex than are conventional ethnographic texts. We do not fall into the trap of thinking that hypertext is the embodiment of post-modernism, nor that it solves all the problems posed by critics of conventional ethnographic epistemology. We do, however, believe that the tasks of cultural exploration and representation will be invigorated by the systematic exploitation of such approaches. Indeed, we believe that in the near future, when virtual reality systems, global information links and the like will be commonplace, the traditional ethnographer, reliant on written texts for the primary means of representation and grounded in realist prose, could well seem like a dreadful anachronism.[1]

Article of Interest

Megan Blumenreich. (2004). Avoiding the pitfalls of "conventional" narrative research: Using poststructural theory to guide the creation of narratives of children with HIV. *Qualitative Research, 4*(1), 77–90.

Traditional narrative research involves telling a story. Whether you do it right depends on how close you get to the truth about that story. This simple, and perhaps comfortable, way of thinking about narrative research—telling stories—has been replaced by more skeptical and more subjective views of what it means to do good narrative research. Blumenreich, who teaches at City College of New York, traces the development of some of the more problematic interpretations of what narrative is, and she suggests using poststructuralist theory as a framework for modifying traditional narrative methods. She illustrates how this can be accomplished through a discussion of her narrative research work with children with HIV. As you read her discussion of Joseph's talks with her, note that she attempts to let Joseph establish meaning for the reader rather than imposing (or structuring) the meaning herself and imposing it on Joseph's narrative. Do you think she was successful? Or is it impossible to keep your own ideas and context out of a story you are telling?

To read the entire article, please go to http://www.sagepub.com/willis_aoi.

Symbolic Interactionism

Denzin (1995, p. 43) lists seven root assumptions of symbolic interactionism:

- "Human beings act towards things on the basis of the meanings that the things have for them."

- "The meanings of things arise out of the process of social interaction."

- "Meanings are modified through an interpretive process, which involves self-reflective individuals symbolically interacting with one another."

- "Human beings create the worlds of experience in which they live."

- "The meanings of these worlds come from interaction, and they are shaped by the self-reflections persons bring to their situations."

- "Such self-interaction is 'interwoven with social interaction and influences that social interaction' (Blumer, 1981, p. 153). This means that symbolic interaction (the merger of self and social interaction) is the chief means 'by which human beings are able to form social or joint acts' (Blumer, 1981, p. 153)."

- "Joint acts, their formation, dissolution, conflict and merger, constitute what Blumer calls 'the social life of a human society.' A society consists of joint or social acts 'which are formed and carried out by the members' (Blumer, 1981, p. 153)."

This framework for qualitative research, and precursors of it, was a popular approach in sociology for much of the 20th century. At times the term has even been used in ways that suggest all qualitative research is based on symbolic interaction theory. That may not be too much of an overstatement, however, because the approach is very broad and has demonstrated facility for evolution. It has much in common with phenomenology and also shares the criticisms made against phenomenology (Denzin, 1994). As in phenomenology, a core of symbolic interactionism is subjective meaning. Symbolic interactionists emphasize that the study of humans is not the study of "real" or concrete events in the external world. In fact, on the Web site of the Society for Study of Symbolic Interactionism the message that crawls across one of the animated panels is "Things are not as they seem." Symbolic interaction research studies human interaction and emphasizes the need to keep in mind that human interaction is not based solely on the way the external world "really" is. That interaction is based, instead, on how humans interpret their world. It is thus symbolic meaning rather than concrete meaning that is most important in symbolic interaction studies. However, that meaning is not individualistic:

Symbolic Interaction Theory is a loose set of assumptions about how symbols are used to create a shared frame of meaning which, in turn, is used to organize and to interpret human behavior in loose and ever changing patterns of work, commerce, family, worship and play. This process, symbolic interaction, is the solid empirical basis for a social magic in which that which does not exist and which has no causal precursors, does in fact come into actuality. It is a remarkable and wonderful process yet it happens everywhere two or more human beings define a situation, reify it by means of belief, organize their behavior as if such a social event were real and, in the consequence, create a fractal, intersubjective social fact. (Young, 1991)

Even with the emphasis on subjective meaning and human interaction, the range of appropriate topics is still broad. There are studies in this tradition on a wide range of topics in psychology, sociology, anthropology, and education. However, additional tenets of symbolic interaction theory address questions such as the purpose of research and the questions that are worth asking. Denzin (1994, p. 44) discusses seven epistemological characteristics of symbolic interaction theory:

• *General theories are not useful.* "They do not write grand or global theories of societies or the individual. They see society, like interaction, as an emergent phenomenon, a framework for the construction of diverse forms of social action. Interactionists, accordingly, study how people produce their situated versions of society."

• *Local understanding is important.* "Rejecting totalizing, grand theories of the social, interactionists, like many poststructural (Foucault) and postmodern (Lyotard) theorists, believe in writing local narratives about how people do things together. These narratives take the form of small-scale ethnographics, life stories, in-depth interviews, laboratory studies, historical analyses and textual readings of bits and pieces of popular culture as given in films, novels and popular music."

• *Objectivity and quantification are not desirable.* "Interactionists do not like theories that objectify and quantify human experience. They prefer, instead, to write texts which remain close to the actual experiences of the people they are writing about. They like texts which express an immediacy of experience, unmediated by the social scientist's interpretations. This means that interactionist narratives often convey pathos, sentimentalism and a romantic identification with the persons being written about.

Interactionists often study the deviant, stigmatized, lonely, unhappy, alienated and powerless people in everyday life."

• *Imported theories from the natural sciences are not desirable.* "Aligning themselves more with the humanities than the natural sciences, interactionists approach their materials from a narrative, textual position, understanding that their texts create the subject matter they write about."

• *Ahistorical theories are inadequate.* "Interactionists do not like theories which ignore history, but they are not historical determinists."

• *Theories that ignore individuals miss much.* "Interactionists do not like theories which ignore the biographies and lived experiences of interacting individuals. They believe that the biographies of individuals articulate specific historical moments. Each individual is a universal singular, . . . expressing in his or her lifetime the general and specific features of a historical epoch. Hence, interactionists don't like sociologies and psychologies which ignore the stories people tell one another about their life experiences."

• *Ask "how" questions, not "why" questions.* "Interactionists don't believe in asking 'why' questions. They ask, instead, 'how' questions. How, for example, is a given strip of experience structured, lived and given meaning?"

Denzin (1994) points out that the likes and dislikes of interactionists mean "they are often criticized for not doing what other people think they should do, like doing macro-studies of power structures, or not having clearly defined concepts and terms, or being overly cognitive, or having emergent theories, or being ahistorical and astructural" (p. 46).

The foundations of symbolic interaction theory are essentially the same as the paradigm we call interpretivism. In many cases, the decision to call something an example of interpretivism or interactionism depends more on which term is most comfortable for the audience than on any real difference between interpretive and interactionist research paradigms. *Interpretivism* is a broader term, but most, if not all, research in the symbolic interaction tradition would also be interpretive research.

As in interpretivism, the research methods used by interactionists vary widely. This type of research is also reported in a number of ways, from traditional studies to poetry.

Symbolic interaction remains a significant influence on qualitative research. The Society for the Study of Symbolic Interaction (http://www .sociology.niu.edu) holds annual meetings, publishes a journal (*Symbolic Interaction*), and hosts an active Web site with numerous links to other relevant sites and a discussion list. (Another journal in this field, published annually, is *Studies in Symbolic Interaction*.)

In response to criticisms that symbolic interaction research has traditionally supported the status quo, some researchers describe themselves as critical symbolic interactionists or feminist symbolic interactionists to indicate that although they use the methods of symbolic interaction, they have also adopted an ideological perspective that opposes the status quo. There are also some variations based on a rejection of linear models of interaction and the adoption of chaos theory as a framework for thinking about symbolic interaction (Young, 1991). Symbolic interaction, more than most of the frameworks discussed in this chapter, appears to be so flexible and elastic that it can respond easily to new perspectives and influences by incorporating them into symbolic interaction rather than rejecting or isolating them.

Articles of Interest

Nick Crossley. (2004). The circuit trainer's habitus: Reflexive body techniques and the sociality of the workout. *Body & Society, 10*(1), 37–69.

Scott Harris. (2003). Studying equality/inequality: Naturalist and constructionist approaches to equality in marriage. *Journal of Contemporary Ethnography, 32*(2), 200–232.

These two articles combine a basic symbolic interaction approach with other methods and frameworks to study everyday events. In Crossley's study the focus is on weekly training classes at a private health and fitness club. One of his concerns is about understanding the class as a social process, and he uses Wittgenstein's concept of language games to frame his exploration of the workout classes. There are many rules and norms for "playing the game" that newcomers to the class must learn.

The second article is about ways of studying equality and inequality. The article is based on the dissertation of the author, Scott Harris, at the University of Oregon. Harris compares two approaches, naturalist and constructionist (which are roughly equivalent to postpositivist and interpretive approaches), and he proposes that the most suitable approach is constructionist. Harris's article includes a detailed overview of the research process, including data collection and analysis, from both postpositivist and constructionist perspectives. Note the differences in the data collection (e.g., interviewing) and data analysis techniques.

As you read these two articles, keep the characteristics of symbolic interaction research in mind. Is there a family resemblance between these studies and the characteristics? Do the studies go beyond those characteristics? Does any aspect of either study contradict the basic guidelines for symbolic interaction research?

To read these articles in their entirety, please go to http://www.sagepub .com/willis_aoi.

Summary

Qualitative research is an approach to understanding human and social behavior that emphasizes the collection of "thick" data. Contemporary qualitative research is the result of more than a hundred years of development, and that history is an important part of the context in which qualitative research is conducted. Qualitative research is also influenced by philosophies of social science (e.g., paradigms) such as critical theory and interpretivism. However, paradigms are general guides. More specific are frameworks such as analytic realism, Eisner's connoisseurship model, semiotics, structuralism, poststructuralism, and analytic induction. All these frameworks are options for a qualitative researcher, and they point toward certain research methods, goals, and topics. Two characteristics—the search for contextual understanding instead of universal laws and a design-as-you-go or emergent approach— help distinguish interpretive, and to some extent critical, approaches to qualitative research from postpositivist quantitative research.

Questions for Reflection

1. Do you think there are any universal laws of human behavior that can be relied on across eras, situations, cultures, and contexts? If there are, do you believe we can discover them through research? How does your view of this issue compare with that of the postpositivists and the interpretivists? Why do you think you take the position you do on this question?

2. The design-as-you-go approach is much more flexible than a technical rational approach to research that requires all the methods to be prescribed beforehand. However, postpositivist researchers would point out that it leaves you open to charges that you may bias your data and thus your conclusions and make it very difficult for someone else to replicate your study. Do you agree with these criticisms? How would you explain your position to someone who is more comfortable with the other approach?

3. Consider each of the frameworks discussed in this chapter. Which one seems most problematic to you? Why? Which one do you find most appealing? Why?

4. Consider a field of research that interests you. Do you think a research career in that field would be most successful if the researcher concentrated on one of the frameworks presented in

this chapter? Which one? Why? Or do you think the researcher would make more progress using different frameworks for different studies in that field? Why?

Note

1. From Coffey, A., B. Holbrook and P. Atkinson, Qualitative Data Analysis: Technologies and Representations, in *Sociological Research Online, 1*(1). Copyright © 1996 by Sage Publications, Ltd.

References

Altheide, D., & Johnson, J. (1994). Criteria for assessing interpretive validity in qualitative research. In N. Denzin & Y. Lincoln (Eds.), *Handbook of qualitative research* (pp. 485–499). Thousand Oaks, CA: Sage.

American Journal of Semiotics. (1998). Retrieved January 27, 2006, from http://www.pdcnet.org/tajs.html

Blumer, H. (1981). Denzin, N. (1995). Symbolic interactionism. In J. Smith, R. Harre, & L. Langenhove (Eds.), *Rethinking psychology* (pp. 43–58). Newbury Park, CA: Sage.

Bruce, C., & Gerber, R. (n.d.). *Phenomenographic research.* Retrieved September 12, 2006, from http://sky.fit.qut.edu.au/~bruce/anabib/intro.html

Coffey, A., Holbrook, B., & Atkinson, P. (1996). Qualitative data analysis: Technologies and representations. *Sociological Research Online, 1*(1). Retrieved January 27, 2006, from http://www.socresonline.org.uk/socresonline/1/1/4.html

Cohen, M., Kahn, D., & Steeves, R. (2000). *Hermeneutic phenomenological research: A practical guide for nurse researchers.* Thousand Oaks, CA: Sage.

Crawford, J. (1990). *The Byzantine shops at Sardis.* Cambridge, MA: Harvard University Press.

Deledalle, G. (2001). *Charles S. Peirce's philosophy of signs: Essays in comparative semiotics.* Bloomington: Indiana University Press.

Denzin, N. (1994). The art and politics of interpretation. In N. Denzin & Y. Lincoln (Eds.), *Handbook of qualitative research* (pp. 500–515). Thousand Oaks, CA: Sage.

Denzin, N. (1995). Symbolic interactionism. In J. Smith, R. Harre, & L. Langenhove (Eds.), *Rethinking psychology* (pp. 43–58). Newbury Park, CA: Sage.

Denzin, N., & Lincoln, Y. (1994). *Handbook of qualitative research.* Newbury Park, CA: Sage.

Denzin, N., & Lincoln, Y. (2005). *The SAGE handbook of qualitative research.* Newbury Park, CA: Sage.

Eisner, E. (1997). *The enlightened eye: Qualitative inquiry and the enhancement of educational practice.* Columbus, OH: Merrill.

Franks, F. (1983). *Polywater.* Cambridge: MIT Press.

Geertz, C. (1973). *The interpretation of cultures.* New York: Basic Books.

Geertz, C. (1983). *Local knowledge: Further essays in interpretive anthropology.* New York: Basic Books.

Giorgi, A. (Ed.). (1995). *Phenomenology and psychological research.* Pittsburgh: Duquesne University Press.

Heidegger, M., & Dahlstrom, D. (2005). *Introduction to phenomenological research.* Bloomington: Indiana University Press.

Karlsson, G. (1993). *Psychological qualitative research from a phenomenological perspective.* Stockholm: Almquist and Wirksell International.

Kvale, S. (1983). The qualitative research interview: A phenomenological and a hermeneutical mode of understanding. *Journal of Phenomenological Psychology, 14,* 171–196.

Lincoln, Y. S., & Denzin, N. K. (1994). The fifth moment. In N. K. Denzin & Y. S. Lincoln (Eds.), *The handbook of qualitative research* (pp. 575–586). Thousand Oaks, CA: Sage.

Miles, A., & Huberman, M. (1994a). Data management and analysis methods. In N. Denzin & Y. Lincoln (Eds.), *Handbook of qualitative research* (pp. 428–444). Newbury Park, CA: Sage.

Miles, A., & Huberman, M. (1994b). *Qualitative data analysis: A new sourcebook of methods* (2nd ed.). Newbury Park, CA: Sage.

Peterson, C., Mailer, S., & Seligman, M. (1995). *Learned helplessness: A theory for the age of personal control.* Oxford: Oxford University Press.

Phillips, D., & Burbules, N. (2000). *Positivism and educational research.* Lanham, MD: Rowman & Littlefield.

Semiotic Society of America. (1996). Proceedings of the 1996 meeting of the Semiotic Society of America. Retrieved January 27, 2006, from http://www.geist.de/langbern/info-D.html#InformationenE

Semiotica home page. Retrieved January 27, 2006, from http://www.arthist.lu.se/kultsem/AIS/IASS4-pub.html

Yore, L., Hand, B., & Florence, M. (2004). Scientists' views of science, models of writing, and science writing practice. *Journal of Research in Science Teaching, 41*(4), 338–369.

Young, T. (1991, March). *Symbolic interactional theory and nonlinear dynamics: Social magic in human activity.* No. 149 in the Transforming Sociology Series. Wiedman, MI: The Red Feather Institute. Retrieved September 23, 2006, from http://critcrim.org/redfeather/chaos/ab-sit.htm

Zigler, E., & Muenchow, S. (1992). *Head Start: The inside story of America's most successful educational experiment.* New York: Basic Books.

CHAPTER 6

General Guidelines for Qualitative Research

This book began with the broad general paradigms that form the overarching structures for different forms of qualitative research. Then chapter 5 focused on a more detailed level: frameworks for qualitative research. This chapter is even more specific and looks closely at a set of general guidelines for qualitative research. Chapter 7 narrows the focus further and looks at specific research methods such as ethnography, historiography, and emancipatory research. Finally, chapter 8 looks at ways of analyzing qualitative data and chapter 9 looks at possible futures.

In dealing with the problem of how to define something, Ludwig Wittgenstein (1978; Zitzen, 1999) rejected the traditional approach of trying to create a set of defining characteristics that precisely distinguish a concept or idea. Instead, he argued that concepts are best defined through *family resemblances*. All members of a particular family may share a set of family characteristics but no single member of a family will have all these characteristics. And there is no single entity such as the shape of the nose, the color of the skin, or a preference for spicy foods that captures the essence of what it means to be an Osgood, or an Ortega, or an Ozkan. Yet when the clan gathers for some family function and there are both blood relatives and in-laws present it is often quite easy to spot the blood relatives. They have family resemblances, characteristics that tend to be more common among that clan than others.

Wittgenstein, who was named one of the 100 most important scientists and thinkers of the 20th century by *Time* magazine, is infamous for his thick, obtuse, and example-sparse writing, in both German and English. Michaela Zitzen (1999), of Heinrich-Heine-Universität in Düsseldorf, provides a more understandable explanation of Wittgenstein's idea of family resemblance that Wittgenstein usually did:

> Wittgenstein was one of the first to doubt and to challenge the Aristotelian theory of categorization which is based on the thesis that a category is defined by a sufficient amount of necessary features. To count something as an instance of a category, it has to consist of a set of criterial features of the category concerned.
>
> Wittgenstein points out that the classical approach is in some ways an inadequate solution for analysing meaning, as he illustrates in a famous passage of his *Philosophical Investigations* where he addresses the question of how to define the term "game" (Wittgenstein 1978, paragraph 66–67). According to his philosophical thoughts, a category is not structured in terms of a set of necessary and sufficient features, but rather by "a complicated network of similarities overlapping and criss-crossing: sometimes overall similarities, sometimes similarities of detail." In other words, the different members of a category are held together by a family resemblance structure, as Wittgenstein calls that phenomenon. Features typically associated with the category are not shared by all members equally. Thus, there are no features common to all the members. . . . Wittgenstein observes that the various members of the category "game" (board-games, card-games, ball-games, Olympic games) do not share a set of common properties on whose basis games can be clearly distinguished from non-games. Therefore Wittgenstein arrives at the conclusion that the category "game" is blurred at its edges:
>
> "What still counts as a game and what no longer does? Can you give the boundary? No, you can not draw one; for none has so far been drawn. (but that never troubled you before when you used the word game.)" (Wittgenstein, 1978, paragraph 67).

Wittgenstein's example of the fuzzy and indefinable category *game* describes not only the internal structure of the category but also how the category *game* might be learned. It cannot possibly be learned in terms of criterial features that uniquely distinguish games from nongames but rather on the basis of similar exemplars.

> "Was bist du für ein Vogel, wenn du nicht fliegen kannst", sagte der kleine Vogel zur Ente. "Was bist du für ein Vogel, wenn du nicht schwimmen kannst", sagt die Ente und tauchte unter. (Prokofiér, S. *Peter und der Wolf*)

"What kind of bird are you if you cannot fly", said the little bird to the duck? "What kind of bird are you when you cannot swim", said the duck, and dove under the water. (S. Prokofiev, *Peter and the Wolf*) [Translation courtesy of Nina Semko]

If Wittgenstein is correct and you cannot use language to precisely define something in the way Zitzen calls criterial, then a foundation for post-positivist research is undermined. If meaning is built from family resemblances rather than criterial specifications, then we are dealing with, at best, partial similarities.

This chapter describes the family resemblances of interpretive and critical qualitative research. As you will see, many of the family resemblances emphasized in one or more of the frameworks discussed earlier are also present here. However, different family resemblances may be barely present, heavily emphasized, or missing altogether in a particular framework.

Resemblances may not be enough to establish a family connection. The idea of family resemblances is a major aspect of Ludwig Wittgenstein's philosophy of meaning, but it has been criticized for opening up the possibility of extending the meaning of an idea infinitely and thus watering it down so much that it becomes meaningless. Some may feel that is true of terms such as *qualitative research* and *interpretivism*. Thomas Kuhn, father of the sociological philosophy of science, extended Wittgenstein's idea of family resemblances to include both resemblances and nonresemblances (e.g., instances and noninstances). This concept was further developed by Hanne Anderson (2000) at the University of Copenhagen. Anderson argues that concepts and their family membership must be understood as progressively developed through history. This chapter presents a set of family resemblances that highlight both how research can share family resemblance with other qualitative studies and how it might have noninstances of resemblance; that is, it might have characteristics that are more like those of other paradigms, such as postpositivism.

Article of Interest

Torrey Shanks. (2004, February). Feminism's family resemblances. *Political Theory, 32,* 109–115.

This article is actually a review of two books written from a feminist theoretical perspective. While a graduate student at Northwestern University, Shanks used Wittgenstein's concept of family resemblance to compare the views of feminism in the two books and analyzed the use of the concept by one of the book's authors, Heyes, to define feminism. Shanks and Heyes are both concerned with the issue of essentialism versus antiessentialism in feminist theory. The issue is this: Essentialism in feminist theory argues that there are certain universal characteristics of women in human society. Those characteristics can be used as a foundation for political action and other efforts to improve the status of women. Antiessentialism is the argument that there is nothing permanent and fixed about the concept *woman*. Accepting that idea will allow women to break out of the stereotypes imposed on them by cultures, thus allowing each woman to develop her own identity. Advocates of each position see a danger in adopting the other position. This is a focus in Heyes's book, and it is also the focus of Shanks's review.

Heyes's solution, to adopt a family resemblance approach to defining *woman,* uses the Wittgensteinian metaphor of a thread that is strong not because one fiber runs through the entire length of the thread but because of the overlapping fibers. This approach provides family resemblances that women share without requiring that certain characteristics be universal. There are no fixed characteristics that all women must share, but political and social action can be based on the family resemblances of women. The author of the second book, Calhoun, does not share the Wittgensteinian approach to defining *woman,* and Shanks suggests that the issue she addresses, the status of lesbian and gay families, would benefit from Wittgenstein's approach to meaning as well. What is your view on the issue of how meaning is attributed to the word *woman?* Are you an essentialist, an antiessentialist, or a Wittgensteinian? Why?

To read the entire article, please go to http://www.sagepub.com/willis_aoi.

Guidelines for Qualitative Research

With due consideration of the idea of family resemblances, in both positive (resemblances) and negative (nonresemblances) ways, this section introduces a set of guidelines that are shared among qualitative researchers in the interpretive and, to a lesser extent, critical traditions. Keep in mind, however, that these are *resemblances,* not *criterial* specifications for what is and is not qualitative research.

Situated or Contextual Understanding, Not Truth, Is the Purpose of Research

In previous chapters the difference between the search for truth that guides postpositivist research and the search for understanding that guides interpretive research has been discussed in detail. A few comments need to be made here about the issue because the search for valid, generalizable truth is the reason there are so many technical details and requirements for positivist and postpositivist social science research. That is not the goal of interpretivist qualitative research. Instead, the goal is to understand a particular context. In the hermeneutic tradition espoused by Gadamer (1975, 1976a, 1976b, 1981), we accomplish this by immersing ourselves in the context we want to understand and by bringing to bear on our efforts all our past experiences and knowledge.

Bilimoria (1998), an Australian scholar from Deakin University, explains how our own experiences and background become a strength instead of a barrier to understanding others:

> What could have presented themselves as the "bitter blockers" to adequate understanding and *Selbstverstandis* (self-understanding)— namely, intentions, subject or "auto" reference, and the embeddedness of a tradition of textual representation in presuppositions, pre-judgments and prejudices, are turned around by Gadamer to become the very links, devices and missing parts that actually enable and are constitutive of understanding. Prejudices are made transparent for what they are, and their limitations are thereby undermined. The walls of traditional framework need not keep the world closed off from hermeneutical access, in understanding and in reflection. This is what Gadamer calls "the happening of tradition" which admits to a kind of hermeneutic self-reflection on the part of language in dialogue with (the authority) of tradition; and here one will notice that the horizons of language and tradition are seen to converge, the world of the reader and the world of the text merge into one another. . . . Gadamer characterised this non-analytic coming-together as the "fusion of horizons" . . . and later commentators have extended the metaphor to signal the meeting of disparate cultures, trans-tradition comparisons, and even the synthesis of the arts of different cultures (as in the "fusion" of world music).

In contrast to the positivist's goals of prediction and control, interpretivist researchers view knowledge as understanding rather than the ability to control. In this approach the distinction between researcher and subject (the term *participant* is a better fit than *subject*) is blurred or even disappears completely in interpretive and critical qualitative research. As you have already learned, however, critical approaches have not given up on the goal of control. However, in critical research the participants often are the disenfranchised, and the goal is not so much control as it is emancipation, which involves taking control from those in power so that the participants become more liberated.

Sometimes contextual understanding is called hermeneutic understanding, ideographic understanding, or *verstehen,* but the essence is the same. Both positivist and interpretive approaches sometimes present generalizations, propose hypotheses and theories to explain patterns of behavior, and suggest additional research. However, there is a difference between the explanatory theory developed by an interpretivist researcher and a theory developed by a postpositivist. The theory proposed by a postpositivist is an attempt to explain a phenomenon in a general or universal way. If the same theory were proposed by an interpretivist the purpose would be to offer a perspective that helps the reader understand particular phenomenon studied. The theory developed may or may not be applicable in similar settings. It is up to the reader, not the writer, to decide how much attention should be paid to the theory when other contexts are considered. Situated understanding, not lawlike generalization, is the outcome of interpretive research. (Note that critical qualitative researchers often fall somewhere between the positivist and the interpretivist. They expect to find local instances of universals such as oppression of the powerless by the powerful.)

Article of Interest

Anshuman Prasad. (2002, January). The contest over meaning: Hermeneutics as an interpretive methodology for understanding texts. *Organizational Research Methods, 5,* 12–33.

Prasad is a professor of management in the School of Business at the University of New Haven in Connecticut. His article on hermeneutics as a research method was written for organizational researchers, but the historical and conceptual framework he presents will be useful to any reader. His historical introduction to hermeneutics begins with the Greeks. He introduces classical hermeneutics, philosophical hermeneutics, and critical hermeneutics before beginning a discussion of contemporary hermeneutics and the issues that surround its use in social science research. As you read this article be sure you understand the differences between various forms of hermeneutics and that you understand words and phrases that have special meaning in the hermeneutic literature, such as *historicality of understanding, hermeneutic horizon, fusion of horizons, understanding as dialogue, authorial intention, critical self-reflexivity,* and *text.* Also, as you read about methodology, think of ways hermeneutic methods could be used to study important topics in your own field of interest.

To read the entire article, please go to http://www.sagepub.com/willis_aoi.

Another way of thinking about this issue is to ask whether the purpose of qualitative research is ideographic or nomothetic. Eisner (1998) argues that good inquiry pays "attention to particulars." However, traditional social science research is nomothetic. A nomothetic study looks at particulars in order to build general rules or laws about human behavior. Eisner tends to emphasize the details of understanding the particular. He is ideographic in his approach. An ideographic study is an effort "not to confirm and expand these general experiences in order to attain knowledge of a law . . . but to understand how this man, this people, or this state is what it has become" (Gadamer, quoted in Fielding & Fielding, 1986, p. 6).

In their chapter on ideography and case study research, Smith, Harre, and Langenhove (1995) point out that the ideographic approach "has been grossly neglected in mainstream psychology" (p. 59). Their approach, which is from the perspective of postmodern psychology, has much in common with Eisner's. They advocate the use of ideographic case studies, which is one concrete way of implementing Eisner's advice to think and write more like novelists and poets. Regardless of how you phrase it—ideographic understanding, knowledge in context, particulars, local truths—the goal is the same.

Accept Multiple Sources of Influence

Qualitative social science research cuts across almost all the disciplines in the field and borrows from almost everywhere, including the arts and the humanities. Because qualitative researchers accept ways of knowing that go well beyond the scientific method, they have been open to the rich traditions of many other disciplines. For example, Eisner (1998) points out that there is much in the way a critic thinks and writes about a work of art or a film that can be used by qualitative researchers in the social sciences.

In his book about the history of the Black Sea, Neal Ascherson (1995) points out that in the English language the term *science* has a much narrower meaning than the equivalent Russian word, *nauka*.

The word in Russian has none of the limitations to physical science or technology which it has acquired in English; a philologist [a language specialist] or an art historian is as much a scientist as a molecular biologist, in the sense of the French word *savant*. Nothing, neither Stalinist terror nor free-market pressures and privations, has been able to rob this Russian term of its majesty. When Mr. Chesnok [an archaeologist on a dig in Crimea] and his colonists spoke about themselves as "scientists," I came to understand that they were talking not only about their research but also about something inward and existential. They meant a sort of marble stele in the mind; incised upon it are the moral commandments to which the life of a scientist is dedicated. These commandments include the commitments to truth, to loyal comradeship, to intellectual and personal self-discipline, to an ascesis indifferent to discomfort or money. . . . At Tanis [the site of the dig] I heard [about] a love affair between a Russian archaeologist and a foreign scholar condemned as "unworthy of a scientist" because it had led the woman concerned to re-time an excavation schedule. (p. 90)

The qualitative researcher's view of research and science is much closer to the meaning of the Russian term than that of the equivalent English word. It embraces all fields of study and many forms and methods of research, and it highlights the commitment to study and thought rather than an emphasis on a particular topic or research paradigm. If you are a *naukovts* ("scientist" in Ukrainian) you are on a quest for knowledge and understanding, and the term means both "a learned person" and "one who studies." It does not imply a certain field of study (sociologist or physicist) or method (experimenter or philosopher).

Expect Multiple Perspectives and Seek Them

A second reason for the diversity of methods in qualitative research is that the underlying epistemology, at least of the interpretivist paradigm, emphasizes the need for multiple perspectives.

Two methodological paradigms that deal with the status quo are the interpretative (or social constructionist) and structural functionalist (or positivist). . . . Interpretivism is nominalist, which means that interpretivist researchers follow a guideline of subjective experience of social reality. This is closely connected to its voluntarist [e.g., "free will"] and idiographic stances; that is, interpretivists hold that human beings have social agency and act on their own initiative, and that social phenomena are best studied by scrutinising one situation in a particular context. Neuman's (1997) definition states that social reality is constructed through interaction, development of shared meaning and communication. This view validates individual experience as not only relevant but crucial to the fabric of social reality in which people develop relationships with one another. In this sense, contrary to positivism, interpretivism is an "inside-out" approach to social science; that is, the reality is dynamic and responsive to the fluctuations of human interaction, perception and creation of meaning. (McQueen, 2002)

Realists see the way the world is as imposing itself on the senses of humans, who then try to figure out just how reality is structured. Within the social sciences some theorists reject this form of reality but do adopt a view that the social structures such as culture, society, and ethnicity determine human reality and impose it on individuals. Both the physical realist and the cultural realist positions are deterministic. That is, something external to the individual determines what she or he believes is real. The physical sciences generally adopt a physical realist position, and critical theorists adopt a position that includes components of both physical realism and cultural realism. For example, critical theorists assert that there are universal aspects of the human world, such as the domination of the disempowered by the powerful. That is an expression of physical realism. However, critical theorists also view research as a two-step process. The first step is to help the powerless understand that their view of reality (e.g., false consciousness) has been imposed on them by the powerful in order to control them. Once praxis or insight is achieved, the next step is to help the powerless emancipate themselves by changing the social order. Both praxis and emancipation are, to a great extent, efforts by the researcher to replace existing beliefs and social structures with new ones they believe are more suited to achieving social justice. This is an example of cultural realism.

Interpretivists generally take a nondeterministic view of things and adopt instead the view that each person can determine his or her own behavior (i.e., each person has free will or has voluntary control over his or her behavior). Furthermore, they assume that the beliefs of groups of people (e.g., nations, regions, ethnic groups, genders) arise from individuals interacting in groups. Thus, the national character of a country is determined by the characteristics of individuals who both influence the groups they belong to and are influenced by those groups. This difference— determinism versus a form of free will—is at the heart of many differences between postpositivism, critical theory, and interpretivism.

From interpretivist and critical perspectives, multiple perspectives often lead to a better understanding of the situation. As Klein and Meyers (1998) put it,

The principle of multiple interpretations requires the researcher to examine the influences that the social context has upon the actions under study by seeking out and documenting multiple viewpoints along with the reasons for them. The analysis of reasons may include seeking to understand conflicts related to power, economics or values. Moreover the researcher should confront the contradictions potentially inherent in the multiple viewpoints with each other, and revise his or her understanding accordingly. This follows from Ricoeur's (1974) work *The Conflict of Interpretations*.

The idea of multiple perspectives derives from the basic belief that external reality is not knowable in any direct and sure way. Therefore, different people and different groups have different perceptions of the world. Acknowledging multiple perspectives recognizes that basic condition of human existence and often helps to elucidate why different individuals and groups behave the way they do. It follows from this that the purpose of seeking multiple perspectives on the same situation or context is not to determine which one is the right perspective. Instead,

> Interpretivist social science is much more inclusive than extreme positivism. From the positivist viewpoint, there is only one "correct" answer; in contrast, the interpretivist paradigm allows multiple positions to be taken into account when attempting to analyse a situation. By extension, "science" is something that all of us do every day, using a combination of common-sense understandings of the world and general laws to create meaning. (McQueen, 2002)

Acceptance of multiple perspectives means, of course, that this paradigm is intensely subjective:

> Interpretivist researchers seek methods that enable them to understand in depth the relationship of human beings to their environment and the part those people play in creating the social fabric of which they are a part. They are not searching for an objective, external answer to their questions, because they view the world through a series of individuals' eyes. In fact, methods that purport to offer objective or "correct" information are contrary to the interpretivist position of subjectivity. People have their own interpretations of reality, and interpretivists choose methods that encompass this worldview. (McQueen, 2002)

This leads interpretivists to prefer certain types of research methods:

> They are interested in using methods that allow them to reflect on an individual's experience in a social context. Ethnography, which uses

the anthropological methods of participant observation and unstructured interviews matches the interpretivist assumptions precisely. By using as the primary data set information from the subject experiences, focusing on how individual decisions affect the broader social reality and searching for deep understanding of a person or group of people, ethnography satisfies the requirements of an interpretivist paradigm. Another key point is that interpretivists do not see themselves separate from the process of research. Participant observation embraces this standpoint and enhances a researcher's ability to probe deeply into the phenomenon under study. (McQueen, 2002)

Article of Interest

T. K. Logan, Lisa Shannon, & Robert Walker. (2005, July). Protective orders in rural and urban areas: A multiple perspective study. *Violence Against Women, 11,* **876–911.**

This study, by a psychologist and two social workers at the University of Kentucky, looks at how protective orders (e.g., restraining orders) are obtained against spouses who pose a threat of violence or disruption. It is a good example of how multiple perspectives enhance a study. The authors were particularly interested in looking at differences between rural and urban areas. The research involved collecting and analyzing several types of data, from police and court data to interviews with court officials, staff at domestic violence centers, health care providers, advocates, and women with protective orders. They also collected data from focus groups of urban and rural women. As you read the analysis of both quantitative and qualitative data you will see that there were important differences between what happens in urban and rural settings. Note how the use of information and perspectives from many different sources added to the richness of the results and the interpretation. Leaving out any source—court data, for example, or focus groups of volunteer women who did not have protective orders—would have reduced the understanding developed by the study.

To read the entire article, please go to http://www.sagepub.com/willis_aoi.

Take a Foundational Rather Than Technique Perspective

An ironic thing about qualitative research is that when it comes to methodology, it would be easy for an impatient person to conclude that there is really nothing there—that there is really no uniquely qualitative method of inquiry. How can that be true when there are hundreds of books and thousands of articles on the topic? This irony—that much is written about qualitative research but there is little that is unique about it—is about the difference between technique and foundation. The foundational beliefs of postpositivism, critical theory, and interpretivism are quite different. Although the interpretive and critical philosophies have enough in common that Eisner (1998) includes both under the term *qualitative inquiry,* there are also so many differences between these two (and between postpositivism and either of them) that few will argue that they are essentially the same. However, the important differences are in the foundations, not in the research techniques. For example, there are postpositivist directions on how to use methods traditionally considered qualitative (Miles & Huberman, 1994a, 1994b), and many qualitative researchers regularly make use of quantitative data. As Bogdan and Biklen (1992) put it, "While conducting studies, the qualitative researcher often comes across quantitative data others have compiled. . . . At times the qualitative researcher finds it useful to generate his or her own numerical data" (p. 147).

Qualitative research typically does not operate within strict technical guidelines. The technical criteria are simply not as important as they are in postpositivist research. In their place are general guidelines or family resemblances. Thus, when interpretive qualitative researchers use the term *research method,* they do not necessarily mean the detailed prescriptions of the quantitative researcher.

> It may be set down as a general rule of interpretation that there are no interpretive rules which are at once general and practical. . . . Every practical rule of interpretations has an implicit "unless" after it, which means, of course, that it is really not a rule. What then is the status of the many traditional canons and maxims of interpretation, and what is their purpose? Clearly, they are provisional guides, or "rules of thumb." (Hirsch, 1967, pp. 202–203)

Qualitative method specialists made the same point in the 1990s:

> "Design" is used in research to refer to the researcher's plan of how to proceed. A qualitative . . . researcher is more like the loosely scheduled traveler than the [traveler who makes] detailed plans, with all the stops (including restaurants) and routes set in advance. . . . Investigators may enter the research with some idea about what they will do, but a detailed set of procedures is not formed prior

to data collection. . . . It is not that qualitative research design is nonexistent; it is rather that the design is flexible. Design decisions are made throughout the study—at the end as well as the beginning. (Bogdan & Biklen, 1992, pp. 58–59)

Novice qualitative researchers often are prepared in departments where the dominant paradigm is quantitative. Sometimes, because of the training and milieu, they try to adapt the structure and rules of postpositivist research to their first qualitative studies.

"When I first wrote up the proposal, etc., I outlined the dissertation in a traditional quantitative way (problem, literature search, methodology, findings, conclusions). My committee laughed me out of the building. They let me know that qualitative research is different. It was okay to talk in the first person! And 'real' qualitative research does not know what the thesis is until the interviews are done and analyzed." (Carol, a doctoral student, quoted in Meloy, 1994, p. 28)

Qualitative research is not based on prespecified methods and detailed hypotheses that will rigidly guide the scholar throughout the study. It is not a sin to change direction in a study and pursue something other than the original topic. In fact, change is encouraged because qualitative researchers assume you will change as you come to know and understand the research context better. In all likelihood the point at which you are the most ignorant about your research setting is before you start the study. Therefore, that is a very bad time to set methods, topics, and hypotheses in stone. A more sensible approach is to have a general idea of what you want to do and how you want to do it. Then, as your work progresses, let the experience guide your decisions about methods and purpose. To some this may seem like a license to do anything you want and to study anything you want regardless of the original intent of the research. As one reviewer of this chapter explained, it seems to allow a student or grant recipient to say he or she is going to study human sexuality and to end up studying mentoring relationships. Suppose that person is completing a dissertation in a program on human sexuality. Does the less rigid, less planned approach proposed here give the student carte blanche? No, it doesn't. If the study of mentoring is simply a topic that caught the student's eye after the dissertation proposal meeting, the switch would not be acceptable. On the other hand, if it turns out that preliminary research suggests that certain types of sexual relationships are, at their core, mentoring relationships, then a shift in focus to look at mentoring in some types of sexual relationships might be not only acceptable but even desirable if it takes the research into new and possibly trailblazing directions. However, the anonymous reviewer had a point when she or he suggested that

> when changes are made in a study, it is only after a great deal of thought about how these changes could affect data collection and future analyses, and the need for change is usually due to unexpected challenges at research sites, difficulty recruiting participants, unanticipated reactions to interview questions, etc., things that have serious effects on study outcomes and success. It may be because data collection in qualitative studies is so prolonged in comparison to most quantitative studies that changing anything is even an option.

The reviewer also rightly raised the issue of ethics and privacy: "Certain procedures MUST be set in stone to protect participants' privacy and well-being." A major change in a research study, regardless of the paradigm or method, should be presented to the institutional review board for approval.

One of the problems University of Houston faculty faced when creating a dissertation committee for a qualitative study was this issue: How much do you prespecify in your proposal? Many faculty who were generally accepting of qualitative data were not so comfortable with a brief dissertation proposal that basically said the student was going to look into a particular area without prespecifying the details of the study. They skirted that problem by including a traditional method chapter in the proposal that included the student's current thoughts on how things might go, but there was always a caveat that the real pattern of the research would emerge across the process. The plan in the proposal was a tentative one that might change radically. This seemed to satisfy anxious faculty.

Qualitative researchers thus take the position that general guidelines are more appropriate than specific technical requirements because each research situation is unique, and you may want to make many decisions on the fly as you conduct your research. For qualitative researchers, such general principles, guidelines, and family resemblances are not concepts that are to be fleshed out by specific, detailed, how-to technical requirements at a later date. The best we can do is to provide guidance, not specific rules. Winn's (1992) distinction between a technical rational and a reflective practice approach to instructional technology is also applicable here. For one approach, technical rationality, the most important thing is to apply tried-and-true solutions to new but familiar problems. For the other, the most important thing is to understand broader ideas and concepts and the implications of those ideas and concepts. That is because the problems you will face are new and unique, so there are no prefabricated methodological solutions stored in some cognitive warehouse that can be ordered up and applied to the problem. In the case of qualitative research methods, there is no Platonic "ideal form" of case study, interview, or emancipatory action research that can be used as a detailed, prescriptive guide in all situations. The best we can do is work from general principles and our base of experience.

As Bogdan and Biklen (1992) put it,

> To state exactly how to accomplish their work would be presumptuous. Plans evolve as [researchers] learn about the setting, subjects, and other sources of data through direct examination. A full account of procedures is best described in retrospect, a narrative of what actually happened, written after the study is completed. Investigators may enter the research with some idea about what they will do, but a detailed set of procedures is not formed prior to data collection. (p. 59)

That does not mean that anything goes, however. As the editor of several scholarly and professional journals I often receive papers that purport to be qualitative research but do not seem to be from that family of research. Some are simply the unreflective opinions of authors who, before submitting them to others for consideration, have failed to think through the ideas. Unexamined conclusions do not constitute qualitative research. In addition, a body of professional practice knowledge has emerged over the past two hundred years that provides general guidelines and suggestions for different types of qualitative research. Those guidelines are not rules, for they are often mangled and broken in the field. However, decisions about methodology should be informed by the available guidelines rather than made in ignorance of them.

To summarize, qualitative research does not generally proceed in prespecified, carefully planned steps, as postpositivist research does (or should according to the underlying theory). Instead, there is a set of foundational beliefs and many guidelines that are often followed (but also sometimes ignored or changed).

Articles of Interest

Immy Holloway & Les Todres. (2003, December). The status of method: Flexibility, consistency and coherence. *Qualitative Research, 3,* 345–357.

Kerry Chamberlain. (2000, July). Methodolatry and qualitative health research. *Journal of Health Psychology, 5,* 285–296.

These two articles, one by a sociologist and psychologist at Bournemouth University in England and one by a psychologist at Massey University in New Zealand, both address the question of what qualitative methods are and how flexible a researcher should be in selecting methods. Holloway and Todres think that the freedom and flexibility qualitative research offers must be counterbalanced by a consideration of the value of consistency and coherence. They approach the issue by suggesting that the epistemological foundations of the research methods be taken into consideration so that a method is not torn from its foundations and used indiscriminately, or even for purposes that are contrary to its foundational assumptions. They explore the implications of their approach for three popular methods in qualitative research: phenomenology, grounded theory, and ethnography. They conclude with a warning against "unreflexive and undisciplined eclecticism."

Chamberlain's article is focused in almost the opposite direction. He is concerned with methodolatry: "the privileging of methodological concerns over other considerations." This has been a charge against postpositivists, but Chamberlain is concerned that it is becoming a problem with qualitative researchers as well. As you read these two articles, do you find the concerns about "undisciplined eclecticism" meaningful and justified? Why? To what extent? Do you find the argument against a strong focus on "correct" and "proper" qualitative methods meaningful and justified. Why? To what extent? After reading these two articles, what would be your personal approach to selecting and adapting a research method for a study in your field?

Finally, if you think about the national character and history of England and New Zealand, do the concerns and arguments in these two articles fit our stereotypes of England and New Zealand?

To read these articles, please go to http://www.sagepub.com/willis_aoi.

Practice Recursive (Iterative) and Emergent Data Collection and Analysis

Another area that has experienced a major shift in perspective is the desirability of recursion or iteration in research. Students trained to conduct traditional quantitative research often want to impose a sequential, linear pattern on the collection and analysis of qualitative data. They want to

1. Develop or adopt a theory about how the world really is.

2. Deduce a testable implication of the theory and make it into a hypothesis.

3. Plan the collection and analysis of data in detail before any data are gathered.

4. Gather data.

5. Then analyze and interpret the data as to whether the theory was supported.

This is sometimes called the hypothetico-deductive model, and the process is linear and sequential. That is, you must start with the proposal of hypotheses that are derived from the theory you want to evaluate. That comes before you plan how you are going to collect data. If you collect some data, do an analysis, and then decide to change your hypotheses and look at the data in a different way, traditional empirical research standards treat those new, post hoc ideas differently. If you did not propose a hypothesis before beginning the study and state beforehand how you would test that hypothesis, the main use of your analysis will be to suggest ideas for further "real" research. Popper (1978, 1979), one of the most influential philosophers of science in the post-positivist tradition, took a clear and unambiguous position on this question: Hypotheses cannot be tested through analysis of data unless they were formed before the data were collected. As Cheyne and Tarulli (1998) put it,

> The Received View of method on this point is clear. An hypothesis can be tested "only after it has been advanced" (Popper, 1968, p. 30). If a novel theoretical perspective occurs to the investigator as a result of the outcome of a particular study then one designs a sub-sequent study optimized to test hypotheses arising from the new theory, whether formal or informal.

However, Cheyne and Tarulli argue that the positivist framework for conducting research in psychology is still preached but not often practiced. They conclude that

> as long as the rhetoric of the social scientific report continues to project an exclusively positivist image of the research enterprise,

the effect of Bem's [author of a guide for graduate students doing research] advice will be to preserve that image while rejecting its substance.

If Cheyne and Tarulli are correct, the traditional or received view of post-positivist research is not always practiced. The all-too-common solution to having standards that cannot be easily implemented is to accept the standards in principle and then ignore them in practice. Qualitative research, particularly interpretive research, takes a different approach. It rejects the principle. It views research as a nonlinear, recursive (iterative) process in which data collection, data analysis, and interpretation occur throughout the study and influence each other. Merriam (1998), among others, argues that working with the data as you collect it gives you the opportunity to develop "emerging insights, hunches, and tentative hypotheses" which "direct the next phase of data collection, which in turn leads to the refinement or reformulation of questions, and so on" (p. 151).

In a qualitative study the process of making meaning is emergent. That is, what you are studying, the data you are collecting, and how those data are to be handled, change and emerge across the life of the study. They are not prescribed in detail beforehand. Instead, they emerge from your exploration of the environment and the data collected. They are constructed in the context of the study.

A number of research procedures support an emergent approach to research. One such approach is grounded theory, or the constant comparative method. In this method the purpose

is to develop theory, through an iterative process of data analysis and theoretical analysis, with verification of hypotheses ongoing throughout the study. A grounded theory perspective leads the researcher to begin a study without completely preconceived notions about what the research questions should be, assuming that the theory on which the study is based will be tested and refined as the research is conducted. (Savenye & Robinson, 1997, p. 1177).

What a difference! In grounded theory what was unacceptable in traditional research is perfectly acceptable, even desirable and required. Grounded theory research is nonlinear; it does not proceed in an orderly manner though a predetermined sequence of steps. The theory you are testing and the questions you ask may change drastically and in unpredictable ways across the study. The study is also recursive (or iterative) because it often goes back to issues that seemed settled but now demand attention again. The grounded theory approach is one of several in qualitative research that allow you to begin with general topics or unformed questions and then refine answers and questions as the study progresses.

Use Multiple Sources of Data

Because interpretivists (and critical theorists) understand that both the data collection techniques used and the participants selected will influence the meaning and understanding developed by the research, multiple sources of data often are used. And because different participants have different views of what really happened, writeups of qualitative research often present more than one perspective. In qualitative studies published to date, the diversity of data sources is amazing. In addition to traditional sources such as participant observations and interviews, there are many others. Personal statements such as diaries, reflective journals, official records, primary and secondary historical sources, pictures, video, and paintings are but a few of the sources.

Think of Research as a Reflective Process:
The Researcher Is the Primary Tool for
Data Collection and Analysis

In traditional quantitative research the method is prespecified, and then the study is conducted. The method of the study is thus an external, preset framework regardless of the approach (e.g., two-group pretest–posttest design, split plot design, or correlational study). In addition, the prespecified method includes details on the statistics that will be used to draw meaning from the data. There are detailed, technical rules for doing analyses of variance on data from a control group and several experimental groups. The researcher strives to do it "right" and thus be able to assert that the research conclusions are valid.

In contrast, qualitative research is recursive and fuzzy. The methods, from technique to purpose, can evolve across the research process. The evolution of the study is in the hands of the researcher (and the participatory team if the study uses one). Similarly, the data analysis almost always depends on the researcher. As you will see in chapter 8, there are a number of frameworks and methods for analyzing qualitative data, but most of them are highly dependent on the researcher. That dependency leads to a major principle of qualitative research: reflection.

Reflection is perhaps the most difficult of the general guidelines for qualitative research to explain. The opposite approach, technical rationality, is easy to explain: "Technical rationality is an epistemology of practice derived from positivist philosophy, built into the very foundations of the modern research university" (Schon, 1987, p. 1). Good research from this perspective involves carefully and precisely defining the problem and then applying clear, well-formed solutions derived from good research to solve the problem.

A reflective model of research assumes that many, if not most, important problems in the social sciences cannot be stated as well-formed issues and solved with preformed solutions. In such a situation,

> The terrain of professional practice, applied science and research-based technique occupy a critically important though limited territory, bounded on several sides by artistry. There are an art of problem framing, an art of implementation, and an art of improvisation—all necessary to mediate the use in practice of applied science and technique. (Schon, 1987, p. 13)

Those arts, of problem framing, implementation, and improvisation, make up reflective practice and reflective research. They are as artistic as they are scientific. That is, they call for decisions in context and on the fly rather than relying on the use of planned sequences of action. They also call for thoughtful and careful attention to, as well as understanding of, the context in which the research occurs. Schon (1987) uses the terms *reflection in action* and *reflection on action* to refer to the type of thoughtful work in context that many interpretivists believe should be important principles in research. He also calls this "artistry" to contrast it with technical approaches. Schon describes reflection on action as a recursive process in which each effort to solve a problem that has not yielded to routine solutions is a trial that presents a reflective opportunity: "But the trials are not randomly related to one another; reflection on each trial and its results sets the stage for the next trail. Such a pattern of inquiry is better described as a sequence of 'moments' in a process of reflection-in-action. Thinking reflectively about what we have done, and are doing, leads to reformulations of the problem as well as to experimentation. New approaches are tried, sometimes discarded, sometimes adopted or revised again" (p. 36). Qualitative researchers in the interpretive tradition are reflective in Schon's sense of the term. They conduct messy, complicated, and sometimes frustrating research that depends on the thoughtful innovation of the researcher rather than the application of technical requirements. Schon's books (1983, 1987) are excellent guides to reflective practice, and much of what he has to say also applies to research.

In qualitative research reflection can happen in many ways, but the core is open and regular attention to the context that allows you to organize, change, and reformulate your perceptions, beliefs, and practices. Reflection can be unstructured and off the cuff, but it is often more structured. It may involve journaling (Lee, 1997) and sharing the journals with others in a support or interest group, for example. Many qualitative researchers recommend that you keep a research diary while you are conducting qualitative research. The diary is different from the data collected and has a different purpose. Writing it helps you organize your thoughts and focus on issues that seem important. It can become a catalyst for insights and lead to reformulations in the purpose and method of your research.

Whatever form reflection takes, it represents an effort to reduce the reliance on pure data in research and to increase the use of reason. Reflection is a major aspect of several frameworks for doing qualitative research, including Eisner's connoisseurship model and most models of action research.

Article of Interest

Natasha S. Mauthner & Andrea Doucet. (2003, August).
Reflexive accounts and accounts of reflexivity in qualitative
data analysis. *Sociology, 37,* 413–431.

Natasha Mauthner teaches at the University of Aberdeen in Scotland, and Andrea Doucet teaches in Canada at Carleton University. Both are sociologists. These authors accept the idea that reflection is an important aspect of data analysis in interpretive qualitative research. However, they do not consider it an easy or straightforward process. In their article they address two major issues related to the role of reflexivity in qualitative research: the conceptual and theoretical implications and the practical issues (or, as they put it, the "nitty-gritty of research practice"). In writing the article they drew on their recent experiences as doctoral students completing dissertations and on the scholarly literature. Do you agree with their position that any methods of data analysis bring with them "the epistemological, ontological and theoretical assumptions of the researchers who developed them" (p. 415)? Does that mean you cannot use data analysis methods developed within a paradigm or framework you are not using in your own research?

Mauthner and Doucet discuss and use their own experiences to illustrate points in their article. In fact, they present their background and experiences as major factors in their research decisions. What in your background and experiences would be major influences on your research decisions? Would they have more or less impact on your decisions that those of Mauthner and Doucet had on theirs? Why?

To read the entire article, please go to http://www.sagepub.com/willis_aoi.

Emphasize Participatory Research

Should researchers remain aloof from the cultures they are studying, or should they actively participate? Some theorists call for a complete detachment from the environment. You observe, take field notes, and no more. Further along this continuum there is participant observation. You participate on some level in the environment you are studying. The extreme of the participatory end of the continuum is what some anthropologists call "going native." There are no universally agreed-upon rules about how much to participate, and the decision can be tricky, as Cecilia Sardenberg (1994) explains,

> Scheper-Hughes (1992) worked in a very poor community in Pernambuco [a Brazilian *favela,* or poor neighborhood] as a Peace Corps volunteer back in the sixties and was then active in community organizing. When she went back to the same place twenty years later to conduct anthropological fieldwork, she tried not to get involved. Here is what happened, in her own words. "On the day before my departure in 1982, a fight broke out . . . outside the creche where I was conducting interviews. . . . When I emerged to see what the commotion was about, the women were ready to turn their anger against me. Why had I refused to work with them when they had been so willing to work with me? Didn't I care about them personally anymore, their lives, their suffering, their struggle? Why was I so passive, so indifferent, so resigned, to the end of UPAC and of [the] creche, the community meetings, and the fiestas? The women gave me an ultimatum: the next time I came back to the Alto I would have to "be" with them—"accompany them" was the expression they used—in their "luta," and not just "sit idly by" taking fieldnotes. "What is this anthropology anyway to us?" they taunted.

In general, qualitative research from a postpositivist perspective tends to be nonparticipative, whereas critical and interpretive research often involves much more participation in the context of research. Some forms of qualitative research are defined in part by how much the observer participates. For example, action research in education (Mills, 2002) generally involves the teacher as a member of the research team. Because the research is generally focused on the classroom, the teacher is a participant observer in the full sense of the term. Often, in fact, the teacher is both the researcher and the focus of the research. Also, the emancipatory approaches (Beresford, 2003) discussed in chapter 7 essentially demand that the researcher be a very active participant.

The issue is a sharp one in the social sciences. Critical researchers often view participation as an important requirement of good research. Postpositivists are generally opposed to participation because it prevents the researcher from maintaining the detachment that is so necessary for objective research. The debate over whether a researcher should remain detached or become involved is also very important today in design, an applied area of qualitative research. In their classic and influential book *Participatory Design: Principles and Practices,* Douglas Schuler and Aki Namoika (1993) describe participatory design as "a new approach towards computer systems design in which the people destined to use the system play a critical role in designing it" (p. xi). They contrast it with other ways of designing:

> Participation stands in contrast to the cult of the specialist. In the specialist model, an expert is sought out. The question is presented to the Expert who will eventually produce the Answer. With this approach, those most affected by the conclusion must sit idly by, waiting patiently for enlightenment. PD, of course, demands active participation. PD, however, is not against expertise. There is no reason or motivation to belittle the role of expertise. Specialized training and experience, both technical and interpersonal, are important. In the participative model, however, this special expertise becomes yet another resource to be drawn on—not a source of unchallenged power and authority. A partnership between implementers and users must be formed and both must take responsibility for the success of the project. (pp. xi–xii)

That is the essence of participatory design, and participatory research is very similar. Involve the participants in the design, execution, analysis, and writeup of the study. They are thus participants, not observers from the sidelines and not objects to be studied.

There are several levels of participatory qualitative research. Participant observation might be called a weak form of participatory research because the researcher can still take somewhat of an expert role.

> The hallmark of participant observation is interaction among the researcher and the participants. The main subjects take part in the study to varying degrees, but the researcher interacts with them continually. For instance, the study may involve periodic interviews

interspersed with observations so that the researcher can question the subjects and verify perceptions and patterns. (Savenye & Robinson, 1997, p. 1177)

In participant observation as generally practiced, the researcher tends to draw the conclusions and seek verification from the participants. The same is true of much of the current generation of action research. The researcher is the expert, and the participants tend to play less central roles. This is still participatory, though a weak form, because there is sharing of the responsibility for the conclusions.

Article of Interest

Leonard Krimerman. (2001, March). Participatory action research: Should social inquiry be conducted democratically? *Philosophy of the Social Sciences, 31,* 60–82.

Krimerman teaches at the University of Connecticut and is an established scholar in the area of participatory democracy. His article focuses on participatory action research (PAR), but it is not so much about the practical aspects of doing PAR as it is about the underlying assumptions of PAR and whether those assumptions should apply to all social science research. He situates his discussion of PAR within Root's discussion of alternative philosophies of social science. Root divides paradigms into those that are *liberal* and insist on value neutrality and those that are *perfectionist* and argue that you cannot separate facts from values. Krimerman sees PAR as an example of the perfectionist tradition. Root actually divides perfectionism into several subgroups. One is *communitarian* or *participatory,* and that is where Krimerman puts PAR. Much of Krimerman's article is an exploration of two questions. "Does it make sense to include as full participants 'those who are inexperienced, if not incompetent, and who have a clear and present stake in the results' in action research" (p. 61)? And "Should perfectionist communitarian philosophies of social science be the guiding framework for all social science research" (p. 61)? Often, Krimerman contrasts his answers to these questions with those of Root. Develop your own answers to the questions. How do they compare with those of Krimerman and Root? What are the critical differences you have with Krimerman, Root, or both that lead you to reject their answers? As you consider the three views—Krimerman's, Root's, and yours—in which of the three major paradigms do they fit best? Interpretive? Postpositivist? Critical?

To read the entire article, please go to http://www.sagepub.com/willis_aoi.

Some action research is much more participatory; the researchers are part of a team in which responsibility is much more evenly distributed (Whyte, 1991). Another approach, cooperative inquiry (Heron, 1996; Reason & Heron, 2001), seems to be a full research equivalent of participatory design. Heron describes cooperative inquiry as a form of participatory research:

> Co-operative inquiry is a form of participative, person-centered inquiry which does research *with* people not *on* them or *about* them. It breaks down the old paradigm separation between the roles of researcher and subject. In traditional research in the human sciences these roles are mutually exclusive: the researcher only contributes the thinking that goes into the project—conceiving it, designing it, managing it and drawing knowledge from it—and the subjects only contribute the action to be studied.
>
> In co-operative inquiry this division is replaced by a participative relationship among all those involved. This participation can be of different kinds and degrees. In its most complete form, the inquirers engage fully in both roles, moving in cycling fashion between phases of reflection as co-researchers and of action as co-subjects. In this way they use reflection and action to refine and deepen each other. They also adopt various other procedures to enhance the validity of the process and its outcomes. (p. 19)

Heron's (1996) book is an introduction to the conduct of research from a participatory or cooperative perspective.

Adopt an Open Approach

Do you explain to the subjects or participants what the purpose of your research is? Can deceit, misrepresentation, or lying to subjects ever be justified? In the first part of this century the qualitative researcher often kept the real purpose of his or her research from the subjects. It was assumed that telling them what you were studying might influence the data you obtained and thus keep you from getting a true impression. This argument for secrecy ignores the fact that the act of coming into an environment is itself an event that is likely to change the situation and thus the data obtained. Even nonparticipant observers change the environments they enter; there is no way to get a true impression in any absolute sense. Current ethical guidelines call for participants to give informed consent to your research, and that generally means they are told what you want to do and why. This is sometimes done grudgingly by researchers, but some forms of qualitative research not only inform the participants but also insist that participants help make decisions about the research process. Thus, if you opt for a participatory approach to research, you will, of necessity, make participants aware of the goals, purposes, and procedures of the study. In some approaches, such as participatory action research, the participants may help define the goals and procedures (for more information, see the annotated lists of online resources about action research at http://www.emtech .net/actionresearch.htm and http://ggsc.wnmu.edu/gap/ar.html). They may even be the primary decision makers and researchers.

Deal With Bias Directly

If it is done well, postpositivist quantitative research is objective at least from a postpositivist perspective. The results do not reflect the biases and values of the researcher. The effort to be unbiased, neutral, and evenhanded is expressed in a number of ways. Most obvious is the insistence on writing in the third person (e.g., "The researcher analyzed the data" instead of "I analyzed the data") and by the exclusion of any personal information or experiences from the research paper (except for some in the Discussion section, where it can be used to back up the quantitative data presented in the Results section or suggest a new line of research). That is not quite how qualitative research works. Qualitative research rejects the very idea that you can be objective and neutral in research. You pick certain things to study because you have an interest. You probably also have an idea about the results and conclusions you will end up with. That makes the study subjective, and hiding behind the third person in the writeup does a disservice because you appear to be objective when that is not the case.

Interpretivists take a different tack: Recognize your biases and values to the best of your ability and acknowledge them. If you are studying a particular subject because you have a relative who has a particular problem, say that in the introduction to your study. If you are a proponent of a particular learning theory—information processing theory, cognitive science, constructivism—say that. Do not pretend to be objective when you are not.

Interpretivists also accept and value personal data. Qualitative researchers sometimes keep a personal journal of reflections about the progress of their research, and they use the journal as well as other forms of data when they write up their study. Research in the social sciences is a subjective activity, and the researcher should make the reader of a study aware of his or her biases. Furthermore, before submitting an article it is often wise to ask others to read it, including those who hold different biases. Their input may point out issues that you have overlooked or ignored.

Select Natural Contexts for Research

All our knowledge is tentative and subjective. That is why qualitative research typically is done in natural or authentic settings. If you want to know something about patterns of leadership in impoverished urban settings, the place to study leadership is in impoverished urban settings. If context is an important mediator of meaning, then it makes sense to study a topic in the setting you want to understand.

Research Should Be Holistic, Not Atomistic

Many forms of traditional empirical research break the subject matter down into small units and study them in "clean," often artificial environments. Qualitative research tends to look at the subject matter holistically and within the larger context in which it resides. This difference in approach is one that has divided social sciences for more than a century. In his study of the 54 most eminent psychologists between the 1880s and the 1980s, Simonton (2000) used a complex statistical analysis to identify six theoretical and methodological characteristics of eminent psychologists. One of the factors Simonton found was "elementaristic versus holistic," which is essentially what is being discussed here. However, when Simonton analyzed the relationships between the six characteristics, he found that much of the difference in eminence was accounted for by one cluster of characteristics. The two extremes of this cluster reflect a scientific emphasis and a humanistic emphasis (see Table 6.1).

Simonton's analyses led him to conclude that the psychologists with extreme scores near the humanistic end of the cluster were rated the most eminent. However, the next highest levels of eminence were associated with psychologists who had very high scores at the scientific end of the cluster. Simonton concluded, "Essentially, there are two kinds of psychology, one leaning toward the hard sciences and the other leaning toward the humanities, in a manner not unlike Snow's (1960) concept of the 'two cultures'" (Simonton, 2000, p. 20). And because I support the humanistic emphasis end of the continuum, I conclude the discussion of Simonton's study by noting that when he compared levels of eminence during two periods (1986–1990 and 1976–1980), he found that "those eminent psychologists who seemed to have lost the most ground across the two periods were those who favored

Table 6.1   Scientific Versus Humanistic Emphasis

Scientific Emphasis	Humanistic Emphasis
Elementaristic	Holistic
Objectivist	Subjectivist
Quantitative	Qualitative
Exogenist (emphasis on environmental determinants and social influences)	Endogenist (emphasis on biological determinants and heredity)
Impersonal (emphasis on the nomothetic, deterministic, abstract, and tightly controlled)	Personal (emphasis on the idiographic, emotional, and unconscious)
Static (emphasis on the normative and stable)	Dynamic (emphasis on motivation, emotion, and the self)

objectivistic, quantitative, elementaristic, impersonal, static, and exogenist psychology" (p. 22). This is perhaps an indication that psychology as a field is shifting from a postpositivist paradigm to interpretivist and critical paradigms.

Article of Interest

Richard Johnson Sheehan & Scott Rode. (1999, July).
On scientific narrative: Stories of light by Newton and Einstein.
Journal of Business and Technical Communication, 13, **336–357.**

University of New Mexico scholars Richard Sheehan and Scott Rode do not completely agree with the division of the social sciences into Simonton's clusters of humanistic and scientific. If you disagree with Simonton, there are three obvious options. You can argue that one of the extremes is not really social science. For example, you could argue that scientific psychology is a natural science (which a number of psychologists do), or you could argue that humanistic social scientists are not really social scientists; instead, they are in the humanities. Sheehan and Rode don't take this route. Instead, they argue that the dichotomy is artificial. They insist that "scientific discourse" is really narrative or storytelling. This is a radical position because storytelling is the goal of many social scientists who use the interpretive paradigm, and most of them probably would not support the idea that the physicist and the chemist are also "telling stories" in their research articles. However, Sheehan and Rode use a research method called narrative analysis to analyze the work of two famous scientists:

Isaac Newton and Albert Einstein. Do you find plausible their thesis that "across scientific eras . . . scientists have used narratives to invent rational interpretations of their experiences with nature" (p. 336)? Why? Do you find this idea—that traditional science is also storytelling—a comfortable one? Discomfiting? Why? Sheehan and Rode's article also provides some insight into one format for a narrative paper. Would this format—beginning with orientation and ending with resolution and coda—be suited to the type of research that interests you? Why?

To read the entire article, please go to http://www.sagepub.com/willis_aoi.

Research Involves More Than Induction and Deduction: Analogical Reasoning, Abduction, and Family Resemblances

Induction involves going from the specific to the general. Deduction starts with the general and goes to the specific. Research in qualitative and quantitative traditions has often been described in terms of whether studies rely on inductive or deductive reasoning.

Traditional quantitative research begins with a broad theory that is tested by data from a specific situation (induction). When the general theory is supported by research, practitioners apply it to a specific practical context (deduction). Qualitative research tends to accept and encourage both induction and deduction in research and practice. In part, this is because qualitative traditions do not distinguish so sharply between research and practice. Another reason is that qualitative research is emergent (scholars often work back and forth between the practice and explanatory theories or understanding), which means the influence can be in either direction. Traditional research is a one-way street for the most part. Research guides practice. In qualitative research, practice can guide and influence research, and vice versa.

The division of reasoning into two types, inductive and deductive, obscures a major difference between quantitative and qualitative approaches, however. Consider this quote from two scholars at the University of Alberta, Walter Archer and Kirby Wright (1999), who are discussing research and its influence on continuing education, a phase in the history of extension education when there was some stability in the field:

The era of continuing education, with its rather routinized creation and operation of courses and certificate programs, was one in which positivist research was done and proved itself at least somewhat useful. This sort of research, derived from the example of the natural sciences, induces general principles from a set of instances and applies them deductively to new but similar instances. . . . Much of the growing body of adult education literature from that era, particularly the literature on program planning, is of this type. A number of models of program planning were developed in the form of rules that could be learned and then applied to practice. However, these sets of prescribed procedures were often honoured more in the breach than the observance.

However, in the era that we now seem to be entering, . . . positivist research of this type is clearly of less value that it was in the era of continuing education. Instead, it seems likely that the interpretive humanism paradigm . . . will become much more important.[1]

The authors go on to say that many of the projects in continuing education today are one-off projects that are not simply recreations of existing methods that have been examined by positivist research studies. They conclude,

If practitioners of university continuing education are doing mainly . . . one-off activities . . . rather than the operation of sets of long-term programs that was typical in the continuing education era, then the type of research that will serve to improve practice may have to change.

When a continuing education unit is running a set of twenty certificate programs, each program fairly similar to the others and to still other programs at other institutions, then inductive/deductive research makes sense. A market survey carried out for certificate program X, for example, can be a replica or slight variation on the ones carried out for certificate programs Y and Z, and many other certificate programs. These programs fit into a category—"certificate program"—so that what has been induced from a study of some of them can be applied more or less directly to all of them. The results of this inductive/deductive research do, in fact, improve practice. . . .

However, when the new program or project under development is so individual that it does not fall neatly into any category, then the basis for research dependent upon inductive/deductive reasoning disappears. Nothing can be induced from some members of a category and generalized by deduction to other members of the category if there is no category. On the other hand, research methods based on analogical thinking—i.e., on the noting of partial similarities between individual phenomena, rather than categories of phenomena—become more useful. Dreyfus and Dreyfus (1986) note that this sort of analogical reasoning is required once practitioners are past the "advanced beginner" stage of competence, and are moving toward the stage of "expert practitioner". . . .

One research method that depends on analogical reasoning—the case study—shows great promise of being a tool that can improve practice in the era of what we refer to as "the new university extension". . . . A number of other practice-oriented academic fields such as Business, Medicine, and Law carry out their research and graduate level instruction, in at least some universities, using the case method. . . .

Finally, we believe that both preparing and publishing case studies based on our own programming as well as reading the case studies published by our colleagues will, in fact, serve to improve our practice of university continuing education. We are not aware of any empirical studies that would offer deductive support for this belief, so we offer instead the analogy with successful case-method business programs (Harvard and Western Ontario, among others) which are recognized for improving the practice of their graduates.[1]

Analogical reasoning is a much looser, less precise approach to inference than either inductive or deductive logic. It involves an acceptance of the idea that we are looking not for certainties but for understanding or partial similarities. This is like early 20th-century philosopher Charles Peirce's idea of abductive reasoning, which involves tentative acceptance of explanations rather than the stronger, surer acceptance associated with deductive, or even inductive, logic. However, Peirce did accept a positivist view of reality: that it is knowable to one degree or another through scientific research. Reasoning by analogy is also similar to Ludwig Wittgenstein's idea of family resemblance (*Familienähnlichkeit*), mentioned at the beginning of this chapter.

To summarize this section on general guidelines for qualitative research, here are 13 guiding principles:

- Situated or contextual understanding, not truth, is the purpose of research.
- Accept multiple sources of influence.
- Expect multiple perspectives and seek them.
- Take a foundational rather than a technique perspective.
- Practice recursive (iterative) and emergent data collection and analysis.

- Use multiple sources of data.
- Think of research as a reflective process: The researcher is the primary tool for data collection and analysis.
- Emphasize participatory research.
- Adopt an open approach.
- Deal with bias directly.
- Select natural contexts for research.
- Research should be holistic, not atomistic.
- Research involves more than induction and deduction; analogical reasoning is important.

The next section turns to another important issue: how qualitative researchers deal with the traditional postpositivist issues of validity and reliability.

Alternatives to Postpositivist Criteria for Believability: Validity and Reliability

In their classic book on research methods, Campbell and Stanley (1963) outlined a framework for evaluating the quality of a research study. Their framework was widely adopted, and it remains in use today. Essentially, they concluded that a study should be judged by how well it deals with potential threats to internal and external validity. Internal validity "is the basic minimum without which any experiment is uninterpretable: Did in fact the experimental treatments make a difference in this specific experimental instance?" (p. 5). Another way to talk about internal validity is to ask whether the study is replicable. If another researcher does the study again, will he or she obtain the same results as the original researcher? If a study is not replicable, it has little value in the postpositivist paradigm. An important aspect of internal validity is the reliability of the data gathered. For example, suppose a certain test of depression yields scores from 1 (no depression) to 10 (severe clinical depression). If a depressed person scores an 8 on the test in the morning, he or she should not score a 2 in the afternoon (unless some impressive treatment has been administered between test administrations). A test that produces such varied results over a short period of time is not reliable. We cannot be sure the person who scores 8 or 9 has a serious depression when he or she scores 1 or 2 in a few hours.

External validity "asks the question of generalizability: To what populations, settings, treatment variables, and measurement variables can this effect be generalized?" (Campbell & Stanley, 1963, p. 5). Much of postpositivist research emphasizes the technical aspects of designing a study so that statistical differences you discover between groups being studied can confidently be attributed to whatever treatment conditions (i.e., independent variables) you are interested in studying. Of course, you are studying the independent variables because you are interested in supporting a theory and the laws or rules or implications of that theory. You study the laws or rules by deriving testable hypotheses and then conducting a research study.

Although there are very specific and detailed rules for research, few research studies in the social sciences are perfect. They usually have one or more problems, and Campbell and Stanley have enumerated a list of threats to internal and external validity. In the face of so many different ways for a study to be invalid, researchers have come up with many creative ways to avoid the dreaded threats to validity. For example, one threat to internal validity is the testing procedures themselves. Suppose you are studying the effectiveness of a new way of teaching a particular course. You randomly assign students to one of two groups: control (uses the standard teaching procedures) or experimental (uses new and untried teaching procedures). Then you administer a pretest on the content of the course and a posttest. This design, a pretest–posttest control group design, to use Campbell and Stanley's terminology, has a major threat to both internal and external validity. Giving a pretest may influence the scores students make on the posttest. For example, it might alert them to topics they should pay attention to. Because this is not the treatment variable in this study, the effect of this variable, giving a pretest, is a confounding variable. You cannot determine whether the results were purely due to the treatment variable (the new way of teaching) or to the pretest. The pretest is also a threat to external validity because it is not a common practice in the settings the researcher wants to generalize to. That is, if the pretest is "reactive" and influences the posttest, you cannot generalize to courses where no pretest is given.

Of course, researchers have come up with a design that deals with the problem of pretesting. In the Solomon Four-Group Design, there are two control and two experimental groups. One of the experimental groups and one of the control groups is pretested; the other two are not. Data from this experiment can be analyzed using standard analysis of variance techniques, and the influence of pretesting can be determined. If the two experimental groups perform essentially the same on the posttest, and the two control groups do likewise, then the pretest probably did not influence the posttest. On the other hand, if the analysis suggests that the pretest did influence posttest behavior, you have an experimental and a control group to compare that did not have a pretest.

This approach to research, of using the scientific method and all the supporting structures that have been created to help us make valid generalizations from our data, is still the dominant paradigm in many areas of the social sciences. Some researchers who use qualitative data take this approach (Miles & Huberman, 1994a, 1994b). In fact, a number of the qualitative researchers cited in this book adopt this approach for some or all of their research. In addition, there are textbooks on qualitative research that adopt a similar perspective. For example, Berg (1998) comments that "qualitative methods can be extremely systematic and thus can be described and potentially reproduced by subsequent researchers. Replication and reproducibility, after all, are central to the creation and testing of theories and their acceptance by scientific communities" (p. 7). In qualitative research, postpositivist perspectives are not dominant, but they do have a presence, as the quote from Berg illustrates. Similarly, Tischler, Whitten, and Hunter's (1983) book introduces sociology as a postpositivist science.

The concepts of validity and reliability are based on the assumption that you are looking for universals—for laws—and therefore want to conduct research that is generalizable and replicable. Interpretive research does not accept either of these as foundational goals of research. The emphasis on generalizability assumes that there are general laws, whereas the interpretivist views our reality as socially constructed. Replicability is a requirement if generalizability is our goal, but it is not if we have other reasons for doing research.

Alternative Approaches to Validity and Reliability: Triangulation and More

I once watched a group of children playing on a long wooden dock that extended into a lake where families from the city came for summer vacations. When they ventured into water over their head for the first time, many did it tentatively. They edged cautiously into the water at a point where it was not over their heads. And as their feet floated in water, free from the comfort and security of the bottom, they held tightly to the dock. Even as they explored this new environment they kept a hand on or near the dock. Only after more experience did they venture out away from the security of the dock, into water over their head and away from dry ground, the muddy bottom of the lake, and the sturdy planks of the dock.

In qualitative research there is an equivalent of the dock. It is a concept called triangulation. It is often used as a qualitative equivalent of validity and reliability. The essential idea of triangulation is to find multiple sources of confirmation when you want to draw a conclusion. Suppose that as you analyze your data you begin to believe that the father in the middle-class families you are studying tends to encourage sons when they try new things and discourage daughters. Before you make that a conclusion of your study, how much data do you need? Triangulation says you need support from more than one source. For example, you could have corroboration from interviews with fathers about parenting, observations in homes of parenting patterns, and interviews with mothers about parenting. If these three sources of information point to it, you are justified in making the conclusion.

There are actually several types of triangulation. Methodological triangulation involves confirmation across three different data collection methods such as interviews, observations, and life histories. "The rationale for this strategy is that the flaws of one method are often the strengths of another, and by combining methods, observers can achieve the best of each, while overcoming their unique deficiencies" (Denzin, 1970, p. 308). Triangulation can also be done across sources of information (e.g., interviews with three different types of respondents), across settings (e.g., observations in the home, at school, and in the neighborhood), across theories, across researchers, and across studies.

As described thus far, triangulation is a dock you can hold on to as you move into water that is over your head. Triangulation is best used in qualitative studies that follow the postpositivist search for generalizations—for laws and truth. If that is your purpose, then triangulating is a conservative way of preventing you from drawing unsupported conclusions from your data. It is a way of dealing with the issue of validity. But what if the goal of your research is understanding, not discovering laws? In that case, triangulation may not be desirable. Bogdan and Biklen (1998) see triangulation this way:

> It has gotten so that it is difficult to find a qualitative research dissertation where the author does not evoke the word in an attempt to convince the reader that his or her work is carefully done. Unfortunately the word is used in such an imprecise way that it has become difficult to understand what is meant by it. . . . Triangulation was first borrowed in the social sciences to convey the idea that to establish a fact you need more than one source of information. . . . When triangulation made its way into qualitative research it carried its old meaning—verification of the facts—but picked up another one. It came to mean that many sources of data were better in a study than a single source because multiple sources lead to a fuller understanding of the phenomena you are studying. Others expanded its use to include using multiple subjects, multiple

researchers, different theoretical approaches in addition to different data-collection techniques. We advise against using the term. It confuses more that it clarifies, intimidates more than enlightens. If you use different data-collecting techniques—interviewing, observation and official documents, for example—say that. . . . In short describe what you did rather than using the imprecise and abstract term *triangulation*. (p. 104)

I agree with Bogdan and Biklen for three reasons. The first is foundational. Triangulation is an extension of the idea of validity in postpositivist research. It is not a core issue in interpretive research. In fact, because interpretivist theory emphasizes that reality is socially constructed, and thus there are multiple perspectives on reality, there is not necessarily a need to try to eliminate all but one true reality from your study's conclusions. Second, it is true that triangulation has so many meanings that it is difficult to know what the term means (however, that can be said about a great many terms in the social sciences). Third, whether to triangulate or not is a local and contextual decision, not one that lends itself to a general rule. A well-done study using one method, such as interviewing, may be far more convincing to readers than a poorly done study using three data collection methods.

Alternatives to Triangulation

Even if triangulation is not a good fit with some forms of qualitative research, especially interpretive, there is still a need to conduct research in such a way that the consumer has some confidence in what you say. There are a number of ways to do that:

• *Member checks.* A more interpretive approach to developing conclusions is called member checks. As you collect and analyze data, check the emerging conclusions with the participants in your study. What do they think about the conclusions?

• *Participatory research.* An even more interpretive approach is generally used in the various forms of participatory research. The participants are not presented conclusions the researcher has formulated, however tentatively. They actively participate in the formulation of conclusions.

• *Extended experience in the environment.* Another way of supporting hermeneutic (understanding) research is to spend time in the environment under study. You do not learn about the culture of a halfway house for drug users, or a microcredit project in Nigeria, by visiting it for a few hours one

Monday and Thursday. The more you experience the environment, the more you have the opportunity to understand it.

• *Peer review.* In addition to member checks and participatory research, you can also involve other scholars in your research. Peer review of your work is a standard aspect of publication in scholarly journals. You submit your paper, and three scholars review it and make recommendations about publication. Peer review should begin much earlier, however. Peers can be part of the participatory research team, or you can involve them regularly in the process as the research proceeds. What are their opinions of the emerging conclusions? Do they have suggestions about the study? The conclusions? Can they suggest different frameworks for analyzing the data? Different methods? How do peers who use a different paradigm feel about your conclusions and methods?

• *Researcher journaling.* Two other interesting approaches to helping you thoughtfully consider and analyze your data are audit trails and journals. Lee's (1997) article is a helpful guide to journaling. Reflective journals are a record of your thinking as you collect and analyze the data. They are often helpful in explaining to others how you arrived at your conclusions (Stake, 1995).

• *Audit trails.* The concept of an audit trail is basic to accounting practice. In essence it means that there is enough information about where money came from and where it was spent to be confident that there are no gaps or omissions that would allow money to be stolen or misspent. An audit trail in qualitative research means essentially the same thing. You should document your work, from the gathering of raw data to the writeup. As your ideas and emerging hypotheses begin to form, keep a record of when they emerged, the data you used to support them, and how they were refined and expanded.

Article of Interest

Robin Whittemore, Susan K. Chase, & Carol Lynn Mandle. (2001, July). Validity in qualitative research. *Qualitative Health Research, 11,* 522–537.

These three authors, from Yale University and the Boston College School of Nursing, present their view on the question of validity in qualitative research. They point out some of the special problems of determining whether a qualitative study is valid when the research must be both rigorous and subjective. If *validity* is just another word for "truthfulness," how can any interpretive qualitative research be valid when the researchers themselves do not believe they have found truth in the study? Should qualitative researchers simply discard the idea of validity?

Can and should the postpositivist concept of validity be translated into something that is compatible with an interpretivist paradigm? How would you do that?

What does *rigor* mean? How can you tell whether a study is rigorous? And is there a real conflict between being rigorous and being creative?

When the authors say, "Verification of personally held belief or theory through a successful demonstration of method does not constitute science" (p. 535), what do they mean?

Finally, does the authors' use of primary and secondary validity criteria make sense? Or is it simply a way of imposing postpositivist validity criteria on interpretive research? Defend your position. Do the techniques proposed by the authors fit your idea of how to demonstrate validity in a qualitative study?

To read the entire article, please go to http://www.sagepub.com/willis_aoi.

Conclusions? Aren't They Generalizations?

The final section of this chapter addresses another aspect of the validity and generalization issue. You may be thinking at this point that any discussion of conclusions is simply the search for generalizable or lawlike statements under another name. It is true that conclusions in a postpositivist study generally involve just that: generalizations that can be used by others. To some extent that is true for interpretive research as well, but the way it works is quite different. Looking for traditional generalizations assumes that individual human and group behavior is characterized by laws that apply across many different settings. What is generalized is abstracted out of the local context in which it was discovered. The abstraction is then communicated by the researcher to other scholars and practitioners. The local context in which it was discovered is less important than the abstraction. In interpretive research the opposite is true. Meaning resides in the context, and it cannot be completely removed from it. Therefore, any conclusion must be made with the context fully in mind. And, as a consumer of the research, you pay special attention to the context in which the study was conducted. You cannot understand the conclusions without understanding the context. The need for contextual detail is one reason that qualitative research articles are often much longer than quantitative articles.

Postpositivist studies try to find abstractions that apply across settings. They become technical rules for practitioner to follow. Follow the rules, and you are practicing correctly. Conclusions from an interpretive study become part of the background, the context, in which a professional makes decisions. They may be helpful, but the practitioner is not working in exactly the same environment as the researcher, and the conclusions may not be applicable. (In fact, even if the practitioner were in the same environment, the conclusions may or may not be applicable. Humans do not always behave in predictable, stable ways.) It is up to the professional to make decisions on the fly in the context of practice, and research is only one source of understanding about how to make those decisions.

Article of Interest

Geoff Payne & Malcolm Williams. (2005, April).
Generalization in qualitative research. *Sociology, 39,* 295–314.

In this article Payne and Williams, both at the University of Plymouth in England, review the debate on generalization in qualitative research. They outline two extremes: interpretive sociology that rejects generalization in the traditional sense and a more postpositivist sociology that views traditional generalization as the *sine qua non* of research. They consider both these extremes unacceptable and begin their article with a discussion of Williams's idea of *"moderantum* generalizations," which are less strict generalizations that do not attempt to rise to the level of lawlike pronouncements. Payne and Williams go on to demonstrate that sociologists tend to make generalizations from their qualitative research results. The authors then make the case for adopting *moderantum* generalization as the preferred framework for qualitative research. For example, they advocate that generalization be planned for when a study is designed and that it be explicitly discussed in every study. And "since we cannot make statistical inferences and therefore calculate probabilistic estimates for a universe, we are constrained to reduce the ambition of our generalization," which means the generalizations from qualitative research are less precise and less assured. Does the approach of Payne and Williams fit an interpretivist paradigm? A critical paradigm? Or is it an attempt to infuse postpositivism into qualitative research? (In another article [Payne, Williams, & Chamberlain, 2004] the authors make a plea for sociology to do more quantitative research and view the dominance of qualitative methods in sociology as a problem. They believe the limited use of quantitative methods will make sociology less relevant in debates over policy issues.) In this book I argue that generalization is the responsibility of the reader rather than the researcher because the reader is the one who has knowledge of the context to which he or she wants to generalize. However, Payne and Williams argue that "despite previous claims that generalization can be left to consumers, provided producers engage in 'thick description,' generalization in qualitative research remains a major problem" (p. 312). Which of these approaches to generalization makes the most sense to you? Or is there a way to combine them that improves on both perspectives?

To read the entire article, please go to http://www.sagepub.com/willis_aoi.

Summary

Qualitative research in the interpretive tradition operates less under rules and regulations than under general guidelines that do not rise to the level of absolute rules. Wittgenstein's concept of family resemblances captures much of the level of structure and direction that qualitative research's general guidelines represent. They are useful but not prescriptive, often followed but not rigidly. Most of the guidelines discussed in this chapter spring directly from the basic ideas of an interpretivist philosophy of social science. These include ideas such as contextual understanding as the purpose of research, the emphasis on participatory research methods, an open, emergent approach to data analysis and interpretation, and the use of multiple sources of data and multiple perspectives. However, when it comes to a discussion of how interpretive and critical paradigms treat postpositivist concepts such as reliability, validity, and generalization, there is less consensus. You have read about several approaches to this issue, from positions that essentially adopt a postpositivist perspective to positions that argue that these are irrelevant concepts, at least in interpretive social science research. Whether the future brings more consensus—and a set of guidelines—or greater diversity remains to be seen.

Questions for Reflection

1. Take one of the guidelines proposed in this chapter and describe a situation in which it would make sense in an interpretive qualitative study. Describe a research study in which it would be better to violate the guideline. Explain why the guideline would or would not be followed.

2. Do you agree with all the guidelines in this chapter? If there are some you do not accept, explain why.

3. Look closely at the guidelines in this chapter. Which have the most impact on the research process? Which are the most important in terms of the impact they have on the purpose of research? The method of doing research? The method of analyzing the data? Which are the most difficult for you to consider seriously? Why?

4. Develop and state in a brief paragraph your position on validity in interpretive qualitative research. Then defend your position against other views expressed in this chapter.

5. Develop and state in a brief paragraph your position on generalization in interpretive qualitative research. Then defend your position against other views expressed in this chapter.

6. Would your response to questions 4 and 5 be the same if you took a critical perspective instead of an interpretive one? How? Why?

Note

1. From Archer, W., & Wright, K. Back to the Future: Adjusting university continuing education research to an emerging trend, in *Canadian Journal of University Continuing Education, 25*(2). Copyright © 1999.

References

Anderson, H. (2000). Kuhn's account of family resemblance: A solution to the problem of wide-open texture. *Erkenntnis, 52*(3), 313–337.

Archer, W., & Wright, K. (1999, June). *Back to the future: Adjusting university continuing education research to an emerging trend.* Paper presented at the Prairie Symposium on Research on University Continuing Education, Winnipeg. Retrieved January 27, 2006, from http://www.extension.ualberta.ca/prairie/ph1p02.htm

Ascherson, N. (1995). *Black Sea.* London: Hill and Wang.

Beresford, P. (2003). User involvement in research: Exploring the challenges. *Nursing Times Research, 8*(1), 36–46.

Berg, B. (1998). *Qualitative research methods in the social sciences* (3rd ed.). Boston: Allyn & Bacon.

Bilimoria, P. (1998). *Towards a creative hermeneutic of suspicion: Recovering Ricoeur's intervention in the Habermas–Gadamer debate.* Paper presented at the 20th World Congress on Philosophy, Boston, August 10–15. Retrieved January 27, 2006, from http://www.bu.edu/wcp/Papers/Cont/ContBili.htm

Bogdan, R., & Biklen, S. (1992). *Qualitative research for education.* Boston: Allyn & Bacon.

Bogdan, R., & Biklen, S. (1998). *Qualitative research for education* (3rd ed.). Boston: Allyn & Bacon.

Campbell, D., & Stanley, J. (1963). *Experimental and quasi-experimental designs for research.* Chicago: Rand McNally.

Cheyne, A., & Tarulli, D. (1998). *Reconciling rhetoric and image in psychology.* Waterloo, Ontario, Canada: Department of Psychology, University of Waterloo. Retrieved January 27, 2006, from http://www.arts.uwaterloo.ca/~acheyne/rhetss.html

Denzin, N. (1970). *The research act: A theoretical introduction to sociological methods.* Chicago: Aldine.

Dreyfus, H. L., & Dreyfus, S. E. (1986). *Mind over machine: The power of human intuition and expertise in the era of the computer.* New York: Free Press.

Eisner, E. (1998). *The enlightened eye.* Upper Saddle River, NJ: Prentice Hall.

Fielding, N., & Fielding, J. (1986). *Linking data.* Thousand Oaks, CA: Sage.

Gadamer, H. (1975). *Truth and method* (trans. G. Barden & J. Cumming). New York: Seabury.

Gadamer, H. (1976a). The historicity of understanding. In P. Connerton (Ed.), *Critical sociology: Selected readings* (pp. 117–133). Harmondsworth, UK: Penguin.

Gadamer, H. (1976b). *Philosophic hermeneutics* (trans. D. E. Linge). Berkeley: University of California Press.

Gadamer, H. (1981). *Reason in the age of science* (trans. F. G. Lawrence). Cambridge: MIT Press.

Heron, J. (1996). *Co-operative inquiry: Research into the human condition.* Thousand Oaks, CA: Sage.

Hirsch, E. (1967). *Validity in interpretation.* New Haven, CT: Yale University Press.

Klein, H., & Meyers, M. (1998). A set of principles for conducting and evaluating interpretive field studies in information systems. *MIS Quarterly.* Retrieved January 27, 2006, from http://www.auckland.ac.nz/msis/isworld/MMyers/Klein-Myers.html

Lee, R. (1997). Journal keeping as an aid to research. Some ideas. *The Weaver: A Forum for New Ideas in Education, 1.* Retrieved January 27, 2006, from http://www.latrobe.edu.au/www/graded/RLed1.html

McQueen, M. (2002). *Language and power in profit/non-profit relationships: A grounded theory of inter-sectoral collaboration.* Ph.D. dissertation, University of Technology, Sydney, Australia. Retrieved January 27, 2006, from http://au.geocities.com/dr_meryl_mcqueen/phd/mcqueen-ch3.htm

Meloy, J. (1994). *Writing the qualitative dissertation.* Hillsdale, NJ: Erlbaum.

Merriam, S. (1998). *Qualitative research and case study applications in education.* San Francisco: Jossey-Bass.

Miles, M., & Huberman, M. (1994a). Data management and analysis methods. In N. K. Denzin & Y. S. Lincoln (Eds.), *Handbook of qualitative research* (pp. 428–444). Thousand Oaks, CA: Sage.

Miles, M. B., & Huberman, A. M. (1994b). *Qualitative data analysis: An expanded sourcebook* (2nd ed.). Newbury Park, CA: Sage.

Mills, G. (2002). *Action research: A guide for the teacher researcher* (2nd ed.). Englewood Cliffs, NJ: Prentice Hall.

Neuman, W. L. (1997). *Social research methods* (3rd ed.). Boston: Allyn & Bacon.

Payne, G., Williams, M., & Chamberlain. S. (2004). Methodological pluralism in British sociology. *Sociology, 38*(1), 191–192.

Popper, K. R. (1968). Epistemology without a knowing subject. In B. Van Rootselaar (Ed.), *Logic, methodology and philosophy of science III* (pp. 333–373). Amsterdam: North-Holland.

Popper, K. (1978). *Unended quest. An intellectual autobiography.* New York: Routledge.

Popper, K. (1979). *Conjectures and refutations: The growth of scientific knowledge*. London: Routledge.

Reason, P., & Heron, J. (2001). *A short guide to cooperative enquiry*. Retrieved January 27, 2006, from http://www.cpct.co.uk/cpct/CiP_anniversary/Co-operative.htm

Ricoeur, P. (1974). *The conflict of interpretations: Essays in hermeneutics*. Evanston, IL: Northwestern University Press.

Sardenberg, C. (1994). Comment on the ANTHRO-L listserv. *ANTHRO-L Archives, 84*. Retrieved January 27, 2006, from http://unauthorised.org/anthropology/anthro-l/january-1994/0082.html

Savenye, W., & Robinson, R. (1997). Qualitative research issues and methods: An introduction for educational technologists. In D. Jonassen (Ed.), *Handbook of research for educational communications and technology* (pp. 1171–1195). New York: Macmillan.

Scheper-Hughes, N. (1992). *Death without weeping: The violence of everyday life in Brazil*. Berkeley: University of California Press.

Schon, D. (1983). *The reflective practitioner*. New York: Basic Books.

Schon, D. (1987). *Educating the reflective practitioner: Toward a new design for teaching and learning in the professions*. San Francisco, CA: Jossey-Bass.

Schuler, D., & Namoika, A. (1993). *Participatory design: Principles and practices*. Hillsdale, NJ: Erlbaum.

Simonton, D. (2000). Methodological and theoretical orientation and the long-term disciplinary impact of 54 eminent psychologists. *Review of General Psychology, 4*(1), 13–24.

Smith, J., Harre, R., & Langenhove, L. (Eds.). (1995). *Rethinking psychology*. Newbury Park, CA: Sage.

Snow, C. P. (1960). *The two cultures and the scientific revolution*. Cambridge: Cambridge University Press.

Stake, R. (1995). *The art of case research*. Thousand Oaks, CA: Sage.

Tischler, H., Whitten, P., & Hunter, D. (1983). *Introduction to sociology*. New York: Holt, Rinehart, and Winston.

Whyte, F. (Ed.). (1991). *Participatory action research*. Thousand Oaks, CA: Sage.

Winn, W. (1992). The assumptions of constructivism and instructional design. In T. Duffy & D. Jonassen (Eds.), *Constructivism and the technology of instruction: A conversation* (pp. 177–182). Hillsdale, NJ: Erlbaum.

Wittgenstein, L. (1978). *Philosophical investigations* (trans. by G. E. M. Anscombe). Oxford: Oxford University Press.

Zitzen, M. (1999). *On the efficiency of prototype theoretical semantics*. Retrieved January 27, 2006, from http://ang3-11.phil-fak.uni-duesseldorf.de/~ang3/LANA/Zitzen.html

Methods of
Qualitative Research

Case 1: Action Research on a Pediatric Surgical Ward

Following the general pattern of use in the literature, in this book the word *method* is used to refer to a particular procedure for collecting and analyzing data. For the same reason, *methodology* is used in discussing the broad principles and guidelines that orient our research work. If we apply those meanings to the title of this chapter, you could reasonably expect the chapter to be a recipe-like description of specific research methods. Unfortunately, things are not so simple. Many qualitative research methods make little sense unless we understand the broader methodologies and paradigms in which they are imbedded. The method used in this first case is a very good example of that point. Participatory action research (PAR) is a popular research methodology and method to address real-world problems. This case is a good example of the careful development and evaluation of action to solve a problem. Rowene Brooker (1997) is a clinical nurse educator on a children's surgical ward in a large teaching hospital. One of her concerns was that nurses and physicians did not always make the best decisions when selecting the types of dressings for different types of wounds. The result was a higher level of complications such as serious infections.

As she began working with staff on the ward, two possible reasons for the problem emerged. One reason was the nursing staff's lack of observation and reflection on their patients' wound care. The second problem was that there were many different types of dressings, many types of wounds, and varying preferences among the surgeons with patients on the ward. Based on these two concerns Brooker initiated an action research project that involved most of the staff working on the ward. She divided her work into a sequence of phases.

Planning. Working with senior nursing staff, Brooker came up with four strategies. A wound survey chart was created that nurses could use to document decisions made about types of dressings applied, types of wounds treated, and any complications. The chart was the main effort to change the way decisions about wound dressing were made. The basic idea was that the chart would help nurses stop and reflect on the best options instead of automatically selecting a dressing without a thorough consideration of the options.

Brooker's group also wrote up a description of the action research project and distributed it to nurses and other staff, including physicians working on the ward. After being told about the study, the head of the surgical department decided to participate himself by collecting data on his patients, including photographs. (He was using a new dressing he thought would reduce scarring.) Finally, members of several hospital committees, such as Infection Control and Wound Care, agreed to do a literature review and present the results to the ward staff.

Implementation: First Cycle. The group began implementation with a 2-week trial of the wound survey chart. The goal of this first trial was to identify and correct any problems with the chart itself and how the nurses used it. No problems were found.

Implementation: First Reflection. After the 2-week trial the research team talked with nurses and asked them to complete a simple questionnaire about the impact of the wound chart. The results were generally positive, but the team also became aware of a problem. Because nurses worked across several shifts and some were on vacation, not all the nurses on the ward were aware of the project and the purpose of the chart. To deal with that problem, written information on the project and the chart was distributed to all nursing staff. However, the nurses' opinion of the chart itself was very positive, and it was not changed.

Implementation: Second Cycle. For another 4 weeks, staff used the wound chart and also participated in reviews of relevant literature such as articles on comparisons of different wound dressings and the process of wound healing.

Implementation: Second Reflection. At the end of the second cycle,

> discussion was again held at a ward meeting. The nurses felt that they had learned more about wound care because of the literature reviews and inservices given by senior staff. These literature reviews

revealed that there was a lot of new theory and knowledge regarding wound healing and management and this challenged one of our current habitual wound practices which we would look into changing. These literature reviews also enthused the senior staff and encouraged more staff into wanting to know more about wound care. . . . As the ward did not have a policy on wound care it was suggested that we develop one out of our readings and research. One of the senior staff members volunteered to take on this task. . . . The facilitator proposed that during the next cycle that the nurses might try and do more reflecting on their nursing practice, and that they could do this by writing their thoughts and feelings in a journal which would be confidential. (Brooker, 1997)

Brooker's research, like most action research, was cyclic. It progressed through a series of cycles that involved reflection on the situation, action to solve a problem, and reflection on whether the action was effective. This cyclic or iterative process is typical of many forms of both emancipatory and participatory research.

Previous chapters have taken a broader approach to qualitative research, beginning with paradigms or philosophies of social science, then narrowing to frameworks for qualitative research, and then narrowing even further to practical guidelines. Part I of this chapter looks at a few popular methods of research: ethnography, case study, interviewing, and historiography (Figure 7.1). These have been the most popular methods for qualitative research. Although the emphasis is on particular methods of research, keep in mind that the methodologies, frameworks, and paradigms these

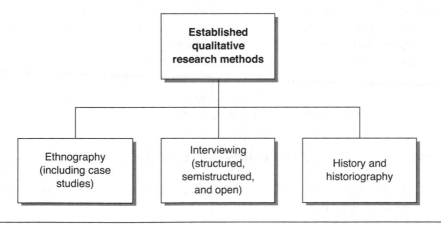

Figure 7.1 Established Research Methods Discussed in Part I of This Chapter

methods belong to must be understood if you are to understand when, how, and where a particular method is appropriate.

There are also some emerging research methods that are becoming more popular today. Part II of the chapter introduces some of these emerging research methods, especially participative and emancipatory methodologies. These were uncommon 20 years ago. However, as interpretive and critical approaches to social science have emerged as strong alternatives to postpositivism, the emphasis has shifted to research in the applied context and to involving people who once would have been the subjects of research more fully in the research process. In fact, the term *participants* or *collaborators* fits better than the word *subjects.*

Participatory research is research that, to some degree, involves the "subjects" in the design, execution, and analysis phases of the research. There are several forms of participatory research—PAR, for example, and participatory instructional design—but they all share the common element of involving those who are being studied or affected in the research process as colleagues and partners.

Emancipatory research developed from critical theory and is based on the assumption that research should lead to greater freedom and control on the part of the participants. An emancipatory researcher who studied the worker–management relationships in a large factory just across the Arizona border in Mexico might involve the workers in designing and carrying out the study. That would be participatory research. If the workers, as a result of the study, began to organize and fight some of the oppressive decisions and policies of management, the research would be emancipatory. The term *false consciousness* often is used to describe the oppressed groups' failure to understand the social and political beliefs and structures that oppress them. In fact, groups often actively maintain and nurture beliefs and practices that oppress them and support those in power over them. An intermediate outcome of emancipatory research is enlightenment and awareness. The oppressed group involved in the research develops an awareness of the oppression and an understanding of the effects of power relationships in their environment. When that understanding is used to overcome the oppression and develop a fairer and more equitable social structure, the process of making that change is called praxis.

Part I. Established Qualitative Research Methods

Part I looks at several traditional qualitative research methods. The first is ethnographic research.

Ethnography

Many of the methods that fall under the general term *observation* are at the core of what qualitative research is. Observational research

- Puts the researcher in the context that is of interest
- Requires the researcher to collect data or participate with others in data collection
- Involves the researcher in the analysis and interpretation of those data

Several types of observation are now used in the social sciences, but the approach originated in anthropology with a method called ethnography.

An Ethnographic Case (Herodotus, 5th Century B.C.E.)

Herodotus was a Greek historian who practiced what we might call today a rough form of ethnography. His book, *Histories,* is still studied and quoted today. Herodotus traveled to the Greek colonies on the northern Black Sea coast in the regions that are now part of Ukraine and Russia but that were then called Thracia and Scythia. The Greek colonies along the coast were trading posts that often purchased basic foodstuffs, such as fish and wheat, and furs from local peoples and shipped them to Greece. While Herodotus was in the Greek colonies he met with and studied the life and customs of the Scythians, who controlled the hinterland behind the Greek coastal cities. The history of the Scythians is important for several reasons. For example, they are one of the ancestors of Slavs such as the Poles, Russians, and Ukrainians. Through observation and interviews, and by living in Olbia, one of the Greek colonies where Scythians traded and interacted with the Greeks, Herodotus developed a detailed story of their culture and lifestyle. Ascherson (1995) repeats one of Herodotus's stories about a Scythian prince who became enamored with life in the Greek city colony. His name was Scyles.

> He became two people. Outside the city walls he was a steppe ruler who commanded a complex traditional [nomadic] society with its wagons and herds and rituals. But within the city walls he became a Greek. Scyles kept a Greek wife in Olbia, and on entering the gates would change his nomad dress for loose Hellenic robes. According to Herodotus, he built an elaborate palace in the town (although no such palace has been found: the private houses of Olbia, as opposed

to the huge municipal buildings and temples, are modest one-story structures without much decoration).

One day, a group of Scythians contrived to peer over the walls into Olbia at the time of the festival of Dionysian mysteries. There they saw Scyles dressed in the regalia of the Dionysian order, reeling through the streets at the head of the sacred procession. To them, or rather to Herodotus reconstructing their reactions, this sign meant that Scyles had crossed an uncrossable frontier: by consenting to become a Dionysian initiate, he had betrayed Scythian identity and become a Greek. When they brought the news home, Scyles' brother assumed power in his place, and Scyles took flight. . . . On the banks of the river, near Istria, Scyles was put to death by his own brother. (Ascherson, 1995, pp. 56–67)

Ascherson uses the *Histories* of Herodotus to explain the origins of the concept of barbarians, and he uses Herodotus's work to show that often the peoples the Greeks called barbarians were actually more "civilized" than the Greeks. Herodotus also tended to cater to Greek sensitivities and interests and to titillate readers with detailed descriptions of the manufacture of drinking cups from human skulls at Gelonus and with his stories of Amazon warriors on the steppe, whose roles in society were quite different from the roles of women in Greek society. Some of his descriptions of Scythian customs have interesting links to contemporary life. In one passage he describes Scythian burial customs that include the use of marijuana:

After the burial . . . they set up three poles leaning together to a point and cover them with woolen mats. . . . They make a pit in the center beneath the poles and throw red-hot stones into it . . . [they] take the seed of the hemp and creeping under the mats they throw it on the red-hot stones, and being thrown, it smolders and sends forth so much steam that no Greek vapour-bath could surpass it. The Scythians howl in their joy at the vapour-bath. (Herodotus, quoted in Ascherson, 1995, p. 79)

By today's standards the ethnographic work of Herodotus was very flawed. He often failed to distinguish between what he observed and what he was told first or second hand. And he includes in his *Histories* as fact what we know to be legends. However, despite his shortcomings the observations of Herodotus remain one of the major sources of knowledge about the times in which he lived.

Although some early psychologists used observation in their work, the field of cultural anthropology is the modern mother of this method. The research of an anthropologist studying a culture is generally called ethnography or cultural ethnography. Essentially it involves making observations (field notes) in an authentic or natural context. The approach began as a way to study other cultures, but it is now used to study everything from the social climate of an inner-city school classroom to the behavior of executives in a large corporation. One of the early ethnographic studies that became world famous is Margaret Mead's (1928) *Coming of Age in Samoa.* Mead traveled to Samoa and spent many months observing and interacting with Samoan children and adolescents. She used her field notes as the basis for her papers and her book. The conclusions she reported challenged many theories of child development, child rearing, and adolescent sexuality that were widely discussed in America. Her findings and conclusions were not accepted by everyone, however. See Freeman (1983) for a critical and detailed attack on both Mead's methods and conclusions.

Article of Interest

I. C. Jarvie. (2001). Freeman and Mead again.
***Philosophy of the Social Sciences, 31*(4), 557–562.**

Jarvie's article is a review of a second book Freeman wrote on Margaret Mead's research in Samoa and a critique of the research of both Freeman and Mead along with a discussion of the harsh and somewhat "unscholarly" criticism Freeman, who taught in Australia, received from American anthropologists. Jarvie comes down on the side of Freeman and concludes that Mead's conclusions are, at best, not confirmed. What do you think of Jarvie's hypothesis about why American anthropologists tried to reject Freeman's ideas? Does an ideology, whether it be positivist or any other, when deeply believed, blind us to evidence that contradicts fundamental tenets of the ideology?

To read the entire article, please go to http://www.sagepub.com/willis_aoi.

The term *ethnography* sometimes is used to mean the same thing as the term *fieldwork,* and sometimes it means all the qualitative methods used to learn about culture (including microcultures such as corporate or school environments). In this broad sense *ethnography* is an umbrella term for fieldwork, interviewing, and other means of gathering data in authentic (e.g., real-world) environments. In this book the terms *ethnography* and *fieldwork* are used as synonyms. At their core, both put the researcher in the settings that he or she wants to study. The research is conducted in the natural environment rather than in an artificially contrived setting.

Ethnography can involve the collection of quantitative as well as qualitative data, but this text concentrates on the qualitative options.

General Framework for Ethnographic Research

Fieldwork often follows a typical pattern. The researcher spends time in the environment and builds a relationship with the participants. As trust develops the participants act more naturally and are more candid when they discuss issues or make decisions while the researcher is watching.

The researcher keeps field notes that summarize what has happened during the observation periods. These are generally rich, or thick, descriptions of what is going on. There is quite a difference between thick and thin data from observations. A positivist researcher might observe in a community center for seniors and use an observation system that requires him or her to look around the room every 30 seconds and count the number of seniors who are engaged in socialization. The result of many hours of observation might then be summarized as a percentage. By contrast, an ethnographer observing at the same center might generate 10, 20, or more pages of notes each day.

Dr. Laura Tamakoshi (1996) has created a Web site on the Internet, "Fieldwork: The Anthropologist in the Field," that includes how-to guidelines that are quite useful. She divides the process of doing fieldwork into four phases:

1. Planning
2. Method
3. Writing
4. Reference

Dr. Tamakoshi then divides each of these phases into more detailed steps. For example, under *Method,* she explains several common tasks:

- Setting up
- Building rapport
- Dealing with culture shock
- Participation in the culture being studied
- Field methods

And finally, under *Field Methods* Dr. Tamakoshi, following Plattner (1989), suggests that an ethnographer should be able to do the following:

- Structured direct observation of events: time allocation analysis, interaction analysis
- Observation and recording of the physical environment, including how to read (and preferably how to draw) topographic and other maps and, as needed, such skills as remote sensing, soil analysis, and biomass transects
- Still photography and, increasingly, video recording
- Approaching informants, maintaining an interview situation, and disengaging from an interview in a manner that leaves open the possibility for further interviewing
- Designing and pretesting interview schedules
- Systematic interview techniques to determine the limits of a domain of study
- Data recording, coding, and retrieval skills, perhaps through a database management system
- Use of personal computers for word processing and data manipulation
- Developing a research design for the quantitative testing of a hypothesis
- Statistical processing of data and interpretation of statistical results

The last two of the items on this list suggest that the work will be done within a positivist paradigm, but even if we focus only on the other activities, it is obvious that this is not a trivial and easily accomplished task. That is true even if the environment we are studying is not another culture in some faraway place but instead a local neighborhood. For a detailed guide to doing ethnographic research, *The Handbook of Ethnography* (Atkinson, Coffey, Delamont, Lofland, & Lofland, 2001) is a valuable resource. A much shorter and more concise book is Alex Stewart's (1998) *The Ethnographer's Method.*

Ethnography is not so much a particular, well-defined method as a family of conceptual and methodological frameworks. There are postpositivist and interpretive versions of ethnology and critical ethnography. There is also ethnomethodology, which is an approach related to ethnography that emphasizes the meaning of discourse. It is based on semiotics (the study of signs and their meaning) and often uses a research technique called discourse analysis. Phenomenological research also has much in common with ethnography but places even more emphasis on communicating the participant's experiences. For example, a traveler's diary of a trip to another country could be written from a phenomenological perspective. Finally, there are many subject-specific forms of ethnography. These subspecialties include ethnoscience, ethnomusic, and ethnohistory.

Each of these subspecialties applies ethnographic methods to a particular subject matter.

Article of Interest

Steven Vanderstaay. (2005, August). One hundred dollars and a dead man: Ethical decision making in ethnographic fieldwork. *Journal of Contemporary Ethnography, 34*(4), 371–409.

The title of this article by Steven Vanderstaay, who teaches at Western Washington University, certainly catches your attention, as do the first two sentences: "In the course of ethnographic research, I inadvertently provided the funds a teenage cocaine dealer used to buy crack from his supplier. This may have begun a horrific sequence of events that included several drug deals, a murder, the arrest and imprisonment of my subject, and the ruin of his mother" (p. 371).

Vanderstaay's focus is on the ethics of ethnographic research, but in the process he also tells the story of his study of a young cocaine dealer. This article illustrates a number of elements of interpretive research. For example, the author tells us about his own background because that is part of the context you need in order to understand what he is saying. He also gives a thick description of Clay and Serena. Is it helpful to us to know Clay wore "a black Oakland Raiders jacket, loose clean jeans, and AirJordan basketball shoes" (p. 385) to his detention hearing? Is the comment Vanderstaay made in his journal after seeing Clay for the first time too much detail? Why did Vanderstaay make personal comments such as "Small, slight, and alcoholic, Serena reminded me of my own mother, who was successfully treated for alcoholism when I was a teenager" (p. 392)? Would this be relevant in a postpositivist study? Why? Why is it relevant in an interpretivist study?

Throughout this article the author points out ethical decisions he makes. There are two levels of those decisions: the rules he follows, such as "do not intervene," and the principles behind those rules. Do you agree with his rules? Do you agree with the underlying principles that are the foundation for them? Would you have used different rules? Different principles? Why?

To read the entire article, please go to http://www.sagepub.com/willis_aoi.

Case Studies: Another Form of Qualitative Observation

Another popular qualitative research method is the case study. A case study is "an examination of a specific phenomenon such as a program, an event, a person, a process, an institution, or a social group" (Merriam, 1988, p. 9). Case studies are

- *Particularistic.* They focus on a particular context such as one person, a family, an office, a company, a classroom, or an apartment building.

- *Naturalistic.* Case studies are about real people and situations, and much of the data collection occurs in real environments.

- *Thick descriptive data.* Sources of case study data include participant and nonparticipant observation, interviews, historical and narrative sources, writing such as journals and diaries, a variety of quantitative data sources including tests, and almost anything else you can imagine.

- *Inductive.* "For the most part, case studies rely on inductive reasoning. Generalizations, concepts, or hypotheses emerge from the examination of data—data grounded in the context itself. Occasionally one may have tentative working hypotheses at the outset of a case study, but these expectations are subject to reformulation as the study proceeds (Merriam, 1988, p. 13).

- *Heuristic.* "Case studies illuminate the reader's understanding of the phenomenon under study. They can bring about the discovery of new meaning, extend the reader's experience, or confirm what is known" (Merriam, 1988, p. 13).

The case study has been one of the most criticized and most used forms of social science research. In Campbell and Stanley's (1963) classic book on experimental research designs in the social sciences, the postpositivist perspective of the authors is quite clear: "Such studies [case studies] have such a total absence of control as to be of almost no scientific value" (p. 6). Campbell and Stanley are quite correct in their assessment if you accept the postpositivist assertion that the scientific method is the only valid and reliable source of knowledge. For Campbell and Stanley even the weakest form of real research, quasiexperimental, always involves "making at least one comparison" (p. 6). They go on to critique case studies as a way of conducting quasiexperimental research that involves comparisons. They assume that the data from a case study will be compared with "other events casually observed and remembered" (p. 6). (That is not an assumption many case study specialists would accept.) In the view of Campbell and Stanley, to be at all creditable a study must have hard data, not memories or casual observations, on at least two groups.

Whereas the postpositivists have little interest in case studies except as sources of ideas that lead to "real" research, both critical and interpretive researchers often use the case study method. For them it has several advantages:

- It allows you to gather rich, detailed data in an authentic setting.

- It is holistic and thus supports the idea that much of what we can know about human behavior is best understood as lived experience in the social context.

- Unlike experimental research, it can be done without predetermined hypotheses and goals.

All these advantages are pluses only if you accept a different purpose for research than the predict and control goals of postpositivism. Interpretivist researchers do not seek to find universals in their case studies. They seek, instead, a full, rich understanding (*verstehen*) of the context they are studying. Case studies are included here because ethnography and case studies are much more similar than dissimilar. However, their heritage is somewhat different. Ethnography comes from anthropology—which is still the discipline that uses this approach the most—whereas case study methodology comes from certain fields in economics, psychology, sociology, and political science. As you will see, there are subtle differences between ethnography, as described earlier, and case study research, but there are also a great many similarities.

General Framework of Case Studies

The term *case study* covers such a broad range of research methods that talking about a general framework is difficult. As Sharan Merriam (1990) puts it, "To some extent, case study has become a catchall category for studies that are not clearly experimental, survey, or historical. Further confusion stems from the fact that *case study* has been used interchangeably with *fieldwork, ethnography, participant observation, exploratory research* and *naturalistic research*."

With the term's diverse meanings, almost everything you can say about case study research has exceptions. That said, however, it may be convenient to think about case studies as involving overlapping phases. The phases are overlapping because you do not complete them in a sequence. Instead, the phases represent needs and issues that may be addressed across the entire research endeavor.

Deciding What to Study, and Where. How do you select a topic for study? There are many ways you can decide what to study. One researcher may do a case study on life in the inner city because he grew up there. Another may study the work setting of assembly line workers because in the critical paradigm he uses, a case study seems appropriate to make clear some of the problems of the work environment that are detrimental to workers. Still another may begin a study because there is an opportunity that she does not want to pass up. (Opportunity, including the availability of grant funds, is probably more often the reason for doing many types of research than is usually admitted.)

Regardless of the way you arrive at a topic of study, the result should be something you find very, very interesting. Case studies, like most qualitative methods, are time intensive and mind intensive. Qualitative studies generally take much longer to complete than quantitative studies, and the data collection and data analysis process is far more dependent on the researcher's thinking. In the middle of their research, many doctoral students completing a qualitative dissertation have yearned for a simple comparison of test scores from two or three groups of subjects. The effort needed to supervise the treatment and control conditions and then perform *t* tests or analysis of variance statistics on the test data is generally much less than that needed to do a qualitative case study on the same topic.

What Data Will You Collect? Case studies typically include multiple sources of data including observations, structured or nonstructured interviews, analyses of documents, historical data, and quantitative data. A case study researcher generally begins with an idea of what data will be gathered. Once the study has begun, however, the initial or tentative plans for data collection may change drastically. For example, if initial data from the case study suggest that historical research would be illuminative, that type of data may be added to the sources for the case study.

Gaining Entry and Maintaining Rapport. Case studies often involve putting yourself in the environment that is being studied. Entry sometimes can be difficult, and acceptance is almost always a problem. Arrogant, demanding researchers can run into major problems gaining entry and cooperation. Also, there are settings where the participants are suspicious of you and are disinclined to be honest and forthcoming. The process of gaining entry calls for an understanding of the context (e.g., who should be contacted for permission, who should be talked to as a courtesy), an ability to communicate your purposes concisely but clearly, and an attitude that tells gatekeepers you will not be a problem. Establishing and maintaining rapport calls for a friendly, flexible attitude and an ability to understand and empathize with participants and hear what they are telling you. These are not easy tasks, and they may be learned best through apprenticeships with experienced researchers. It would be difficult to learn these skills just by reading a book.

Data Collection, Data Analysis, and Writeup. These three activities often are treated as separate parts of the case study process. First you collect the data, then you do your data analysis, and then you write the paper. This clean, neat, linear presentation of how it is done does not reflect the reality of case study research. You do not collect data in some abstract, detached manner and then analyze it. You are analyzing as you gather data, and you are thinking about how to write it up. The bulk of data analysis generally comes after a significant amount of data has been gathered, but there are times when your data analysis suggests that additional interviews or observations should be made to clarify an issue. Therefore, these activities—data collection, data analysis, and writeup— are integrated. While you are focusing on one, you may be doing the others as well.

If you would like more information on case study methodology, see Jacques Hamel's (1993) short book titled *Case Study Method* or the second edition of Robert Yin's (2004) *Applications of Case Study Research*. A longer but particularly readable book is Robert Stake's (1994) *The Art of Case Study Research*. For more in-depth coverage of case study methodology see Yin's (2002) *Case Study Anthology* and Gomm, Hammersley, and Foster's (2000) *Case Study Method*.

Variations in Case Study Research

Thus far the discussion of case study research has looked at commonalities. Like *ethnography, case study* is a broad term, and others have defined several special types of case study (Bogdan & Biklen, 1992; Merriam, 1988):

• *Ethnographic case study.* This type of case study emphasizes sociocultural issues. "Concern with the cultural context is what sets this type of study apart from other qualitative research" (Merriam, 1988, p. 23).

• *Microethnographic case study.* Ethnographic case studies look at large social groups such as communities. Microethnographic studies look at much smaller units. They may study two children with attention deficit disorder in a fifth-grade classroom, for example.

• *Situational analysis.* Situational cases concentrate on a single event, such as the riots at the Democratic National Convention in Chicago or the development of a civilian police force in Kosovo.

• *Historical case study.* "This type of research employs techniques common to historiography—in particular the use of primary source material" (Merriam, 1988, p. 24). "Historical case studies may involve more than a chronological history of an event. . . . To understand an event and apply one's knowledge to present practice means knowing the context of the event, the assumptions behind it, and perhaps the event's impact on the institution and participants" (p. 24).

- *Historical organizational case studies.* "These studies concentrate on a particular organization over time, tracking the organization's development" (Bogdan & Biklen, 1992, p. 65).

- *Life history case study.* "The researcher conducts extensive interviews with one person for the purpose of collecting a first-person narrative. . . . When this type of interviewing is done by historians it is referred to as oral history. . . . Sociological or psychological first-person life histories collected through case study interviewing are usually directed at using the person as a vehicle to understand basic aspects of human behavior or existing institutions rather than history" (Bogdan & Biklen, 1992, p. 65).

- *Psychological, sociological, and educational case studies.* These case studies are characterized by the use of concepts and topics that are typical of a particular discipline. Psychological case studies generally look at individuals; sociological studies look at groups, their interrelationships, and patterns; and educational case studies focus on learning and educational contexts.

Of course, these categories can overlap. The categories are a convenient way of thinking about case studies, but few cases are actually instances of pure categories.

Another way of looking at case studies is based on the way the data will be used:

- *Descriptive case study.* These are called observational case studies by Bogdan and Biklen (1992), and the purpose of this type of research is to provide a rich, detailed description of the case. There is no effort to begin with a theory or to develop theory as the case progresses.

- *Interpretive case study.* Interpretive studies gather and analyze thick data sources, just as descriptive studies do. Interpretive studies go further, however. They use the descriptive data to "develop conceptual categories or to illustrate, support, or challenge theoretical assumptions held prior to the data gathering" (Merriam, 1988, p. 28). The focus is on understanding the intricacies of a particular situation, setting, organizations, culture, or individual, but that local understanding may be related to prevailing theories or models.

┌───┐

Article of Interest

Christine Benedichte Meyer. (2001, November).
A case in case study methodology. *Field Methods, 13*(4), 329–352.

Norwegian researcher Christine Meyer accomplishes two goals in this article. She offers a succinct but broad overview of what case study research is, and she takes us through the process of conducting one case study on corporate mergers and acquisitions in Norway. Do you agree with her assessment of the strengths of case studies in addressing "how" and "why" questions? Did you find the decisions she made about the design of her study reasonable? Would you have made different decisions? Why? What about her data analysis methods? Did the way she treated the data make you more or less confident of her conclusions? Why? Were you comfortable with her approach to whether she tries to be objective or accepts subjectivity as a matter of course? Meyer uses Mitchell's ideas on how the results of a qualitative study can be generalized. Do you agree with this approach to generalizability? Why?

To read the entire article, please go to http://www.sagepub.com/willis_aoi.

└───┘

Interview Research

Much of qualitative research involves forming questions and asking them. The result is often powerful stories that both inform and inspire. Take Glesne's (1997) interviews of Dona Juana, an 86-year-old Puerto Rican researcher and educator. Through five poetic transcriptions that provide varied portraits of Dona Juana, Glesne takes us on a warm journey of introspection and connection where we hear a "third voice that is neither the interviewee's nor the researcher's but is a combination of both" (p. 203). Another admirable piece is Bochner's (1997) questioning of himself, his divided self, which starts with the death of his father while he was attending a conference. Throughout his writing, Bochner confronts the divisions, gulfs, and dismemberment in our private and professional lives that we never question and presents a personal narrative that is poignant and insightful.

Glesne and Peshkin (1992) appropriately name their chapter on interviewing "Making Words Fly" and compare it to playing ball. However, the researcher is unlike the baseball pitcher, whose "joy derives from throwing balls that batters never touch" (p. 118). Instead, you "toss questions which you want your respondents to hit and hit well in every corner of your data park, if not clear out of it—a swatted home run of words" (p. 118). The world view within which you are conducting research plays a defining role in how you prepare for the interview, who you choose as interviewee, what questions you ask, how you structure the interview, and how you interpret the data.

One way of organizing your thinking about the different types of interviewing that are possible is to look at the degree to which they are structured. Much of the literature on interviewing is about how to conduct very structured interviews.

> There is a large and varied literature which collects strategies, recipes and advice on how to conduct interviews. Writers who put the research project in first position generally promote predesigned, standardized interview schedules, while those who stress a natural expression of the life world favor open or semi-structured interviews. In both, the interview itself is seen strategically, as a designable course of events (either pre-designed or locally steered), serving transcending purposes. But, whatever the strategy chosen, on the ideological or the practical level, some tensions between the three worlds—life world, interview situation and analytic framework—seem to remain. (Mazeland & ten Have, 1996)

Interviews may be highly structured, semistructured, or open. Structured interviews and surveys that ask participants to select answers to questions from a list of options are common tools for the postpositivist researcher. The idea is that if enough effort is invested in writing good interview or survey questions, the interview or survey should capture some of the reality of the situation. In fact, once the right combination of questions is in place, they can be used in the form of a mail survey, phone interview, or World Wide Web survey. It's all in the framing of questions. But interpretivists believe otherwise. They tend to prefer semistructured and so-called open or unstructured interviewing. As Mazeland and ten Have (1996) emphasize, the less structured approaches to interviewing always involve some tension or conflict between the three contexts of the interview: life world, interview situation, and analytic framework.

Unfortunately, most of our exposure to interviewing and surveying today involves answering questions put to us by hourly wage workers who ask about our preferences for politicians, bathroom cleanser, and deodorants (Stumpf, 1966).

> Understanding gang members or hoboes through interviews lost importance; what became relevant was the use of interviewing in

survey research as a tool to quantify data. This was not new; opinion polls and market research had been doing it for years. But during World War II there was a tremendous increase in survey research, as the U.S. armed forces hired great numbers of sociologists as survey researchers. More than half a million American soldiers were interviewed in one manner or another, . . . and their mental and emotional lives were reported in a four-volume survey, *Studies in Social Psychology in World War II*. The research for the first two volumes of this study, titled *The American Soldier,* was directed by Samuel Stouffer. This work had tremendous impact and led the way to a widespread use of systematic survey research. (Fontana & Frey, 1994, p. 362)

The following is a list of guidelines that were given to a group of interviewers during their training to conduct structured interviews. It is a valuable list that describes what interpretivist research is not. Simply delete the *nevers* and *don'ts* and you get the essence of interviewing in the interpretivist world.

- Never get involved in long explanations of the study; use the standard explanation provided by the supervisor.
- Never deviate from the study introduction, sequence of questions, or question wording.
- Never let another person interrupt the interview; do not let another person answer for the respondent or offer his or her opinions on the question.
- Never suggest an answer or agree or disagree with an answer. Do not give the respondent any idea of your personal views on the topic of the question or survey.
- Never interpret the meaning of a question; just repeat the question and give instructions or clarifications that are provided in training or by supervisors.
- Never improvise, such as by adding answer categories, or make wording changes. (Fontana & Frey, 1994, p. 364)

This basically defines a postpositivist approach to asking questions and getting answers. Instead of never doing those things, do all of the above, and you will be close to an interpretive approach to interviewing. That said, however, there are projects that entail the interviewing of an inordinate number of people, and this calls for trained interviewers. Depending on the data desired, the number of interviewers and interviewees, and the project budget, prudent, even cautious decisions must be made about how structured the interview should be.

Interviewing is so common and may seem so simple that it is easy to treat the method lightly. Collecting good interview data is actually difficult and takes practice and effort. If you would like more information about interviews in research, there are many books and articles on the process. However, different authors tend to take quite different, even contradictory, approaches to what should and should not be done. Herbert and Irene Rubin's (2004) book *Qualitative Interviewing: The Art of Hearing Data* is a very good introduction to open interviewing in the interpretive tradition. Gubrium and Holstein's (2003) *Postmodern Interviewing* is another source of guidance for interpretive and critical interviewing. For help on how to use interviewing, both semistructured and more tightly structured, to make inferences about the theory, see Wengraf's (2001) *Qualitative Research Interviewing: Biographic Narrative and Semi-Structured Methods.*

Historiography

Case 2: Racial Gerrymandering in Cincinnati

Patricia Leigh, a professor at Iowa State University, grew up in Cincinnati, Ohio. Dr. Leigh, an African American, had often wondered as a child why the schools in the area where she lived were so different from schools in other parts of the greater Cincinnati area. In general, whatever money bought, the schools in her area didn't have. To discover why there was such a disparity, Leigh (1997, 2004) looked at the history of that school district and the behavior of civic and business leaders in Cincinnati since the Civil War. She located many types of public records, checked newspaper accounts, read journals, found city plans, and interviewed people who knew some of the history of the area. What she discovered was decades of discrimination and abuse of public trust that had pushed Black citizens of Cincinnati into one area of the town. In that area a separate school district was created that served a predominantly Black population. However, the tax base was inadequate to support a decent school system.

She begins her case study with the creation of inferior school systems for Black students after the Civil War that emphasized trade or vocational education. These school systems generally operated fewer months a year than schools for Whites and received far less funding from White-dominated school boards. Leigh concluded that when the emphasis on learning a trade in poorly supported schools for Blacks was combined with highly prejudiced attitudes among most of the White leadership in

Cincinnati, the result was a job market in which most Blacks could find only low-paying jobs.

Using both primary and secondary sources of data, Leigh found that the situation was made worse in the early 20th century by

> the efforts of city planners to segregate the populations of their municipalities along racial lines. . . . With Blacks relegated to low-income communities, school boards were free to establish districts with minimal and substandard resources, accomplishing de facto segregation without the appearance of malice. (Leigh, 1997, p. 123)

Leigh's historical case study shows how decisions by city officials, bankers, civic betterment leagues, employers, and much of the White population led to the isolation of Blacks in Cincinnati in the late 1800s and early 1900s. The result was Lincoln Heights, a Black community. She then documents how decisions about the city limits of Lincoln Heights isolated this predominantly Black area from more prosperous White areas around it. To cite just one example, before 1950 students from Lincoln Heights could attend schools in surrounding White communities because the school district lines overlapped. In 1950 the county reorganized school districts. It created a predominantly White school district in the area, Woodlawn. When the lines were redrawn for that district and Lincoln Heights, Woodlawn had 17% of the students and 54% of the tax base to support the schools. Lincoln Heights had 83% of the students and only 48% of the tax base in the area. As a result, Woodlawn could spend $8,801 per pupil per year, whereas Lincoln Heights had $1,544 per pupil.

Leigh concludes her study with this comment:

> The hidden economic and political forces that gave rise to the school district serving Lincoln Heights' children actually determined the paths and patterns of their lives. In a nation where many espouse the virtues of rugged individualism and self-empowerment, it is important to expose those often overwhelming but hidden forces that are external to the individual and that oppose self-empowerment and agency. (Leigh, 1997, p. 134)

Dr. Leigh's historical research is one example of the type of work that can be done when there are questions about the past and its influence on today. In her conclusions, Dr. Leigh briefly discusses the question of whether the patterns of discrimination she found in her study had continued in the 1970s, 1980s, and 1990s, but her focus was on documenting what happened in Cincinnati from the Civil War to the 1960s. The next case study is quite different. It emphasizes the present and uses the past to help us understand and interpret the present and the future.

Case 3: Black Participation in South African Policymaking

Dr. Sipho Seepe is a professor at the University of Venda in South Africa. He grew up during the apartheid era in South Africa and lived in Soweto, the best known of the Black townships where South Africa's Black citizens were segregated. There was great hope when Nelson Mandela was elected president of South Africa in the first election open to all citizens. However, Seepe and many others became concerned that, even with the election of Mr. Mandela, the pace of change in South Africa has not been very fast. He believes one of the reasons is the lack of participation in policy discussions by the Black intelligentsia. A portion of his article (Seepe, 1998) is reproduced here. He begins with a discussion of comments made by then–Deputy President Thabo Mbeki (the person who became president after Mr. Mandela):

> Deputy President Thabo Mbeki decried the fact that the black intelligentsia is conspicuous by its absence in public forums and policy debates in this country. . . .
>
> Having decried the paucity of black intellectuals, Mbeki went further to suggest that the few intellectuals who are prominent, those promoted by the media, "are an acute embarrassment" to the black majority.
>
> These sweeping and unfortunate remarks do not augur well for the African renaissance, precisely because they stigmatize every black intellectual who dares to question the dominant paradigms and discursive practices in this country.
>
> An African renaissance, or any renaissance for that matter, requires an environment that encourages a flourishing of ideas. It requires an environment that promotes robust and vibrant intellectual engagements.
>
> It requires the pitting of ideas in the marketplace, so that the best ideas may win the day. It also requires tolerance of ideas, even the ideas we strongly disagree with.
>
> It is therefore unfortunate that Mbeki—a man credited for championing, reformulating and reintroducing the African renaissance—could be seen as joining those bent on stifling intellectual discourse in this country.

Let me make this quite clear, we need to distinguish labeling and stigmatizing people's ideas from the process of engaging and challenging ideas with which we differ. Robust engagement demands us to rigorously expose the limitations, or bankruptcy, of such ideas.

Simply labeling them does not advance our arguments, it closes a discussion and introduces a culture where might, power and privilege determine right. (p. 3)

Seepe then discusses in some detail whether the views of leaders who were forced into exile or jailed by the apartheid regime deserve any higher status than the views of those who were not. He is particularly concerned that the leaders of Mr. Mandela's party, the African National Congress, do not accept as worthy of consideration the views of other leaders outside their party.

What makes some voices more authentic than others? How are we to interpret "peacetime revolutionary," a label often thrown at Africans who hold different opinions to the dominant ones? More importantly, how do we define and prescribe "acceptable" black intellectual activity?

Divergent Opinions

Unless these questions are addressed and space is created for divergent opinions, we risk saturating the country with praise singers and zombies, not critical thinkers.

It is probably pertinent at this point to extend a dialogue on the role and challenges of black intellectuals. Simply put, intellectuals are individuals who are fascinated by ideas, and are in the habit of toying and engaging with ideas. . . .

Briefly, the role of intellectuals is to critique and define social problems, and to suggest solutions to these problems. . . .

Anticipating criticism from those who correctly argue that intellectual activities are ideologically grounded, Mosala comments further (. . . quoting Said).

He said the intellectual's consciousness is "a spirit in opposition, rather than accommodation, that grips me because the romance, the interest, the challenge of intellectual life is to be found in dissent against the status quo at a time when the struggle on behalf of under-represented and disadvantaged groups seems so unfairly weighted against them." . . .

Because of their shared history and experience of oppression and racism, black intellectuals have an added responsibility to come with a black agenda that would contribute to the development of black people.

The agenda should of necessity address poverty, illiteracy, economic underdevelopment and intellectual dependence— challenges derived from a legacy of oppression and colonialism.

This agenda would of necessity involve an interrogation of the hegemonic practices in our public and private institutions. As could be expected, this engagement would be contested and challenged by those who have benefited from the oppression of the majority in this country. . . .

African intellectuals, academics and professionals should feel challenged and move from the sidelines, and assume centre stage in the public debates and forums.

They need to ensure that the objectives informed by this reawakening are not hijacked, commercialized and compromised. (p. 3)[1]

These two examples of historical research have several things in common. Both take a critical perspective. Both are also concerned with the history of Black oppression. However, these two articles are also very different. Dr. Leigh takes a traditional approach to historical case study research. She tells her story through a narrative that begins with the Civil War and ends in the 1960s. She makes her points and supports them with both primary and secondary citations. The result is an article that can be understood even if you do not know the history of Black oppression in America. Dr. Seepe's article deals with a contemporary issue in South Africa's postapartheid society. He does not cite many sources for his conclusions, but the article is steeped in the history of South Africa. The better readers understand the last two hundred years of South African history, the better they will understand Seepe's perspective and viewpoint.

As the two cases show, historical research is quite diverse. It can be anything from an article on the history of a particular school district to a psychological analysis of a major leader in a social movement. Gall, Borg, and Gall (1996) define historical research as "a process of systematically searching for data to answer questions about a past phenomenon for the purpose of gaining a better understanding of present institutions, practices, trends, and issues" (p. 644). Although the term *systematic* may not apply to all forms of historical research—much of it involves hard work and effort that progresses in a more nonlinear than linear fashion—this definition captures much of the essence of historical research.

Historical Research and Paradigms

Gall et al. (1996) give several reasons why historical research is similar to other forms of qualitative research:

- It emphasizes context.
- It looks at behavior in natural rather than artificial or laboratory settings.
- It is more holistic than atomistic.
- Interpretation is critical; the meaning of the data is not obvious.

With those characteristics you would think that historical research would fit nicely into the interpretive and critical paradigms. However, Gall et al. (1996) think that "historical research tends to be postpositivist rather than purely interpretivist. That is, historians acknowledge fallibility and bias in human observation, but nonetheless believe that it is possible through careful analysis and multiple sources of evidence to discover what 'really' happened during a given time period with respect to the phenomenon being investigated" (p. 644). Before the 20th century an even more rigorous and narrow version of objectivism dominated historical research. History generally involved the study of great events (especially diplomatic and political events) and great men (as opposed to great women or ordinary people). The result of historical research was generally "facts." When historians disagreed—for example, German historians and French historians— the disagreement was generally considered to be over facts rather than interpretations.

An alternative way of thinking about history emerged in France, in part because of the work of Marc Bloch and Lucien Febvre. Bloch was one of the first to point out that written documents from a particular period of history were not primary sources that reflected fact. They were, instead, secondary sources that reflected the authors' subjective impression of events (or expressions of the public stance on an issue). Bloch also studied topics, such as life in rural France, that had not been considered appropriate topics before his pioneering work. Bloch and Febvre founded the journal *Annales d'Histoire Economic et Social* in 1929 and helped link history to other social sciences.

It is ironic that Bloch, who pushed history away from the idea of treating one interpretation of history as *the* interpretation, died because of a movement that took the opposite view. After Nazi Germany conquered France and took over the political machinery of northern France, the anti-Semitic laws that were passed forced Bloch to leave his professorship at the

University of Paris. As persecution of Jews and others increased in France under Nazi rule, he joined the resistance movement. He was captured by the Germans in 1944 and shot by a firing squad.

The ideas of Bloch and others who advocate a more interpretive approach are not without competition today. Gall and his colleagues may be correct that much of historical research today is still in a postpositivist tradition. However, there are also many instances of research from interpretive and critical frameworks (Iggers, 1997). For example, the two articles at the beginning of this section were based on a critical paradigm (or "new historicism") rather than a postpositivist paradigm.

The role postpositivism and positivism have played in historical research is still a topic of debate in the field. In his book *That Noble Dream: The "Objectivity Question" and the American Historical Profession,* Peter Novick (1988) traces the role of objectivity (positivism) in American historical research. He believes American historians adopted the objectivist approach of German history, in which the purpose of history was to discover *wie es eigentlich gewesen* ("the way it really was"). Although the objective approach to historical research dominated much of the 20th century, Novick points out that by the early 1900s some historians had questioned our ability to find objective historical facts. Between the two world wars he believes American historians embraced an interpretive approach that acknowledged multiple perspectives and the subjective nature of historical interpretation. However, World War II and then the perceived threat of Communism in the 1950s bolstered the objectivist approach. Today, according to Novick, interpretivists (he uses the term *relativists*) and objectivists have split the field so badly that students completing graduate programs in history do not have much of a common core when they are trained by members of different theoretical camps.

Many qualitative researchers are more sympathetic to the interpretive and critical approaches to history. Historical researchers have increasingly acknowledged that there are multiple perspectives on most issues. Instead of trying to find a single "truth," many papers and monographs seek to represent the perspectives of different groups. For example, the winter 1998 issue of the journal *Configurations* contains a number of articles about Thomas Kuhn and his influence on the philosophy of science. Taken together these articles present multiple perspectives on both what science is and the history of scientific thought. For interpretive historians, doing research involves constructing history as much as discovering it. This idea, which has been encouraged and reinforced in history by a number of postmodern movements in the humanities, is not universally accepted. Despite its sensationalist subtitle, Keith Windschuttle's (1997) book *The*

Killing of History: How a Discipline Is Being Murdered by Literary Critics and Social Theorists is a thoughtful but aggressive critique of the basic positions taken in this book. The strong emotion attached to the issue of what history is and how we can think about it is also illustrated in Victor Hanson's (1997) review of Windschuttle's book:

> Out here in the heartland (I live and teach in Fresno, Calif.), the feuds of theorists and traditionalists over academic turf are of little interest to our students, who desperately wish to learn first something of culture, any culture, before they are taught how to tear it down.
>
> We care little whether Mr. Derrida got his honorary degree at Cambridge, or who does and does not get invited to the Princeton Institute. When on rare occasions I am asked about post modernism by a few of my history students, it is usually from the very practical angle of, "Who are these people and why do they write these silly things?" I answer not to worry, that these are just parlor games of the desk-bound class. After all, the majority of unworldly theorists are patently worldly in that most left-wing literary critics like Frederick Jameson and Stanley Fish or meta historians like Hayden White, despite their nihilism, demand high salaries and do little undergraduate teaching in the here and now. In short, they live lives quite different from those of students at Fresno State. . . .
>
> How much easier, Windschuttle reminds us, it is to write opaquely than clearly, how much less work there is in dismissing positivist historians than in actually reading them—suggesting that much of theory's appeal among the young is in its sheer laxity.
>
> And there are more heads to the hydra of theory. For relativists, who profess no belief in absolute values or humanism, Windschuttle shows that there is an awful lot of hand-wringing about Western exploitation—hand-wringing that exemplifies timeless and universal notions about human decency.
>
> We need more Keith Windschuttles, hundreds more of them. In the field of classics, if it were not for the two recent volumes of refutation by Mary Lefkowitz, we would still be subject to the untruth of Martin Bernal and his glitzy pseudo-history of an African-Asiatic origin of Greek culture. If it were not for the systematic demolition of the "liar's school of Herodotus" by W. K. Pritchett—hard at work in his 80s—we would still be reading that the history of the Persian Wars is but a fictive discourse without any historical substance.

The shoots of untruth and false knowledge sprout forth in ever more disturbing shapes each season, but they always must be identified and cut back. This endless and often tedious work, like pruning vines, is no fun, but the alternative is a rank and savage wild.[2]

Nihilism

This is an extreme form of skepticism based on the idea that we cannot know anything and that all our beliefs and values are without foundation. This skepticism erodes belief in the progress of society and encourages a tendency to prefer destructive rather than constructive actions. However, for the pure nihilist any purpose, any reason for living, is futile and worthless. The term is rarely used by someone to characterize his or her own beliefs. Instead, it is typically used by critics of a particular philosophical, social, or political view that includes skepticism about foundational beliefs. German philosopher Nietzsche argues that nihilistic views would destroy the moral and religious foundations of society and precipitate a major crisis because of the despair and loss of will it inspired. In the 1800s the term was applied to a group of Russian anarchists who rejected the authority of both the Orthodox church and the tzarist regime.

In the 20th century the term *nihilism* often was used to describe the situation in which established foundations (e.g., religion, political systems) for beliefs have been swept away and replaced by skepticism. In the first half of the 20th century critics often considered the subjectivity and relativism of nihilism as potential sources of the destruction of society. However, by the end of the century much of the discussion about nihilism was less apocalyptic. For example, in his book *Shows About Nothing: Nihilism in Popular Culture From* The Exorcist *to* Seinfeld, Thomas Hibbs (2000) traces the influence of nihilism in movies and other popular culture through chapters with titles such as "The Revenge of a Dark God," "The Recovery of Film Noir," "The Romantic Revival and the Banality of Goodness," and "America as Semiotic Hell." And in their book *Laughing at Nothing,* Marmysz and Marmysz (2003) show us how the anxiety and despair of modern nihilism can lead us to humor and activity.

As Peter Novick (1988) points out, there is not one type of history research; there are many. History has been a subject of study in itself for centuries, but today there are many specialized forms of history research. In addition to specialty areas such as the history of science and the history of medicine, there are thriving groups of researchers who do research from a particular ideological perspective. Feminist history is just one of many specialties that concentrate on a particular topic and use a particular paradigm.

Newton's (1988) three basic principles of a feminist critical history (new historicism) are summarized on Barbara McManus's Web site (http://www.cnr.edu/home/bmcmanus) at the College of New Rochelle. The quotations in this list are from Newton's original 1988 paper:

- "That there is no trans historical or universal human essence and that human subjectivity is constructed by cultural codes which position and limit all of us in various and divided ways" (p. 88). Instead of the autonomous "self" or "individual," these critics speak of topics, ideas and people that are socially and linguistically constructed, created by various discourses of a given culture. Feminist critical historians were influenced by the work of the French theorist Michel Foucault, who focused upon the intricately structured power relations in a given culture at a given time to demonstrate how that society controls its members through constructing and defining what appear to be "universal" and "natural" truths. These critics are skeptical toward any "universalizing" or "totalizing" claims, focusing rather on the specificities of a particular historical and cultural context.

- "That there is no 'objectivity,' that we experience the 'world' in language, and that all our representations of the world, our readings of texts and of the past, are informed by our own historical position, by the values and politics that are rooted in them" (p. 88). Feminist critical historians emphasize the necessity for self-awareness on the part of the critic, who must be constantly aware of the difficulties of seeing the past except through the lenses and cultural constructs of the present.

- "That representation 'makes things happen' by 'shaping human consciousness' and that, as forces acting in history, various forms of representation ought to be read in relation to each other and in relation to non-discursive 'texts' like 'events'" (pp. 88–89). In the process of creating thick, rich descriptions, they link literary works with many other cultural phenomena of a period, including the discourse of "popular culture" and of areas like economics, law, medicine, politics, etc.

The approach, called new historicism, shares these three assumptions with what is often called cultural studies, but cultural critics are even more likely to emphasize the present implications of their study and to position themselves in opposition to current power structures. They often work to empower traditionally disadvantaged groups. Cultural critics also downplay the distinction between "high" and "low" culture and often focus particularly on popular culture.

Newton's position on what history is from a critical feminist perspective is an example of the thinking of one subgroup within the broad field of historical research. There are many other groups, and quite a few have adopted a form of critical theory as a foundation.

However, other subgroups base their work on an interpretive paradigm. For example, Steven Harris (1998) discusses current issues in the subfield generally known as the history of science. According to Harris, that discipline is in the middle of a major debate about the foundations on which historical research is based. There are two sides in this debate:

> On the one hand, we find a powerful alliance of historians, philosophers, and sociologists of science—as well as most practicing scientists—who share a more or less consistent set of philosophical assumptions regarding the nature of modern sciences. [They take a positivist perspective that is] characterized by commitments to realism, rationality, objectivity, and method and the ability of science to generate a cumulative, progressive body of knowledge. (p. 131)

On the other side of the debate are what Harris calls social constructivists. This group rejects the idea of a grand narrative of science that is universal. Instead, they emphasize research about specific contexts

> because of a general commitment to an epistemology of situated or embedded knowledge and what might be called a "localist hermeneutic." In an interpretive strategy that seems equally indebted to Clifford Geertz and Tip O'Neill, constructivists maintain that if all knowledge is local and all politics is local, then scientific knowledge—like legislation—is drafted, negotiated, and ratified in the immediate, face-to-face sociopolitical world of the laboratory. (p. 132)

In biting prose Harris shows just how opposed these two paradigms are to each other:

> If positivists invoke the trans- or ahistorical categories of reason, objectivity, method, and nature in their rational reconstruction of scientific progress, then constructivists deem any such appeals to transcendent categories as extra historical and illegitimate: scientific knowledge resides not "out there" in transcendent or disembodied ideas, but "down here" in mundane, socially embedded practices. If positivists seek to remove the subjective, social, and political elements to the margins of their favorite genre (method and discovery stories), then constructivists dismiss method stories as fundamentally circular and Whiggish and strive to reposition the subjective

and sociopolitical at center stage—and, indeed, to make objectivity, rationality, and facticity themselves into artifacts of social relations and moral economies. If positivists have expended prodigious amounts of energy maintaining the divide separating science from other forms of human activity, constructivists eagerly seek to erode such demarcation and delight in accentuating its mundane existence. Where positivists insist that nature (when properly interrogated by experiment or observation) settles all scientific disputes, constructivists are reluctant to give nature a speaking role at all—let alone an independent voice, since the "language of nature" is nothing more than the mundane, human, and rhetorical language of social discourse. In short, while positivism celebrates the universality of nature, science, reason, and method, constructivism insists upon their particularity. (p. 135)

Transcendent Categories

A transcendent category is one that is understood widely or universally and treated as a permanent entity. For example, if *self* refers to something every person has, and perhaps it is even God-given, then it is transcendent. On the other hand, if the term *self* refers to a socially constructed concept that has meaning in some cultures but not others, it is not transcendent. Similarly if you see terms such as *race, ethnicity,* and *gender* as referring to characteristics that are standard across situations and cultures, you are using the terms transcendently. You are not if you see their meaning as defined significantly by the cultural context in which they are used.

Whiggish

The term derives from British politics in the 17th through the 19th centuries. Whigs tended to favor liberal reforms, whereas the Tories supported the established structure of society, including the church and the then current political format. For example, Whigs supported giving the vote to more citizens. Whigs also tended to favor Protestantism and opposed giving the crown to James because he was a Catholic. Some Whigs did not like the term and adopted the term *Liberal* instead. The first British prime minister who officially called himself a liberal was William Gladstone in 1868, but the Liberal Party was essentially the Whigs with a new name. Thus to be Whiggish is to look at the world from liberal, progressive perspective that tends to favor reform, even revolution, and to advocate greater representation in government over absolute rights of either a monarch or a religion. The term was also used during the American Revolution to signify someone who favored revolution and was against the rule of England. Later, several members of the Whig Party became president, including William Henry Harrison and the last Whig president, Millard Fillmore.

The original meaning of the term *Whig* has evolved into a more specific and more negative meaning over the 20th century. It is usually applied to someone who is looking at history. A "Whig approach to history" means the person is interpreting historical events so that they support and validate the liberal, progressive approach, or any contemporary approach the writer considers desirable. For example, a Whig approach to Greek history might treat the democracies of the Greek city states (polis) as if they were modern capitalist Western democracies, ignoring the many differences between Greek and Western systems that share the name. The term *Whig* is now a term of derision in some quarters and is applied to scholars when the critic believes they have overinterpreted the past in ways that support their favored modern position (whether it be Western democracy, the scientific method, or something else).

For a thoughtful and thorough overview of the influence of postmodern movements in literature and the impact of multiculturalism and feminism on history, see Berkhofer (1997). Strong critical and interpretive influences came to history a bit later than they did to the humanities and some of the other social sciences. Today, however, these movements have had enough influence to inspire strong and spirited responses (Zagorin, 1999). One of the better books on alternative ways of thinking and doing historical research is *The Postmodern History Reader,* edited by Keith Jenkins (1997).

Historiography: The Research Methods of History

Historical research uses some of the methods that have already been discussed, such as interviews, but it also has its own set of methods and procedures. All the methods of the history researcher are called *historiography,* and there are a number of good books on this type of research. For example, Martha Howell and Walter Prevenier's (2001) book *From Reliable Sources: An Introduction to Historical Methods* is a good overview of the entire process that presents both postpositivist and interpretive frameworks for doing historical research. If you would like an introduction to several forms of history, from postpositivist to Marxist, Freudian, and ethnohistory, Anna Green and Kathleen Troup's (1999) book *The Houses of History: A Critical Reader in Twentieth-Century History and Theory* is a good place to start. Another interesting book that presents a range of methods, grouped under the term *new history,* was edited by Cambridge professor Peter Burke (2001). *New Perspectives on Historical Writing* introduces a number of approaches to historical research that have in common a rejection of the traditional objective stance of historical research and an acceptance of a more subjective, relativistic approach. Finally, another appealing book on historical research is Georg Iggers's (1997) *Historiography in the Twentieth Century: From Scientific Objectivity to Postmodern Challenge.* Iggers traces the development of historical research from its beginnings to the contemporary period and explains the shift from a positivist framework to critical and interpretive approaches.

Article of Interest

Madeline H. Caviness. (2003, August). Iconoclasm and iconophobia: Four historical case studies. *Diogenes, 50,* 99–114.

Caviness, an art history professor at Tufts University, was interested in iconoclasm (literally, "breaking of icons") and iconophobia (the fear of icons). The term *iconoclasm* is often traced back to a conflict in the Byzantine Empire over whether there should be icons in Christian churches. Caviness wanted to understand better the ways iconoclasm and iconophobia develop and are expressed. She created four case studies. One dealt with the attack on the Templars in the 14th century and the Lollards because they were "desecrating" the Christian symbol, the crucifix. Another was about the odd application of Reformation iconoclasm by Puritans in the New World, and a third focused on the use of iconoclasm in the French Revolution, when the king and queen were icons that were first destroyed as icons and then physically destroyed. The fourth case study was about the heads of kings that were broken off statues at Notre Dame Cathedral during the French Revolution and then discovered in a mass "grave" in 1977. As you read this article, what do you see Caviness doing? Telling a story? Making points by selectively highlighting certain events in history? Building a theory? Advocating a policy? Something else?

To read the entire article, please go to http://www.sagepub.com/willis_aoi.

Part II. Innovative Methods: Participatory Qualitative Research

Forms of qualitative research such as ethnography, interviews, case studies, and historical research are all very well established. However, other methods are less established (Figure 7.2). One group of these emerging research methods is participatory research. Participatory research reflects a shift from the perspective that the researcher knows best to one in which the researcher is part of a team that, collectively, can accomplish much more when each person is a full participant instead of either an object of study or a researcher. This shift from expert–object to expert–expert is reflected in a number of qualitative approaches to research, including action research and constructivist instructional design. Participant observation, which was discussed earlier, might be called a weak form of participatory research because the researcher still takes an expert role.

> The hallmark of participant observation is interaction among the researcher and the participants. The main subjects take part in the study to varying degrees, but the researcher interacts with them continually. For instance, the study may involve periodic interviews interspersed with observations so that the researcher can question the subjects and verify perceptions and patterns. (Savenye & Robinson, 1997, p. 1177)

In participant observation as generally practiced, the researcher tends to draw the conclusions and then seek verification from the participants. The same is true of much of the current generation of action research, which focuses on solving a practical problem in a real-world context. The researcher is the expert, and the participating teachers (in school-based action research) tend to play less central roles. This form of action research is still participatory, though a very weak form, because there is some sharing of the responsibility for the conclusions.

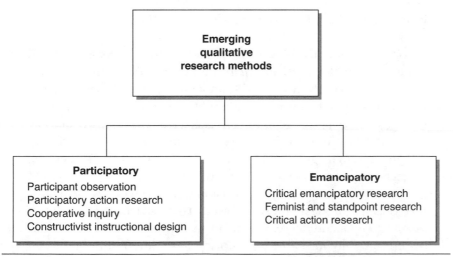

Figure 7.2   Emerging Qualitative Research Methods Covered in Part II of This Chapter

┌───┐
│ **Article of Interest**

Randy Stoecker. (1999, February). Are academics irrelevant? Roles for scholars in participatory research. *American Behavioral Scientist, 42,* 840–854.

Stoecker, who teaches at the University of Toledo, introduces the concept of participatory research and traces the history of its development. He views participatory research (PR) as democratizing the research process. He tends to view PR through the lens of critical theory, and he worries about the useful roles academics can play in PR. He takes the critical theory perspective that a very important goal of PR is to produce knowledge that helps oppressed groups throw off oppression. And because academics often have been part of the elitist groups that dominated, he questions how academics fit into PR. He proposes several potential roles for academics. What do you think of the roles he proposes for academics? Do they make sense from a critical perspective? From an interpretive perspective? Postpositivist?

　　To read the entire article, please go to http://www.sagepub.com/willis_aoi.
└───┘

Although many forms of action research are somewhat participatory, another research method, cooperative inquiry (Heron, 1996), is an example of an even stronger form of participatory research.

Cooperative Inquiry

Heron (1996) describes cooperative inquiry this way:

Co-operative inquiry is a form of participative, person-centered inquiry which does research *with* people not *on* them or *about* them. It breaks down the old paradigm separation between the roles of researcher and subject. In traditional research in the human sciences these roles are mutually exclusive: the researcher only contributes the thinking that goes into the project—conceiving it, designing it, managing it and drawing knowledge from it—and the subjects only contribute the action to be studied.

　　In co-operative inquiry this division is replaced by a participative relationship among all those involved. This participation can be of different kinds and degrees. In its most complete form, the inquirers engage fully in both roles, moving in cycling fashion between phases of reflection as co-researchers and of action as co-subjects. In this way they use reflection and action to refine and deepen each other. They also adopt various other procedures to enhance the validity of the process and its outcomes. (p. 19)

Heron's (1996) book is a detailed introduction to the conduct of research from a participatory or cooperative perspective. He summarizes cooperative inquiry as follows:

- It involves two or more people researching a topic through their own experience of it.
- It consists of a series of cycles in which participants move between this experience and reflect together on it.
- Each participant is a co-subject in the experience phases and a co-researcher in the reflection phases.

The fundamental goal of cooperative inquiry is to develop self-directing capacity (Heron, 1996, p. 3). That is a local or individualistic goal, as opposed to developing generalizations and laws of human behavior. According to Heron, it is best achieved by interactions that involve *fully reciprocal human relationships* in which we learn and change by democratically interacting with others.

As noted earlier, participatory qualitative research involves the researcher and other stakeholders in a collaborative process. This is an active and growing area of social science research, and the methods in this area can be divided somewhat arbitrarily into three groups: PAR, cooperative inquiry, which has already been discussed, and constructivist instructional design.

Article of Interest

Peter Reason. (1999). Integrating action and reflection through co-operative inquiry. *Management Learning, 30,* **207–226.**

Bath University's Peter Reason is a leading light in the development of cooperative inquiry. In this article he provides a comprehensive introduction to the approach, including the underlying assumptions. Are some aspects of the paradigm he proposes particularly appealing to you? Why? Are there aspects that you reject? Why? What about the research method itself? Is it really research? Or is it just good professional practice? Why? Can you think of a topic, question, or problem in your field of interest that would be appropriate to cooperative inquiry research? What makes it appropriate? Can you think of something that would not be appropriate? What makes it inappropriate?

To read the entire article, please go to http://www.sagepub.com/willis_aoi.

Participatory Action Research

Cooperative inquiry focuses on particularistic and "local" issues, but the researcher may also be interested in developing theories and models that are of interest in other contexts. This postpositivist tint is less apparent in another participatory approach, action research.

All forms of action research have an emphasis on real-world problems. It is most often used in education, international development, and health care to address professional practice problems. Participatory Action Research (PAR) is the result of several trends, some of them new and others much older. For much of the 20th century the positivist and post-positivist paradigms emphasized the technical qualities of research. Hundreds of thousands of studies were published that met technical criteria such as random assignment to groups and tight control of the research environment. Unfortunately, meeting the technical criteria for a "good" study often meant the research had to be done in artificially controlled environments. Often, the research was done on a different species, such as rats and pigeons, and the results generalized to humans.

In the last quarter of the 20th century there was a strong reaction against the out-of-context, out-of-species research model. Many argued that it is more important to study complex phenomena in their natural settings, even if it means there is not total control, than to create special, artificial environments where control can be maintained. Much of the push for looking at phenomena in context comes from the interpretive and critical theories that emphasize meaning in context.

This push for meaning in context was one of the factors that contributed to action research. Some attribute the rise of interest in action research to the theories of Kurt Lewin (Kemmis & McTaggart, 1988). Lewin was a Gestalt psychologist who emphasized the need to understand the context instead of concentrating on a single element in a social situation. Masters (1995) lists a number of other theorists who contributed to this approach but credits Lewin with creating a theory of action research that includes

- A spiral approach that proceeds through a series of steps that include planning, action, evaluation of the action, and then another cycle through the process

- The inclusion of practitioners in the process of designing and conducting research because they will be the ones who implement any changes that are suggested by the research

Gestalt Psychology

This movement in psychology came into prominence in the first half of the 20th century. It was founded by German psychologists, including Max Wertheimer, Kurt Koffka, and Wolfgang Kohler. A major idea of Gestaltists was that you lose something if you break things down into component parts. They argued that there is meaning in the whole that is lost when the whole is destroyed. Some trace the beginning of Gestalt psychology to a train trip Wertheimer took from Vienna. He was going to the Rhineland for a vacation. However, as he looked out the window of the train he noticed that the telephone poles along the track did not always look the same. Sometimes they appeared to be moving, and sometimes they even looked as if they were bending. Wertheimer named the phenomenon he observed *apparent motion* and got off the train in Frankfurt instead of going on vacation. At the University of Frankfurt he met Kurt Koffka and Wolfgang Kohler and told them about his ideas. Gestalt psychology grew out of that meeting and is still a potent force in the social sciences. The Gestaltists approached perception as a psychological rather than a simple physical process, and they developed a number of rules for human perception that explained figure-ground phenomena and how objects are perceived as groups (e.g., the law of proximity). These ideas were also applied to areas such as problem solving. For example, Gestalt psychologists argued that rote learning and learning a sequence of steps that would be followed precisely to solve a problem were both undesirable. They argued instead that creative problems should be presented and solved holistically.

Postpositivist Action Research

Lewin's two assumptions are a foundation for postpositivist action research. Postpositivist action research is technical in nature; it seeks a correct answer to a practical problem, and the researchers assume the solution is best found by studying the problem in the real world. In a typical study researchers from a university would enter a setting such as a public housing project or a school and seek input from the practitioners there as they developed a research idea.

> The underlying goal of the researcher in this approach is to test a particular intervention based on a pre-specified theoretical framework. The nature of the collaboration between the researcher and the practitioner is technical and facilitatory. The researcher identifies the problem and a specific intervention, then the practitioner is

involved and they agree to facilitate the implementation of the intervention. (Masters, 1995)

This type of action research is solidly within the standard postpositivist social science research tradition. For example, there is a clear distinction between the researcher and other "junior" members of the team.

Much of the standard scientific method, including the reasons for doing research, are preserved. The researcher still has a special status. The primary differences between this and mainstream postpositivist research is that

- Researchers give up some control in order to do the research in the natural environment.

- Practitioners from the natural environment have an opportunity to participate in the study under the direction of the researcher.

- There is a focus on a technical solution for practical problems rather than on a search for broad, universal truths.

Even these concessions are sometimes called into question by action researchers who still accept the postpositivist paradigm. Kock, McQueen, and Scott (1997) summarize criticisms of action research (AR):

- *Research findings are local;* you can't generalize from the settings where the study occurred to other contexts.

- *The experimental setting is not well controlled.* "This lack of control is one of the main reasons for AR being seen as inappropriate to test or produce strong theories, or build up research models based on solid evidence."

- *Personal overinvolvement may hinder research.* "The usual personal over-involvement of researchers with client organisations in AR projects may hinder good research by introducing personal biases in the conclusions."

Kock and his colleagues enumerate a number of other weaknesses of action research, such as the "unplanned and informal structure" and the time it takes to do a typical study. To deal with these weaknesses Kock et al. (1997) suggest ways of "improving" action research so that it meets more of the requirements of positivist research. Their main suggestion is to use iteration: "We argue that the progress through iterations allows the researcher to gradually broaden the research scope and in consequence add generality to the research findings."

Fixing action research so that it is more like traditional postpositivist research is one approach, but to many scholars who use AR it is akin to trying to make modern chemistry more alike alchemy. Another option is to reject the postpositivist paradigm and base action research on an alternative foundation.

Article of Interest

Linda Dickens & Karen Watkins. (1999, June). Action research: Rethinking Lewin. *Management Learning, 30,* **127–140.**

In this article the authors trace the development of action research from the work of Gestalt social psychologist Kurt Lewin in the 1940s. They describe the basic approach Lewin proposed and introduce a number of variations on action research. Two that are based on a positivist paradigm are *action science* and the *professional expert model of action research.* How do these differ from other approaches that are more interpretive or critical, such as PAR?

What do you see as the most innovative aspect of action research? Is it iteration? Research in the field rather than the lab? The group or collaborative aspects? The reflective part of the process? Is action research, particularly PAR, a good way to create generalizable knowledge? Or is it primarily a way of solving a problem in a particular applied setting? Finally, how would you characterize the action research reported at the end of the article in terms of what you define as the family characteristics of PAR? For example, was there participation on the part of the stakeholders?

To read the entire article, please go to http://www.sagepub.com/willis_aoi.

Interpretivist Action Research

When action research is based on the interpretive paradigm, it generally has five characteristics:

• *The setting is naturalistic.* The research is conducted in real-world contexts.

• *The process is participatory.* If the research is in a health care setting, the staff will be involved in the design, execution, and analysis of the study. "In action research, all actors involved in the research process are equal partners, and must be involved in every stage of the research process" (Grundy & Kemmis, 1982, p. 87).

- *Phronesis is the goal.* Instead of looking for a technical solution for practical solutions, the emphasis is on less sure and more contextual understanding, or *phronesis,* which is often called practical judgment. "While phronesis results in a doing-action or praxis, and is therefore product centered, the 'idea' in the interaction is personal, subjective and never fully formed, rather it is constantly being formed and being influenced by the situation" (Masters, 1995).

- *The work is collaborative.* "The researcher and the practitioners come together to identify potential problems, their underlying causes and possible interventions. . . . Collaborative participation in theoretical, practical and political discourses is a hallmark of action research and the action researcher" (Grundy & Kemmis, 1982, p. 87).

- *Theory and practice interact.* Preconceived theory does not always guide the research as it does in traditional postpositivist action research. Instead, the dialog between participants in the research project may be the source of a theory, and the research may lead to radical reformulation of the explanations and understandings participants have.

Article of Interest

Karen Healy. (2001, January). Participatory action research and social work: A critical appraisal. *International Social Work, 44,* 93–105.

In this article, Karen Healy, a social work professor at the University of Sydney, evaluates the relationship between the principles of social work and PAR. She deals with two forms of PAR: the Southern version, which is more influenced by critical theory, and a Northern variation that draws from a broader range of theories. Healy's overview of PAR emphasizes the critical framework (sometimes to the exclusion of other paradigms), and one of her concerns is the rhetoric of critical PAR about giving power to the participants, as compared to the many reports in the literature that describe researchers and academics taking the lead in PAR. What is your position on this issue? Using her critical perspective, Healy says the goal of PAR is the development of knowledge and "transformation of the social order" (p. 94). Other proponents of PAR would argue that the goal of PAR is the solution of real problems. What do you see as legitimate goals of PAR? Finally, what other aspects of Healy's discussion of PAR are the result of critical theory? How would that aspect of her analysis be different if she had taken an interpretive approach?

To read the entire article, please go to http://www.sagepub.com/willis_aoi.

Critical-Emancipatory Action Research

This type of action research is based on critical rather than interpretive theory. It will be discussed in more detail in the section on emancipatory research.

Ways of Doing Action Research

Masters (1995) makes the point that differences in the three ways of doing action research (postpositive, interpretive, and critical) are "not in the methodologies . . . but rather in the underlying assumptions and world views of the participants that cause the variations in the application of the methodology." However, there are some differences in the methods used by the three paradigms, and this section focuses on the methods of participatory and emancipatory action research.

Seymour-Rolls and Hughes (1995), using a framework developed by Kemmis and McTaggart (1988), divide the typical PAR project into four moments: reflecting, planning, acting, and observing. These four moments form a continuing spiral.

> *Reflect.* You begin with reflection on the issues. "The group undertaking PAR identifies a thematic concern through discussion and reflection. These concerns are integrated into a shared or common goal. The group agrees to collaborate and participate in a PAR project because of this integrated goal" (Seymour-Rolls & Hughes, 1995).
>
> *Plan.* Then the collaborative group plans a way to improve the situation. "The group and the members of the group are thus empowered to plan and act to create a social change" (Seymour-Rolls & Hughes, 1995).
>
> *Act.* The third moment involves putting the plan into action. "A change in practice is affected and observed using an appropriate research tool" (Seymour-Rolls & Hughes, 1995).
>
> *Observe.* The final moment in one cycle of the spiral is observation of the effects of the change.

Observation ends one of the cycles, but the process spirals back to reflection, and the project may continue for a number of cycles as new options and revisions are planned, implemented, and evaluated. One cycle of PAR becomes the background and foundation for the next cycle.

An alternative to Kemmis and McTaggart's four moments of PAR is outlined by Yoland Wadsworth (1998). Wadsworth's version of PAR has six phases:

- [PAR] commences—ironically—with stopping. That is, we do not begin to inquire until we actually suspend our current action because of the:
- raising of a question; which then provokes us to go about:
- planning ways to get answers—ways which will involve identifying and involving "questioners," "the questioned" and an idea of for who and for what we desire answers;
- engaging in fieldwork about new, current or past action in order to get answers and improve our experiential understanding of the problematic situation;
- generating from the "answers" an imaginative idea of what to do to change and improve our actions;
- the putting into practice of the new actions (followed by further stopping, reflecting and possible "problematisation"). (Wadsworth, 1995)

As you can see, each of the PAR models emphasizes the recursive nature of the process. PAR involves completing a number of cycles as you try out options, decide whether they worked, and think about how they can be improved. Then you try again. PAR is a powerful way of trying to improve practice. If you would like more information on PAR, Stringer's (1996) book is an excellent source of additional information. There are more than 400 other books on different forms of action research, however. Many are quite specialized. More general guides to action research that emphasize participatory forms include books by Atweh, Kemmis, and Weeks (1998), Lomax (1996), McNiff (1995), Schmuck (1998), and Whyte (1991). Most of the books are edited compilations that present several models or frameworks for thinking about PAR. Schmuck's book is a very good general introduction to action research that was written as a college text. It is a good place to start if you are a novice and want a solid foundation in action research. The 45-chapter *Handbook of Action Research,* edited by Peter Reason and Hillary Bradbury (2001), is also a good choice for those who really want to learn about action research. The chapters are organized into four sections that deal with alternative paradigms, methods of doing action research, exemplars of action research, and the competencies needed to do action research. If you are interested particularly in the idea of teachers as researchers, the book *Teachers Investigate Their Work: An Introduction to the Methods of Action Research* (Altrichter, Posch, & Somekh, 1993) is an excellent resource. *The Action Research Dissertation: A Guide for Students and Faculty,* by Kathryn Herr and Gary Anderson (2005), may be of particular interest to Ph.D. students in the social sciences and faculty who supervise action research dissertations.

Participatory and Constructivist Instructional Design

Traditionally, the process of design has not been considered research in the social sciences. That is due in part to the predominant view that the purpose of research is to find universals. A product is not a universal, so design of products cannot be research. Design is research in many other fields, however. Industrial design, architecture, art, graphic design, most fields of engineering, some fields of agriculture, areas in business such as marketing, many specialties in health care, computer science, commercial art, and several areas of communication and journalism all focus on design. Design may involve anything from the creation of a coffee pot or the design of a work environment to the building of software. Outside the traditional social sciences, design is a critical outcome of scholarship in many different disciplines.

Today, as ideas about scholarship become more open and flexible, design work is increasingly accepted in the social sciences as valid research. Thirty years ago many social science scholars, for example, did not consider writing a successful undergraduate textbook to be scholarship because it did not involve the creation of new knowledge. Now, the idea of scholarship has been broadened to include effective dissemination of knowledge, and textbook authorship is accepted as scholarship at many research universities. Some have even given this type of work a name: the *scholarship of teaching* or, more broadly, the *scholarship of professional practice*. This pattern of increasing acceptance also applies to the creation of educational software. Not long ago a chemistry professor at a research university who wrote an innovative piece of software for an undergraduate organic chemistry class might have been able to count it on her annual report as either teaching or service but not as research. Today at least some research universities would accept the design and development of high-quality educational software as scholarship. For that reason, this section on instructional design (ID) is included.

Formalized ID has been around since the early 1960s, but most of the models for design have been based on the postpositivist research paradigm and behavioral psychology (Dick & Carey, 1996). More recently, several approaches to ID have been developed that use an interpretive paradigm and constructivist theories of learning. One of them is the Reflective and Recursive Design and Development (R2D2) model (Colon, Taylor, & Willis, 2000; Willis, 1995, 2000; Willis & Wright, 2000). Like a number of emerging ID models, R2D2 is based on a participatory model. However, participatory models developed in other fields of design before they were created in ID.

In their classic and influential book *Participatory Design: Principles and Practices,* Douglas Schuler and Aki Namoika (1993) describe participatory design as "a new approach towards computer systems design in which the people destined to use the system play a critical role in designing it" (p. xi). They contrast it with other ways of designing.

> Participation stands in contrast to the cult of the specialist. In the specialist model, an expert is sought out. The question is presented to the Expert who will eventually produce the Answer. With this approach, those most affected by the conclusion must sit idly by, waiting patiently for enlightenment. PD, of course, demands active participation. PD, however, is not against expertise. There is no reason or motivation to belittle the role of expertise. Specialized training and experience, both technical and interpersonal, are important. In the participative model, however, this special expertise becomes yet another resource to be drawn on—not a source of unchallenged power and authority. A partnership between implementers and users must be formed and both must take responsibility for the success of the project. (pp. xi–xii)

That is the essence of participatory design: Involve the users in design as participants, not as observers from the sidelines and not as objects to be studied. User involvement has been promoted and studied in software engineering and industrial design, but ID has been slower to consider the full possibilities of user involvement, perhaps because behavioral theories have dominated that field longer and more deeply than in other design disciplines. In addition to participation, the R2D2 ID model is based on three other guiding principles: recursion, nonlinearity, and reflection.

Recursive (Iterative), Nonlinear Design

Most ID models are based on the assumption that a somewhat linear approach is best. That is, there are steps in the model, and those steps are best carried out in a particular sequence. Braden (1996) is one of the clearest proponents of linear ID: "Linear instructional design and development (LDD) is what we commonly call basic instructional design, basic instructional development, or just basic ID" (p. 5). Braden's detailed description of a linear ID model is one of the best presentations of a design model based on the assumption that linear is better.

If nonlinear ID seems chaotic to many, it is perhaps not surprising that a source of support for it is chaos theory. You (1994) points out that

> the conventional model of ISD [instructional systems design] takes the form of a straight line through a relatively linear sequence of

procedures. . . . Within the linear ISD model, the second step cannot be implemented without carrying out the first step because the first step is antecedent to the second. [This] is one of the major shortcomings of traditional ISD models. . . . A linear approach is not sufficiently flexible for working with environmental turbulence or sophisticated educational systems. . . . The linear ISD process imposed upon a dynamic system typically overlooks one or more "messy" variables that interfere at each stage of design and development. (p. 20)

You (1994) proposes the use of nonlinear ID models because they "can represent the dynamic interrelationship and interdependence among their components" (p. 20).

An aspect of nonlinear ID is recursion. The R2D2 model is also recursive. The same issues are addressed over and over across the entire design and development process. For some, the approach seems chaotic. It is chaotic in the sense that it does not prescribe in advance a specific pattern. It suggests instead that you let the project guide your decisions. What you should do next depends on the situation. This makes nonlinear ID much like other forms of qualitative research that are not completely planned.

Combine participation with iteration, and the result is a process for developing instructional material that allows both users and experts to fully participate in the process of revision and reformulation. This may happen at many levels. Members of the design team may initially look at little more than scribbles on a flip chart. More accurately, they create the scribbles on the flip chart through collaborative development of the concept for the material. Later they may go through a scenario that tells the story of how the material would be used in a class and revise their conceptions of what they will create. Still later they might look at rough and then progressively more complete prototypes of the material. Finally, alpha and beta versions of the material would be tried out and revised.

Reflection

A reflective model of practice assumes that many, if not most, important problems in professional practice cannot be well formed and solved with preformed solutions. In such a situation,

The terrain of professional practice, applied science and research-based technique occupy a critically important though limited territory, bounded on several sides by artistry. There is an art of problem framing, an art of implementation, and an art of improvisation—all necessary to mediate the use in practice of applied science and technique. (Schon, 1987, p. 13)

Those arts, of problem framing, implementation, and improvisation, make up reflective practice. They are as artistic as they are scientific, and they call for thoughtful and careful attention to, and understanding of, the context in which the professional work occurs. Schon (1987) uses the terms *reflection in action* and *reflection on action* to refer to the types of thoughtful work in context that should be an important principle in design work. Schon also calls this artistry, to contrast it with technical approaches. Schon describes reflection on action as a recursive process in which each effort to solve a problem that has not yielded to routine solutions is a trial that presents a reflective opportunity.

But the trials are not randomly related to one another; reflection on each trial and its results sets the stage for the next trial. Such a pattern of inquiry is better described as a sequence of "moments" in a process of reflection-in-action. Thinking reflectively about what we have done, and are doing, leads to reformulations of the problem as well as to experimentation. New approaches are tried, sometimes discarded, sometimes adopted or revised again. (p. 13)

The R2D2 ID model incorporates Schon's concepts of reflection in the design and development of instructional materials.

To read a case study about the application of the R2D2 model, see Colon et al. (2000). For information about another constructivist instructional design model that emphasizes participation, see Cennamo, Abell, and Chung (1996).

Emancipatory Research

Throughout this text three paradigms have framed the discussion of research methods: postpositivism, interpretivism, and critical theory. In this chapter, traditional action research has already been discussed. It is based in the postpositivist paradigm. Participatory forms of research—cooperative inquiry and PAR, as well as constructivist instructional design—typically use an interpretive and constructive foundation. The third type of scholarship explored in this chapter is emancipatory research. It is based on critical theory.

Emancipatory research is an effort to help oppressed groups become aware of their oppression (overcome a false consciousness or acquire emancipatory knowledge) and develop ways of overcoming that oppression (praxis). In rural development work, for example, this form of research has "contributed to awakening or heightening poor people's awareness about the conflicts and contradictions existing in their situation and ways to overcome these" (Huizer, 1997).

Patti Lather's (1991) book *Getting Smart: Feminist Research and Pedagogy With/in the Postmodern* is one of the more powerful expressions of this approach to research. Lather, who works from a feminist postmodern perspective, advocates research that takes a stand politically and brings about change—emancipation—in the environment studied.

From Lather's perspective emancipation is not only a possibility, it is virtually a necessity if you are going to do meaningful research. To do this type of research you obviously must abandon any pretense of detached objectivity. The researcher is personally, subjectively, and intensively involved with the people at the center of the study. The researcher is intrusive in that there is no effort to leave the situation as it is. There is no *Star Trek* Prime Directive.

Good emancipatory research thus violates almost all the basic assumptions of good postpositivist research. In fact, some advocates of emancipatory research think traditional training in social science research makes it more difficult for researchers to take an emancipatory stand:

> However, practising this view . . . is often difficult as a consequence of the ways in which the social sciences are generally being taught and implemented. At present social scientists are amply trained in tabulating, drafting questionnaires, observation and interviewing, but there is hardly any systematic training to become sensitive to the needs and values of fellow human beings, individually or in groups. Even less attention is given to oneself, as a researcher and as a human being, grown up with all the biases one's society imposes.
>
> Similarly neglected is development of the capacities to bring "experiences," impressions and biases through introspection and discussion in small groups into the "objective" sphere, something that can be learnt like good interviewing as is amply demonstrated by many feminist consciousness-raising groups. Such "sensitivity-training" is probably a good way to overcome the alienating, dehumanizing effects of most of the current social research methodology which is basically manipulative and not emancipatory. Introducing such a sensitive methodology, in addition to possibly helping the people being researched, may well have a liberating effect on the social scientists concerned themselves. (Huizer, 1997)

The negative view of emancipatory researchers toward traditional social science methods is returned by supporters of postpositive research. Hammersley (1995), for example, considers emancipatory research an abandonment of the basic principles of research that set this particular type of truth seeking (e.g., scientific research) apart from other paths to knowledge. He is particularly concerned that emancipatory researchers take a political position that guides their work. He believes politicization of research may actually threaten the survival of research in the social sciences.

Hammersley's argument is a natural response if you accept a postpositivist perspective on what good research is: objective, unbiased, and empirical. Emancipatory researchers reject his criticism of their approach in part because they believe all research is political:

> In contrast to the position represented by Hammersley, theorists in the "emancipatory" camp argue that all research is value-laden and is inevitably political, since it represents the interests of particular (usually powerful, usually white male) groups. Neutrality is seen as problematic, arising from an objectivism which assumes scientific knowledge is free from social construction. What is required is research which "brings to voice" excluded and marginalized groups as subjects rather than objects of research, and which attempts to understand the world in order to change it.
>
> Critical, feminist, participatory and anti-racist approaches to research all have this explicit purpose as a fundamental and legitimate premise. Lather says "Rather than the illusory 'value-free' knowledge of the positivists, praxis-oriented inquirers see emancipatory knowledge . . . [which] increases awareness of the contradictions distorted or hidden by everyday understandings, and in doing so it directs attention to the possibilities for social transformation" (Lather, 1991, p. 52).
>
> What Lather attempts to do in her book is to bring together three "discourses of emancipation" in order to draw out an approach to research which is genuinely liberatory. These perspectives are feminism, neo-marxism, and post-structuralism. (Humphries, 1997)

If you are interested in pursuing the idea of emancipatory research, Lather's (1991) book is especially recommended. Other good sources of information that take a slightly different perspective include Harvey's 1990 book on critical social research and a series of articles in 1997 and 1998 in *Sociological Research Online* (http://www.socresonline.org.uk) that debate the issue of whether emancipatory research is a meaningful concept or a problem.

Critical Emancipatory Action Research

Emancipation is the ultimate goal of critical research, so it is not surprising that it is also the goal of critical action research. The main difference between critical and interpretive action research is in the ultimate purpose. Interpretive researchers accept that there may be multiple perspectives that must be represented—that the situation can be viewed from several different perspectives. However, the research can still lead to better understanding of the situation, and that understanding can be the basis for practical knowledge, or phronesis.

Critical research accepts that assumption as well but tends to make choices based on power relationships. The goal is to empower those who are oppressed. In a classroom study where teachers have limited power and work in an authoritarian district, the emphasis might be on empowering teachers. Another action research project might emphasize the empowerment of students who are seen as oppressed or disenfranchised by the school and by teachers. As Kemmis and McTaggart (1988) put it, this research is "collective, self-reflective enquiry undertaken by participants in social situations in order to improve the rationality and justice of their own social . . . practices" (p. 5).

Some action research scholars argue that the original work of Kurt Lewin in the 1940s and 1950s was really critical action research rather than postpositivist or technical action research (Kemmis, 1993). Kemmis points out that Lewin, a Jewish scholar who emigrated to the United States from Nazi Germany in the 1930s, saw action research as a way of achieving social justice. However, in the climate of the United States in the 1950s, anything that seemed "leftist" was suspect. Thus "it is hardly surprising that some advocates of action research would de-emphasize the link between action research and social justice movements" (Kemmis, 1993). However, Kemmis points out that even during the McCarthy era in the 1950s some scholars such as educator Stephen Corey (1953) and sociologist Abraham Shumsky (1958) emphasized the power of action research for social justice and emancipation.

Corey and Shumsky were exceptions, however. In general, the link between emancipation and action research was ignored or denied. As a result "action research began to seem more like 'amateur' or 'poor man's' research, to be distinguished from the Real Thing" (Kemmis, 1993). Kemmis believes the current climate supports three types of action research: technical, which is based on positivism; practical action research, which is in the interpretive tradition and is similar to Donald Schon's reflective practice; and emancipatory or critical action research. Kemmis advocates emancipatory action research, which

> is always connected to social action: it always understands itself as a concrete and practical expression of the aspiration to change the social (or educational) world for the better through improving shared social practices, our shared understandings of these social practices, and the shared situations in which these practices are carried out. It is thus always critical, in the sense that it is about relentlessly trying to understand and improve the way things are in relation to how they could be better. But it is also critical in the sense that it is activist: it aims at creating a form of collaborative learning by doing (in which groups of participants set out to learn from change in a process of making changes, studying the process and consequences of these changes, and trying again).

Emancipatory action research often uses the forms and approaches used in interpretive and participatory action research. It shares with PAR an emphasis on participation (in fact, it is often called PAR) and the concern with changing conditions in the real world.

A number of the books on action research take an emancipatory or critical perspective. For more information on how to conduct emancipatory action research, see Greenwood and Levin's (1998) book *Introduction to Action Research: Democratizing the Research Process,* Noffke and Stevenson's (1995) *Educational Action Research: Becoming Practically Critical,* and McTaggart's (1997) *Participatory Action Research: International Contexts and Consequences.*

Summary

A number of qualitative research methods are well established and widely used today. These include ethnography or observation, interviews, case study, and historiography. All these methods have long histories and many variants. When you look for additional information on these methods, be sure to think about which variant interests you, because there will be guides, handbooks, and manuals on how to do research from a number of different perspectives, including postpositivist, critical, and interpretive.

There are also a number of less established but emerging qualitative research methods. Many of the most interesting can be organized into two overlapping groups: participatory and emancipatory. Participatory research has emerged over the past 15 years as a major way of conducting research based on interpretive and critical paradigms. There are versions of participatory research that address basic theoretical questions in the social sciences (e.g., cooperative inquiry), but most participatory research is practical in nature, with PAR being the most common. Another variant of participatory research is constructivist instructional design, which is emerging as an alternative form of scholarship that focuses on the creation of educational materials. Instructional design is increasingly accepted as scholarship as ideas about what constitutes scholarship are becoming broader and more inclusive.

Finally, critical theory is the foundation for the other type of research discussed in this chapter. Emancipatory research is participatory and emphasizes both the development of a critical consciousness and praxis or action to achieve social justice. Interpretive scholars generally accept critical research, but some postpositive scholars believe the political agenda that is acknowledged in emancipatory research makes it something other than research.

Questions for Reflection

1. Select an area of scholarship that interests you and describe two issues or questions that might lend themselves to ethnographic research. Why does ethnographic research seem particularly suited to approaching those issues or questions? What theoretical framework would you use in the research? Why?

2. Develop a one- to two-page plan for a research study of a topic that interests you. The study should involve interviews as a major source of data. Use what you have learned in this chapter to develop a tentative topic focus, identify whom you would interview and how you would collect your data, and the way you would organize notes as you read your source material.

3. Suppose someone at a party made the comment, "Historical research is neither real research nor very useful to anyone except those who write it." As a warm, perhaps even heated, discussion begins, what position would you take? Why?

4. Take a topic you would like to know about that can be studied using historiography and explain how a positivist, an interpretivist, and a critical researcher would approach the topic. Would their purposes be different? Their methods? Their means of analysis? The way they write their reports?

5. Cooperative inquiry and PAR have many similarities. However, the possibility of studying basic questions is inherent in cooperative inquiry but not as much in interpretive and critical forms of PAR. What basic question would interest you that would be suited to study by cooperative inquiry? How would you go about conducting such a study? What would be the basic framework and approach? Also, what related practical or applied question could you study using PAR?

6. Definitions of things such as AR are always debatable because they attempt to define something that has many variations, some based on opposing theoretical foundations. However, please throw caution to the wind and develop three definitions of AR: one that postpositivists would be comfortable with, one for interpretivists, and one for critical theorists. Is there anything these three approaches to AR share, or is postpositivist AR something quite different from interpretive AR and interpretive different from critical AR?

7. In this chapter several models or plans for action research were presented. Select an interesting topic that is appropriate for AR and write a brief fictional account of how you did an AR study on the topic. Justify the sequence of activities and relate the model you used to the models presented in the chapter. Did you pick one of the models and use it? Did you develop your own? Did you use another model from the literature? Did you combine elements of several models? Why?

8. What is your response to the question of whether instructional design is scholarship? Would someone in your field who developed a college textbook or an outstanding educational software package be doing research? Would opinions about this vary with the setting (research university, teaching university, liberal arts college)? Justify your views.

9. Is emancipatory research really research? Or is it political action masquerading as research? Take a position on this issue. Then write a response that takes the opposite view and defends that position.

Notes

1. From Seepe, S. Critical thinkers needed, in *Sowetan* 9/15/1998. Used with permission.
2. From Hanson, V., Windschuttle's Warning: In Praise of the Killing of History, in *The Weekly Standard*, copyright © 1997. Used with permission.

References

Altrichter, H., Posch, P., & Somekh, B. (1993). *Teachers investigate their work: An introduction to the methods of action research.* London: Routledge.

Ascherson, N. (1995). *Black Sea.* London: Hill and Wang.

Atkinson, P., Coffey, A., Delamont, S., Lofland, J., & Lofland, L. (2001). *Handbook of ethnography.* Thousand Oaks, CA: Sage.

Atweh, B., Kemmis, S., & Weeks, P. (Eds.). (1998). *Action research in practice: Partnerships for social justice in education.* New York: Routledge.

Berkhofer, R. F. (1997). *Beyond the great story: History as text and discourse.* Cambridge, MA: Harvard University Press.

Bochner, A. P. (1997). It's about time: Narrative and the divided self. *Qualitative Inquiry, 3*(4), 418–438.

Bogdan, R., & Biklen, S. (1992). *Qualitative research for education* (2nd ed.). Boston: Allyn & Bacon.

Braden, R. (1996, March–April). The case for linear instructional design and development: A commentary on models, challenges, and myths. *Educational Technology, 36*(2), 5–23.

Brooker, R. (1997). *Improving wound care in a paediatric surgical ward.* Retrieved January 27, 2006, from http://www.beh.cchs.usyd.edu.au/~arow/Reader/Brooker.htm

Burke, P. (2001). *New perspectives on historical writing* (2nd ed.). University Park, PA: Penn State University Press.

Campbell, D., & Stanley, J. (1963). *Experimental and quasi-experimental designs for research.* Chicago: Rand McNally.

Cennamo, K., Abell, S., & Chung, M. (1996). A "layers of negotiation" model for designing constructivist learning materials. *Educational Technology, 36*(4), 39–48.

Colon, B., Taylor, K., & Willis, J. (2000, May). Constructivist instructional design: Creating a multimedia package for teaching critical qualitative research. *The Qualitative Report, 5,* 1, 2. Retrieved January 27, 2006, from http://www.nova.edu/ssss/QR/QR5-1/colon.html

Corey, S. (1953). *Action research to improve school practices.* New York: Teachers College Press.

Dick, W., & Carey, L. (1996). *The systematic design of instruction* (4th ed.). New York: HarperCollins.

Fontana, A., & Frey, J. H. (1994). Interviewing: The art of science. In N. K. Denzin & Y. S. Lincoln (Eds.), *Handbook of qualitative research* (pp. 361–376). Thousand Oaks: Sage.

Freeman, D. (1983). *Margaret Mead and Samoa: The making and unmaking of an anthropological myth.* Cambridge, MA: Harvard University Press.

Gall, M., Borg, W., & Gall, J. (1996). *Educational research: An introduction* (6th ed.). New York: Longman.

Glesne, C. (1997). That rare feeling: Representing research through poetic transcription. *Qualitative Inquiry, 3*(2), 202–221. Glesne, C., & Peshkin, A. (1992). *Becoming qualitative researchers: An introduction.* New York: Longman.

Glesne, C., & Peshkin, A. (1992). *Becoming qualitative researchers: An introduction.* White Plains, NY: Longman.

Gomm, R., Hammersley, M., & Foster, P. (Eds.). (2000). *Case study method.* Thousand Oaks, CA: Sage.

Green, A., & Troup, K. (Eds.). (1999). *The houses of history: A critical reader in twentieth-century history and theory.* Albany: State University of New York Press.

Greenwood, D., & Levin, M. (1998). *Introduction to action research: Democratizing the research process.* Thousand Oaks: Sage.

Grundy, S., & Kemmis, S. (1982). *Educational action research in Australia: The state of the art.* Paper presented at the Annual Meeting of the Australian Association for Research in Education, Adelaide. Cited in J. Masters. (1995). *The history of action research.* Retrieved January 27, 2006, from http://www.beh.cchs.usyd.edu.au/~arow/Reader/rmasters.htm

Gubrium, J., & Holstein, J. (2003). *Postmodern interviewing.* Thousand Oaks, CA: Sage.

Hamel, J. (1993). *Case study method.* Thousand Oaks, CA: Sage.

Hammersley, M. (1995). *The politics of social research.* Thousand Oaks: Sage.

Hanson, V. (1997, September 22). Windschuttle's warning: In praise of *The Killing of History. The Weekly Standard.* Retrieved January 27, 2006, from http://www.cspc.org/books/reviews/history.htm

Harris, S. (1998). Introduction: thinking locally, acting globally. *Configurations, 6*(2), 131–139.

Harvey, L. (1990). *Critical social research.* London: Unwin Hyman.

Heron, J. (1996). *Co-operative inquiry: Research into the human condition.* Thousand Oaks, CA: Sage.

Herr, K., & Anderson, G. (2005). *The action research dissertation: A guide for students and faculty.* Thousand Oaks, CA: Sage.

Hibbs, T. (2000). *Shows about nothing: Nihilism in popular culture from* The Exorcist *to* Seinfeld. Dallas: Spence.

Howell, M., & Prevenier, W. (2001). *From reliable sources: An introduction to historical methods.* Cornell, NY: Cornell University Press.

Huizer, G. (1997). *Participatory action research and people's participation.* Retrieved January 27, 2006, from http://www.fao.org/WAICENT/faoinfo/susdev/Ppdirect/Ppre0021.htm

Humphries, B. (1997). From critical thought to emancipatory action: Contradictory research goals? *Sociological Research Online, 2*(2). Retrieved January 27, 2006, from http://www.socresonline.org.uk/socresonline/2/1/3.html

Iggers, G. (1997). *Historiography in the twentieth century: From scientific objectivity to postmodern challenge.* Hanover, NH: Wesleyan University Press/University Press of New England.

Jenkins, K. (Ed.). (1997). *The postmodern history reader.* New York: Routledge.

Kemmis, S. (1993, January 19). Action research social movement: A challenge for policy research. *Educational Policy Analysis Archives, 1*(1). Retrieved January 27, 2006, from http:///olam.ed.asu.edu/epaa/v1n1.html

Kemmis, S., & McTaggart, R. (1988). *The action research planner* (3rd ed.). Geelong, Australia: Deakin University.

Kock, N., McQueen, R., & Scott, J. (1997). *Can action research be made more rigorous in a positivist sense? The contribution of an iterative approach.* Retrieved January 27, 2006, from http://www.cis.temple.edu/~kock/public/jsit97/is-arw6.htm

Lather, P. (1991). *Getting smart: Feminist research and pedagogy with/in the postmodern.* New York: Routledge.

Leigh, P. (1997). Segregation by gerrymander: The creation of Lincoln Heights (Ohio) school district. *Journal of Negro Education, 66*(2), 121–136.

Leigh, P. (2004). *Fly in the ointment: School segregation and desegregation in the Ohio Valley.* New York: Peter Lang.

Lomax, P. (Ed.). (1996). *Quality management in education: Sustaining the vision through action research.* New York: Routledge.

Marmysz, J., & Marmysz, J. (2003). *Laughing at nothing: Human as a response to nihilism.* Albany: State University of New York Press.

Masters, J. (1995). *The history of action research.* Retrieved January 27, 2006, from http://www.beh.cchs.usyd.edu.au/~arow/Reader/rmasters.htm

Mazeland, H., & ten Have, P. (1996). Essential tensions in (semi-)open research interviews. In I. Maso & F. Wester (Eds.), *The deliberate dialogue: Qualitative perspectives on the interview.* Brussels: VUB University Press. Retrieved January 27, 2006, from http://www2.fmg.uva.nl/emca/ET.htm or http://www.paultenhave.nl

McNiff, J. (1995). *Action research: Principles and practice.* New York: Routledge.

McTaggart, R. (Ed.). (1997). *Participatory action research: International contexts and consequences.* Albany: State University of New York Press.

Mead, M. (1928). *Coming of age in Samoa.* New York: Morrow.

Merriam, S. (1988). *Case study research in education: A qualitative approach.* San Francisco, CA: Jossey-Bass.

Merriam, S. (1990). *Qualitative research and case study applications in education.* San Francisco, CA: Jossey-Bass.

Newton, J. (1988). History as usual?: Feminism and the "new historicism." *Cultural Critique, 9,* 87–121.

Noffke, S., & Stevenson, R. (Eds.). (1995). *Educational action research: Becoming practically critical.* New York: Teachers College Press.

Novick, P. (1988). *That noble dream: The "objectivity question" and the American historical profession.* New York: Cambridge University Press.

Plattner, S. (1989). Commentary: Ethnographic method. *Anthropology Newsletter, 32,* 21, 30.

Reason, P., & Bradbury, H. (2001). *Handbook of action research.* Thousand Oaks, CA: Sage.

Rubin, H., & Rubin, I. (2004). *Qualitative interviewing: The art of hearing data.* Thousand Oaks, CA: Sage.

Savenye, W., & Robinson, R. (1997). Qualitative research issues and methods: An introduction for educational technologists. In D. Jonassen (Ed.), *Handbook of research for educational communications and technology* (pp. 1171–1195). New York: Macmillan.

Schmuck, R. (1998). *Practical action research for change*. Thousand Oaks, CA: Corwin.

Schon, D. (1987). *Educating the reflective practitioner.* San Francisco: Jossey-Bass.

Schuler, D., & Namoika, A. (1993). *Participatory design: Principles and practices.* Hillsdale, NJ: Erlbaum.

Seepe, S. (1998, September 15). Critical thinkers needed. *Sowetan* (Soweto, South Africa), 3.

Seymour-Rolls, K., & Hughes, I. (1995). *Participatory action research: Getting the job done.* Retrieved January 27, 2006, from http://www.beh.cchs.usyd.edu/au/~arow/Reader/rseymour.htm

Shumsky, A. (1958). *The action research way of learning.* New York: Teachers College Press.

Stake, R. (1994). *The art of case study research.* Thousand Oaks, CA: Sage.

Stewart, A. (1998). *The ethnographer's method.* Thousand Oaks, CA: Sage.

Stringer, E. (1996). *Action research: A handbook for practitioners.* Thousand Oaks, CA: Sage.

Stumpf, S. E. (1966). *Socrates to Sartre, a history of philosophy*. New York: McGraw-Hill.

Tamakoshi, L. (1996). *Fieldwork.* Retrieved June 21, 2005, from http://www.melanesia.org/fieldwork/tamakoshil/default.htm

Wadsworth, Y. (1998). What is participatory action research? *Action Research International,* Paper 1. Retrieved January 27, 2006, from http://www.scu.edu.au/schools/gcm/ar/ari/arihome.html

Wengraf, T. (2001). *Qualitative research interviewing: Biographic narrative and semi-structured methods.* Thousand Oaks, CA: Sage.

Whyte, F. (Ed.). (1991). *Participatory action research.* Thousand Oaks, CA: Sage.

Willis, J. (1995). A recursive, reflective instructional design model based on constructivist–interpretivist theory. *Educational Technology, 35*(6), 5–23.

Willis, J. (2000). The maturing of constructivist instructional design: Some basic principles that can guide practice. *Educational Technology, 40*(1), 5–16.

Willis, J., & Wright, K. E. (2000). A general set of procedures for constructivist instructional design: The new R2D2 model. *Educational Technology, 40*(2), 5–20.

Windschuttle, K. (1997). *The killing of history: How a discipline is being murdered by literary critics and social theorists.* New York: Free Press.

Yin, R. (2002). *Case study anthology.* Thousand Oaks, CA: Sage.

Yin, R. (2004). *Applications of case study research* (2nd ed.). Thousand Oaks, CA: Sage.

You, Y. (1994). What can we learn from chaos theory? An alternative approach to instructional design. *Educational Technology Research and Development, 41*(3), 17–32.

Zagorin, P. (1999, February). History, the referent, and narrative: Reflections on postmodernism. *History and Theory, 38,* 1–24.

Sources of Additional Information

Action Research International. This is an online electronic journal (http://www.scu.edu.au/schools/gcm/ar/ari/arihome.html) and discussion list where participants can comment on and discuss articles submitted to the journal and raise other issues related to action research.

Educational Action Research. This journal, published by Triangle Journals in the United Kingdom, began publication in 1993. It publishes research articles and theoretical conceptual articles on all aspects of action research in education. Some of the articles in this journal are available online from the publisher's Web site (http://www.triangle.co.uk).

Institute for Developmental Studies. IDS supports a Web site that includes links to several types of resources on both action research and international development. The address is http://nt1.ids.ac.uk/eldis/pra/pra.htm.

CHAPTER 8

Approaches to Data Analysis and Interpretation

Qualitative researchers sometimes look fondly at the clean, structured lines of basic quantitative research. The positivist or postpositivist approach lends itself to the creation of detailed technical rules for conducting research. If you can find (or get closer and closer to) truth about the topics you study, you should also be able to find truth about how to do research and communicate it to others. Interpretivism and critical theory do not lend themselves to a recipe or technical approach. Both are open when it comes to methodology and data collection and analysis.

That openness has led to many different forms of data collection and analysis. However, most of the specific approaches are used in the context of a broader research family. A research family may focus on a particular research method, such as grounded theory, or a broad psychological or sociological theory, such as structuralism. However, all the research families discussed in this chapter are not so much sets of detailed, technical directions for how to analyze data as they are sets of related principles and concepts.

That there are both research families and strategies for data analysis can be confusing. In fact, the whole process of qualitative research, including data analysis and interpretation, can be confusing and frustrating. It is difficult to get at the "right" answer because there are so many right answers. One way to bring some sense of order to the process is to think about qualitative research, especially data collection and analysis, as a process that involves decisions about six different types of issues:

- *Epistemology.* Which philosophy of science, world view, or ideological perspective have you adopted?

- *Purpose.* What is the general purpose of the research? To describe a setting, to develop a theory of explanation, to tell a story? Something else?

- *Research methods.* What methods of research will you use? Case study, emancipatory, ethnographic, participatory action research?

- *Research framework.* There are a number of well-established qualitative research frameworks that include procedures for analyzing data. Grounded theory, analytic induction, hermeneutics, and poststructural analysis are examples of these general frameworks.

- *Data analysis strategies.* In addition to frameworks there are also sets of data analysis strategies in common use today. Several of these will be introduced in this chapter.

- *The audience for your ideas and the form used to communicate them.* Although most qualitative studies are published as journal articles or monographs, there are other ways of communicating your work to a range of audiences. You must decide what forms to use when disseminating your work.

Purpose of Research

Most of the six decisions you must make about your qualitative research study have been discussed already. One, in particular, calls for more exploration: the purpose of research. There are many traditions in qualitative data analysis, but most of them fit into one of two broad categories: holistic or atomistic. These two traditions differ in many ways, including the underlying philosophies of science that support them. A question that encapsulates many of the differences between these two approaches is what we expect to gain from research. There are five basic answers to this question. Each is based on a general philosophy of social science and has many implications for how the research is conducted and how data are analyzed and written up.

General Theory

The purpose of postpositivist quantitative research is to discover general laws or lawlike relationships. You do a study to test a theory about how the world behaves. The local context is not so important because the reason we do research is to find truths that can be generalized. Qualitative research based on this approach (Miles & Huberman, 1994; Smith, 1993) is done for the same purpose as traditional quantitative research. Approaches such as grounded theory (Strauss & Corbin, 1997) often have general theory as a purpose.

Article of Interest

Vera Lopez & Edmund Emmer. (2000, June). Adolescent male offenders: A grounded theory study of cognition, emotion, and delinquent crime contexts. *Criminal Justice and Behavior, 27*(3), 292–311.

This article is based on the dissertation of Vera Lopez, who was a student at the University of Texas at Austin. It is a good illustration of research that attempts to develop a general theory. In this case the theory had to do with the context of criminal behavior by young males. Lopez used semistructured interviews to collect her data, and she described her data analysis as grounded theory. As she reviewed her interview data she created and applied codes to segments of the data. For example, when a respondent talked about the benefits of committing a crime, she coded that comment as relating to "Crime Reward." After she had coded the data she began to look at the data with an eye toward developing a general theory of "delinquent cognition." However, she soon concluded that there was no one explanatory framework that applied to all crimes. Eventually she began to develop a typology that included two factors in her coding: type of crime and motivation for doing the crime. For example, she found three types of motives: emotion driven, belief driven, and reward driven. By combining type of crime and motive, she came up with three major types of crimes (e.g., emotion-driven violent assault). Using her data, Lopez then created a set of characteristics that are typical of each type of crime. In the discussion Lopez and Emmer present their findings as an alternative to other theories of delinquency and suggest that their emphasis on the context in which the crimes occurred yields a superior theory.

We would like to make two more comments about the study. The first is that although the methodology was described as grounded theory, the study may not meet the criteria in some definitions of grounded theory. Several involve evaluating a theory by comparing its predictions with the results from a subset of the available data. The theory is then modified as needed, and another subset of the data is used to validate the revised theory. For example, Charmaz (2005) says grounded theory is "a set of flexible analytic guidelines that enable researchers to focus their data collection and to build inductive middle-range theories through successive levels of data analysis and conceptual development" (p. 507). It is the phrase *successive levels* that is in question here.

Although it is not completely clear, it appears that in this study the authors used all of the data to develop the theory, then tested the revised theory against all the data—the same data that were used in the first round of analysis. Is this a minor variation? Does this qualify as grounded theory? Charmaz goes on to argue that "grounded theory methods consist of simultaneous data collection and analysis, with each informing and focusing the other throughout the research process. . . . As grounded theorists, we begin our analyses early to help us focus further data collection" (p. 508). This again seems to imply a process that weaves analysis and data collection into an ongoing process rather than collecting data and then doing the data analysis. However, Atkinson and Delamont (2005) offer a much broader explanation of grounded theory: "Grounded theory does not refer to some special order of theorizing per se. Rather, it seeks to capture some general principles of analysis, describing heuristic strategies that apply to any social inquiry independent of the particular kinds of data: indeed, it applies to the exploratory analysis of quantitative data as much as it does to qualitative data" (p. 833). This seems to describe a grounded theory tent that is certainly large enough to house Lopez's research. However, the authors go further: Grounded theory "captures the *abductive* logic through which analysts explore the social or natural world through practical engagements with it, derive working models and provisional understandings, and use such emergent ideas to guide further empirical explorations" (p. 833). What is given in the first quotation seems to be taken back in the second. There is again the idea of *successive levels* of data analysis. What do you think? There is nothing inherently wrong with Lopez's approach, but is it grounded theory? And does it matter whether it is? Finally, if you read Rennie's article (discussed later in this chapter), ask yourself whether this study meets his revised expectations of a typical grounded theory study.

The other comment has to do with the believability of the data. Lopez asked delinquents to tell about their crimes and then tended to treat the verbal explanations as accurate reflections of how the delinquent perceived and felt about the crime. Some might question whether that is a wise assumption. Would the story have been the same had the delinquent been telling the story to a friend, fellow gang member, or girlfriend? For a postpositivist reader the issue at hand is whether what the delinquents said is an accurate or true indicator of their cognitive processing. For an interpretive reader the question is whether what the delinquents said is *the* true indicator of their cognitive processing or just one of many, each of which reflects not only internal cognitive processing but also the social and cultural context in which the statements were made. The authors seem to use the data as if it were *the* true indicator. Are you comfortable with that approach? If not, how would you approach the interpretation of these data?

To read the entire article, please go to http://www.sagepub.com/willis_aoi.

Local Theory

Most qualitative researchers acknowledge that a single study in a specific setting cannot produce truth that can be generalized directly to other settings. In fact, they question whether any studies can produce general truth. Therefore, some attempt to develop a rich understanding of the local context instead of generalizable laws or rules. They search for truths about the local context. Collins (1998) points out that it is common practice to use interview data to discover facts about a situation in an effort to build local theory (or general theory). The purpose of this form of interviewing is to mine the sources of data in order to understand what is really happening and then to communicate the essence of this to others. Other than accepting the limited generalizability of the results, local theory studies follow essentially the same guidelines as general theory research. Collins, who advocates thinking of qualitative interviewing as a way of understanding a story you are going to tell, believes it is impossible even to get at local theory because interviewing is not an objective process; it is a very subjective and complex act of human interaction.

Article of Interest

Kathryn A. Sielbeck-Bowen. (2000, May). Development of local program theory: Using theory-oriented evaluation to make a difference. *Field Methods, 12,* 129–152.

Sielbeck-Bowen's article looks for local theory. She is concerned with the correspondence between the theories of practice held by the staff of a program for pregnant teenagers in New York and how the program really worked. She used several different research methods in this study: analysis of text documents, concept mapping by staff, interviews, a review of participants' charts, and home visits.

Sielbeck-Bowen used the data she collected to build a local theory of how the program was to work. This theory represented the staff's view of both the way the program operated and the impact of the program. She then created a description of the program's operation and impact from the other data she collected. She treated this description as an empirically derived explanation of how the program really worked. She assumed that "disparity between staff members' local program theory and empirical data would be indicative of program weaknesses and point to potential problems in fully implementing the program" (p. 131). Her conclusions are interesting in part because they highlight the complexity of program evaluation. After you read this article, what is your option about whether the program was effective? Why? Do you accept the author's approach of comparing the subjective local theory of the staff to the way things really are, as evidenced by her data analysis? And do you agree with her recommendations?

To read the entire article, please go to http://www.sagepub.com/willis_aoi.

Objective Description

General and local theory research involves inference. You develop generalizations from the raw data and emphasize those generalizations in the writeup. A third approach, also based on the assumption that qualitative research can lead to the truth about a situation, focuses on accurate description of the situation under study. Description is at the basis of both general and local theory research, but it can be a goal in itself. From the point of view of interpretive and critical researchers, trying to stick to simple, "objective" descriptions does not work. Description is not, in the words of Sergeant Friday on the old *Dragnet* television program, "just the facts, ma'am." Description is selective, it is the interpretation of the describer, and therefore it is subjective. For this group, there is no possibility of objective description.

Article of Interest

Judie A. Heinschel. (2002, December). A descriptive study of the interactive guided imagery experience. *Journal of Holistic Nursing, 20,* 325–346.

Heinschel did this study as her dissertation in nursing at the University of Colorado. The article retains some of the structure of a dissertation, with sections such as "Review of the Literature" and "Procedure." Her goal was to generate a rich description of interactive guided imagery (IGI) from the point of view of the patient. IGI is a revision of relaxation training that has been used to treat many illnesses, often with the purpose of reducing anxiety or the perception of pain. Heinschel gathered her data using semistructured interviews. Audiotapes of the interviews were transcribed, and she used an inductive procedure to move from the details of the descriptions provided by patients to general "patterns, categories, and themes." These emerged from the data as she coded and worked with her transcripts. She worked with segments of the data "until the interpretive truth" (p. 328) was revealed. Her approach was iterative. That is, rather than coding data once and then attempting to draw final conclusions from that set of codes, she revised her coding structure and recoded several times. "Initial data were gathered and analyzed, then the emerging findings were used to guide the gathering of further data, followed by a return to analyzing again, and so on, in an ongoing fashion until categories, subcategories, and themes" (p. 328) became clear.

Based on her analysis Heinschel developed a description of the IGI experience that had six major themes. A section of the article describes those themes. Is Heinschel's research an example of objective description—"just the facts?" Or did she do more? Is the organizing of information about IGI into themes such as "the guide–client relationship" and "the lived experience" something the researcher imposed on the data, or was it in the data and Heinschel just found it?

To read the entire article, please go to http://www.sagepub.com/willis_aoi.

Hermeneutic (*Verstehen*) Understanding

The purpose of descriptive and theory-based research is to identify the truth of the matter, or at least get as close as possible to it. That truth exists separately from the people who are studied, and it is separate from the researcher. Although this may be a defensible position in the physical sciences, it is less likely when humans are studied because humans are reactive; their perspectives and views influence what they do, and their experiences influence their perspectives. The purpose of hermeneutic research, or to use a slightly more general word in German, *verstehen,* is to understand the perspectives of humans. And because understanding is situational, hermeneutic research tends to look at the details of the context in which the study occurred. The result is generally rich data reports that include multiple perspectives. There can also be efforts to develop theories and test hypotheses, but as Kelle (1997) points out, "the theories and hypotheses of hermeneutic research are not the same as the theories of descriptive and theory-based research. Hermeneutic theories are more like fuzzy, tentative explanations that ebb and flow, merge and diverge, as research progresses." In the tradition of the scientific method used by quantitative researchers, the theories and hypotheses must be precisely defined before the research is conducted, and they must be linked to well-defined, observable behavior. This is not common in holistic qualitative research in the hermeneutic tradition. The hypotheses and theories qualitative researchers typically work with often are vague

assumptions and conjectures about possible relations between certain domains. To examine these hypotheses means to return to the material in order to explore this possible relationship by a thorough analysis of textual data. This interpretive analysis of text (segments) may then form the basis for the clarification and modification of the researchers' initial (general or vague) assumptions. The notion of hypothesis testing would be rather misleading here, if one understands it as an attempt to falsify an empirically contentful statement. (Kelle, 1997)

When *verstehen* is the purpose of research, the researcher may work with fuzzy, incomplete, and emerging ideas that are called theories or hypotheses. However, they are quite different from the theories and hypotheses researchers use when they are seeking truth (e.g., general theory, local theory).

Often the result of hermeneutic research is not anything close to a theory. Often the result is a list of exemplars rather than generalizable truths (Smith, 1993). Postpositivists are generally uncomfortable with the idea of leaving lists of exemplars as the final product of research; they would like to transform them into theories that represent universals.

Interpretivists, of course, will have none of this at any level. They agree with Feyerabend (1981) when he says that, for certain traditions, . . . "a list is not a mistaken first step on the way to a more appropriate definition: it is the only adequate form of knowledge". . . . One learns to use a list, and thereby becomes part of a practical tradition, by playing around with or applying the list in interaction with others. (Smith, 1993, p. 141)

However, lists are not simply different forms of postpositivist universals. "Items on a list are not rules that foreclose or predetermine the kind of judgments people make, they are values that influence those judgments" (Smith, 1993, p. 141).

Article of Interest

Darren Langdridge & Trevor Butt. (2004, February).
A hermeneutic phenomenological investigation of the
construction of sadomasochistic identities. *Sexualities, 7,* 31–53.

This study is an example of hermeneutic phenomenological research. The authors, both at the University of Huddersfield in England, looked at Web sites on sadomasochism to develop an understanding of this "sexual story." Although most of the research on sadomasochistic behavior comes from interviews, Langdridge and Butt thought they would learn a lot from the material on Web sites devoted to sadomasochistic interests.

What do you think about the authors' concepts such as "sexual stories" and "sexual citizenship" and the reasons they give for an increase in the number of people who want to express and live out sexual preferences that are not "in the mainstream"? What do the authors mean when they talk about the "social construction of sadomasochism" (p. 32)? Do you think the research method—locating and analyzing text on Internet sites—was effective for accomplishing the purpose of the research? Why? Does the hermeneutic phenomenology method of Paul Ricoeur (1974) seem particularly suited to the purpose of this study? Why? What, exactly, was the purpose of the research? Please note also that the attitude of these researchers, who use a hermeneutic approach, toward sexual preferences that are not "vanilla" is quite different from the attitudes of many researchers who use more traditional research methods. In this article the authors note that some believe approaches that define certain sexual behaviors as pathological "serve not to describe and explain but construct and control sexuality for the service of political and economic imperatives" (p. 34). The more open and accepting attitudes of these authors toward nonstandard behavior is typical of many forms of qualitative research. Some critical theorists might well argue that traditional postpositivist research often supports the status quo while focusing on ways of coercing the individual to conform to the standards set by the groups in power.

To read the entire article, please go to http://www.sagepub.com/willis_aoi.

Storytelling and Narrative

Collins's (1998) work on job loss and stress is an example of storytelling as qualitative research. He insists that meaning exists only in context and that qualitative interviewing does not uncover preexisting truths. Instead it is a social process that constructs meaning through interaction. This approach does not attempt to present the *truth of the matter* as objective description does. Instead, it is an effort to represent in detail the perspectives of participants in the process or setting being studied. Whereas description produces one truth about the topic of study, storytelling may generate multiple perspectives, interpretations, and analyses by the researcher and participants. Storytelling has much in common with hermeneutic research, but it puts more emphasis on representing the perspectives of the participants in a context of details about the setting or situation. Charmaz (2005) points out that in the past qualitative researchers have used *story* as a "metaphor for varied qualitative data such as interview statements, field note descriptions, or documents" (p. 526). However, she believes that we have moved to another phase in which "we cease to use the term 'story' as metaphor and have come to view it as concrete reality, rather than a construction we place on these data" (p. 526). Charmaz's views illustrate how deeply the idea of stories as an outcome of research has become embedded in the qualitative tradition.

Articles of Interest

Pat Sikes. (2005, February). Storying schools: Issues around attempts to create a sense of feel and place in narrative research writing. *Qualitative Research, 5,* 79–94.

Morten Skjørshammer. (2002, September). Understanding conflicts between health professionals: A narrative approach. *Qualitative Health Research, 12,* 915–931.

These two articles are both examples of telling stories or, to use a more professional term, they are examples of narrative research. Some scholars make a sharp distinction between storytelling and narrative research, with narrative research being more structured, detailed, and systematic. Others, such as Rankin-Brown (2006), do not: "Narrative research involves using stories to inquire about events, feelings, thoughts, and the meaning of a story with another. Narratives attempt to connect individuals with others, develop creativity and critical thought, and transcribe academic research and writing for a larger, public audience. Narrative research recaptures the art of storytelling and draws attention to its important role in sharing knowledge with others" (p. 3). These two articles are examples of storytelling and narrative research from the perspective Rankin-Brown takes.

Pat Sikes, a professor of education at the University of Sheffield in England, tells the story of a visit to a high school for boys with behavior problems. The article begins like a short story or novel, with a richly described scene in a fast-moving car. After she tells the story of her visit to the school, she then discusses some of her concerns about narrative representations of a context, particularly the issues of "creating a sense of 'feel' and 'place.'" Her concerns and how she handled them provide a good introduction to some of the goals of narrative research methods. What purposes can this type of narrative research method meet in your field?

Morten Skjørshammer's article also tells a story. As a public health professional, he is concerned with conflicts between health care providers at a Norwegian hospital. He collected more than 100 stories of conflict between professionals at the hospital, and he selected one to illustrate his understanding of how conflicts are resolved. Note that whereas Sikes tells the story in her own words and from her own perspective, Skjørshammer uses quotes from interviews and his own comments and interpretations to tell the story. He thus presents multiple perspectives of what was happening. He then uses the multiple perspectives to illustrate the application of a theory of conflict resolution to this story. However, even his application of theory is done in a narrative or storytelling style, and he points out common elements in conflict stories such as emplotment, temporal development, diversions, and struggle for the dominant story version. In the discussion, Skjørshammer criticizes theories of conflict resolution based on positivist models and argues that "within a narrative paradigm . . . the parties' stories are not considered anecdotes standing in the way of the real issues and arguments but are an important part of it." Do you agree with his view of the advantages of a narrative perspective? Are you comfortable with his comment that "within the narrative paradigm, there is no clear difference between fact and fiction? Both history as 'true' and story as 'fiction' share a common narrative structure"?

Are these two narrative research studies based on the same underlying assumptions? Do they have similar purposes?

To read these articles, please go to http://www.sagepub.com/willis_aoi.

The purposes of research point toward certain types of data analysis. If you want to build a general or local theory (or an accurate description) that explains the truth of what you are studying, you may want to consider emphasizing atomistic approaches to data analysis. Atomistic approaches generally involve breaking the data down into segments, adding codes to the data segments, and then looking at relationships between the codes.

On the other hand, if you take a hermeneutic, narrative, or storytelling approach, some of the more holistic methods may be most appropriate. Holistic approaches tend to leave the data intact and to emphasize that meaning must be derived for a contextual reading of the data rather than the extraction of data segments for detailed analysis.

Data Analysis Families

The purpose of your research will determine how you analyze the data to some extent. Data analysis is not simple, however. Several sometimes contradictory families of data analysis methods are introduced here. These families vary in terms of whether they advocate a detailed or atomistic approach or a holistic approach. Some emphasize the development of broad understanding of what the data tells us without much effort to deal with all the details in some specific way. Other approaches put a great deal of emphasis on coding all the data and then building theories or explanations through analysis of the codes. Still others emphasize a certain type of issue or data or focus on certain types of research questions. This section is not a how-to guide to research within these families. Rather, it is an effort to introduce you to these families so that you can decide which ones are interesting enough to merit further study. It begins with the more holistic approaches and progresses toward more atomistic approaches to data analysis.

Eyeballing the Data

In the field of applied behavior analysis (ABA), an extreme form of behaviorism, the data collected are generally a count of certain behaviors such as out-of-seat behavior in a classroom or the number of problems completed in a math lesson. Data in ABA studies are generally presented in graphic form, such as a chart of the percentage of time a student was on task across no-treatment and treatment periods. To determine whether the treatment had an impact on the student, you look at the graphic pattern of the data. Eyeballing is all that is used in many ABA studies. The results are considered obvious to anyone who understands the graph.

This same approach is used in qualitative studies. You become familiar with your data and then write a paper based on your impression of the data and what it says to you. Generally the paper that results from such a study cites examples of the data to support the conclusions made. Although some consider this less than adequate as a research technique, there are many topics for which the approach seems to work well.

Sometimes, however, the debate about whether the eyeball approach is acceptable clusters around extremes. Eyeballers reject the more structured approaches to analysis that break down the data into small units and, from the perspective of the eyeballers, destroy the wholeness and some of the meaningfulness of the data. On the other hand, those who advocate more structured approaches sometimes imply that if you do not do it their way, then you are simply expressing your opinions and need not have gathered any data at all. It is true that the frameworks for qualitative data analysis tend to fall into two broad categories, holistic and atomistic, but these are actually two ends of a continuum. Eyeballers are at one end of that continuum, and many postpositivist researchers who use statistical tests to make decisions about what their data say are at the other. There is a vast and fruitful landscape of approaches between these two extremes, however. If you tend toward the holistic end of the continuum but are uncomfortable with what you see as anarchy inherent in the eyeball approach, there are other options, including a framework called the connoisseurship model.

Article of Interest

Louisa Allen. (2005). Managing masculinity: Young men's identity work in focus groups. *Qualitative Research, 5,* 35–57.

This is an example of an eyeball approach to data analysis. New Zealand researcher Louisa Allen was interested in how young men manage their sexual identities. She used data from her dissertation research to explore this topic. Her data source was the transcripts of talk in four focus groups that discussed sexuality. As you read this article, note that Allen draws conclusions based on her reading and rereading of the focus group transcripts. She uses quotes from the transcripts to illustrate her conclusions and to convince you that she is correct in her interpretation. Allen also critiques existing theories about male sexual identity and rejects some theories while supporting others. How believable is Allen's work? Is it less believable because she used an eyeball approach? Or is it more believable because she looked at the data holistically instead of breaking them down into pieces by coding them and then analyzing the code patterns?

To read the entire article, please go to http://www.sagepub.com/willis_aoi.

Article of Interest

Yvonna S. Lincoln & Gaile S. Cannella. (2004). Qualitative research, power, and the radical right. *Qualitative Inquiry, 10,* 175–201.

Whereas the previous article of interest, by Louisa Allen, defined a precise data set that she eyeballed to come up with her conclusions, this article, by Lincoln and Cannella, does not. They draw from a number of sources, including news reports, initiatives and policies of the federal government, speeches by national figures, and articles in the scholarly literature. In fact, they used almost everything they were aware of to support their conclusions. Some might consider this an essay rather than a research article, but the boundary between essays and research articles is blurred in qualitative research. As you read this article note that Lincoln (a major figure in qualitative research circles) and Cannella establish their ideological bias early in the article and then detail their view of the current climate in America for qualitative researchers. They also try to convince you that their view is accurate. As you read this article, ask yourself whether the evidence they use to support their view could be interpreted differently by those who oppose Lincoln and Cannella's ideological stance. Also, do you agree with their definition of terms such as *liberal* and *conservative?*

To read the entire article, please go to http://www.sagepub.com/willis_aoi.

Connoisseurship: A Global Perspective

Some of the approaches you will read about later emphasize breaking down data into components, or units, and then looking for relationships between the components. Elliot Eisner's (1998) approach, connoisseurship, does not emphasize breaking things down as much as it promotes developing a contextual, holistic understanding of the research context. Eisner's approach is one of the best examples of the more holistic approaches to qualitative research. Grounded theory, which is discussed later, is an example of the opposite: the creation of understanding through a detailed process of coding and logical inference.

Another way to highlight the differences between connoisseurship and other frameworks is to ask, "How does understanding emerge from a qualitative study?" Some scholars advocate emulating the postpositivist approach of starting with very definite, specific hypotheses (or developing them quickly from the first data you gather) and then testing your hypotheses or theories against new data. As the data suggest that your hypotheses or theories are incorrect, you revise them and test them against new data. This process involves moving from specific to specific, from one detailed hypothesis or theory to another. This is very similar to the process a postpositivist researcher would use across a series of separate studies on the same topic.

Another alternative is not to develop specific theories and hypotheses in the beginning. Instead, let your understanding emerge gradually across the data collection and analysis process. Although Eisner sees much value in both specific-to-specific and emergent approaches, his framework tends to emphasize emergent understanding. Eisner's approach has matured and evolved over the past two decades (Eisner, 1985, 1998; Flinders & Eisner, 1994). It was originally known as aesthetic inquiry, and it emphasized the use of methods from the humanities and the arts. He has also used the term *educational criticism*. In his latest book, *The Enlightened Eye: Qualitative Inquiry and the Enhancement of Educational Practice* (1998), Eisner uses the terms *educational criticism* and *educational connoisseurship*. His approach will not be discussed in detail here. However, it is one of the emerging frameworks that is growing in popularity today.

Eisner's framework, which is deeply rooted in interpretivist epistemology, reflects a healthy respect and appreciation for critical theory as well. It is probably the best-known and most widely used holistic approach to qualitative inquiry in education. The next framework, hermeneutics, is less frequently used in education but shares many things with Eisner's model, including the emphasis on meaning in context.

Hermeneutics as a Data Analysis Method

Hermeneutics has already been discussed. The approach strives for understanding—*verstehen*—in context, as opposed to searching for universals. It has

> always stressed that ambiguity and context-relatedness have to be regarded as central characteristics of everyday language use. . . . It is impossible to make sense of written or spoken messages in everyday contexts—an operation which forms the core of hermeneutic *Verstehen*—without a "tacit knowledge" which cannot easily (if at all!) be formalized. (Kelle, 1997)

Tacit knowledge is knowledge you construct through experience. It is not overt. Tacit knowledge may be important, or even critical, but it cannot be found in an employee manual, a software guide, or some other formal source of knowledge. It is learned in context and may guide the way we do things even if we are completely unaware of that knowledge.

Article of Interest

Seonjin Seo & Mirka Koro-Ljungberg. (2005, Summer).
A hermeneutical study of older Korean graduate students' experiences in American higher education: From Confucianism to Western educational values. *Journal of Studies in International Education, 9*(2), 164–187.

Seonjin Seo was a doctoral student at the University of Florida when she wrote this article, and Mirka Koro-Ljungberg is a professor of qualitative research methodology at the same institution. The article deals with an important topic—how students from one culture adapt and relate to higher education in a different culture—and it is a good example of hermeneutic research. As you read this article, write a brief description of a hypothetical hermeneutic study that would interest you. Use the same general method as the authors did but select your own topic. Are there any aspects of the general method the authors used that do not fit your study? For example, would the critical incident method work well for you? If you needed to, how would you have to adapt the research procedures to make them work in your hypothetical study?

Finally, in your hypothetical study do you think you would find a cultural force that is a major influence, as the authors of this article did with Confucianism? Can you explain your response?

To read the entire article, please go to http://www.sagepub.com/willis_aoi.

Like most of the frameworks discussed in this chapter, hermeneutics is related to others. In the case of hermeneutics, it shares a great deal with phenomenology and interpretivism. Some (e.g., Neyland, 1992) put interpretivism and hermeneutics together to form one major paradigm of research.

Although there is a natural fit between interpretive and hermeneutic perspectives, there are also very strong connections between hermeneutics and critical theory. Critical hermeneutics marries the focus of understanding in context with critical ideology. Today, hermeneutics is a strong and continuing influence on work in both the interpretivist and critical traditions. This point is illustrated by Sohng (1995), a social worker at the University of Washington, in her discussion of the foundations for participatory research that includes an emancipatory or community action component:

> In contrast [to approaches that look for an out-there truth], participatory research regards that truth is not referenced simply or directly to an external, independently existing reality but is a way to consider the dynamic and changing, historically and socially constructed patterns that influence our daily lives. These patterns are objective, however, in the very sense that they have been historically and socially formed through human struggles. Subjective, on the other hand, directs attention to what is inside people, the interests and purposes that allow them to make sense of their day-to-day lives. . . . As we have learned from hermeneutics, the only criterion for the "rightness" of an interpretation is "intersubjective," that is, that it is right for a group of people who share a similar world. But it is also important to realize that when considering the validity of an interpretation we are not solely concerned about "being right," as Torbert (1981) points out. Being right has to be contextually valid. Is our way of framing the research questions fruitful and meaningful? That is, a key validity criterion has to consider not only "is it right?" but also "is it useful" and "is it illuminating?"
>
> A dialectic view of truth must include the notion that there are always emerging possibilities which are not yet visible. This requires a bold shift in evaluating the validity of knowledge, from "Does this research correspond with the observable facts?" to "To what extent does this research present new possibilities for social action?" and "Does it stimulate normative dialogue about how we can and should organize ourselves?" This is termed catalytic validity.

For an excellent and detailed history of the influences of hermeneutics in psychology and psychiatry see Phillips (1996). From a methodological perspective, one of the most important contributions of hermeneutics is the idea of the hermeneutic circle. It is expressed in many approaches to qualitative research. For example, it was one of seven principles proposed by Klein and Meyers (1998) as a framework for doing interpretive research in the information sciences:

> The most fundamental principle of hermeneutics is that of the hermeneutic circle. This principle is foundational to all interpretive work of a hermeneutic nature and is in effect a meta-principle upon which the following six principles expand. The idea of the hermeneutic circle suggests that we come to understand a complex whole from preconceptions about the meanings of its parts and their interrelationships. To clarify its generality it is best to relate to Gadamer's (1976) example of how we are to translate the meaning of a sentence into a foreign language. As a case in question, consider the sentence "they are playing football." In order to understand the individual parts of the sentence (i.e. whether the football is a round ball, an egg-shaped ball or no ball at all), we must attempt to understand the meaning of the sentence as a whole. The process of interpretation moves from a precursory understanding of the parts to the whole and from a global understanding of the whole context back to an improved understanding of each part, i.e. the meanings of the words. The sentence as a whole in turn is a part of some larger context. If from this context it is clear that nobody is engaged in sport at all, then we can conclude that the meaning of "they are playing football" must be metaphorical. To apply the metaphor, one needs to interpret "football" as an issue which is contested which in turn involves a new understanding of the meaning of the term "playing" as involving something abstract which is being "thrown or kicked around." Also, "playing" no longer means physical movement on a grassy field. "Thus the movement of understanding is constantly from the whole to the part and back to the whole. Our task is to extend in concentric circles the unity of the understood meaning. The harmony of all the details with the whole is the criterion of correct understanding. The failure to achieve this harmony means that understanding has failed" (Gadamer, 1976, p. 117). In Gadamer's description of the "hermeneutic circle," the terms "parts" and

"whole" should be given a broad and liberal interpretation. They can be parts of a historical story, and then the whole is the proper perspective of the historical context. . . . Alternatively, the parts can be the interpretive researchers' and the participants' preliminary understandings (i.e. pre-understandings) in the study. The whole consists of the shared meanings that emerge from the interactions between them. Note that participants appropriate (i.e. make their own) ideas from the researcher and vice versa. Hence, in a number of iterations of the hermeneutic circle, a complex whole of shared meanings emerges. This interpretation should be used in applying the principle of interaction between the researchers and subjects. During repeated cycles of the hermeneutic circle all of the suggested principles can be applied iteratively forming a complex web of interpretations.[1]

You will find both forms of the hermeneutic circle expressed in many types of qualitative research. For a critique of the usefulness of these two forms of the hermeneutic circle (whole–part and researcher–subject interaction) in historical research, see Megill (1999). Megill, a professor of history at the University of Virginia, points out that Richard J. Bernstein distinguished

between pre- and post-Heideggerian notions of the hermeneutic circle. In many standard characterizations, the circle runs between part and whole within the reality that the investigator seeks to understand. For instance, a historian or a textual critic will come to understand one sentence in a document in light of the document as a whole. But in its wider, post-Heideggerian sense, the circle runs between the investigator and what is being investigated. The investigation will be prompted by the traditions, commitments, interests, and hopes of the investigator, which will affect what the investigator discovers. Conversely, the process of historical research and writing will change both the investigator and the audience—at least, it will do so if the inquiry is more than trivial. To come to grips with the interpretive aspect of inquiry, one must make a reflexive move, looking at the way the inquirer's point of view enters into the investigation. The long historiographic tradition that holds to the fiction of an objective narrator feigning to be silent before the truth of the past resists self-reflexive sensitivity.

Article of Interest

**Donald Polkinghorne. (2000). Psychological inquiry
and the pragmatic and hermeneutic traditions.**
Theory & Psychology, 10(4), 453–479.

Donald Polkinghorne, who teaches at the University of Southern California, has written a number of influential books and articles on hermeneutic and narrative research. In this article he contrasts the standard approach to psychological research, "producing valid and reliable general knowledge," with doing research that produces the "kind of inquiry used by psychological practitioners." Polkinghorne's "practitioner inquiry" is very different from "research inquiry," and much of this article is an exploration of his ideas about why we should adopt the practitioner inquiry model of research in psychology (the logic also applies to other social sciences). Do you find his philosophical arguments persuasive, particularly his discussion of the alternatives to "the end of epistemology"? Why? Do you agree with his preference for the second rather than the first philosophic response to the end of epistemology?

Do you find the author's use of Aristotle's concepts of phronesis and techne appealing? Why? What are the implications of adopting Polkinghorne's views on techne and phronesis?

Polkinghorne tries to blend Dewey's pragmatism and Gadamer's hermeneutics to produce a form of hermeneutic inquiry that focuses on how humans come to acquire practical knowledge. If this idea suddenly became the paradigm of research in your field, what types of research would be popular? What types would be rejected or ignored? Can you think of some topics that would become more important? Less important? How would studies of those more important topics be conducted?

To read the entire article, please go to http://www.sagepub.com/willis_aoi.

Article of Interest

**Melissa Freeman. (2001). "Between eye and eye stretches
an interminable landscape": The challenge of philosophical
hermeneutics.** *Qualitative Inquiry, 7*(5), 646–658.

When she wrote this article, Freeman was a doctoral student at the State University of New York at Albany. Some of her research involved interviewing parents with children in school. As she did this research she came to understand the complex challenges involved in understanding the communication of the parents. This article addresses her concerns and challenges through a series of poems. What is your general response to this article, which alternates poems and reflective commentary? Is the article legitimate? Is it scholarship? Is it research? If you were a professor, and a student turned in something like this as a research paper, would you accept it?

To read the entire article, please go to http://www.sagepub.com/willis_aoi.

If you would like more information on how to do hermeneutic data analysis, the short book by Cohen, Kahn, and Reeves (2000) covers the entire research process including data analysis. A longer book that is more theoretical and also more focused on data analysis and interpretation is Max Van Manen's (1990) *Researching the Lived Experience*. Finally, a number of short books in Sage's Qualitative Research Methods series also deal with hermeneutic data analysis.

Grounded Theory

Grounded theory (Glaser & Strauss, 1967; Strauss, 1987) is a way of developing theory through analysis of qualitative data. Using this approach, researchers work with successive waves of data to develop theory. For example, a researcher might look at the first wave of data from a study, develop a tentative theory based on those data, and then collect more data to test the theory. If the current version of the theory also fits the new data, the researcher proceeds to the next wave of data. If it does not fit the new data, the researcher modifies the theory so that it fits both the original and the new data and then checks it against more new data. This process continues until there are no revisions to the theory or no more new data. The goal is to build a theory that fits every set of data and thus is generalizable.

The theories developed by grounded theory studies are more specific and detailed—closer to practice—than the grand theories that were popular in psychology in the 20th century (e.g., Tolman's purposive behaviorism, Skinner's behaviorism, and Kohler's Gestalt theory). However, the grounded theories are still meant to be generalizable to other settings.

Grounded theory is a general framework that guides the research process. However, there are more detailed and specific frameworks commonly associated with it. They deal with the process of data analysis. One of the most widely used is the constant comparative method. Using comments from one of the developers of the method (Glaser, 1978) and from Bogdan and Biklen (1998), the constant comparative method can be summarized in six recursive steps:

1. Start data collection.

2. Organize the data into units such as sentences, events, or paragraphs.

3. Associate similar units and develop categories for the data.

4. Look for links, associations, and relationships between the categories.

5. Develop broader, more general explanations from the categories and their relationships.

6. Repeat the process.

Organizing the constant comparative method into six easy steps is a gross oversimplification of the process, but it does illustrate the link between theory and data. Data drives theory development. However, theory does not come directly from the data. First, categories emerge from the data. Categories are one level up in generalization from the data themselves. For example, you might observe teachers in a classroom as they work with students in small collaborative groups and begin to create a set of categories of teacher behavior. One category that emerges from the raw data might be facilitative behavior. The category named *facilitative behavior* could include a wide range of behaviors—asking the right question to help students think through a problem, not answering questions students need to puzzle through themselves, encouraging a group in work that gets them closer to their goal—but the behaviors in that category would share many common characteristics.

Once you have categories, the relationships between categories emerge. For example, you might find that facilitative behaviors often lead to certain types of student behavior. From that you develop broader theories that attempt to explain the way things are in that particular situation. Theories are general explanations that are specific enough to generate hypotheses that can be tested by being applied to additional data. In the classroom study, for example, a tentative hypotheses derived from your developing theory might be that facilitative teacher behavior sets the scene for the emergence of certain types of student behavior. As you collect more data that hypothesis could be tested and the theory modified as necessary.

Criteria for judging the theory developed through grounded theory research have been discussed by several authors (Glaser, 1993; Glaser & Strauss, 1967; Merriam, 1998). They include

- *Parsimony.* Does it provide the simplest, most straightforward explanation that is meaningful?

- *Scope.* How broad is the theory? Can it be applied to a wide range of contexts?

- *Overall explanatory power.* How much of the situation does the theory explain? A little? A lot?

- *Degree of generalization.* Does at least some of the theory seem helpful when it is applied to similar situations?

- *Logical internal consistency.* Does the theory hang together as a coherent whole? Are the different components logically interrelated?

These five criteria are all discussed by one or more authors as desirable characteristics of the theories that emerge from grounded theory research. The better a theory scores in these five areas, the stronger the theory. However, these characteristics are not always the five characteristics that should guide our judgment. They fit well with a postpositivist approach to research that emphasizes the creation of broad generalizations that apply across many contexts. Three of the five criteria relate to generalization (scope, overall explanatory power, and degree of generalization). The other two relate to how well the theory hangs together internally (parsimony and internal consistency). Translated into the language of postpositivist research, the five criteria deal with internal and external validity. Nothing in the list is very far outside the traditional postpositivist framework.

Although they may sometimes be appropriate, they may also mislead and misdirect. Consider scope and parsimony. The broader the theory, the broader the scope. Is that an appropriate criterion for judging a theory? Not always. Sometimes a theory is useful precisely because it is narrow, not broad. It gives us a rich, complex way of looking at a particular situation. But the narrowness that helps us see and understand what we are interested in may also limit the scope of the theory. The same theory may also be complex and detailed, which would mean it is not as parsimonious as other competing theories. If we assume human behavior is simple rather than complex and well structured rather than ill structured, then the search for parsimony is generally desirable. If we assume human behavior is complex and ill structured, the emphasis on parsimony may actually lead us astray.

This does not mean that any of these criteria are necessarily inappropriate or undesirable. The point is that they cannot be used as if they were already established as criteria that everyone should use. They are not. When used, they should be justified. And when alternative criteria, even criteria opposite to these five, are used, researchers should justify them as well, and readers should be open to accepting those criteria for the quality of a theory.

In concluding the section on grounded theory, note that the constant comparative method is not associated solely with grounded theory. It is widely used in qualitative research even when the purpose is not theory development.

Articles of Interest

David L. Rennie. (2000, August). Grounded theory methodology as methodical hermeneutics: Reconciling realism and relativism. *Theory and Psychology, 10,* 481–502.

Judith Y. Weisinger & Paul F. Salipante. (2005, March). A grounded theory for building ethnically bridging social capital in voluntary organizations. *Nonprofit and Voluntary Sector Quarterly, 34,* 29–55.

These two articles are both about grounded theory, but they approach the topic in very different ways. Rennie, a psychologist at York University in Canada, sees grounded theory as a way to deal with the realism versus relativism issue that haunts every social science discipline. The article by Weisinger and Salipante, on the other hand, is a study that illustrates how grounded theory methodology is used in research.

Rennie's article explores the underlying assumptions of grounded theory and the implications of the approach if certain assumptions are modified. For example, he believes that the original conception of grounded theory does not adequately address the question of whether the results of the method should be considered real (realism) or subjective (relativism). (In fact, the originators did view the results as interpretive or subjective, but Rennie does not like that assumption.) He views grounded theory as an inductive process (going from specifics to broad generalizations) rather than deductive (beginning with a broad generalization such as a theory and checking to see whether the implications match the specifics of data collected in a specific situation). However, he modifies the assumptions of grounded theory, using Peirce's (a founder of semiotics) theory of meaning and pragmatism and philosophical hermeneutics to justify a position that the inductively oriented grounded theory method is a way of obtaining reliable and valid (e.g., accurate or truthful) knowledge. Central to Rennie's effort to make grounded theory an acceptable realist research method is his use of Peirce's idea of abductive inference as an alternative to induction and deduction. What do you think of his argument? Does he make a good case for inductive methods being "self-correcting" and thus able to bear the weight of responsibility for finding truths about our world? Is it an "objective" research method? Also, does it make sense to consider it a (or *the*) hermeneutic method? Are the assumptions of a hermeneutic approach compatible with Rennie's revised assumptions for the grounded theory research method?

Weisinger and Salipante's article is a study of how to build "ethnically bridging social capital." In other words, the authors are saying that organizations need social capital ("connections among individuals—social networks and the norms of reciprocity and trustworthiness that arise from them") that help ethnically diverse groups work and play together in ways that foster positive interaction and understanding. The focus of their study was a Girl Scout troop, and they studied both members of the troop and the volunteers who ran it. However, their real purpose was not to understand the inner workings of that particular troop. Weisinger and Salipante make it clear that their goal was to "develop theory," and they begin with an existing theory of social capital that, when applied to their data, does not fit. In the end they suggest a revised version of the theory that is more promising. Did the approach to data analysis in this article illustrate a grounded theory approach? Why? Do you consider this a qualitative, quantitative, or mixed study? Why? Did you find the failure of Adler and Kwon's original theory of social capital convincing? Did the theory really fail to explain the data gathered? And does the new theory proposed by Weisinger and Salipante do a better job of fitting the data?

To read these articles, please go to http://www.sagepub.com/willis_aoi.

Analytic Induction

This approach begins with a question or problem (Bogdan & Biklen, 1998). The purpose of the research is to deal with that question or problem. Analytic induction involves a series of steps in data analysis to move from the raw data to proposed answers or solutions. It is a multicase approach in that you gather data from one participant or group of participants (e.g., you interview one worker in a *maquiladora* on the Mexico–USA border). Once you have used those data, you gather more data (e.g., interview another worker) and use them to refine and reformulate the theory or model you developed. Briefly, analytic induction involves six steps:

1. *Data collection.* Data that should be relevant to the question or problem are gathered.

2. *Data analysis.* The raw data are used to create a descriptive and explanatory model that represents the first case (or cases).

3. *Gather data* on another case.

4. *Apply the model* to the new case.

5. *Revise the model* if necessary.

6. *Complete Steps 1–4* again and again. In the beginning new cases may be similar to the existing cases, but as work progresses you may want

to look for cases that are quite different. Cases that may challenge the theory you are developing are particularly valuable.

As you have probably noticed, analytic induction has some things in common with the grounded theory method. Grounded theory studies do not necessarily move on to a new case for each cycle. They can involve collection of additional data in the same setting. Researchers may even divide up data they have already collected into different sets and use one set at a time to test the current version of their theory. On the other hand, there are many similarities between analytic induction and grounded theory. Both are recursive (you complete some of the steps several times), and both are emergent (your ideas, categories, and focus may change drastically across the study). You do not necessarily stick with your original theory or hypothesis.

Article of Interest

Niki Tsangaridou. (2002, February). Enacted pedagogical content knowledge in physical education: A case study of a prospective classroom teacher. *European Physical Education Review, 8,* 21–36.

Tsangaridou teaches in the Department of Education at the University of Cyprus and is concerned about teachers' knowledge, particularly content knowledge, and the way it is expressed during teaching. The author studied one student who was preparing to be a teacher. The researcher observed the student while she was practice teaching, read documents such as her lesson plans and reflective journals, and interviewed her. Tsangaridou used analytic induction and the constant comparative method to analyze the data and presented the results in a "realist type of case narrative." How did Tsangaridou use the results from this study? Was the goal hermeneutic or interpretive understanding of this teacher's use of content expertise? Or was it to support a broad or universal theory of teachers' use of content expertise? Was the goal an appropriate one for the study? Why?

To read the entire article, please go to http://www.sagepub.com/willis_aoi.

The Ethics of Research

Most of the major associations for social scientists and education researchers (e.g., American Anthropological Association, American Educational Research Association, American Historical Association, American Psychological Association, American Sociological Association, British Psychological Society, British Sociological Association, Canadian Association of Anthropology and

Sociology, Indian Council of Medical Research, International Sociological Association, World Medical Assembly) have a set of guidelines for the ethical conduct of research. There is even an Association of Research Ethics Committees, based in the United Kingdom, that helps with and coordinates the development of ethical guidelines for research. These guidelines cover everything from what volunteer participants in a study must be told to how authorship credit is to be assigned. In addition to those guidelines, most universities have one or more research committees that must approve a study before you begin research. This generally involves preparing an application for the committee that covers the details of the study. Most universities base their guidelines and procedures on national requirements that apply to all organizations and institutions that receive national funding for research.

Some researchers consider the process of obtaining approval to do research an irritating and time-consuming task, but there are too many examples of egregious harm done to research subjects to accept this view. One of the most famous examples of a research study gone grotesquely awry is the Tuskegee Study. This was a study by the U.S. Health Service on the long-term effects of syphilis. Poor and ill-educated Blacks around Tuskegee, Alabama, were recruited to participate when the study began in the early 20th century. Those who were diagnosed with syphilis were offered free medical care for the duration of the study, which lasted for decades. However, they were not told they had syphilis, and one of the reasons they were offered free medical care was to prevent them from learning they had syphilis and seeking treatment elsewhere. When the study began the only common treatment for syphilis was a form of arsenic, which was a major poison itself. There was a question about whether the treatment did more harm than the disease. So the study was begun. However, in the 1940s penicillin became widely available, and it was an effective, inexpensive cure for syphilis and a host of other diseases. The researchers and administrators of the Tuskegee Study could have told the participants in the study they had this disease and even provided penicillin to them, particularly because the main reason for the study—a treatment that might be worse than the cure—was no longer valid. They did not do that. Instead, they kept their secrets and continued to study the effects of untreated syphilis on their subjects while providing them with medical care for everything but that disease. Of course, many died of complications of syphilis. Some of the people who conducted the study are still alive, and some still defend their decision because it provided important scientific information. However, that researchers would do that in a supposedly democratic nation where everyone has equal protection under the law is one reason that there are strict guidelines for ethical research today. In fact, today such a study could not be conducted because every set of guidelines requires informed consent of the subjects. That is, the subjects must be fully informed about the study, and they must particularly be told about any dangers.

A detailed overview of the ethics of qualitative research will not be presented here. There are many sources of information about research ethics today (Bosk & De Vries, 2004; Cushman, 2004; Detardo-Bora, 2004; Emihovich, 1999; Helgeland, 2005; Oakes, 2002; Weisburd, 2003). However, it is important to recognize that there can be major differences of opinion about whether a study is ethical that depend on the paradigm you are using. A brief summary of an anthropological study carried out over decades by Wolfgang Feurstein (1992), a German researcher who became interested in a small ethnic group called the Lazi who live along the Black Sea coast in Turkey, illustrates this point. This description of his work is taken from Neal Ascherson's (1995) outstanding book *Black Sea.* As a nation Turkey is young. It emerged from the Ottoman Empire in the mid-1920s after two major military events. The first was World War I, in which the Ottoman Empire fought on the side of Germany and lost. At the end of the war much of the Ottoman Empire was carved up, leaving a smaller and struggling country in Asia Minor to rebuild itself. As the country struggled, Greece, with the encouragement of the British, invaded with the goal of creating a "Greater Greece" that included much of the lands in Asia Minor that had been part of Greece in antiquity. The Ottoman Empire dissolved at this point, but a daring military leader, who became known as the "father of the Turks," Kemal Atatürk, rallied the Turkish army and led campaigns that were so successful that the Greek army was decisively defeated. As part of the Treaty of Lausanne in 1923, almost a million Greeks living in what became Turkey were expelled to Greece, and about half that many Turks were expelled from Greece to Turkey. (Actually, the exchange of citizens was based on religion [Islam versus Christianity] instead of ethnic group membership.) Atatürk established the Turkish Republic with the motto "Turkey for the Turks," and he insisted that Turkey was a monocultural state made up of Turks. Turkish laws forbid "political party platforms suggesting 'that minorities exist in the Turkish Republic based on national, religious. confessional, racial or language differences,'" any "'written or oral propaganda, along with meetings, demonstrations and marches, that have the goal of destroying the indivisible unity of the state' and any action that 'incites people to enmity and hatred by pointing to class, racial, religious, confessional or religious differences'" (Kinzer, 2001, pp. 147–148). Until a rash of changes in the laws in late 2002 designed to support Turkey's application for membership in the European Union, it was illegal to teach in the language of a minority such as Kurdish. As recently as early 2002, one of the senior leaders of Turkish education branded as traitors students who had signed a petition to allow the teaching of Kurdish language and literature in the nation's universities.

The Turkish government has suppressed any effort to distinguish one group of Turkish citizens from another:

> Writers, journalists and politicians who criticize the status quo are packed off to prison for what they say and write. Calls for religious freedom are considered subversive attacks on the secular order. Expressions of ethnic or cultural identity are banned for fear that they will trigger separatist movements and ultimately rip the country apart. (Kinzer, 2001, p. 12)

Advocating "separatism," as it was called, in almost any form was a crime that brought down the wrath of many law enforcement groups. I remember talking in 2001 to a well-educated Turkish university official who insisted that there was little need in Turkey for the multiculturalism taught in America because Turkey was a monocultural nation.

It was into this context that Wolfgang Feurstein came in the 1960s and learned about the Lazi, a group of about 250,000 who speak a non-Turkic language and have separate cultural traditions. The Lazi, living on isolated farms and villages in a remote area of the Turkish Black Sea coast, have maintained their cultural and linguistic differences by keeping "these differences to themselves, like some ancestral wedding dress, which is of no interest to anyone outside the family. Given the paranoia of the Turkish state about differences, this has been prudent" (Ascherson, 1995, p. 197). However, Feurstein realized that the culture and language were disappearing as modern communication technologies such as satellite TV came to the area and more and more Lazi moved away to cities such as Istanbul. In a few decades he knew the language of the Lazi, which is pre–Indo-European, would cease to exist because there was no written form, and the last speakers would die. Ascherson points out that several languages have disappeared recently. The last speaker of Ubykh, for example, died in 1992. He also points out that the Lazi have survived as a separate culture because they were

> safely settled in their remote corner of Turkey, [and] they behaved as if the private language of home and the public language of schools and jobs would remain indefinitely in equilibrium. But then, in the late twentieth century, the balance began to tip. The coming of television and the huge expansion of the Turkish economy

during the last twenty years have served the Lazi notice that a choice is becoming inevitable. The past suggested that they would choose passive assimilation [into Turkish culture and language]. (Ascherson, 1995, p. 203)

Feurstein resolved to do something about this. He began to study the culture and learn the language. However, "News of his interests and movements came to the Turkish authorities. Framed by the security police for 'illegally entering a frontier district,' he was arrested, beaten up, threatened with death and then, after a brief imprisonment, expelled" (Ascherson, 1995, p. 202). This did not deter Feurstein. He returned to Germany, and in the small village of Schopfloch he created a center of Lazi cultural studies. Thus far he and a small group of Lazi expatriates have developed an alphabet for the Lazi language, published a dictionary, created schoolbooks for teaching written and spoken Lazi, and begun developing a history of the Lazi people. These materials have been smuggled back into Turkey and made available to Lazi who want to study or use them.

The story of the Lazi and Feurstein is included in this chapter to illustrate an important issue in social science research: Both interpretive and critical paradigms come to different conclusions about the ethical nature of his work than do many postpositivists.

To his critics, who include some Western academics, what Feurstein is doing is morally and scientifically wrong. Their crudest argument is that nationalism is in all circumstances evil, and that to encourage it is therefore unpardonable. The second, more formidable line of objection is that any student of another society has an obligation to do no more than study. It may be inevitable that the very presence of a foreign researcher will to some extent contaminate and modify the behaviour under examination, but to take sides in that society's disputes, still more to set out to change its attitudes irrevocably, is a monstrous intrusion and a violation of scientific responsibility. (Ascherson, 1995, p. 207)

The second line of criticism identified by Ascherson derives from objectivism. To a postpositivist the researcher is an uninvolved, objective observer who "tells the truth" about the data gathered. This idea was a central issue in one of the more popular science fiction television series, *Star Trek*. The Prime Directive on the voyage of discovery through the universe was to do nothing that would interfere with the natural path of development of any culture encountered. This was a central issue in many episodes.

Star Trek's Prime Directive is a pure expression of postpositivist ethics. On the other hand, both interpretive and critical paradigms allow for, and may even insist on, the involvement and participation of the researcher in the context of study. As Feurstein (1995) sees it, "I did not wish to write about a people, but for a people" (p. 207). He is proud that his alphabet and his textbooks are being used in Lazi homes and by teachers in classrooms populated by Lazi children.

Ascherson (1995) aptly characterizes the question of whether Feurstein is ethical or not:

> This is a dilemma as old as the social sciences—which are not very old, but already battle-scarred. It sounds like a dispute over professional ethics, but it is really an argument about cognition. One side defends the idea that "facts speak," and that the scholar must therefore listen to them in impartial silence. The other side retorts that facts say almost anything the investigator wants, and that what he hears in the silence is no more than the mutter of his own unacknowledged prejudices. (p. 207)

Ascherson's prose illustrates the depth of his commitment to the ideas of participative qualitative research when he comments that for Feurstein "a scientist is not a camera, and the scientist's duty to a vanishing culture is not only to record but to offer wisdom and to say: 'This end is not inevitable. There is a way to survive, and I can point you towards it'" (1995, p. 209).

Doing ethical research is thus not as simple as following a set of rules. In fact, there are some rules that vary from one paradigm to another. You should not necessarily adopt Feurstein's participative approach to qualitative research, but it is important for you to know the ethical guidelines of your field and to make reasoned and thoughtful decisions about them. And when there is a question of ethics with competing answers, you should understand why there is an argument and make informed choices.

Summary

Approaches such as hermeneutics and connoisseurship have been treated in this chapter as frameworks for data collection and analysis. They are not necessarily limited to that level of influence (e.g., data collection and analysis) in qualitative research, however. In other publications some of these frameworks may be appropriately treated as paradigms, research methods, or data analysis strategies. However, they are discussed in this chapter because they are important frameworks for thinking about qualitative data.

The frameworks discussed are only a small sample of those in use today. They could be organized along a number of continua. For example, some are based on the idea that better understanding emerges if the data are treated holistically. Others break the data down into small units and then build broader and broader generalizations as the data analysis proceeds. That is the way the frameworks were generally organized in this chapter: from loose and holistic to structured and atomistic. Another continuum is foundational. Some approaches are based on phenomenological and structural theories and thus look for universals. Others are based on interpretive theories and look for contextual understanding.

There is also a third general issue that complicates matters and makes it especially difficult for novices to make choices about frameworks. That issue is the overlap between the frameworks. As you read about the different frameworks, you probably noted that the basic principles of many of them are very similar. An emphasis on understanding or meaning in context, for example, is a core belief of several frameworks. Therefore, these are not a set of frameworks that represent totally different approaches. Some seem almost identical in core beliefs but tend to emphasize certain types of subject matter or certain research methods. Others differ from similar frameworks more in their origins than anything else. That is, a framework that grew out of sociology may be very similar to one that emerged from psychology or anthropology, but the two frameworks generally show up in different journals and have different supporting organizations. All this makes thinking about frameworks complex.

Additionally, many of the frameworks have developed their own specialized language, or jargon. For example, hermeneutic jargon is not always the same as the jargon of semiotics even when one is discussing essentially the same thing. Doing research in some frameworks calls for the acquisition of a new vocabulary in which there are new terms to learn and new meanings for many old, established terms.

Fortunately, the purpose of this chapter was not to present all the options in some organized fashion and then present the right one for you to learn. There is no single framework for doing qualitative research. For example, you probably noticed that some of the frameworks discussed in this chapter do not agree with some of the family resemblances of qualitative research discussed earlier. There are many frameworks, and the decisions you make about them are not simply technical ones. In fact, most involve fundamental beliefs and an appreciation of the particular nuances of a framework. You should think about these frameworks not as watertight compartments that are distinct and separate but as advocacy groups for particular viewpoints and areas of emphasis. The framework you decide to use in your own research may not reflect the beliefs of any single framework. Instead, it may be a reflection of your own thinking that draws from and is based on the scholarship in several different compatible frameworks.

Questions for Reflection

1. Of the six types of decisions you must make to do qualitative research, which are you most sure of at this point? Why? Which are you least sure of? Why?

2. When you think of the purposes of research—from general theory to storytelling—which purposes are you most comfortable with? Why? Which are you least sure are appropriate for social science research? Why?

3. Which data analysis methods seem most compatible with your approach to social science research? Why? Are you completely comfortable with that method, or do you have some concerns? Why?

4. After reading the section on the ethics of research, what would be the most likely conflict you as a researcher would have with standard ethical guidelines? Can you see ways of dealing with the issues that would be ethical to you and to those who initially disagree with you?

Note

1. From Klein, H. K., and Myers, M. D., A set of principles for conducting and evaluating interpretive field studies in information systems, in *MIS Quarterly*, *23*(1), 67–93, copyright © 1999. Used with permission.

References

Ascherson, N. (1995). *Black Sea.* London: Hill and Wang.

Atkinson, P., & Delamont, S. (2005). Analytic perspectives. In N. Denzin & Y. Lincoln (Eds.), *The SAGE handbook of qualitative research* (3rd ed., pp. 821–840). Thousand Oaks, CA: Sage.

Bogdan, R., & Biklen, S. (1998). *Qualitative research for education* (3rd ed.). Boston: Allyn & Bacon.

Bosk, C., & De Vries, R. (2004, September). Bureaucracies of mass deception: Institutional review boards and the ethics of ethnographic research. *Annals of the American Academy of Political and Social Science, 595,* 249–263.

Charmaz, K. (2005). Grounded theory in the 21st century. In N. Denzin & Y. Lincoln (Eds.), *The SAGE handbook of qualitative research* (3rd ed., pp. 507–535). Thousand Oaks, CA: Sage.

Cohen, M., Kahn, D., & Reeves, S. (2000). *Hermeneutic phenomenological research.* Thousand Oaks, CA: Sage.

Collins, P. (1998). Negotiating selves: Reflections on "'unstructured'" interviewing. *Sociological Research Online, 3*(3). Retrieved April 13, 2006, from http://www.socresonline.org.uk/socresonline/3/3/2.html

Cushman, T. (2004, March). Anthropology and genocide in the Balkans: An analysis of conceptual practices of power. *Anthropological Theory, 4,* 5–28.

Detardo-Bora, K. (2004, September). Action research in a world of positivist-oriented review boards. *Action Research, 2,* 237–253.

Eisner, E. W. (1985). *The educational imagination* (2nd ed.). New York: Macmillan.

Eisner, E. (1998). *The enlightened eye: Qualitative inquiry and the enhancement of educational practice.* Upper Saddle River, NJ: Merrill.

Emihovich, C. (1999). Compromised positions: The ethics and politics of designing research in the postmodern age. *Educational Policy, 3,* 37–46.

Feurstein, W. (1992). Mingrelisch, Lazisch, Swanisch: Alte Sprachen und Kulturen der Kolchis vor dem baldigen Untergang. In G. Hewitt (Ed.), *Caucasian perspectives* (pp. 285–328). Unterschleissheim, Germany: Lincom Europa.

Feurstein, W. (1995). Quoted in N. Ascherson, *Black sea.* London: Hill and Wang.

Feyerabend, P. (1981). *Problems of empiricism* (Vol. 2). Cambridge: Cambridge University Press.

Flinders, D. A., & Eisner, W. E. (1994). Educational criticism as a form of qualitative inquiry. *Research in the Teaching of English, 28*(4), 341–361.

Gadamer, H. (1976). The historicity of understanding. In P. Connerton (Ed.), *Critical sociology: Selected readings* (pp. 117–133). Harmondsworth, UK: Penguin.

Glaser, B. (1978). *Theoretical sensitivity: Advances in the methodology of grounded theory.* Mill Valley, CA: Sociology Press.

Glaser, B. (1993). *Examples of grounded theory: A reader.* Mill Valley, CA: Sociology Press.

Glaser, B., & Strauss, A. (1967). *The discovery of grounded theory.* Chicago: Aldine.

Helgeland, I. (2005, August). "Catch 22" of research ethics: Ethical dilemmas in follow-up studies of marginal groups. *Qualitative Inquiry, 11,* 549–569.

Kelle, U. (1997). Theory building in qualitative research and computer programs for the management of textual data. *Sociological Research Online, 2*(2). Retrieved April 13, 2006, from http://www.socresonline.org.uk/socresonline/2/2/1.html

Kinzer, S. (2001). *Crescent and star: Turkey between two worlds.* New York: Farrar, Straus, & Giroux.

Klein, H., & Meyers, M. (1998). A set of principles for conducting and evaluating interpretive field studies in information systems. *MIS Quarterly*. Retrieved April 13, 2006, from http://www.auckland.ac.nz/msis/isworld/MMyers/Klein-Myers.html

Megill, A. (1999). [No title.] Retrieved April 13, 2006, from http://www.people.virginia.edu/~adm9e/articles/

Merriam, S. (1998). *Qualitative research and case study applications in education.* San Francisco: Jossey-Bass.

Miles, A., & Huberman, M. (1994). *Qualitative data analysis: A new sourcebook of methods* (2nd ed.). Newbury Park, CA: Sage.

Neyland, M. (1992). *Educational computing research: A non-universal methodology.* Paper presented at the annual joint conference of the Australian Association for Research in Education and the New Zealand Association for Research in Education. Retrieved April 13, 2006, from http://www.swin.edu .au/aare/conf92/NEYLM92.269

Oakes, J. (2002, October). Risks and wrongs in social science research: An evaluator's guide to the IRB. *Evaluation Research, 26,* 443–479.

Phillips, J. (1996). Key concepts: Hermeneutics. *Philosophy, Psychiatry, & Psychology, 3*(1), 61–69. Retrieved April 13, 2006, from http://muse.jhu.edu/demo/ philosophy_psychiatry_and_psychology/3.1phillips.html

Rankin-Brown, M. S. (2006). *Increasing awareness of self and culture through writing research.* Paper presented at the 2006 California Teaching English as a Second Language Conference. Retrieved September 22, 2006, from http://www.catesol.org/Rankin-Brown_2.pdf

Ricoeur, P. (1974). *The conflict of interpretations: Essays in hermeneutics.* Evanston, IL: Northwestern University Press.

Smith, J. (1993). *After the demise of empiricism: The problem of judging social and educational inquiry.* New York: Ablex.

Sohng, S. (1995). *Participatory research and community organizing.* A working paper presented at the New Social Movement and Community Organizing Conference, University of Washington, Seattle, November 1–3, 1995. Retrieved April 13, 2006, from http://weber.u.washington.edu/~jamesher/sue.htm

Strauss, A. (1987). *Qualitative analysis for social scientists.* Cambridge: Cambridge University Press.

Strauss, A., & Corbin, J. (1997). *Grounded theory in practice.* Thousand Oaks, CA: Sage.

Torbert, W. R. (1981). Why educational research has been so uneducational: The case for a new model of social science based on collaborative inquiry. In P. Reason & J. Rowan (Eds.), *Human inquiry* (pp. 141–152). New York: Wiley.

Van Manen, M. (1990). *Researching the lived experience.* Albany, NY: SUNY Press.

Weisburd, D. (2003, June). Ethical practice and evaluation of interventions in crime and justice: The moral imperative for randomized trials. *Evaluation Review, 27,* 336–354.

CHAPTER 9

21st-Century Social Science Research

Peering Into the Future

In the 20th century social scientists experienced many paradigm changes and conceptual revolutions and an explosion of methodological developments. The century ended not so much on a single pleasing note as with a cacophony of loud, diverse, and uncoordinated notes. Those notes are the many different paradigms, subparadigms, methodological groups, and topic or discipline groups that make up what we generally call social science.

However, the social sciences are so diverse, and there is so much disagreement about what constitutes social science, what it should study, and what constitutes valid and meaningful research that some may think there really is nothing we can call social science. Pushed to its logical but extreme conclusion, this line of thought leads to the belief that we should get rid of the term *social science* altogether because it has no real meaning. However, the problem is more that *social science* has too many meanings. Associated with each of those meanings is a group of methods, metaphors, and basic assumptions that proponents attempt to neatly package and offer to unwary college students who happen to wander into graduate and undergraduate courses in one of the social sciences.

Will the Cacophony Continue?

Western thought tends to make two assumptions that are so deeply embedded in the culture that they are often hard for us to separate from other important issues in order to discuss and critique them separately. The first assumption is that competition usually is the best way to make choices. The American and Western European emphasis on sports—from the Olympics, to cricket, to soccer, to American football—is an obvious example of how competition is emphasized. However, there are many other examples. Our criminal justice system has two groups, prosecutors and defense attorneys, who compete for the jury's vote. Our system of government is also competitive: Candidates must compete with others running for the same office, and the one with the highest number of votes wins the election (at least theoretically). Similarly, the capitalist economic system is based on the idea that "marketplace competition" will encourage efficiencies in the system and result in the best products at the best prices for the most people.

There are hundreds of other examples of the deeply embedded assumption that competition is the best way of making choices. Academic life is also competitive. We present our ideas, research, interpretations, and methods to an audience and hope that the audience will decide that what we communicate warrants their attention. However, in almost every situation, valuing what we say means the audience must ignore or reject what another group is saying about the same topic. Even before readers can make a decision about what to value, a group of referees will review a paper submitted to a journal and decide whether it merits being published. And when a faculty member is considered for annual merit salary increases, promotion, or tenure, his or her publications often are ranked according to whether they are in the top journals in their field or in lower-ranked journals. This is all part of competition. This competitive aspect of social science (which is also an element in almost every other human endeavor in the West) is one reason social science, for the foreseeable future, will be an intellectual landscape where there are many competing views that call for a reasoned and thoughtful selection process on the part of the audience. However, the idea that this form of competition leads us inevitably to selecting the best research to be distributed to other social scientists is not difficult to challenge. In the 20th century, when B. F. Skinner and his followers had difficulty publishing their research about the influence of reinforcement schedules on the behavior of pigeons, they established a new journal, *The Journal for the Experimental Analysis of Behavior,* which is still in print. And when applied behaviorist researchers began to study the impact of token reinforcement systems and other types of contingency management procedures on the behavior of humans with problems, they also had difficulty getting published in the top journals in their field. They established *The Journal for Applied Behavior Analysis,* which is also still in print. These two journals are now the top journals for scholars and researchers who work within a Skinnerian paradigm. Competition for space in the journals, for slots at conferences, and for attention from readers clearly is not a total meritocracy; it is determined at least in part by the values of the community of scholars that evaluate your work. It would be rare, if not impossible, for the same paper to be accepted by the journal *Qualitative Inquiry* and by *The Journal of Experimental Psychology,* even if the topic of the paper was appropriate for both journals. The dominant paradigms in the two journals are different, and it is the ideology, the preferred paradigm, that guides reviewers when they judge a paper, not some generally agreed-upon and universal standard for what constitutes good research.

Within your field, whether it be economics, history, sociology, education, or another social science, there will be important questions of substance, theory, practice, and research methodology that are answered very differently by different groups within your field. Someone looking for an emerging consensus, even within just one of the social sciences such as psychology, will be disappointed in the 21st century. Diverse perspectives, contradictory answers to important questions, and continued debates about the "right" way to do research in the social sciences will continue for the foreseeable future. To some extent that is to be expected in a culture that values competition highly.

Why Can't the Social Sciences Converge on the Answer?

The second tendency in Western thought is linearity. Western scholars tend to think in linear ways, from a start to an end. Even the dominant, Judeo-Christian religion has a story of the beginning of everything and an assumption that the physical world as we know it will come to an end. As Carol Bell at Louisiana State University points out, not all religions assume that there was a beginning and that there will be an end. This linear form of thought is replaced by cyclic models of existence in some religions, for example. A soul, spirit, or person may be born, live, die, be born another time, live, die, and so on through an unending number of cycles.

We want the social sciences to converge on the answers to questions that concern us in part because we have absorbed the Western assumption of linearity. In modernist versions of social science, one way linearity is expressed is in the belief in progress, the idea that we are gradually learning more and more about ourselves and the world around us. (A further assumption of modernist perspectives is that more knowledge is good because it supports "progress," which is good.)

This belief in linear progress can even lead to efforts to force everyone to accept what those in power consider to be the answer. However, as Paulo Freire (1997) points out in *Pedagogy of the Heart,* "Authoritarian regimes are enemies of curiosity. They punish citizens for displaying it. Authoritarian power is prying, not curious or questioning" (p. 99). Freire was talking about governments, but his concerns also apply to the academic world. Imposing a hegemony of either a social science research method or a paradigm is unlikely to bring about long-lasting, beneficial change. At the turn of the century, the Bush administration's efforts to impose a postpositivist approach to research on education led, inevitably, to a strong and aggressive counterattack. The flyer advertising a book titled *Qualitative Inquiry and the Conservative Challenge* (Denzin & Giardina, 2006) begins with this paragraph:

> This volume is a call to qualitative researchers to respond to the political and methodological conservatism of the new millennium. Scholars from five countries and many academic disciplines address how qualitative inquiry can maintain its forward-looking agenda, its emphasis on ethical practice, and its stance in favor of social justice in a world where conservatives control the political system, the university, and grant agency purse strings.

The advertising flyer gives you a flavor of how easy it is to mythologize a favored view and demonize the opposition. For example, the ethical practice of research is a concern in all paradigms, but the definition of what is ethical may be different. However, the aggressive tone of the flyer is mild compared with some of the commentary from supporters of opposing views. Consider these quotes from Roger Kimball's (1998) book *Tenured Radicals:*

> The situation is far graver today than it was a decade ago when exotic phenomena such as Afrocentrism, Queer Theory, Critical Legal Studies, and the attack on science by so-called humanists were just beginning to gather steam. Now more than ever those dominating the discussion in academia are committed to discrediting the ideals of objectivity and disinterested scholarship by injecting politics into the heart of the educational enterprise. . . .
> Like most modern tyrannies, the dictatorship of the politically correct has freely used and abused the rhetoric of virtue in its effort

to enforce conformity and silence dissent. This is part of what makes it so seductive. . . . But the union of moralism and radicalism . . . is particularly destructive when applied to institutions dedicated to intellectual inquiry. Not only does it foster an atmosphere of intimidation and encourage slavish conformity, but it also attacks the very basis for the free exchange of ideas. . . .

Such vertiginous nonsense—ranging over disciplines as various as literature, law, history, and the social sciences—now constitutes a large proportion of what is taught and pursued as "scholarship" in the academy. Typically combining hermetic jargon and a profound animus against the achievements of the Western moral and intellectual tradition, such politicized rhetoric governs the teaching of the humanities from the ground up. . . .

Indeed, for the gender–race–class cadres that now dominate the discussion in the university, all social, artistic, and intellectual life must be subjected to a battery of political tests. This marks what we might call the Sovietization of intellectual life, where the value or truth of a work is determined not by its intrinsic qualities (many deny that "intrinsic qualities" even exist) but by the degree to which it supports a given political line. . . .

In preparing this new edition I have again and again been reminded that if things were bad in 1990 they are much worse today. This is largely because the radical trends that seemed startling in 1990 have by now thoroughly established themselves. They are part of the ambient cultural poison surrounding us: so familiar as to be barely detectable, but progressively damaging nevertheless. . . . The story that this edition of *Tenured Radicals* tells is the same: an unhappy tale of intellectual chicanery, pedagogical dereliction, and moral irresponsibility. (pp. x–xix)

With such rhetoric from an opposing viewpoint, it is little wonder that opponents also engage in aggressive rhetoric. However, the Denzin and Giardina book itself is a thoughtful response to a multilevel, aggressive, and powerful effort to give preference to one ideological framework, from funding to influence at the tables of policymakers. Both sides in the debate, what Denzin and Giardina (2006) call the conservative challenge on one side, and the interpretive and critical coalition of social scientists and humanists who oppose them, tend to see this as a competition in which one side must "win" and another must lose. That is the nature of competition in the Western intellectual tradition. There is also an element of linear thinking in this way of looking at the competition between different paradigms or philosophies of social science. The competing paradigms propose what they think is true and expect that more scholarship will eventually show that one is true and the other is wrong. This is a rather simplistic view of how science, natural or social, works. In most cases the competing paradigms are both replaced by a third that eventually offers more than either of the existing paradigms. The third paradigm often incorporates aspects of all the paradigms it replaced. Thus, although protagonists in the paradigm wars don't usually see it this way, there is usually some value and meaning in each of the paradigms that compete for our attention and fealty. If we accept that assumption, a highly competitive approach to selecting the "best" paradigm or research method may not make sense because none of the competing paradigms are completely wrong or completely right. Also, none of the competing paradigms are completely finished. They are all in the process of changing, evolving, and adapting.

Dialog as an Alternative to Competition

Paulo Freire worked within the critical theory paradigm for most of his life, but he also emerged from the liberation theology movement (C. Underwood, personal communication, 2006) that, until it was strongly discouraged by the Vatican several years ago, provided a framework for Catholic activism with South American urban and rural poor. Like the conservative challenge addressed by Denzin and Giardina, both critical theory and liberation theology have at times been confrontational and aggressive in their efforts to liberate the oppressed. However, in one of the last books he wrote, Freire (1997), who remained a committed leftist, said,

> No leftist party can remain faithful to its democratic dream if it falls into the temptation of rallying cries, slogans, prescriptions, indoctrination, and the untouchable power of leaderships. Such temptations inhibit the development of tolerance, in the absence of which democracy is not viable.
>
> No leftist party can remain faithful to its democratic dream if it falls into the temptation of seeing itself as possessing a truth outside of which there is no salvation, or if its leadership proclaims itself as the avant-garde edge of the working class. . . .
>
> An authentic progressive party must not become sectarian, for that would represent a move away from its normal radical position. Radicalness is tolerant, sectarianism is blind and antidemocratic. (pp. 82–83)

In *Pedagogy of the Heart,* Freire (1997) imparts some of the lessons he learned both as a leftist activist who was imprisoned and then exiled from his native Brazil by the CIA-backed right-wing military junta that took control of the country in 1964 and later as a member of a leftist Worker's Party government in the city of São Paulo in the 1980s. Freire's advice was for those active in politics, but it also applies to social science scholars who must decide what paradigms they will use and which ones they will ignore or reject. Freire talks about "unity within diversity" to emphasize that we must not be so sectarian that we reject both valuable sources of knowledge and even whole communities of scholars who may have something to share with us. He also speaks about the need for humility in our self-valuation because that is a precondition for something he values highly: tolerance.

Humility and tolerance are in turn prerequisites for what Freire calls dialogism, which he views as an essential aspect of human knowing. He views it as a critical method of teaching and learning. For Freire, dialogism is a "requirement of human nature" and the foundation of the democratic process, and it involves a permanent search for knowledge in which humans reflect on and interact with their world and with each other.

> A dialogic relationship—communication and intercommunication among active subjects who are immune to the bureaucratization of their minds and open to discovery and to knowing more—is indispensable to knowledge. The social nature of this process makes a dialogical relationship a natural element of it. In that sense, authoritarian antidialogue violates the nature of human beings, their process of discovery, and it contradicts democracy. . . . Dialogue . . . is full of curiosity and unrest. It is full of mutual respect between the dialoging subjects. Dialogism presupposes maturity, a spirit of adventure, confidence in questioning, and seriousness in providing answers. (p. 99)

Freire's idea of coming to know through humility, tolerance, and dialog with others and with the world around us may be a good general guide for social science scholars. However, this approach requires us to stop deifying two foundations of Western thought—linearity and competition—and one of the major implications of those two foundations: the assertion that we steadily progress toward absolute and general truths about our world and ourselves. This is not easy, however, in part because its history in Western thought involves choices made long ago.

Three Approaches to Knowing in Greek Thought

Three traditions in Greek thought have had a profound influence on both the natural and the social sciences. One was the approach of Plato, who rejected the study of the physical world as a source of true knowledge.

Instead, he proposed that we use dialog and our rational skills to understand the "ideal forms" that are the perfect, nonmaterial instances of everything from a horse and a government to the concept of virtue. Aristotle, on the other hand, rejected Plato's emphasis on contemplation, reflection, and dialog as the primary sources of truth. Instead, he took a much more empirical approach to knowledge development. In Aristotle's system, "ideal forms" were to be found in careful observations of the material world.

The ideal forms are really another way of talking about absolutes. Both Aristotle and Plato were searching for absolute truths, but they disagreed on the best ways to arrive at those truths. One sought knowledge through contemplation, thought, and dialog; the other emphasized empirical study of the world around us. Some have described Plato's approach as mystical or as emphasizing received wisdom, but it comes closer to what we think of as philosophy today.

Aristotle and Plato also disagreed on the value of a third source of knowledge for the ancient Greeks: the humanities. Plato considered all "poets" to be liars, and in *The Republic* he even proposed that they be expelled from the ideal Greek polis (city state) because they were likely to mislead citizens. In Greek, the word translated as *poet* literally means "maker," and it applied to many types of authors. Plato's rejection of poets was thus a rejection of much of what we call the humanities today. Aristotle, on the other hand, wrote the first piece of literary criticism, *Poetics,* and explained in some detail the value of Greek prose and poetry.

In the 20th century social science made some choices about issues that go all the way back to Plato and Aristotle.

Accepting Plato, Aristotle, and the Humanities: There Is Absolute Truth

All three traditions—Plato, Aristotle, and the Greek humanities—tried to find and express enduring and universal truths. For the most part the social sciences have also accepted this as a goal. The empirical approach of Aristotle has dominated the Western intellectual tradition for the last 300 years, but the other two have always been there as well. A modern approach with much in common with Plato's rational idealism is Ayn Rand's Objectivist philosophy. Her novels, such as *Atlas Shrugged* and *The Fountainhead,* are still widely read, and her philosophy is a favorite of libertarian, minimalist government advocates. In 2006 a new journal, *The Objective Standard: A Journal of Culture and Politics* (http://www.theobjectivestandard.com/), began publication. It is based on Rand's approach, which seeks absolute truth through an approach that has more in common with Plato than with either Aristotle or the Greek humanists. In his introduction to the journal, Craig Biddle (2006) describes the journal's foundational philosophy:

> It is widely believed today that our cultural and political alternatives are limited either to the ideas of the secular, relativistic left—or to those of the religious, absolutist right—or to some compromised mixture of the two. In other words, one's ideas are supposedly either extremely liberal or extremely conservative or somewhere in-between. We at *The Objective Standard* reject this false alternative and embrace an entirely different view of the world.
>
> Our view is fully secular and absolutist; it is neither liberal nor conservative nor anywhere in-between. Our philosophy uncompromisingly recognizes and upholds the natural (this-worldly), factual, moral foundations of a fully free, civilized society.
>
> Culturally, we advocate scientific advancement, productive achievement, objective (as opposed to "progressive" or faith-based) education, romantic art—and, above all, reverence for the faculty that makes all such values possible: reason. Politically, we advocate pure, laissez-faire capitalism—the social system of individual rights and strictly limited government—along with the whole moral and philosophical structure on which it depends. In a word, we advocate Objectivism, the philosophy of Ayn Rand, and apply its principles to the cultural and political issues of the day.
>
> Ayn Rand described Objectivism as "a philosophy for living on earth." The reason why it is a philosophy for living on earth is that its every principle is derived from the observable facts of reality and the demonstrable requirements of human life and happiness.
>
> As a philosophical system, Objectivism includes a view of the nature of reality, of man's means of knowledge, of man's nature and means of survival, of a proper morality, of a proper social system, and of the nature and value of art. Ayn Rand presented her philosophy in her many fiction and nonfiction books, such as *The Fountainhead, Atlas Shrugged, Philosophy: Who Needs It?, The Virtue of Selfishness, Capitalism: The Unknown Ideal*, and *The Romantic Manifesto*.

Rand's Objectivist philosophy is not the only modern Platonic alternative, however. In *Christianity and the Soul of the University: Faith as a Foundation for Intellectual Community* (Henry & Beaty, 2006), a group of authors explain why the Christian faith should be the foundation for the intellectual communities that have become modern universities. The approach advocated by these authors represents another version of Plato's approach that comes to quite different conclusions. It is based on Christian thought, which was influenced by Plato through the neo-Platonists. The Christian concept of The Word, which derives from Plato's idea of Logos, is the foundation for a prescription for universities that is quite different from the model that emerges from Ayn Rand's ideology, yet both have Platonic roots.

Rejecting Plato, Accepting Aristotle: Empiricism (and Later the Scientific Method) Is the Royal Road to Knowledge

The dominant 20th-century traditions in social science rejected Plato's Idealism and his heavy reliance on contemplation and dialog. Instead, social science has tended to follow Aristotle and to emphasize empirical data collection as the preferred, even exclusive source of knowledge.

Accepting Plato, Rejecting Aristotle: Social Science Is Separate From the Humanities

In terms of their relationship with the humanities, the social sciences have generally followed Plato and rejected the humanities as a source of knowledge. Typically, the social sciences have considered the humanities as a way of expressing truths that were discovered in some other way. The idea that a novelist, for example, might actually be someone who can discover knowledge and communicate it to us was not acceptable to most social scientists in the 20th century.

Suppose We Chose Poorly?

In the movie *Indiana Jones and the Last Crusade,* the Templar knight, who had for hundreds of years guarded the sacred cave in the Egyptian desert, commented, "He chose poorly" after the wealthy Nazi collaborator shriveled and turned to dust in one of the special effects scenes Hollywood values so highly today. That was after the man had selected a beautiful chalice and drunk from it on the assumption that it was Christ's chalice. Christ's chalice was actually the most humble of those arrayed around the room. Thus, the Grail Knight commented, "He chose poorly."

Suppose social science in the Western tradition has chosen poorly and that we should have made different choices?

Rejecting the Fundamentalism of Both Aristotle and Plato: The Search for Knowing Is Continuous

Despite Freire's identity as a leftist activist, his theory of knowledge emphasizes that we must never become doctrinaire and "sectarian" in our beliefs. Richard Rorty (2006) makes the same point over and over again when he urges all the sciences, including the social sciences, to reject the idea of absolute truth and instead to encourage democratic dialog as a means of better understanding the world. The title of Rorty's (2006) book, *Take Care of Freedom and Truth Will Take Care of Itself,* expresses his view. Giving up the belief that social science can find, and then communicate, absolute truths may be the most important but most difficult step to take, especially because the two major Greek foundations for Western thought, Plato and Aristotle, both accepted the idea that humans can know absolute truth. However, the fact that they sought it in very different ways and had different definitions of what that truth was indicates how contentious the idea is. The position succinctly expressed by Denzin and Lincoln (2005) sums up the alternative to absolute truth in social science:

> It is . . . clear that there is no single "truth." All truths are partial and incomplete. There will be no single conventional paradigm . . . to which all social scientists might ascribe. We occupy a historical moment marked by multivocality, contested meanings, paradigmatic controversies, and new textual forms. This is an age of emancipation, freedom from the confines of a single regime of truth, emancipation from seeing the world in one color. (p. 189)

Rejecting Aristotle and Plato Again: Value Many Sources of Knowledge, Not Just One

As the quote from Denzin and Lincoln suggests, if social science accepts that the search for absolute truths is doomed to failure, an important implication for research is that we cannot trust any particular research method or technique. Plato was very skeptical of Aristotle's belief in the empirical study of the physical world, and Aristotle was skeptical of Plato's belief in rational reflection and dialog as a path to truth. Perhaps a desirable alternative to both positions is to respect and value multiple sources rather than just one. Kincheloe and Berry (2004) argue against "monological knowledge" that involves taking "unilateral perspectives." They view the subject matter of social science as complex and argue that such subject matter cannot be understood through unilateral perspectives. What happens if we heed the advice of scholars such as Kincheloe and Berry? In the social sciences this would mean scholars in the qualitative tradition, for example, would pay attention to quantitative research, and vice versa. Even more important, no particular paradigm can be taken for granted as *the* correct world view. If we are, as Freire explains it, on a continuing search that has no end (and thus is not necessarily linear), we can never be completely sure of our foundations—even if we believe there are no absolute foundations. Two contemporary trends that express this view are the mixed-method approach to research (Tashakkori & Teddlie, 2002) and a framework for research called bricolage (Kincheloe & Berry, 2004).

The saying that "to someone with only a hammer, the whole world looks like a nail" aptly expresses what movements such as mixed methods and bricolage are trying to avoid. As Kincheloe and Berry (2004) explain, a bricoleur

> labours to expose the various structures that covertly shape our own and other scholars' research narratives, [and] the bricolage highlights the relationship between a researcher's ways of seeing and the social location of his or her personal history. . . . The researcher-as-bricoleur abandons the quest for some naïve concept of realism, focusing instead on the clarification of his or her position in the web of reality and the social locations of other researchers and the way they shape the production and interpretation of knowledge. (p. 2)

Kincheloe and Berry (2004) take a nonfoundational, contextual approach to the relationship between theory and research data, which means you cannot disentangle your theory from your data. Thus, the possibility of objectivity is lost, and that has implications for how researchers should be trained.

> The education of researchers demands that everyone take a step back from the process of learning research methods. Such a step back allows us a conceptual distance that produces a critical consciousness. Such a consciousness refuses the passive acceptance of externally imposed research methods that tacitly certify modes justifying knowledges that are decontextualized and reductionistic. (p. 3)

In the place of a search for reductionistic knowledge, Kincheloe and Berry (2004) propose that we use several tools, including context and discourse to both understand our own subjectivity and the subjectivity of the truths we derive from data.

> Whether one is attempting to make sense of a novelist, an interviewee, or a historical manuscript, discourse and context are central dimensions of the interpretative act. . . . The bricoleur's attention to discursive and contextual dimensions of knowledge production does not make one anti-empiricist or anti-quantitative. Instead, such concerns make the bricoleur more attentive to the various dynamics that shape what is called empirical knowledge. In this context such a researcher is less willing to make a final statement of truth or meaning based on the empirical investigations in which she has engaged. The bricoleur knows that empirical data viewed from another perspective or questioned by one from a different background can elicit fundamentally different interpretations. (p. 7)

Kincheloe and Berry's (2004) interpretation of bricolage makes awareness and use of different methods, different viewpoints, and different scholarly literatures a virtue. They do not reject Aristotle's empirical study of the physical world; they are not antiquantitative even though they are qualitative researchers. They go even further and argue that "philosophical research" is also important to a social scientist. By that phrase they mean "the use of various philosophical tools to help clarify the process of inquiry and provide insight into the assumptions on which it conceptually rests" (p. 8). Thus, unlike Aristotle, Kincheloe and Berry do not reject Plato's ways of knowing.

> The bricolage makes use of philosophical research into the boundary between the social world and the narrative representation of it. Such explorations provide profound and often unrecognized knowledge about what exactly is produced when researchers describe the social world. Rigor, I [Kincheloe] assert, is impossible without such knowledge and discernment. Exploring this complex, ever shifting boundary between the social world and the narrative representation of it, philosophically informed bricoleurs begin to document the specific influences of life history, lived context, race, class, gender and sexuality on researchers and the knowledge they produce. (p. 8)

Kincheloe's bricoleur thus represents a social scientist who expresses the humble, tolerant, nonsectarian values advocated by Freire. Both Plato's and Aristotle's ways of knowing are valued.

Rejecting Plato and Accepting Aristotle's Advice About Poets: Link Closely With the Humanities

In 1962 C. P. Snow published *The Two Cultures and the Scientific Revolution,* a book in which he asserts that there are two cultures in universities: the sciences and the humanities. These two cultures do not speak the same languages, study the same problems, or advocate the same answers. Snow's solution to this situation was to suggest that the humanities learn to be like the sciences. That is still considered a desirable suggestion by some natural scientists. A sizable percentage of social scientists today probably would not accept humanities as a source of knowledge in the same way that social sciences such as sociology, history, economics, and psychology are. This is the modern expression of Plato's view of the humanities. But what if Aristotle was right and the poet is an important source of understanding and wisdom? Gruenwald (2005) thinks Aristotle was correct. In an article titled "The Third Culture" he argues that the natural sciences and the humanities are valid and worthwhile sources of knowledge in the social sciences.

At this point it is important to note that the separation of social science from the humanities is more a problem in the English-speaking thread of the Western tradition. The close linkage of social and natural science that is characteristic of English scholarly traditions is not so dominant in other language groups, nor is the strong boundary between the social sciences and the humanities. In Russian, for example, the term *gumanitarnyje nauki,* or "humanitarian sciences," includes literature, linguistics, sociology, psychology, anthropology, philosophy, history, economics, law, education, and more. The German word *geisteswissenschaften* covers a similarly broad range of what the British and Americans separate into social sciences and humanities.

If we accept the idea that multiple sources of knowledge ought to be valued, social science should not break completely with the methods and models of natural science. The historic links should be kept, and social science, practiced as if it were a natural science based on the scientific method, should be valued as a potential source of understanding and knowledge (but not as the sole source of knowledge or the source of absolute truths). However, that openness to the natural sciences and their methods should be balanced on the other side by an openness not only to qualitative research and what Kincheloe and Berry call "philosophical research" but to the humanities in general. Both Denzin and Lincoln (2005) and Kincheloe and Berry (2004) make strong arguments for the social sciences becoming closer and more attentive to the humanities. Thomas Gould's (1991) book *The Ancient Quarrel Between Poetry and Philosophy* traces the history of the humanities since they were rejected by Plato and praised by Aristotle. When Gould discusses two visions of the world, that of the poet and that of the philosopher, what he says about philosophers also applies to many social scientists today:

> Philosophers, unlike poets, usually hunger for a single, internally consistent explanation for truth and are therefore apt to be hostile to the one or the other vision. There are exceptions, of course. Nietzsche tries hard to accept both visions. A few philosophers champion "poetry" against "philosophy" (Heidegger is an obvious example); but most in essence champion "philosophy" only. (p. 207)

Interestingly, Gould's analysis of the "quarrel" between the poet and the philosopher is carried out from the perspective of a social science: psychology. His is a psychoanalytic interpretation of the history of the relationship between philosophy and the humanities.

Denzin and Lincoln (2005) specifically make the case for linking the humanities and the social sciences. They note several movements in the social sciences that have encouraged greater involvement with approaches normally associated with the humanities:

> The postmodern and postexperimental moments [eras in the history of the social sciences] were defined in part by a concern for literary and rhetorical tropes and the narrative turn, a concern for storytelling, for composing ethnographies in new ways. . . . In the blurred genres phase, the humanities became central resources for critical, interpretive theory, and the qualitative research project broadly conceived. The researcher became a bricoleur, . . . learning how to borrow from many different disciplines. . . . A kind of methodological diaspora took place, a two-way exodus. Humanists migrated to the social sciences, searching for new social theory, new ways to study popular culture and its local, ethnographic contexts. Social scientists turned to the humanities, hoping to learn how to do complex, structural and poststructural readings of social texts. From the humanities, social scientists also learned how to produce texts that refused to be read in simplistic, linear, incontrovertible terms. The line between text and context blurred. (p. 3)

Denzin and Lincoln also point out that Clifford Geertz's (1973, 1983) pioneering theoretical work helped establish modern qualitative concepts of social science research and went on to propose that the boundaries between the social sciences and the humanities had become blurred. Social scientists were now turning to the humanities for models, theories and methods of analysis (semiotics, hermeneutics). A form of genre diaspora was occurring: documentaries that read like fiction (Mailer), parables posing as ethnographies (Castaneda), theoretical treatises that look like travelogues (Lévi-Strauss). (pp. 17–18)

Also in the 3rd edition of *The SAGE Handbook of Qualitative Research,* Denzin and Lincoln (2005) describe writing as "a new method of inquiry" and note, "New forms [of inquiry] include authethnography, fiction stories, poetry, drama, performance texts, polyvocal texts, readers' theater, responsive readings, aphorisms, comedy and satire, visual presentations, conversation, layered accounts, writing stories, and mixed genres" (p. 912). Laurel Richardson and Elizabeth Adams St. Pierre's (2005) chapter in the *Handbook,* titled "Writing: A Method of Inquiry," is a very good introduction to the integration of humanities methods and meanings in social science. Richardson's book (2004), written with her husband, Ernest Lockridge (who is a novelist and professor of English), titled *Travels With Ernest: Crossing the Literary/Sociological Divide,* is an interesting example of an effort to link the literary genre and social science through the vehicle of a travelogue that covers the couple's trips in Europe and the Middle East.

Two Theories That May Help Us Build 21st-Century Social Science

If we are correct and 21st-century social science continues to be multiparadigmatic and competitive, it will be difficult to adopt the three suggestions discussed in the previous section: reject absolutes; respect multiple ways of knowing across quantitative, qualitative, and philosophical ways of knowing; and reduce the barriers between social science and the humanities. However, the critical and interpretive paradigms are evolving even further toward multivocality and respect for multiple perspectives and methods. And if books such as D. C. Phillips and Nicholas Burbules's (2000) *Postpositivism and Educational Research* are any indication, even postpositivists are moving toward a "kinder and gentler" view of fundamental issues such as the nature of truth and the range of methods and purposes that are appropriate in social science research. Two emerging theoretical perspectives provide a framework for doing that: poetic logic and chaos or complexity theory. We will end the book with a brief exploration of these two emerging theoretical perspectives.

Poetic Logic

In his review of Paul Colilli's (1997) book *The Idea of a Living Spirit: Poetic Logic as a Contemporary Theory,* Daniel Kim (1998/1999) defines poetic logic this way:

> "Poetic logic'" is distinguished from classical rationalism's mathematically "clear and distinct thinking'" in being a mode of signification and cognition that is variously metaphorical, tropological, figurative, mythopoeic. Its processes of troping and metaphoric coupling draw from our so-called primal and primary modes of experience and memory—via the human sensorium, imagination, spirit, and unconscious. Rational thought in comparison results from subsequent and increasing abstraction and mediation. From banishment under Enlightenment rationalism, "poetic logic" rescues contradiction, difference, silence, the everyday and its banality, along with ancient mysteries, the sacred, and the spiritual.

In essence, Kim and Colilli are describing an alternative to rational–empirical logic. As Kim (1998/1999) explains,

> Colilli takes contemporary Western thought to be in a state of crisis and proposes a cure: "poetic logic." The crisis, of course, is one in which the scientific world-view and the rationalism that dominates its ontology and epistemology have "tor[n] the mind from body; philosophy from poetry; and in general, art from science." Following this line, the Enlightenment's contemporary legacy is a reduced, dehumanized phenomenological reality: "we have thus entered the third age in Vico's chronology of human and cultural development, an age where reason is completely severed from the temporal and spiritual realities of the human body." Colilli therefore offers "poetic logic" as an alternative mode of thought and cognition that can "salvage from obscurity and oblivion all those elements of human experience that have been marginalized by the ratiological mind-set that has dominated the Western tradition."

The Vico that Kim mentions is Giambattista Vico, an 18th-century Italian scholar who wrote *The New Science* (1725), which was actually less an effort to advance the cause of the emerging sciences than it was a statement of support for existing sources of knowledge. Vico's new science was partly a response to Descartes's hypothetico-deductive view of how knowledge is constructed from basic, "clear and distinct" ideas such as "I think, therefore I am." Vico did not think all knowledge could be reduced to precise mathematical or logical language, and he thought that adopting such criteria for true knowledge would mean that other forms of valuable knowledge would be ignored or denigrated. Vico called the idea of reducing knowledge to mathematics "conceit" on the part of humans, and he argued that an important aspect of the creation of knowledge is the fact that humans are social beings. Instead of going back to Aristotle or Plato, Vico relied heavily on Homer and the Homeric epics such as the Odyssey for many of his examples and illustrations. He suggested that poetic logic, which is not "scientific" in Descartes's meaning of the term, is an important component of full knowledge and that it must particularly be considered when we are dealing with knowledge of human behavior. Poetic knowledge is more felt and imagined than it is found in the analysis of hard data. It is often expressed in literary genres and in myths that capture important aspects of a culture. Vico accepted that the emerging scientific sources of knowledge might discover universal laws and knowledge about the world, but he argued that another, more particularistic type of knowledge is also important and must be considered valid truth as well. His universal and particular knowledge presages both the search for universal knowledge that characterizes postpositivist social science and the search for understanding and local knowledge that is the goal of interpretive scholarship.

Vico's idea of poetic knowledge was not very influential while he was alive, but since the 18th century it has been very influential. Marcel Danesi's (2004) book *Poetic Logic* is subtitled *The Role of Metaphor in Thought, Language, and Culture.* In it he traces the history of poetic logic through the centuries and makes a strong case for including it as an important way of knowing in the social sciences. He also emphasizes the importance of metaphor in poetic ways of knowing. Metaphor becomes a way of understanding the unknown by linking it to what is known:

> Like Aristotle, Vico saw metaphor as a strategy for explicating or exemplifying an abstract notion such as life. However, he went much further in claiming that the strategy itself resulted from an association of sense between what is unknown and what is familiar. (p. 15)

Danesi (2004) also points out that

> Vico's view of metaphor was largely ignored by his contemporaries. Mainstream philosophers of the era, and of the immediately succeeding one [e.g., Hegel, John Stuart Mill], continued to insist

that metaphor was no more than a decorative accessory to literal language. (p. 15)

However, Danesi notes that Kant, like Vico, believed that metaphor (figurative language) was a natural or innate way humans tried to understand the unfamiliar. Danesi's book is a very readable treatment of the concept of poetic logic and the history of its development over the past 2,500 years. Martha Nussbaum's (1995) book *Poetic Justice: The Literary Imagination and Public Life* is a more artistic defense of poetic logic in the social sciences. She uses novels such as those of Charles Dickens to make the point that we understand a situation differently when sympathy (or pathos, as Aristotle called it when he was discussing Greek tragedy) is elicited by the story being told. She criticizes the social sciences for leaving out precisely that component, which poetic logic does not, and argues that a fully developed and human social science must include it. Using examples from Walt Whitman, Charles Dickens, and E. M. Forster, she concludes that

> literary works that promote identification and emotional reaction . . . [require] us to see and to respond to many things that may be difficult to confront—and they make this process palatable by giving us pleasure in the very act of confrontation. (p. 6)

The title of her last chapter, "Poets as Judges," indicates her feelings about the importance of poetic logic. Also, if you are interested in the application of poetic logic to economics, see Tyler Cowen's (2005) paper "Is a Novel a Model?"

Perhaps even more appropriate to this discussion of the importance of literary forms in the social sciences, Jorn Barger (2006) describes poetic logic in the first few lines of a poem about how to make decisions while developing computer programs. Barger coined the term *weblog* to describe a form of Internet-based communication that has become a worldwide phenomenon. There are hundreds of thousands of blogs today, and some are read regularly by millions of people. Barger published his poem on the auxiliary site for the Robot Wisdom blog (see http://robotwisdom2.blogspot .com/2006/01/poetic-logic.html).

Finally, in Jane Hamilton's (1994) novel *A Map of the World,* the main character, Alice, is jailed and awaits trail after being charged with child sexual abuse. She is innocent. When her husband asks her what she would like him to bring her while she is in jail, she replies "Books." He thinks she wants law books to prepare her defense, but she tells him no, she wants novels.

To summarize, poetic logic is a different way of knowing, and many think it should be incorporated into the social sciences. And if poetic logic is incorporated into the ways of knowing of the social sciences, all three of the suggestions for the future of the social sciences discussed earlier become more meaningful and more essential. However, we do not want to go as far as Oscar Wilde in his use of literary standards in the social realm. In the preface to *The Picture of Dorian Gray* (published in 1890), he commented that

> There is no such thing as a moral or an immoral book. Books are well written, or badly written.
>
> That is all.
>
> The nineteenth century dislike of realism is the rage of Caliban seeing his own face in a glass.
>
> The nineteenth century dislike of romanticism is the rage of Caliban not seeing his own face in a glass.

(Note: Caliban is a mythical monster in English literature. His most common representation is as a slave character in Shakespeare's *The Tempest,* where he lives in a cave. He is crudeness personified—a monster who is deformed, half-human, half-beast.)

Chaos and Complexity Theory: Another Route to a Nonlinear Social Science

Since Pythagoras, Western thought has had a strong reductionist thread that views the world as a mathematical formula. In this tradition, the world, when it is fully understood, can be reduced to mathematics. Nina Semko (personal communication, 2005) remembers Flitta Lubov, her high school Russian literature teacher in Kiev, Ukraine, telling the story of her college professor in Siberia (Flitta's father was an exile there in the 1930s). The professor was studying Pushkin's epic poem *Eugene Onegin.* A major plot line is the love story between Tatiana and Eugene. Much to the amusement of his students, the professor was working on a mathematical formula and graph to quantitatively chart Tatiana's love for Eugene across the poem.

The scientific method has several foundations, including materialism, determinism, and empiricism, but among those foundational beliefs is a faith in quantification, in mathematics, as an essential aspect of understanding. The scientific revolution of the Enlightenment emphasized careful observation and experiments. That was one of the first steps in the scientific revolution. Another was the increasing reliance of quantification and statistics. David Salsburg's (2002) easy-to-read book, *The Lady Tasting Tea: How Statistics Revolutionized Science in the Twentieth Century,* traces the development of statistical thinking and the use of statistical probabilities to determine what is true.

For much of the 20th century, quantification dominated the methodologies of social science, but there have always been countercurrents. For example, from the perspective of economics, Drechsler (2000) makes a cogent argument that a social science founded on quantitative mathematical foundations is not possible. His logic follows Hans Gadamer and the hermeneutic tradition in arguing that the social sciences seek a different form of knowledge than the natural sciences. However, Drechsler emphasizes the importance of one of Aristotle's forms of knowledge, phronesis, which is more local and more contextual than the types of knowledge sought by the natural sciences.

Quantification has even been challenged as the foundation for the natural as well as the social sciences. In several books with titles such as *The Rise of Statistical Thinking, Trust in Numbers,* and *The Modern Social Sciences,* Theodore Porter argues that the quantification of both the natural and the social sciences, beginning in the 18th century, was not due solely to the demonstrated value of quantification in the natural sciences. In fact, he has doubts that there is any core of quantification that cuts across all genres of the natural sciences. His well-documented view is that there were social and cultural reasons for the "experts" in both the natural and social sciences to quantify; the major one is that it gave the impression of objective, solid evidence that made people listen to what the scientists said. Porter's polite analysis of the history of quantification gives way to a more aggressive interpretation of history in Mary Poovey's (1998) *A History of the Modern Fact: Problems of Knowledge in the Sciences of Wealth and Society.* Like Porter, she considers the rise of statistical thinking in the 1830s to be very important in the history of the sciences. However, Poovey traces the quantification of the social sciences back to double-entry bookkeeping, which emerged in 16th century to establish credibility, economic advantage, and prestige on the part of practitioners who had to prove themselves to their employers and superiors. Like Porter's, her analysis emphasizes the social and cultural context and reasons for quantification as determining factors in the move toward mathematics as the foundation of social science research.

Mathematics and the quantification of the social sciences took an unpredicted turn in the last half of the 20th century when a group of theories, often called chaos theory or complexity theory, developed in the "hard" sciences and began to be applied in the social sciences. Some scholars are particularly sensitive to the term *chaos theory* because they think it is too colloquial. Therefore, the editors of a new journal avoided both *chaos* and *complexity* and named their journal *Nonlinear Dynamics, Psychology, and Life Sciences.* The journal is sponsored by the Society for Chaos Theory in Psychology and Life Sciences and was founded in 1997. In the first issue of the journal, editor Stephen Guastello (1997) introduces the journal and the topic this way:

> Nonlinear dynamical systems (NDS) theory, colloquially known as "chaos theory," is a hybrid of mathematical concepts and developments concerning attractors (some of which are chaotic), bifurcations, structural stabilities and instabilities (some of which involve chaos in the literal sense), fractals, catastrophes, self-organizing processes, cellular automata, genetic algorithms and other evolutionary processes, and neural networks. The scientists whose work will appear in *Nonlinear Dynamics, Psychology, and Life Sciences* will be using the products of these mathematical efforts to explain or explore phenomena of widespread interest. The journal is thus dedicated to the advancement of both the theory and experimental knowledge base of NDS in a wide range of disciplines spanning from biology, through psychology, to economics, sociology, and political science. The broad mixture of disciplines represented here is a recognition that many bodies of knowledge share common principles. By juxtaposing developments in different fields within the life and social sciences, the scientific communities may obtain fresh perspectives on those common principles and their implications.

Note that although many comments about the inappropriate role of quantification have been made in this book, mathematics is a crucial component of chaos or complexity theory. However, traditional views of determinism, rationality, absolute truth, and linearity that are usually associated with a "quantitative" approach are all rejected or heavily modified by this theory. Chaos or complexity theory has become an alternative to the positivist and postpositivist paradigms in social science, and by rejecting the foundational beliefs of those paradigms, it has much in common with interpretivist approaches to the social sciences. Space is not available here to explore chaos or complexity theory in detail, but there are a number of excellent resources on the subject. The Society for Chaos Theory in Psychology and Life Sciences has a number of good introductory tutorials on its Web site at http://www.societyforchaostheory.org.

Article of Interest

Daniel Weigel & Colleen I. Murray. (2000, June).
**The paradox of stability and change in relationships:
What does chaos theory offer for the study of romantic
relationships?** *Journal of Social and Personal Relationships, 17,* 425–449.

In this article, the authors, who are at the University of Nevada Reno, look at
how chaos theory can help us understand romantic relationships. Does your
own experience with romance, and that of your friends, suggest that a theory that
expects nonlinear patterns that can be chaotic and change rapidly might be
helpful to understanding? Does one of the general linear stage models described
in the article fit you? Or are you an outlier? Or perhaps you aren't an outlier who
does not fit the expected linear, phase pattern? Perhaps romance is chaotic. Can
you see things such as phase shifts, strange attractors, and self-organization in
the romantic relationships you have had an opportunity to observe? Suppose
romance is a chaotic, nonlinear process. What types of research in your field of
social science would help us understand them better?

   To read the entire article, please go to http://www.sagepub.com/willis_aoi.

In terms of books, James Gleick's (1988) *Chaos: Making a New Science*
is still one of the most entertaining and readable introductions to the topic.
However, David Byrne's (1998) *Complexity Theory and the Social Sciences*
deals specifically with the social sciences, and Bolland and Atherton's (1999)
article explores chaos theory as an alternative paradigm for social work
research and practice.

Some Core Concepts in Complexity and Chaos Theory

Although no brief overview can capture the full implications of chaos or
complexity theory, several key ideas are particularly important to the social
sciences. This section explores four of them briefly and notes some of the
implications for social science research.

Sensitive Dependence on Initial Setting
Conditions: The Butterfly Effect

This concept is often called the butterfly effect, in reference to the dis-
coverer of the effect, Edward Lorenz. In 1972 he presented a paper at the
annual meeting of the American Association for the Advancement of Science

titled "Predictability: Does the Flap of a Butterfly's Wings in Brazil Set Off a Tornado in Texas?" Lorenz is a meteorologist who studied weather patterns. While using computer simulations for a research study he accidentally discovered that the impact of prior weather conditions on future weather is not linear. That is, large weather events that happen just before the time when you want to predict the weather should be the most powerful predictors if the process is linear. However, what Lorenz found was that very small events that happened many months earlier had a huge impact on the weather for that day. Thus, a butterfly flapping its wings in the Brazilian rainforest months before a tornado in Texas could have been a major factor in the creation of the tornado. Although at first this seems strange, many theories in social science follow this same logic. For example, Freud's psychodynamic theory assumes that childhood experiences, even seemingly minor ones, may have major effects on the adult behavior of humans. Jung's theories go even further and assert that the experiences of generations of humans have an impact, through archetypes, on the thinking of humans today. Similarly, in history what appears to be a small difference at the moment—such as the English kings turning over some power to the nobles while the French kings were less willing—is now used as one of the reasons why there was a French Revolution but the United Kingdom still has a monarch.

The butterfly effect is also in direct opposition to some social science theories. For example, Skinner's schedules of reinforcement and Pavlov's classical conditioning are based on contrary assumptions about time and influence. For an interesting example of a phenomenon that fits the butterfly effect concept more than it does either Skinnerian or Pavlovian conditioning, see Seligman and Hager's (1972) discussion of what Seligman calls the sauce béarnaise syndrome. Note, however, that chaos or complexity theory does not insist that the butterfly effect is a replacement for Skinnerian and Pavlovian conditioning or anything else. It is simply another way of trying to understand behavior.

Perhaps the most important implication of the butterfly effect for social science research is that the degree to which it reflects the patterns of determination in social behaviors is the degree to which it will be very difficult, if not impossible, to develop a social science that can precisely predict and control behavior. "Chaos theory has not led to precise prediction, and by its nature, cannot do so since it does not rest on the idea of linear cause and effect. It is, however, useful in understanding" (Bolland & Atherton, 1999, p. 367). Rosenberg (1995) makes the same point about the social sciences in general: "Unlike the natural sciences, which aim at causal theories that enable us to predict and control, the social sciences seek to explain behavior by rendering it intelligible" (p. 19).

The human behavior equivalent of a butterfly flapping its wings cannot be measured 6 months, a year, or decades before you want to predict behavior. The only hope for completely fulfilling the behavioral psychologist's goal of prediction and control of behavior is if measurable behaviors that occur close in time to the behavior to be predicted or controlled actually exercise a great deal of control over what you want to predict. If the butterfly effect applies to human and social behavior, prediction and control become much more problematic. In their discussion of social work, Bolland and Atherton (1999) put it this way:

> Social work (and much of social science) still has a heavy commitment to linear cause-and-effect explanations for a wide range of human and social processes. By "linear" explanations, we mean explanations that claim or suggest that there are, if we could discover them, straightforward causes for all effects. We believe that chaos theory is a viable alternative to those linear deterministic models that impose simplistic cause-and-effect thinking on the complex and uncertain situations commonly encountered in social work. (p. 369)

The butterfly effect is one of several concepts in chaos or complexity theory that challenge the idea of linearity and support nonlinear thinking. As Guastello (1997) puts it,

> A nonlinear relationship between two variables is one where an incremental change in one is not met with a proportional change in the other. Rather, a small change in one variable, at the right place and time, can produce a large effect elsewhere in the system. Alternatively, a large change in one variable could produce a negligible impact on another. Although nonlinear phenomena abound in nature, they are often treated as quaint curiosities in a relentlessly linear world view. (p. 4)

Article of Interest

Hal Gregersen & Lee Sailer. (1993, July). Chaos theory and its implications for social science research.
Human Relations, 46, 777–802.

The authors introduce chaos theory and then argue that prediction and control simply are not a meaningful goal for social science because what we try to predict and control does not obey the linear laws that traditional social science assumes to exist. If you have a limited mathematics background, some of the material in this article will be difficult to deal with, and you can skim over those sections and concentrate on the concepts instead. Are the arguments against prediction and control convincing? Why or why not? What about the six implications at the end of the article? Do they all flow naturally from an acceptance of chaos theory? Why? Which of them would be the easiest, and which the most difficult, for a postpositivist to accept? A critical theorist? An interpretivist?

To read the entire article, please go to http://www.sagepub.com/willis_aoi.

Strange Attractors: Another Challenge to Linearity

The idea of strange attractors (also called chaotic attractors in some of the literature) may seem at first to fit best in a romance novel about couples who enter romantic relationships when all their friends cannot figure out what attracted them to each other. There is actually some association between the romance novel instance of "strange attractors" and the concept of strange attractors in chaos or complexity theory. A strange attractor is a state, condition, or location that a variable tends to gravitate around. This abstract definition has little meaning without some more explanation. Consider the Marxist theory of history. A core assumption is that there is a set of linear phases of social order that human groups inevitably pass through. Initially there is a primeval communal order, which is tribal. Then comes feudalism, followed by capitalism (and the last stage of capitalism, which is imperialism), followed inevitably by socialism and then communism. This is a linear, deterministic model of human history. Suppose that this is not the model human history follows. Suppose, instead, that the history of government tends to move back and forth between two types of organization: one that strives toward unification across many groups and another that strives toward more local control based on similarities between those who are governed. As this was being written, the European Union had just approved more nations for candidate status, including the first candidate that is primarily in Asia, Turkey. And the tiny Republic of Montenegro had voted to become an independent nation (the last nation to pull out of what was Yugoslavia, leaving Serbia by itself) and began a campaign to become part of the European Union. If this cyclic explanation were a better explanation of political history, we might call the two tendencies—toward large, interethnic governments and toward small, local governments—strange attractors because history seems to move back and forth between various versions of these two options. Many metaphors are used to explain strange attractors, including the pattern of moths as they fly around a bright light, but the most important implication of strange attractors for social science is that the concept is an alternative to straight, linear models of behavior. Looked at through the lens of chaos or complexity theory, a pattern that seems chaotic and random may actually illustrate a pattern or path around one or more strange attractors. That pattern is often illustrated with an illustration such as the one in Figure 5 on the Web site http://www.ib .cnea.gov.ar/~thelerg/rueda_loca.php, which graphically represents the pattern of a variable moving over time around two strange attractors.

Fractal Geometry and Social Behavior

Strange attractors actually are one aspect of a broader concept, that of fractals. An IBM scientist, Benoit Mandelbrot, is credited with the modern creation of a new field of mathematics, fractal geometry, which has now been applied to many fields, from astronomy to the social sciences. In essence, a fractal is a shape that has several characteristics:

Fractals Can Be Described by a Simple Mathematical Formula. "Seemingly random shapes, such as those found in living tissue structures, lightning bolts, plant structures, and the shape of islands can actually be generated by relatively simple equations that characterize the fractal structures" (Guastello, 1997). On many Web sites, you can view versions of a fractal named the Barnsley fern. Michael Barnsley developed the formula for it at Georgia Institute of Technology. The pattern generated is very close to that of a black spleenwort fern. On his Web site about fern fractals (http://www.home.aone.net.au/~ byzantium/ferns/fractal.html) David Nicholls explains how to enter data into the freely available program Fractint (http://www.fractint.org) and create your own versions of the fern leaf. Using fractal geometry, you can create complex images using simple mathematical formulas. Some scholars think fractal geometry may be a foundation for the genetic codes stored in DNA because they can create very intricate patterns from small amounts of data. In the social sciences it might also be a way of understanding phenomena such as juvenile delinquency, economic growth patterns, or the emergence of new forms of popular music.

Fractals Repeat Patterns From One Level to Another. "Fractal structures are self-repeating over space, and self-similar over levels of magnification. This principle has widespread implications for the analysis of the time series data taken from complex adaptive systems" (Guastello, 1997). This concept is illustrated by fractals created by a Venezuelan teacher, Marcello Anelli, using a program named Ultrafractal (http://www.ultrafractal.com). You can view many of Anelli's fractals on his Web site (http://fractal.marceloanelli.com/). As already noted, one characteristic of some fractals is that they repeat at different levels. If you zoomed in on some fractal images, you might find that the same pattern you see at one level is duplicated at another more detailed level. Zoom in to see even more detail, and the pattern is repeated again at a third level. The reverse is also true: Zoom out and again the pattern is duplicated at a another level. If you would like to explore this characteristic of some fractals in more detail, take Guided Tour #1 at the Welcome to Fractal Explorer Web site (http://www.geocities.com/Cape Canaveral/2854/). The tour lets you zoom to different levels of a colorful Seahorses Valley fractal.

Fractals Created by the Same Equation Share Family Resemblances, but They Are Not Identical. Much of nature is like that. When you look out the window at the leaves on a large oak tree, one of the striking things about them is that although they are all obviously the leaves of an oak, none of them are identical. They are all unique, like snowflakes. The fern leaf fractals created by Barnsley are unique. If you ran the program that created any of them again, even using exactly the same data, the leaf image produced would not be exactly the same. The two leaves would be similar but not identical. This characteristic of fractals helps explain how there can be such infinite variety in nature and yet similarities (family resemblances) as well. Look at a cauliflower, the face of a cliff or mountain, foam on the sea, clouds, the coastline, or the circulatory system in your body, and you will see fractals. Felix Golubov at the Warner Music Group has created a Fractal Landscapes Creator that you can use online (http://www .geocities.com/felixgolubov) to create several types of landscapes. This program illustrates some of the power of fractal geometry. It has become a very powerful way of creating realistic but fictional landscapes for movies. One beautiful illustration of how fractal geometry can create fictional landscapes is *American West,* an image created by Junpei Sekino, a professor of mathematics at Willamette University. The image is shown in color on Dr. Sekino's Web site (http://www.willamette.edu/~sekino) along with many other landscape fractals. Although Dr. Sekino used a simple formula to create the landscape, you can see that the images produced are far from simple.

Chaotic Systems Have Special Characteristics

The final concept of chaos or complexity theory to be discussed here is the idea that chaotic systems behave in unusual ways when they are unstable or far from equilibrium. Much of the research in the social sciences tries to discover the characteristics of stable systems. Those systems may be married couples, a workgroup in a research center, or political groups in a stable democracy. However, many systems studied by social scientists are not in equilibrium; that is, they are not stable. Traditional social science theory tends to look at change as happening in a slow, Darwinian evolutionary mode, but more and more evidence suggests that social systems may change quickly and violently after periods of seeming stability. Few experts predicted the rapid disintegration of the Soviet Union in the early 1990s, for example. Chaos or complexity theory looks at the behavior of systems that are not in equilibrium, including those that are in transition between chaos and equilibrium and those far from equilibrium. In these stages, systems behave differently than they do under stable conditions. "Systems in a state of chaos, or far-from-equilibrium conditions, self organize by building feed-back loops or other synergetic coupling among the subsystems. These feed-back loops serve to control and stabilize the system in a state of lower entropy" (Guastello, 1997). As used here the term *entropy* refers to the amount of slippage or ineffectiveness in a system. A system with lower entropy is thus a system that "works better." Chaos or complexity theory suggests that chaotic systems become less chaotic over time through feed-back loops between the different components of the system. Such a system is thus self-organizing. Chaos or complexity concepts of self-organizing chaotic systems are already being applied in the social sciences. Williams (2003) describes how self-organizing systems help us understand human behavior: "It is manifestly true that we are physical entities, but that is only part of it. If we get hung up on the obvious, we miss an awful lot which is not obvious, but which is no less real for not being obvious." This, put in rather more technical language, is the message of the Belgian chemist Ilya Prigogine, who was awarded a Nobel Prize for his work on self-organizing systems. Prigogine found as the result of his investigations that it is impossible to derive a fundamental level of description from which to explain the behavior of self-organizing systems. Thus they will always be somewhat unpredictable. The reason for this, as Williams put it, is that "there are always levels of organization that we don't know about but which are, potentially, just as important to the functioning of the system as the level that we do know about." Prigogine argues that although we can learn a lot about self-organizing systems, such as people, we will never find the basic or foundational level that, when studied, will unlock all the secrets of that system. Some researchers may study humans at the molecular level, others at the biological level, others at the psychological level, and still others at the social and cultural level, but there "can be no 'officially correct' level of organization upon which to predicate understanding" (Williams, 2003). Williams goes on to explain in some detail how a multilevel, nonlinear way of thinking about mental illness leads us to radically different ways of formulating both the questions and the potential solutions.

Although this chapter has only scratched the surface of both poetic logic and chaos or complexity theory, you can already see how both support different ways of studying social science. Both of these emerging frameworks can support and even expand the two major paradigms discussed in this book: critical theory and interpretivism. As you consider your perspective on social science research, poetic logic and chaos or complexity theory are both worthy of your attention. If you would like to read more about chaos or complexity theory, a special issue of the journal *Theory, Culture & Society* (2005, vol. 22[5]) was devoted to this topic.

Summary

In the 21st century social science will continue to diversify, with many different research methods, paradigms, and ideologies competing for the attention of individuals and groups of social scientists. On the issues that divided Aristotle and Plato, the social sciences have tended to choose the search for absolute truth that both philosophers advocated. However, social science has tended to opt for Aristotle's empiricism over Plato's reflective idealism and for Plato's rejection of the humanities over Aristotle's warm endorsement of them. This chapter explored the implications of making the other choices: a rejection of intellectual fundamentalism that insists there are absolute truths humans can know with certainty, acceptance of multiple sources of knowing, and closer relationships with the humanities. These alternative choices are appealing, and two emerging frameworks for thinking about social science research, poetic logic and chaos or complexity theory, both offer some support for a 21st-century social science that is quite different from the social science of the previous century.

Questions for Reflection

1. Consider the three choices discussed in the early part of the chapter. Would you vote a "straight ticket" on them? That is, would you also make the same choices made by 20th-century social science? Or would you select the opposite three? Why? Or, in the tradition of chaos theory, would you select a different set of answers, or different answers altogether? What would your choices be, and how would you make them?

2. Has the case for poetic logic been made in your mind? Why or why not? How? Is poetic logic really different from rational and empirical judgment? How? If there are different forms of knowledge, should there be a hierarchy, with one form being better than another or taking precedence? Why?

3. Finally, how does chaos or complexity theory fit with interpretivism? With postpositivism? With critical theory? Do you have to give up these paradigms to adopt chaos or complexity theory? Or is it compatible with interpretivism, critical theory, or postpositivism? Does it help us build bridges across these paradigms?

References

Barger, J. (2006). *Poetic logic.* Robot Wisdom auxiliary. Retrieved September 23, 2006, from http://robotwisdom2.blogspot.com/2006/01/poetic-logic.html

Biddle, C. (2006, Spring). Introducing *The Objective Standard. The Objective Standard, 1*(1). Retrieved September 23, 2006, from http://www.theobjective standard.com/issues/2006-spring/introducing-the-objective-standard.asp

Bolland, K., & Atherton, C. (1999, July/August). Chaos theory: An alternative approach to social work practice and research. *Families in Society, 79,* 367–373.

Byrne, D. (1998). *Complexity theory and the social sciences.* New York: Routledge.

Colilli, P. (1997). *The idea of a living spirit: Poetic logic as a contemporary theory.* Toronto: University of Toronto Press.

Cowen, T. (2005). *Is a novel a model?* Unpublished paper, George Mason University, Department of Economics. Retrieved September 23, 2006, from http://www .gmu.edu/jbc/Tyler/Model.doc

Danesi, M. (2004). *Poetic logic: The role of metaphor in thought, language, and culture.* Madison, WI: Atwood.

Denzin, N., & Giardina, M. (2006). *Qualitative inquiry and the conservative challenge.* Tucson: Left Coast Press/University of Arizona Press.

Denzin, N., & Lincoln, Y. (Eds.). (2005). *The SAGE handbook of qualitative research* (3rd ed.). Thousand Oaks, CA: Sage.

Drechsler, W. (2000). On the possibility of quantitative-mathematical social science, chiefly economics: Some preliminary considerations. *Journal of Economic Studies, 27*(45), 246–259.

Freire, P. (1997). *Pedagogy of the heart.* New York: Continuum.

Geertz, C. (1973). *The interpretation of cultures.* New York: Basic Books.

Geertz, C. (1983). *Local knowledge.* New York: Basic Books.

Gleick, J. (1988). *Chaos: Making a new science.* New York: Viking/Penguin.

Gould, T. (1991). *The ancient quarrel between poetry and philosophy.* Princeton, NJ: Princeton University Press.

Gruenwald, O. (2005). The third culture: An integrative vision of the human condition. *Journal of Integrative Studies, 17,* 139–160. Retrieved September 23, 2006, from http://www.jis3.org/samplearticle.htm

Guastello, S. (1997). Science evolves: An introduction to *Nonlinear Dynamics, Psychology, and Life Sciences. Nonlinear Dynamics, Psychology, and Life Sciences, 1*(1), 1–6. Retrieved September 23, 2006, from http://www.society forchaostheory.org/ndpls/editorial_1997.pdf

Hamilton, J. (1994). *A map of the world.* New York: Doubleday.

Henry, D., & Beaty, M. (Eds.). (2006). *Christianity and the soul of the university.* Grand Rapids, MI: Baker Academic.

Kim, D. (1998/1999, Winter). Letters in Canada. *University of Toronto Quarterly, 68*(1). Retrieved September 23, 2006, from http://www.utpjournals.com/product/utq/681/theory16.html

Kimball, R. (1998). *Tenured radicals* (revised ed.). Chicago: Elephant Paperbacks/Ivan R. Dee.

Kincheloe, J., & Berry, K. (2004). *Rigour and complexity in educational research: Conceptualizing the bricolage.* New York: Open University Press.

Nussbaum, M. (1995). *Poetic justice: The literary imagination and public life.* Boston: Beacon.

Phillips, D., & Burbules, N. (2000). *Postpositivism and educational research.* Lanham, MD: Rowman & Littlefield.

Poovey, M. (1998). *A history of the modern fact: Problems of knowledge in the sciences of wealth and society.* Chicago: University of Chicago Press.

Porter, T. (1988). *The rise of statistical thinking.* Princeton, NJ: Princeton University Press.

Porter, T. (1996). *Trust in numbers.* Princeton, NJ: Princeton University Press.

Porter, T., & Ross, D. (2003). *The modern social sciences.* Cambridge: Cambridge University Press.

Richardson, L., & Adams St. Pierre, E. (2005). Writing: A method of inquiry. In N. Denzin & Y. Lincoln (Eds.), *The SAGE handbook of qualitative research* (3rd ed., pp. 959–978). Thousand Oaks, CA: Sage.

Richardson, L., & Lockridge, E. (2004). *Travels with Ernest: Crossing the literary/sociological divide.* Walnut Creek, CA: AltaMira.

Rorty, R. (2006). *Take care of freedom and truth will take care of itself: Interviews with Richard Rorty* (E. Mendieta, Ed.). Stanford, CA: Stanford University Press.

Rosenberg, A. (1995). *Philosophy of social science.* Boulder, CO: Westview.

Salsburg, D. (2002). *The lady tasting tea: How statistics revolutionized science in the twentieth century* (2nd ed.). New York: Owl Books.

Seligman, M. E. P., & Hager, J. L. (1972, August). Biological boundaries of learning: The sauce-béarnaise syndrome. *Psychology Today,* 59–61, 84–87.

Tashakkori, A., & Teddlie, C. (2002). *Handbook of mixed methods social and behavioral research.* Thousand Oaks, CA: Sage.

Vico, G. (1984). The new science of Giambattista Vico (3rd ed., T. G. Bergin & M. H. Fisch, Trans.). Ithaca, NY: Cornell University Press. (Originally published 1725)

Williams, N. (2003). Psychological entropy. *New Alchemy, 5.* Retrieved September 23, 2006, from http://web.ukonline.co.uk/phil.williams/psychologicalentropy.htm

Index